Everlasting Love

オレのずっと好きな人

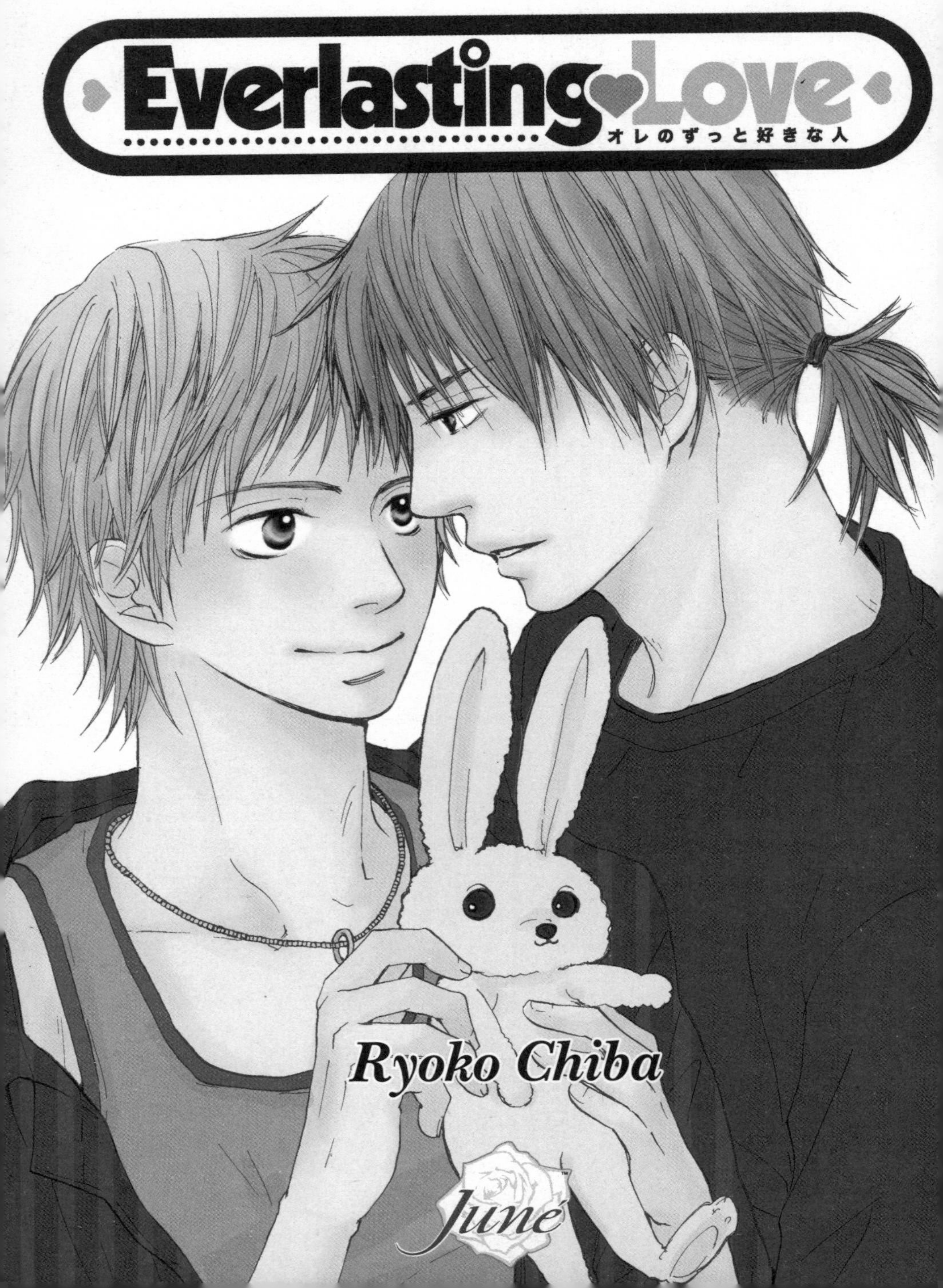
Ryoko Chiba
June

•Everlasting♥Love•

オレのずっと好きな人

Translation .... Andrew Marshall
Lettering .... Tawnie Wilson
Graphic Design ...Matt Akuginow / Daryl Kuxhouse
Editing .... Daryl Kuxhouse
Editor in Chief .... Fred Lui
Publisher .... Hikaru Sasahara

English Edition Published by
DIGITAL MANGA PUBLISHING
A division of DIGITAL MANGA, Inc.
1487 W 178th Street, Suite 300
Gardena, CA 90248

www.dmpbooks.com

First Edition: January 2008
ISBN-10: 1-56970-778-2
ISBN-13: 978-1-56970-778-4

1 3 5 7 9 10 8 6 4 2

Printed in China

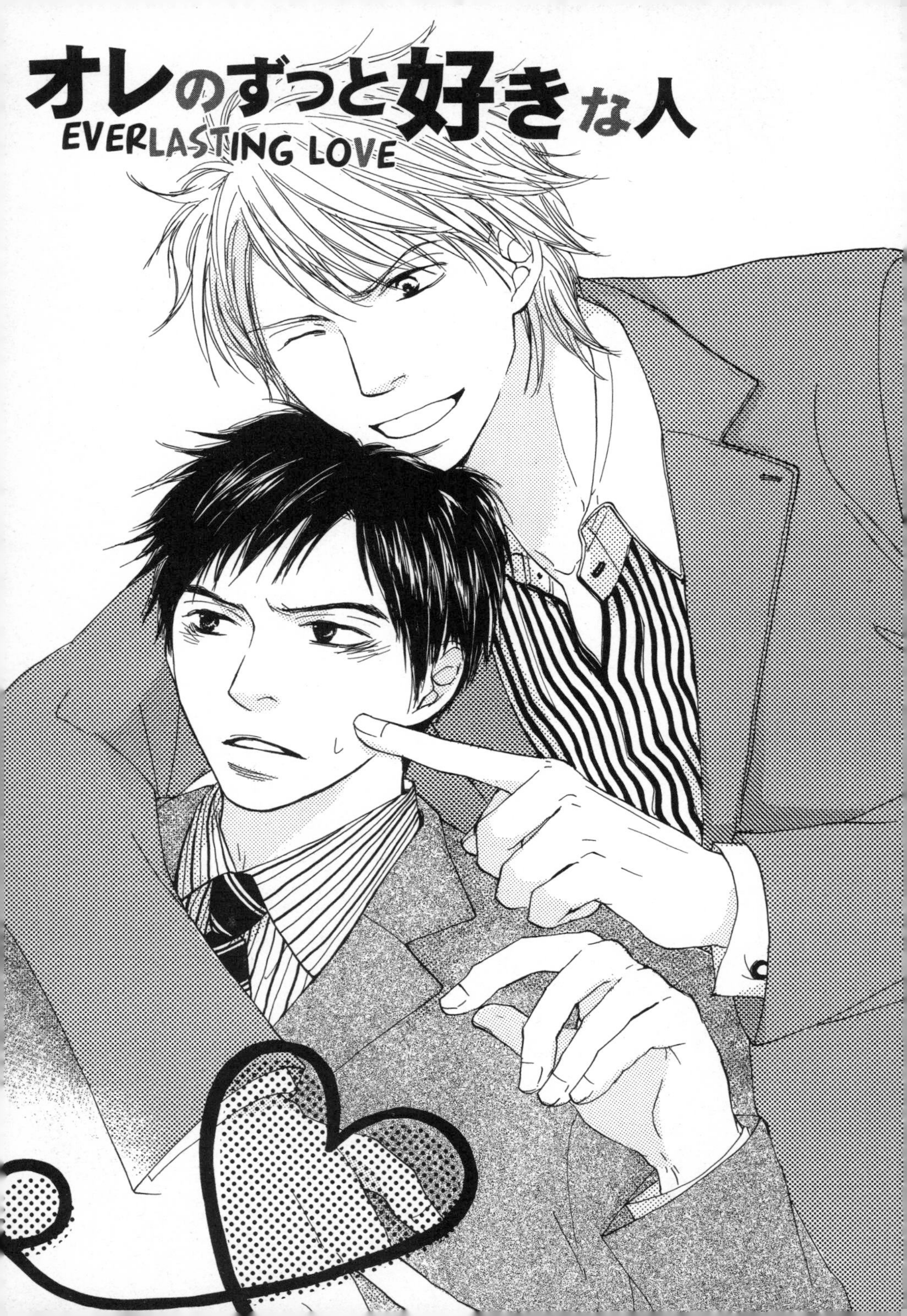
オレのずっと好きな人
EVERLASTING LOVE

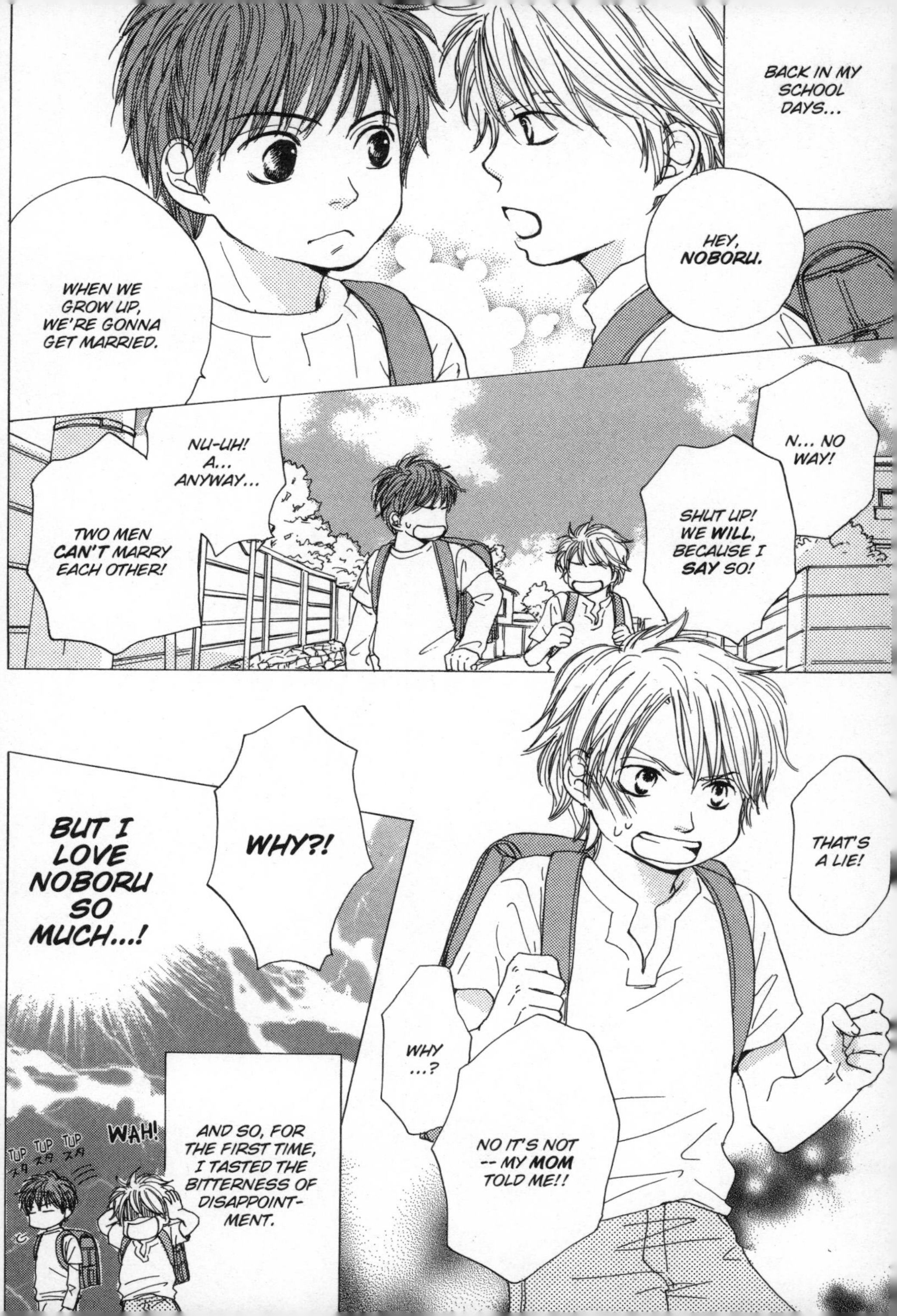
BACK IN MY SCHOOL DAYS...
HEY, NOBORU.
WHEN WE GROW UP, WE'RE GONNA GET MARRIED.
N... NO WAY!
SHUT UP! WE WILL, BECAUSE I SAY SO!
NU-UH! A... ANYWAY...
TWO MEN CAN'T MARRY EACH OTHER!
THAT'S A LIE!
WHY ...?
NO IT'S NOT -- MY MOM TOLD ME!!
WHY?!
BUT I LOVE NOBORU SO MUCH...!
AND SO, FOR THE FIRST TIME, I TASTED THE BITTERNESS OF DISAPPOINT-MENT.
WAH!
TUP TUP TUP

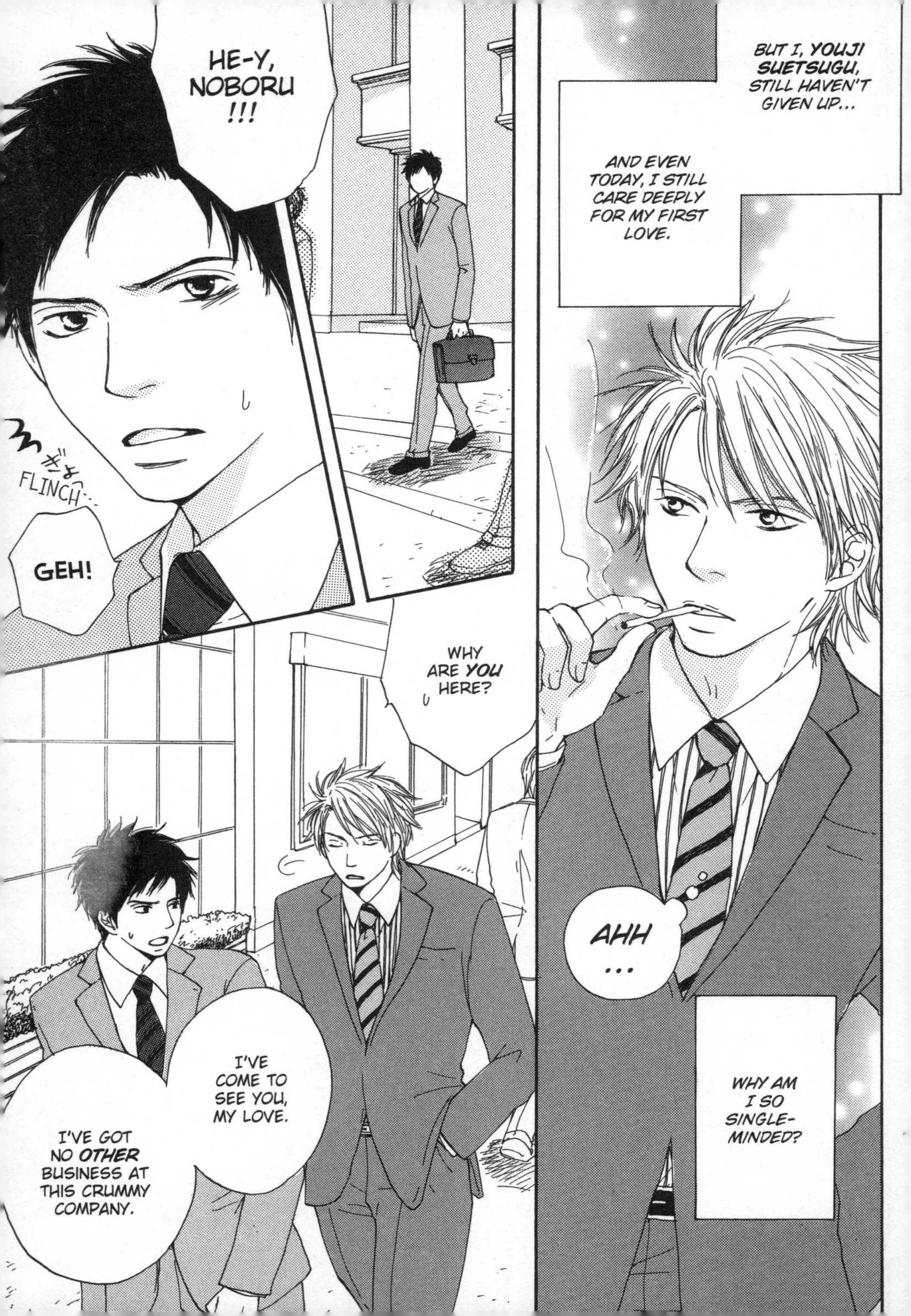
BUT I, YOUJI SUETSUGU, STILL HAVEN'T GIVEN UP...
AND EVEN TODAY, I STILL CARE DEEPLY FOR MY FIRST LOVE.
AHH ...
WHY AM I SO SINGLE-MINDED?
HE-Y, NOBORU !!!
ぎょ
FLINCH...
GEH!
WHY ARE YOU HERE?
I'VE COME TO SEE YOU, MY LOVE.
I'VE GOT NO OTHER BUSINESS AT THIS CRUMMY COMPANY.

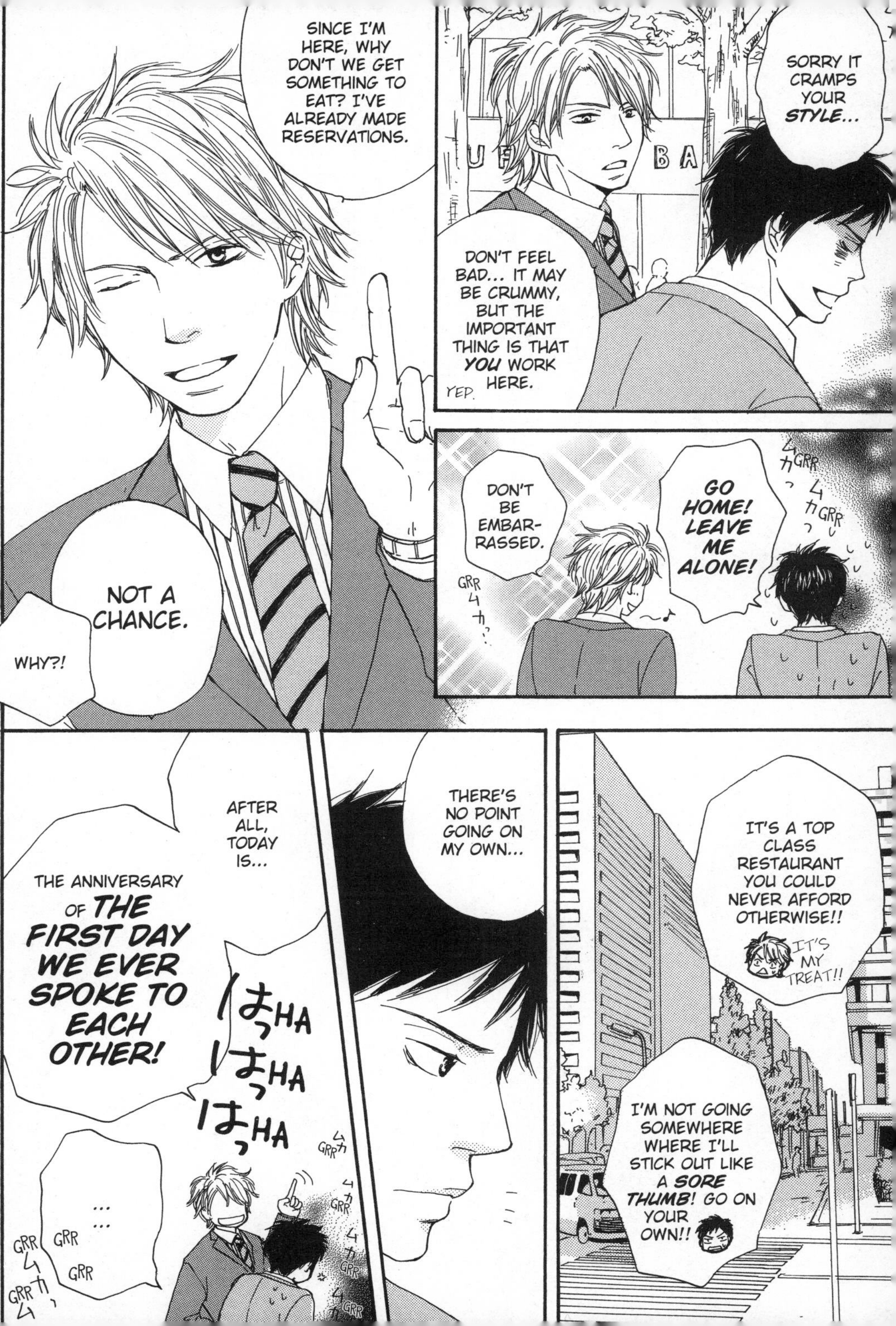
SORRY IT CRAMPS YOUR STYLE...
DON'T FEEL BAD... IT MAY BE CRUMMY, BUT THE IMPORTANT THING IS THAT YOU WORK HERE.
YEP.
ムカッ GRR ムカッ GRR
GO HOME! LEAVE ME ALONE!
DON'T BE EMBARRASSED.
GRR ムカッ
SINCE I'M HERE, WHY DON'T WE GET SOMETHING TO EAT? I'VE ALREADY MADE RESERVATIONS.
NOT A CHANCE.
WHY?!
IT'S A TOP CLASS RESTAURANT YOU COULD NEVER AFFORD OTHERWISE!!
IT'S MY TREAT!!
I'M NOT GOING SOMEWHERE WHERE I'LL STICK OUT LIKE A SORE THUMB! GO ON YOUR OWN!!
THERE'S NO POINT GOING ON MY OWN...
AFTER ALL, TODAY IS...
THE ANNIVERSARY OF THE FIRST DAY WE EVER SPOKE TO EACH OTHER!
はっHA はっHA はっHA
ムカ GRR ムカ GRR ムカ GRR
......
GRR GRR GRR ムカッ

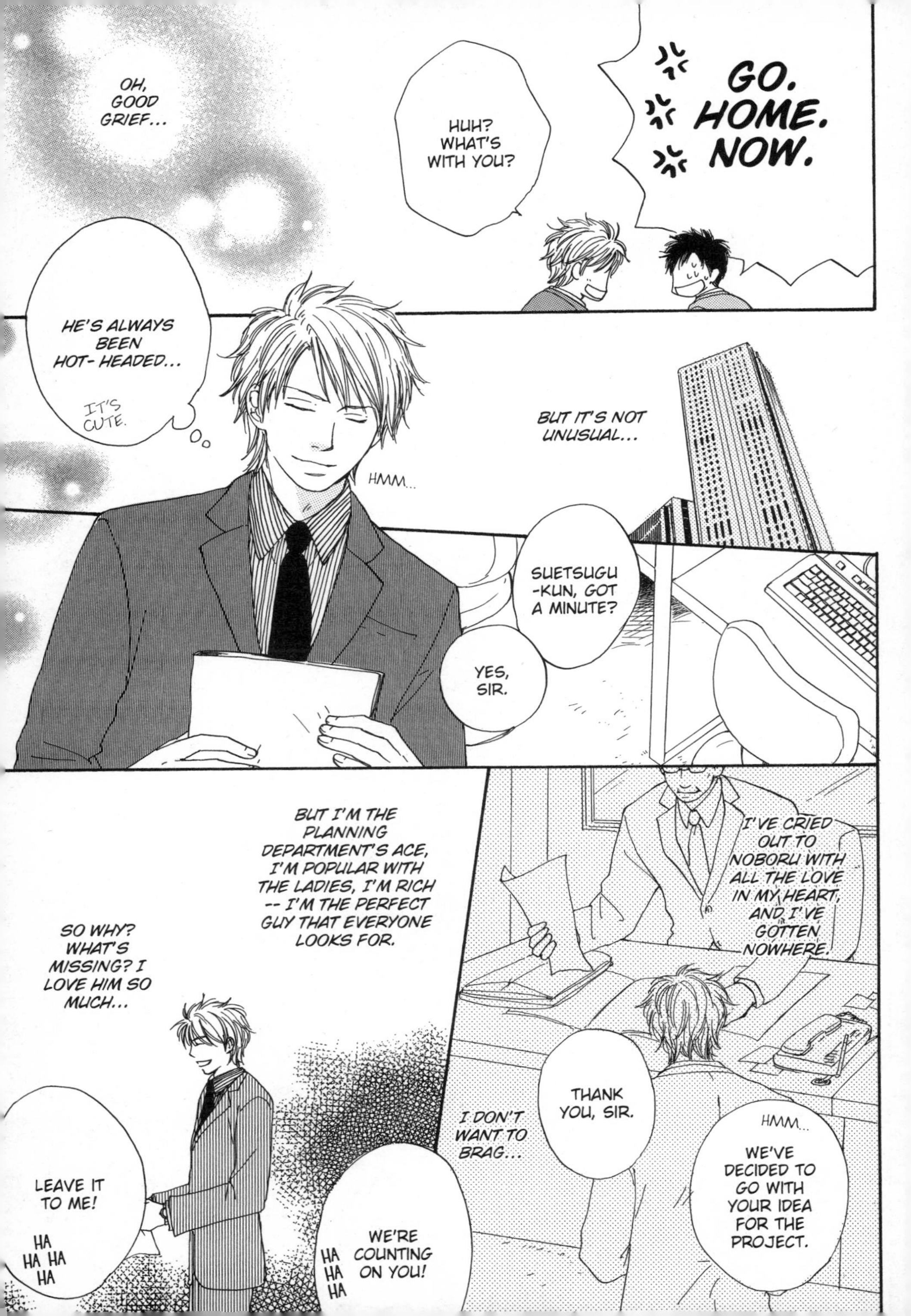
GO. HOME. NOW.
HUH? WHAT'S WITH YOU?
BUT IT'S NOT UNUSUAL...
SUETSUGU-KUN, GOT A MINUTE?
YES, SIR.
OH, GOOD GRIEF...
HE'S ALWAYS BEEN HOT-HEADED...
IT'S CUTE.
HMM...
I'VE CRIED OUT TO NOBORU WITH ALL THE LOVE IN MY HEART, AND I'VE GOTTEN NOWHERE.
HMM...
WE'VE DECIDED TO GO WITH YOUR IDEA FOR THE PROJECT.
THANK YOU, SIR.
I DON'T WANT TO BRAG...
BUT I'M THE PLANNING DEPARTMENT'S ACE, I'M POPULAR WITH THE LADIES, I'M RICH -- I'M THE PERFECT GUY THAT EVERYONE LOOKS FOR.
SO WHY? WHAT'S MISSING? I LOVE HIM SO MUCH...
WE'RE COUNTING ON YOU!
HA HA HA
LEAVE IT TO ME!
HA HA HA HA

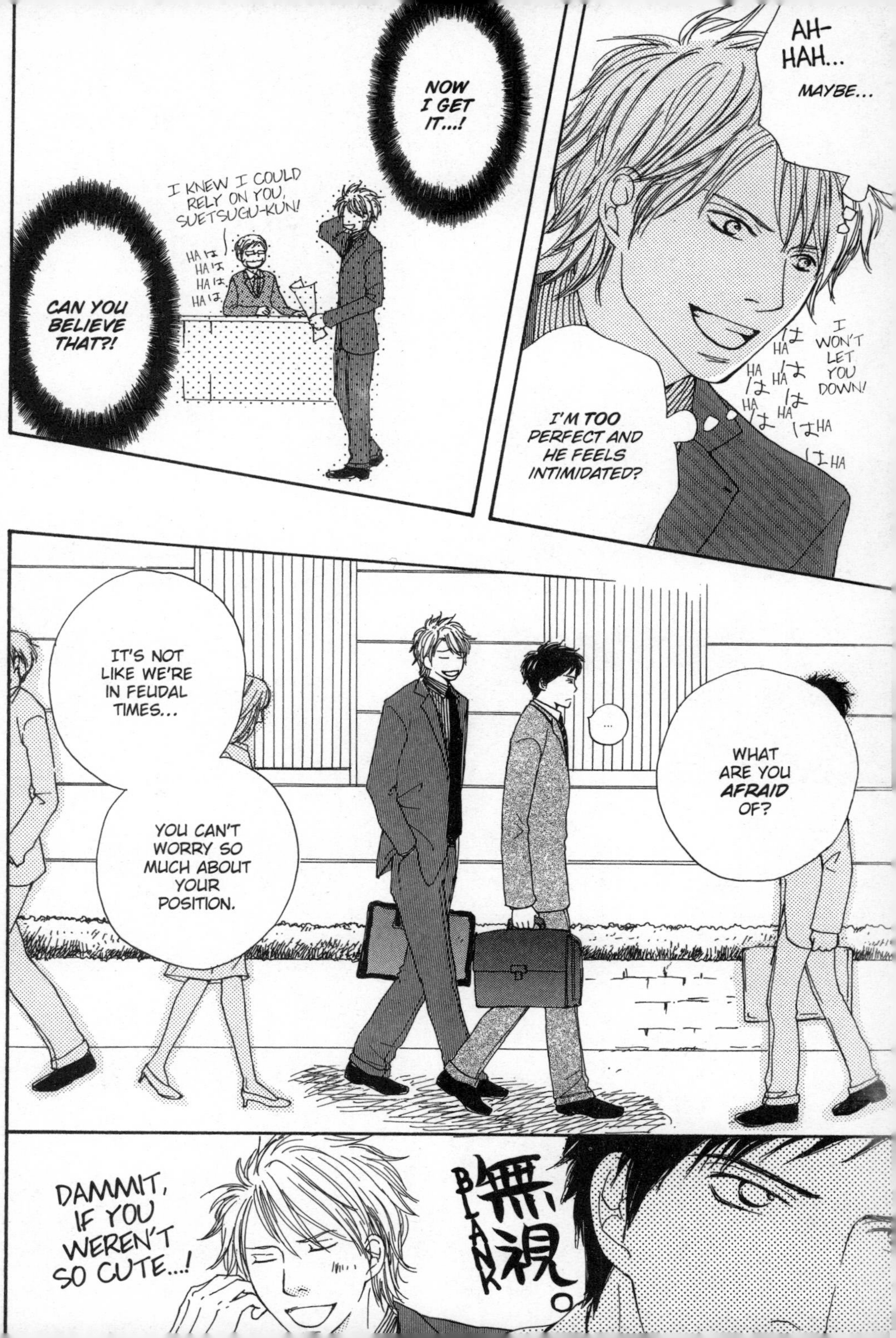
AH-HAH...
MAYBE...
I'M TOO PERFECT AND HE FEELS INTIMIDATED?
はHA はHA はHA はHA はHA はHA はHA
I WON'T LET YOU DOWN!
NOW I GET IT...!
I KNEW I COULD RELY ON YOU, SUETSUGU-KUN!
HAは HAは HAは HAは
CAN YOU BELIEVE THAT?!
WHAT ARE YOU AFRAID OF?
...
IT'S NOT LIKE WE'RE IN FEUDAL TIMES...
YOU CAN'T WORRY SO MUCH ABOUT YOUR POSITION.
無視。
BLANK
DAMMIT, IF YOU WEREN'T SO CUTE...!

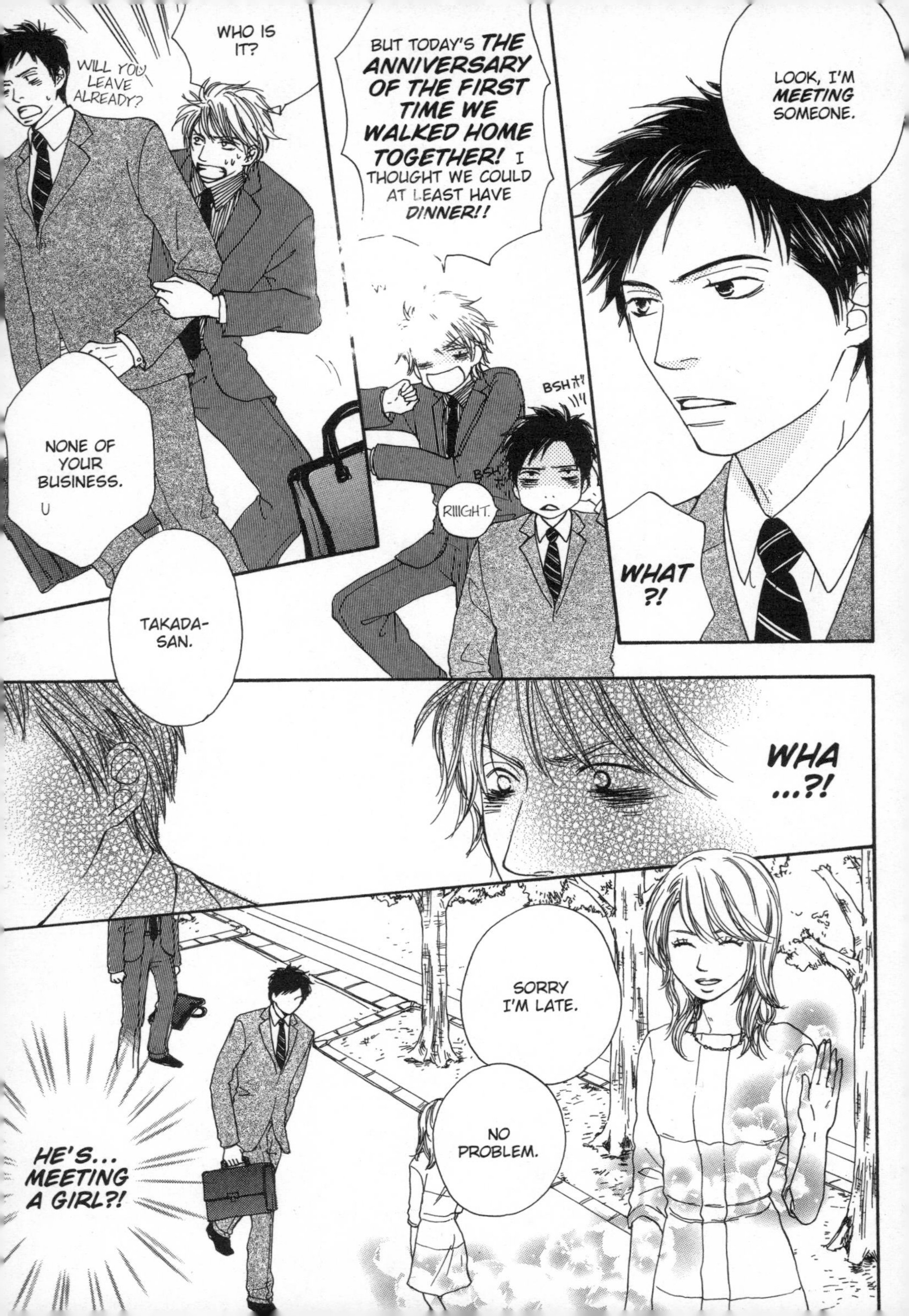
LOOK, I'M MEETING SOMEONE.
WHAT ?!
BUT TODAY'S THE ANNIVERSARY OF THE FIRST TIME WE WALKED HOME TOGETHER! I THOUGHT WE COULD AT LEAST HAVE DINNER!!
RIIIGHT.
WHO IS IT?
WILL YOU LEAVE ALREADY?
NONE OF YOUR BUSINESS.
TAKADA-SAN.
WHA ...?!
SORRY I'M LATE.
NO PROBLEM.
HE'S... MEETING A GIRL?!

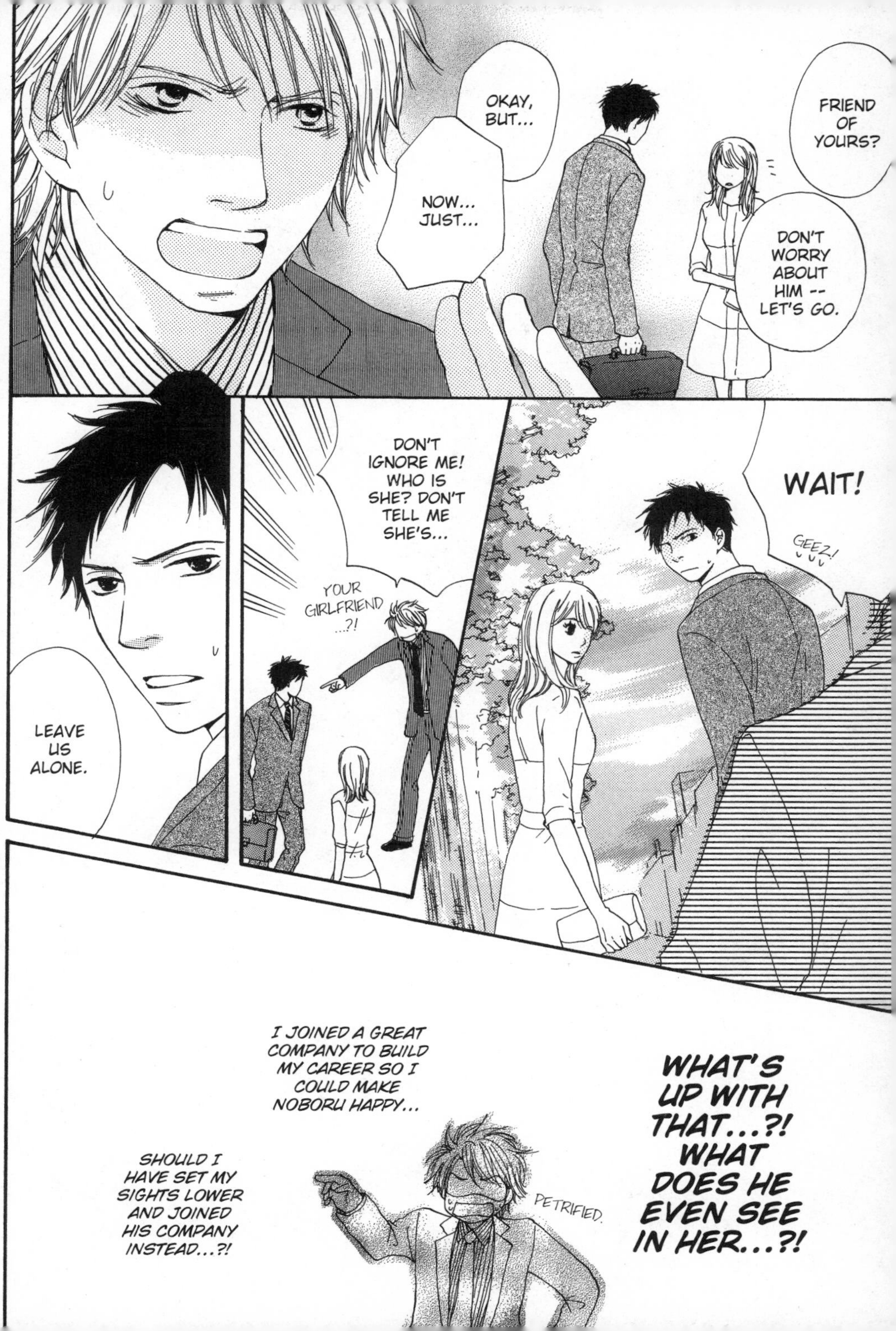
FRIEND OF YOURS?
DON'T WORRY ABOUT HIM -- LET'S GO.
OKAY, BUT...
NOW... JUST...
WAIT!
GEEZ!
DON'T IGNORE ME! WHO IS SHE? DON'T TELL ME SHE'S...
YOUR GIRLFRIEND ...?!
LEAVE US ALONE.
WHAT'S UP WITH THAT...?! WHAT DOES HE EVEN SEE IN HER...?!
PETRIFIED.
I JOINED A GREAT COMPANY TO BUILD MY CAREER SO I COULD MAKE NOBORU HAPPY...
SHOULD I HAVE SET MY SIGHTS LOWER AND JOINED HIS COMPANY INSTEAD...?!

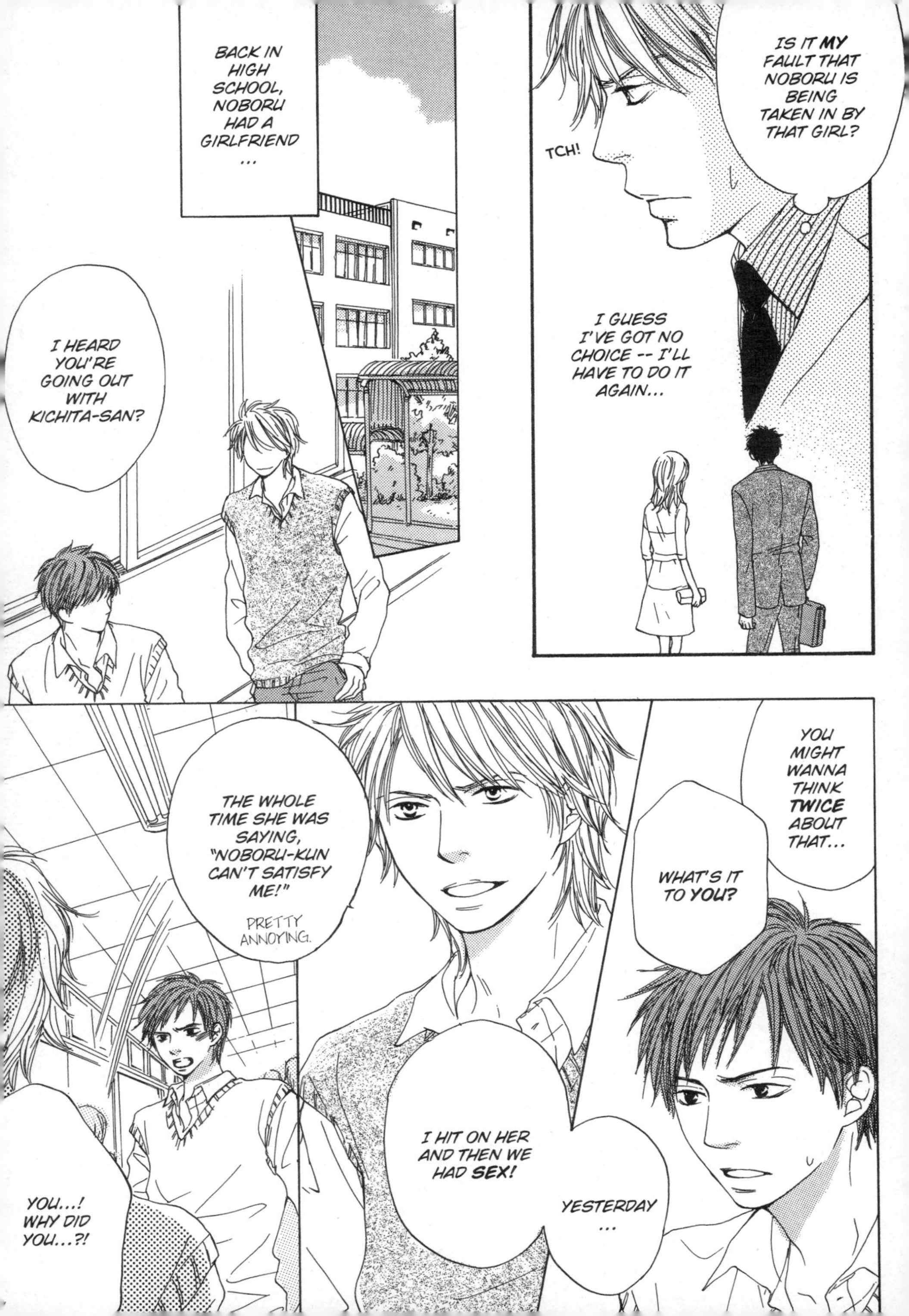
IS IT **MY** FAULT THAT NOBORU IS BEING TAKEN IN BY THAT GIRL?
TCH!
I GUESS I'VE GOT NO CHOICE -- I'LL HAVE TO DO IT AGAIN...
BACK IN HIGH SCHOOL, NOBORU HAD A GIRLFRIEND...
I HEARD YOU'RE GOING OUT WITH KICHITA-SAN?
YOU MIGHT WANNA THINK **TWICE** ABOUT THAT...
WHAT'S IT TO **YOU?**
YESTERDAY...
I HIT ON HER AND THEN WE HAD **SEX!**
THE WHOLE TIME SHE WAS SAYING, "NOBORU-KUN CAN'T SATISFY ME!"
PRETTY ANNOYING.
YOU...! WHY DID YOU...?!

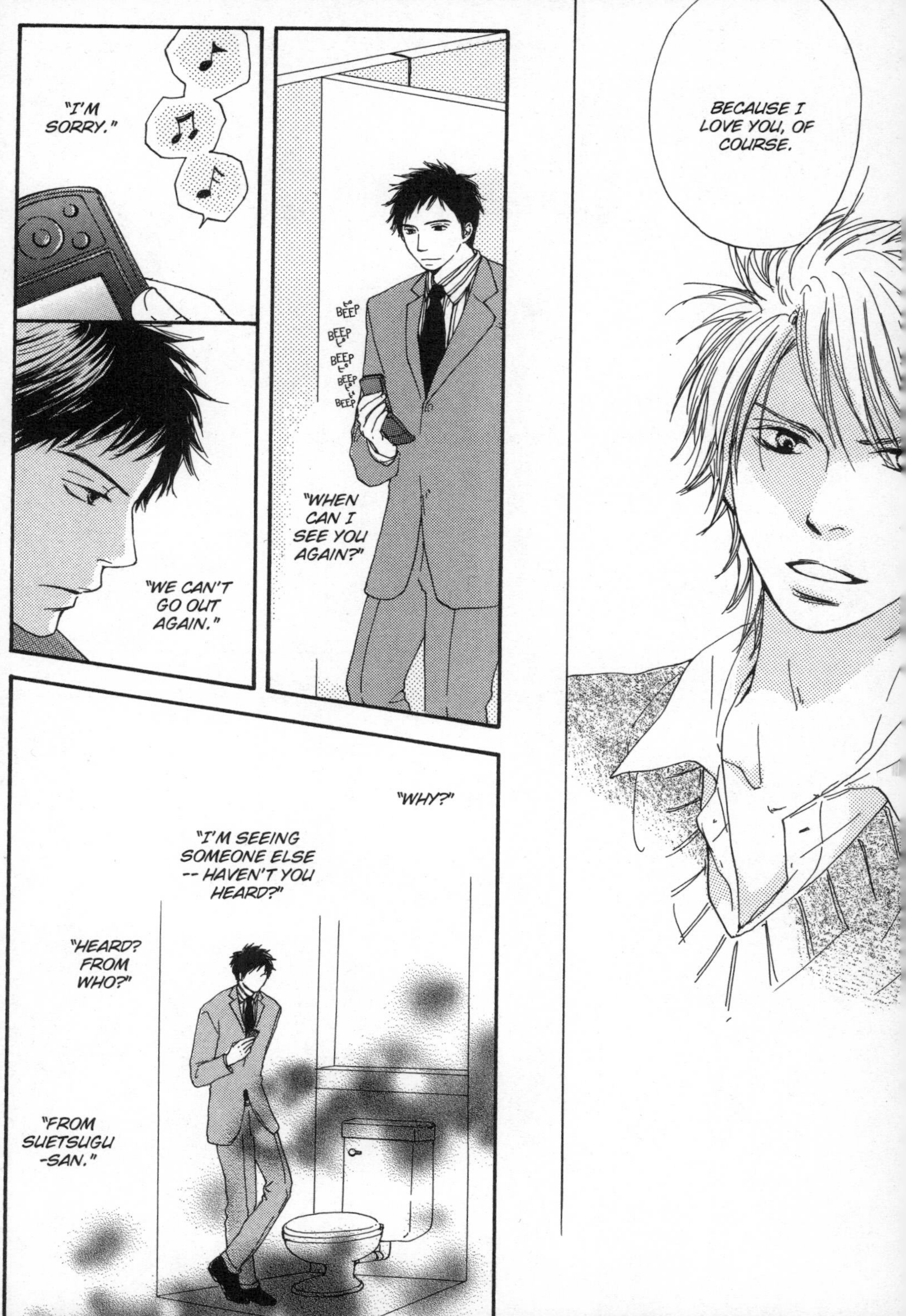
BECAUSE I LOVE YOU, OF COURSE.
BEEP BEEP BEEP BEEP BEEP
"WHEN CAN I SEE YOU AGAIN?"
"I'M SORRY."
"WE CAN'T GO OUT AGAIN."
"WHY?"
"I'M SEEING SOMEONE ELSE -- HAVEN'T YOU HEARD?"
"HEARD? FROM WHO?"
"FROM SUETSUGU -SAN."

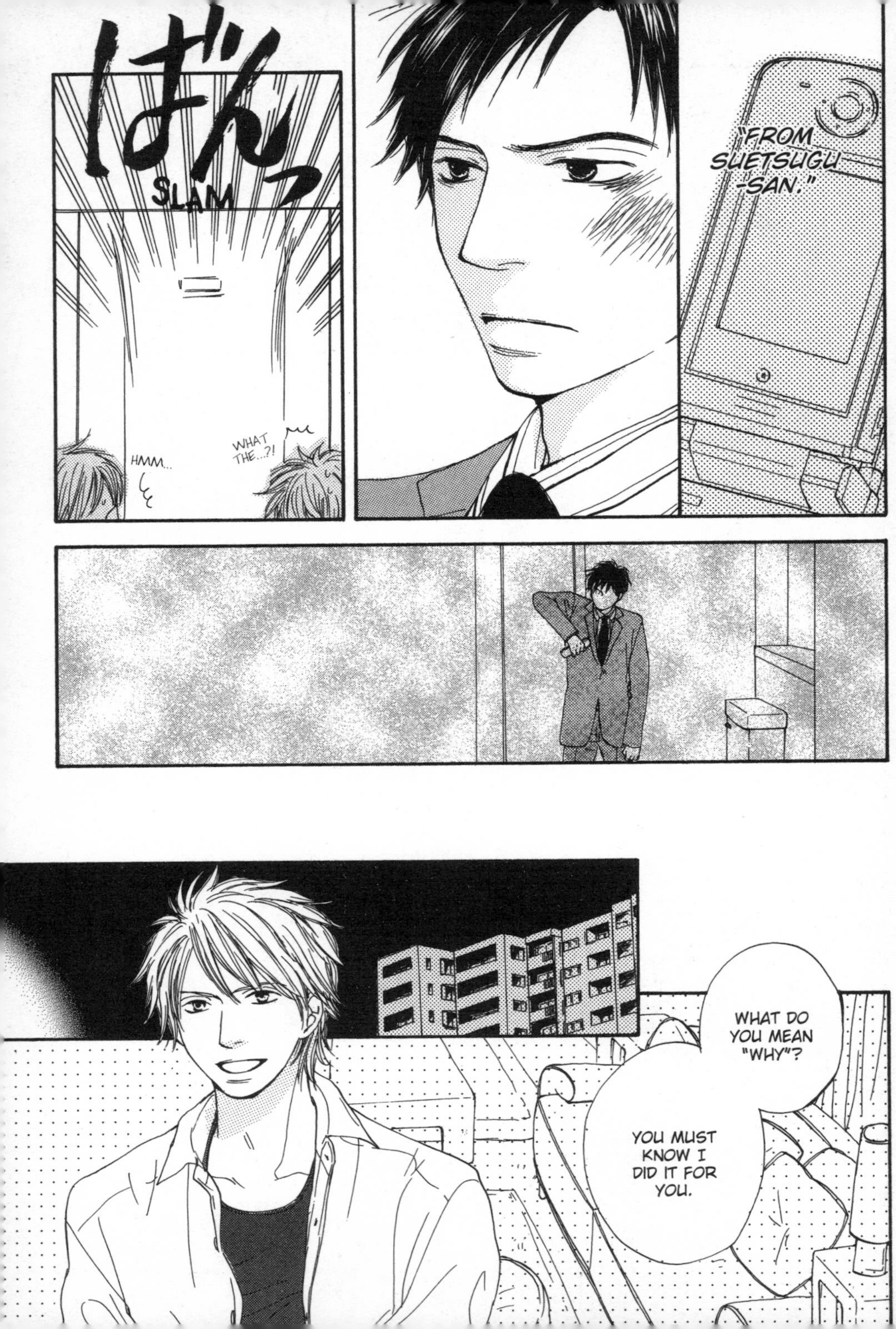
"FROM SUETSUGU-SAN."
ばんっ
SLAM
WHAT THE...?!
HMM...
WHAT DO YOU MEAN "WHY"?
YOU MUST KNOW I DID IT FOR YOU.

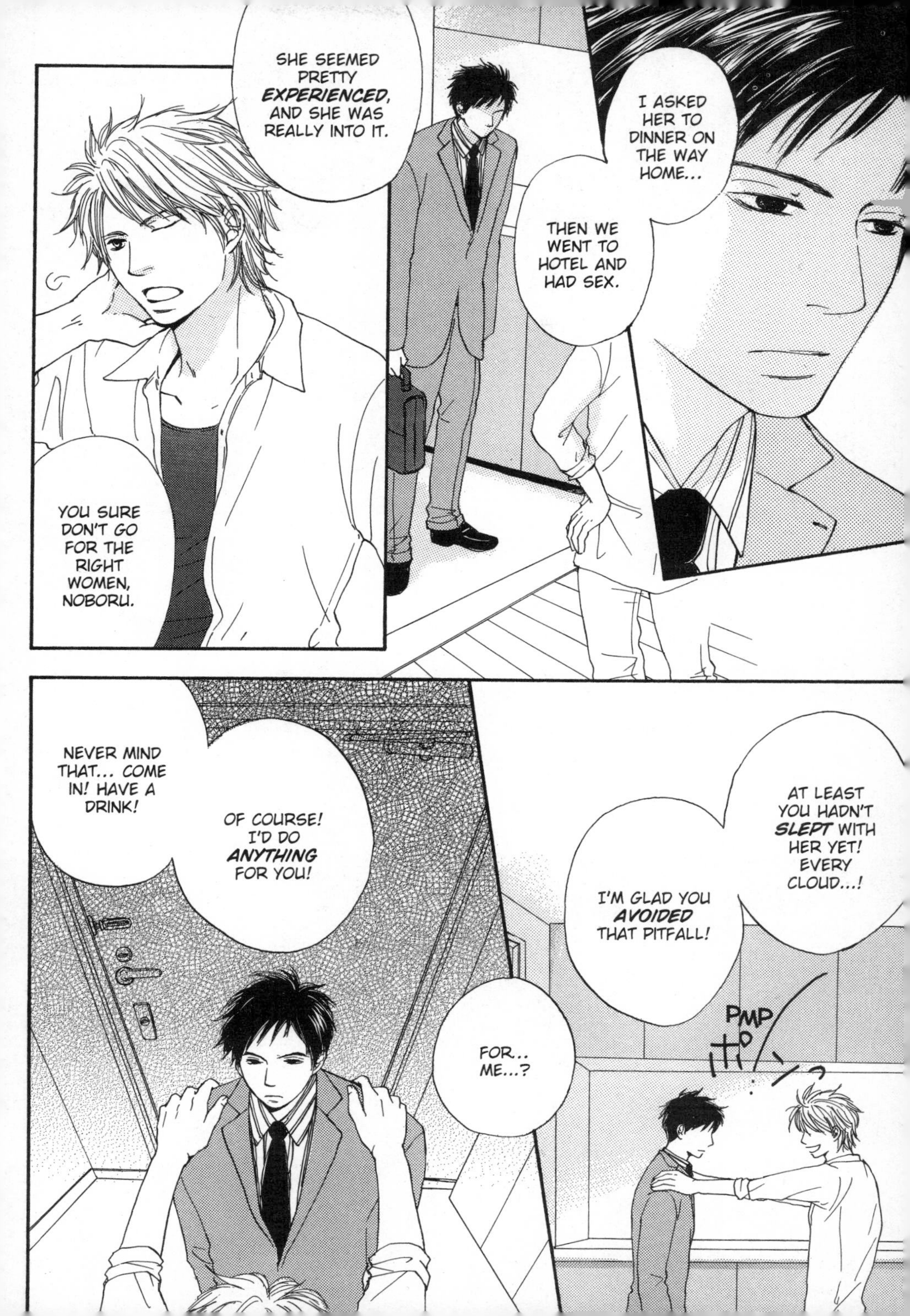
I ASKED HER TO DINNER ON THE WAY HOME...
THEN WE WENT TO HOTEL AND HAD SEX.
SHE SEEMED PRETTY **EXPERIENCED**, AND SHE WAS REALLY INTO IT.
YOU SURE DON'T GO FOR THE RIGHT WOMEN, NOBORU.
AT LEAST YOU HADN'T **SLEPT** WITH HER YET! EVERY CLOUD...!
I'M GLAD YOU **AVOIDED** THAT PITFALL!
PMP
FOR.. ME...?
OF COURSE! I'D DO **ANYTHING** FOR YOU!
NEVER MIND THAT... COME IN! HAVE A DRINK!

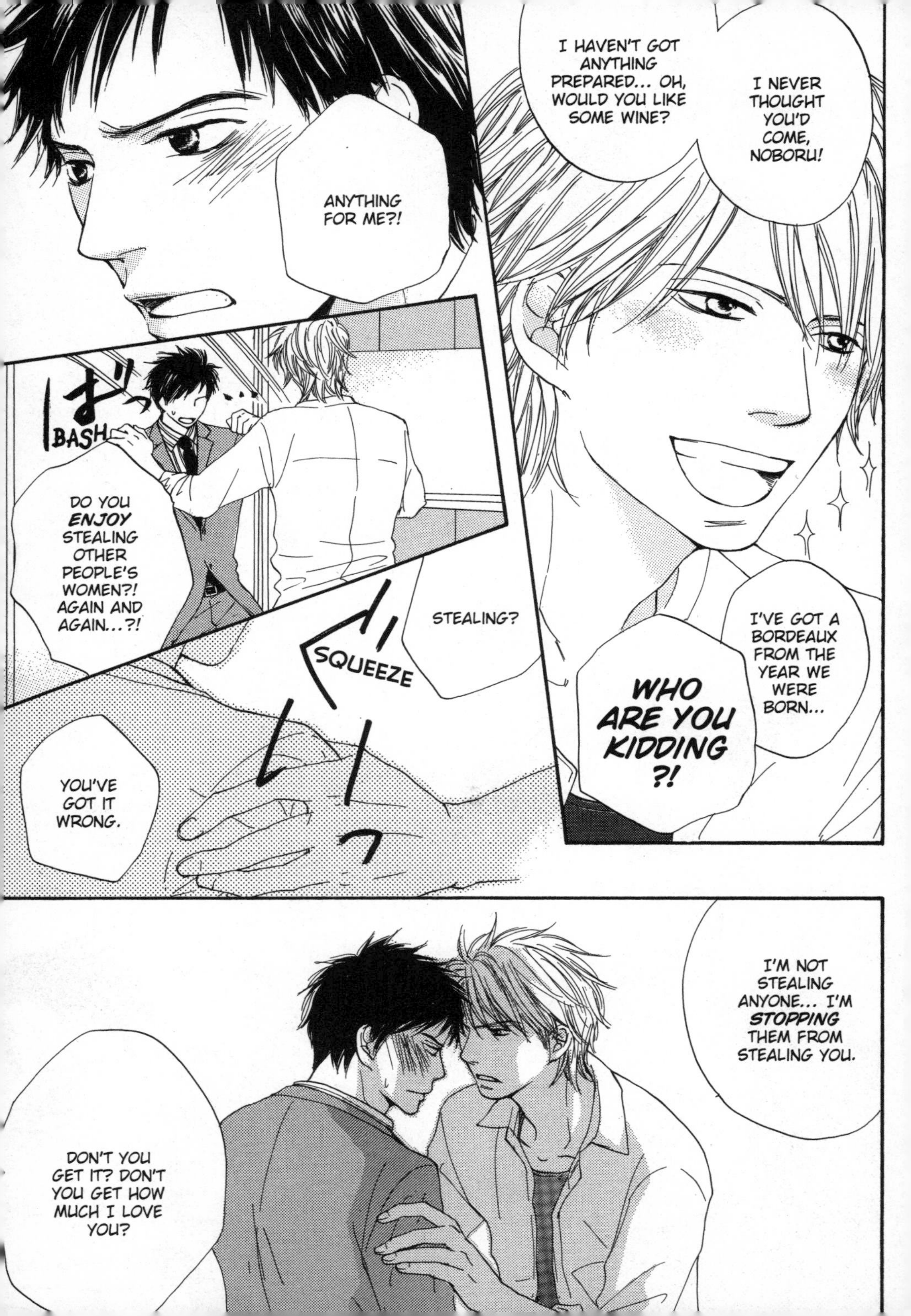
I NEVER THOUGHT YOU'D COME, NOBORU!
I HAVEN'T GOT ANYTHING PREPARED... OH, WOULD YOU LIKE SOME WINE?
I'VE GOT A BORDEAUX FROM THE YEAR WE WERE BORN...
WHO ARE YOU KIDDING?!
ANYTHING FOR ME?!
BASH
DO YOU ENJOY STEALING OTHER PEOPLE'S WOMEN?! AGAIN AND AGAIN...?!
STEALING?
SQUEEZE
YOU'VE GOT IT WRONG.
I'M NOT STEALING ANYONE... I'M STOPPING THEM FROM STEALING YOU.
DON'T YOU GET IT? DON'T YOU GET HOW MUCH I LOVE YOU?

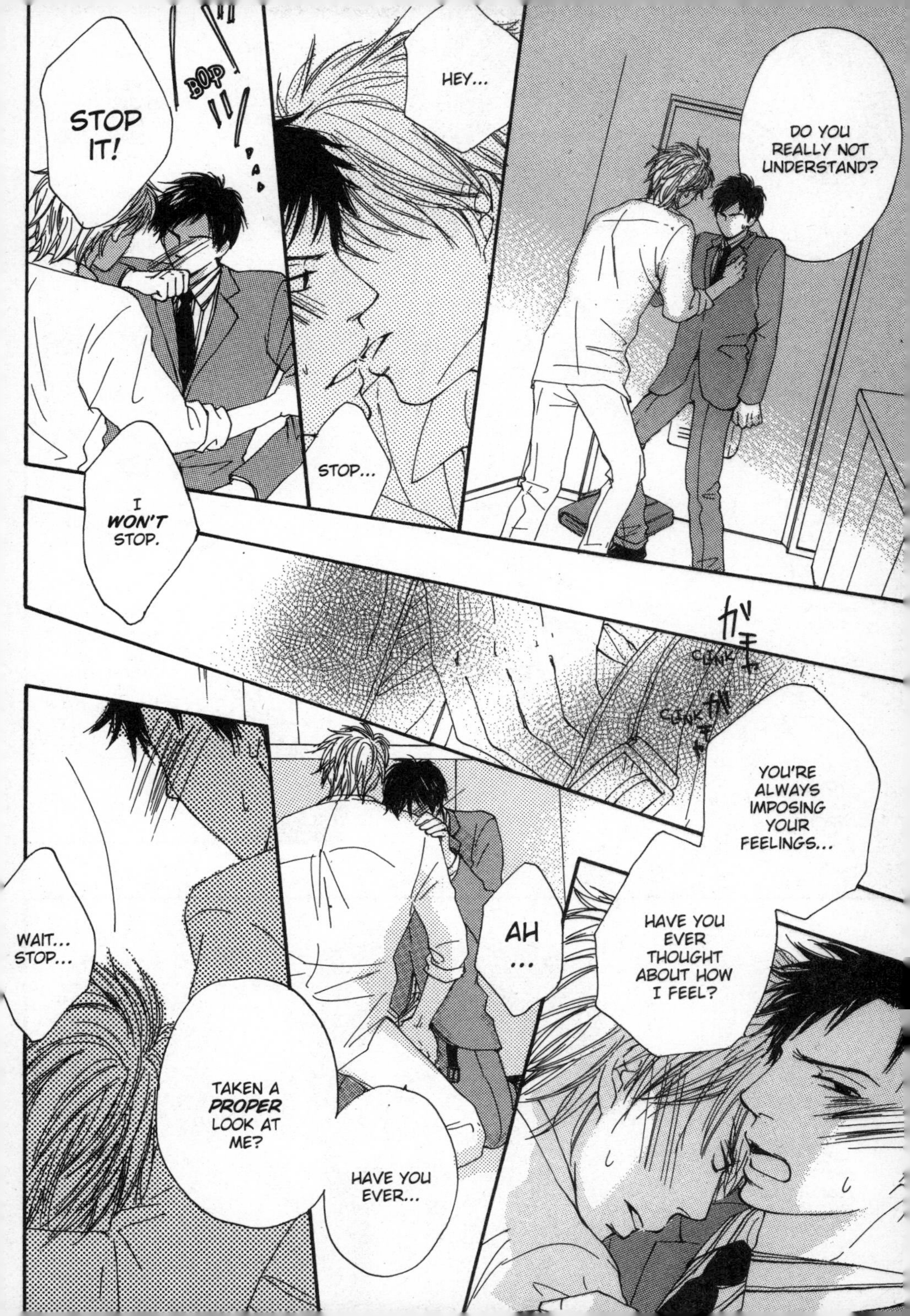

DO YOU REALLY NOT UNDERSTAND?
HEY...
STOP...
BOP!!
STOP IT!
I WON'T STOP.
CLINK
CLINK
YOU'RE ALWAYS IMPOSING YOUR FEELINGS...
HAVE YOU EVER THOUGHT ABOUT HOW I FEEL?
AH...
HAVE YOU EVER...
TAKEN A PROPER LOOK AT ME?
WAIT... STOP...

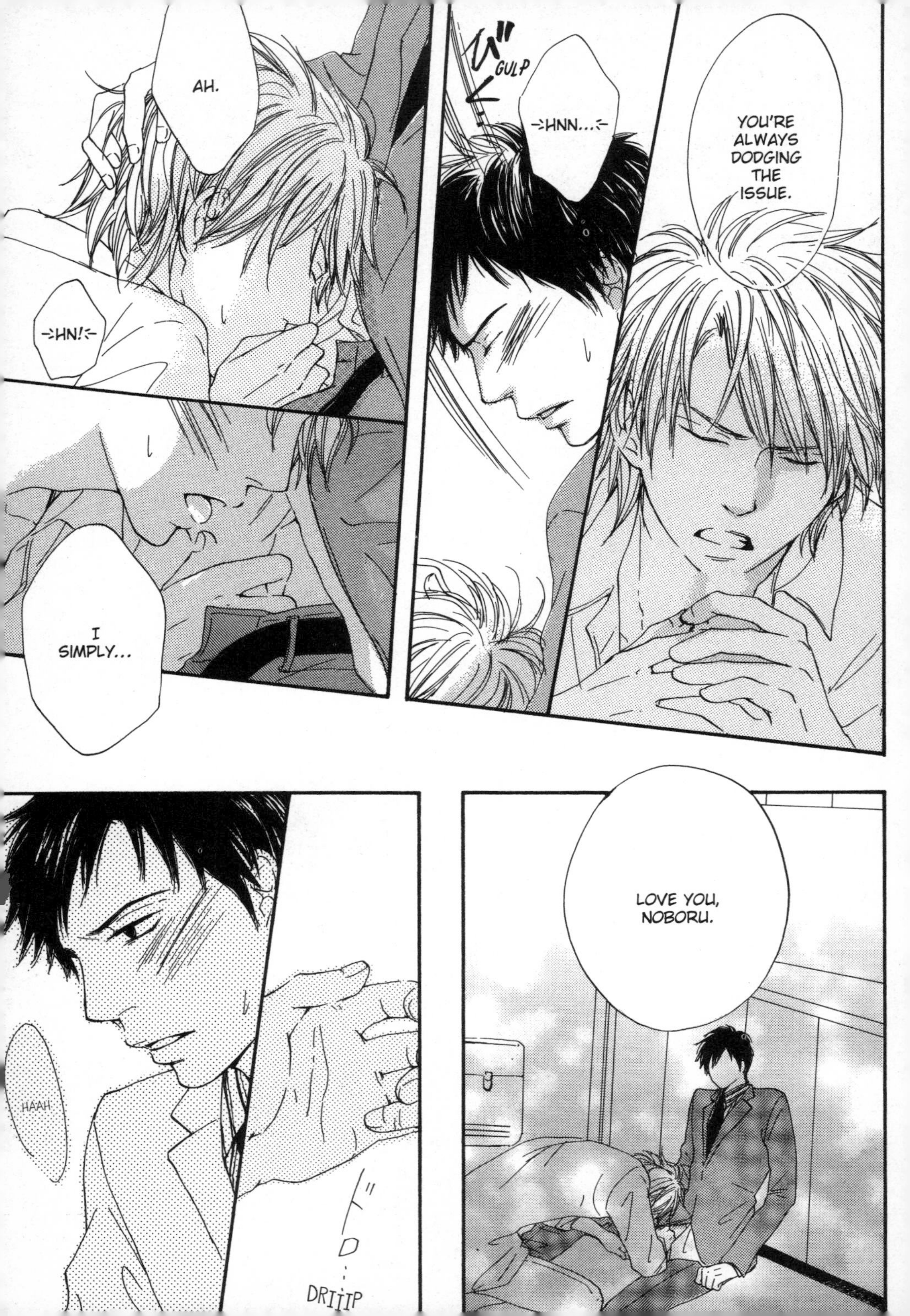
YOU'RE ALWAYS DODGING THE ISSUE.
GULP
HNN...
AH.
HN!
I SIMPLY...
LOVE YOU, NOBORU.
HAAH
DRIIIP

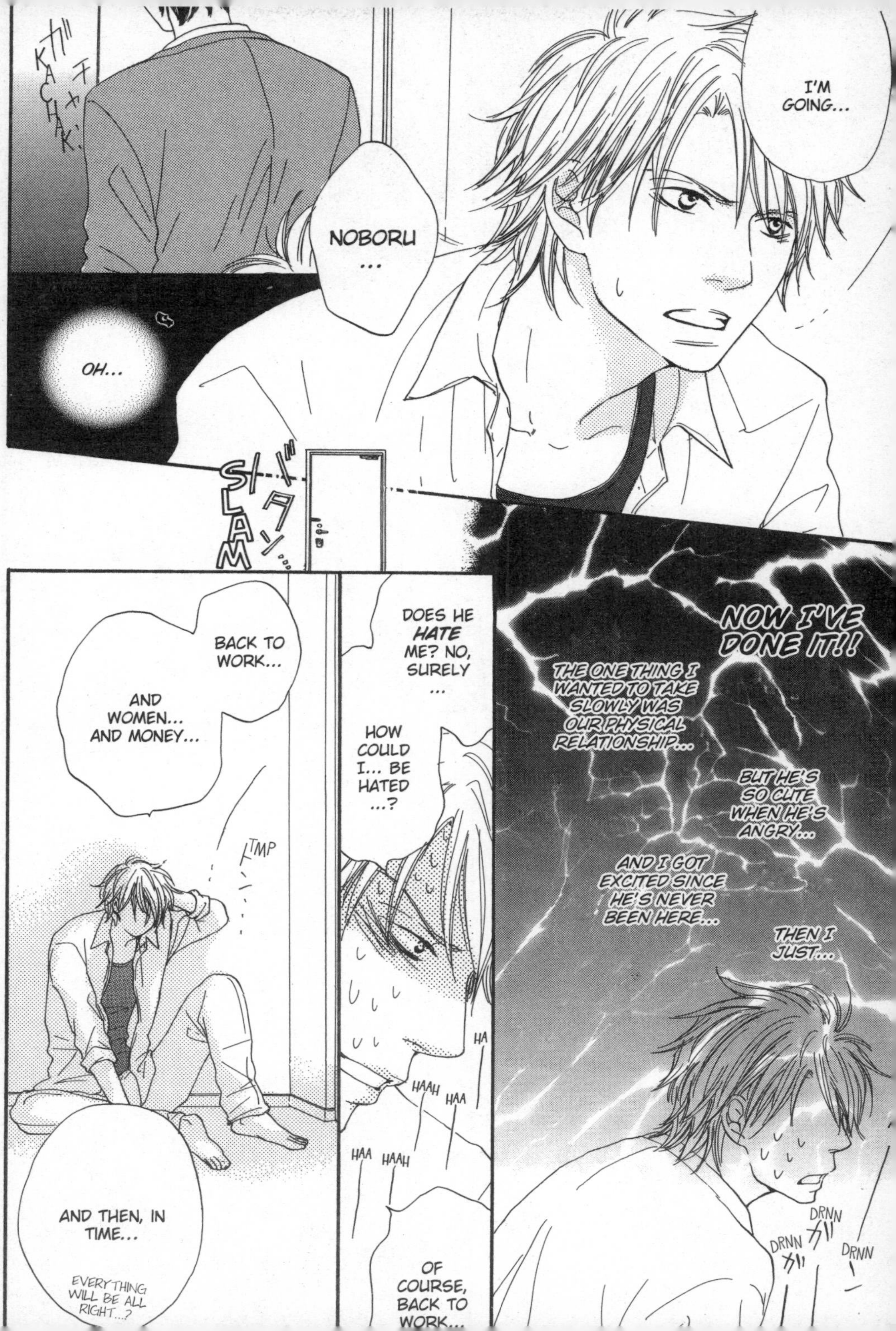
I'M GOING...
NOBORU...
KACHAK
OH...
SLAM
NOW I'VE DONE IT!!
THE ONE THING I WANTED TO TAKE SLOWLY WAS OUR PHYSICAL RELATIONSHIP...
BUT HE'S SO CUTE WHEN HE'S ANGRY...
AND I GOT EXCITED SINCE HE'S NEVER BEEN HERE...
THEN I JUST...
DRNN DRNN DRNN
DOES HE HATE ME? NO, SURELY...
HOW COULD I... BE HATED...?
HA
HAAH HAA
HAA HAAH
OF COURSE, BACK TO WORK...
BACK TO WORK...
AND WOMEN... AND MONEY...
TMP
AND THEN, IN TIME...
EVERYTHING WILL BE ALL RIGHT...?

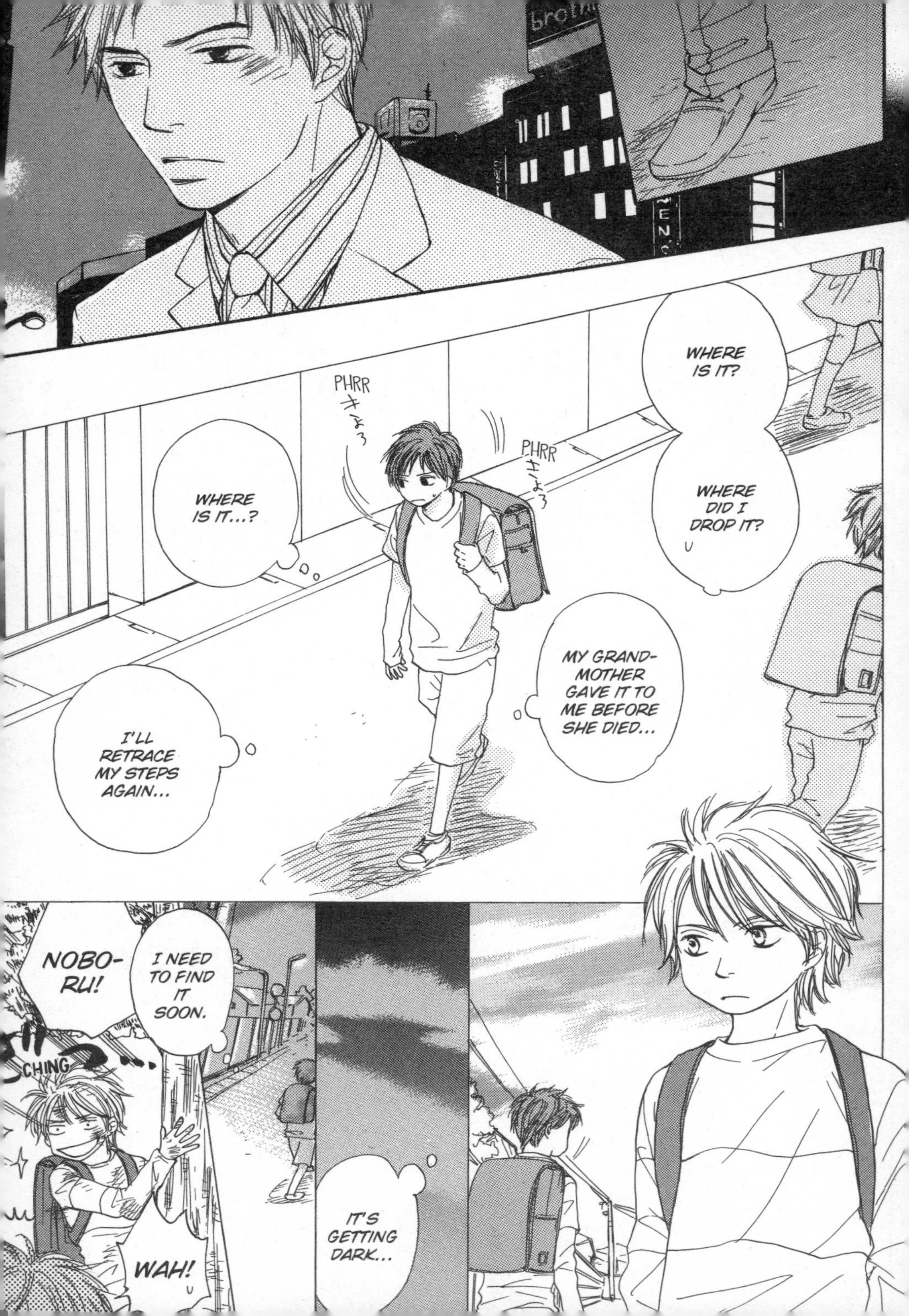
WHERE IS IT?
WHERE DID I DROP IT?
PHRR
PHRR
WHERE IS IT...?
MY GRAND-MOTHER GAVE IT TO ME BEFORE SHE DIED...
I'LL RETRACE MY STEPS AGAIN...
IT'S GETTING DARK...
I NEED TO FIND IT SOON.
NOBO-RU!
CHING
WAH!

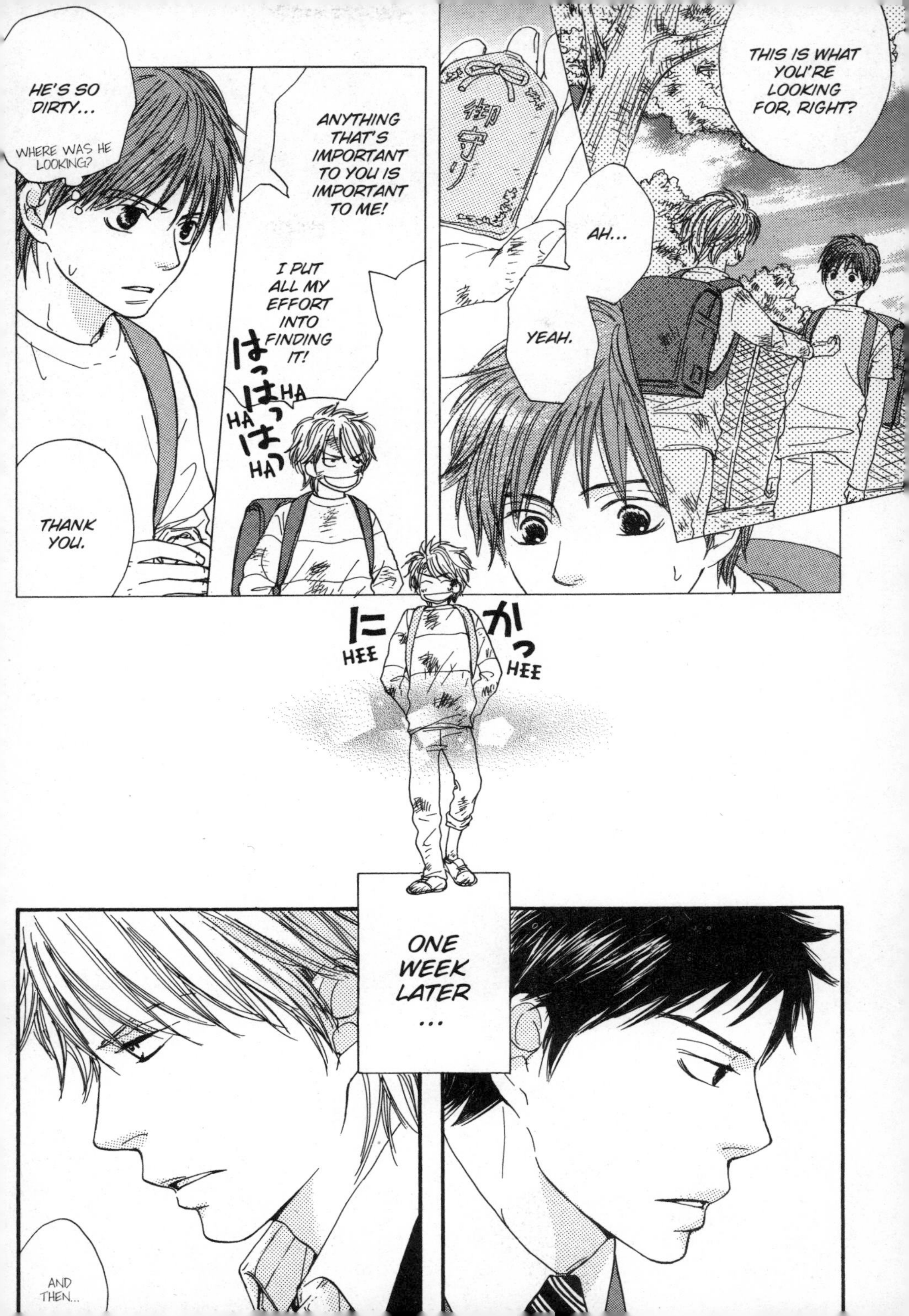
THIS IS WHAT YOU'RE LOOKING FOR, RIGHT?
御守り
AH...
YEAH.
ANYTHING THAT'S IMPORTANT TO YOU IS IMPORTANT TO ME!
I PUT ALL MY EFFORT INTO FINDING IT!
はっはっ
HA HA HA HA
HE'S SO DIRTY...
WHERE WAS HE LOOKING?
THANK YOU.
にかっ
HEE HEE
ONE WEEK LATER ...
AND THEN...

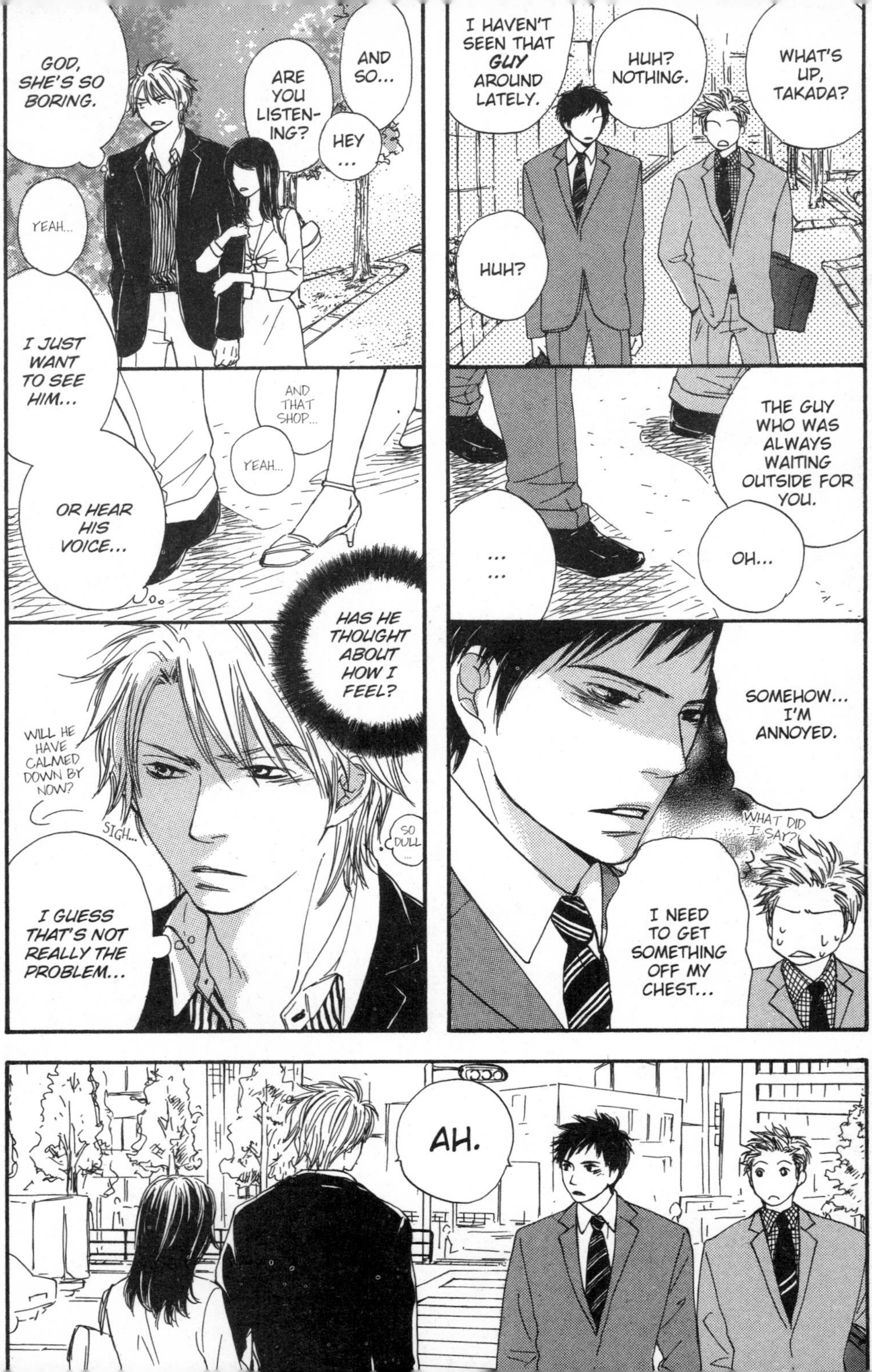
WHAT'S UP, TAKADA?
HUH? NOTHING.
I HAVEN'T SEEN THAT GUY AROUND LATELY.
HUH?
AND SO...
ARE YOU LISTENING?
GOD, SHE'S SO BORING.
HEY ...
YEAH...
I JUST WANT TO SEE HIM...
THE GUY WHO WAS ALWAYS WAITING OUTSIDE FOR YOU.
OH...
... ...
AND THAT SHOP...
YEAH...
OR HEAR HIS VOICE...
SOMEHOW... I'M ANNOYED.
WHAT DID I SAY?
I NEED TO GET SOMETHING OFF MY CHEST...
HAS HE THOUGHT ABOUT HOW I FEEL?
SO DULL ...
WILL HE HAVE CALMED DOWN BY NOW?
SIGH...
I GUESS THAT'S NOT REALLY THE PROBLEM...
AH.

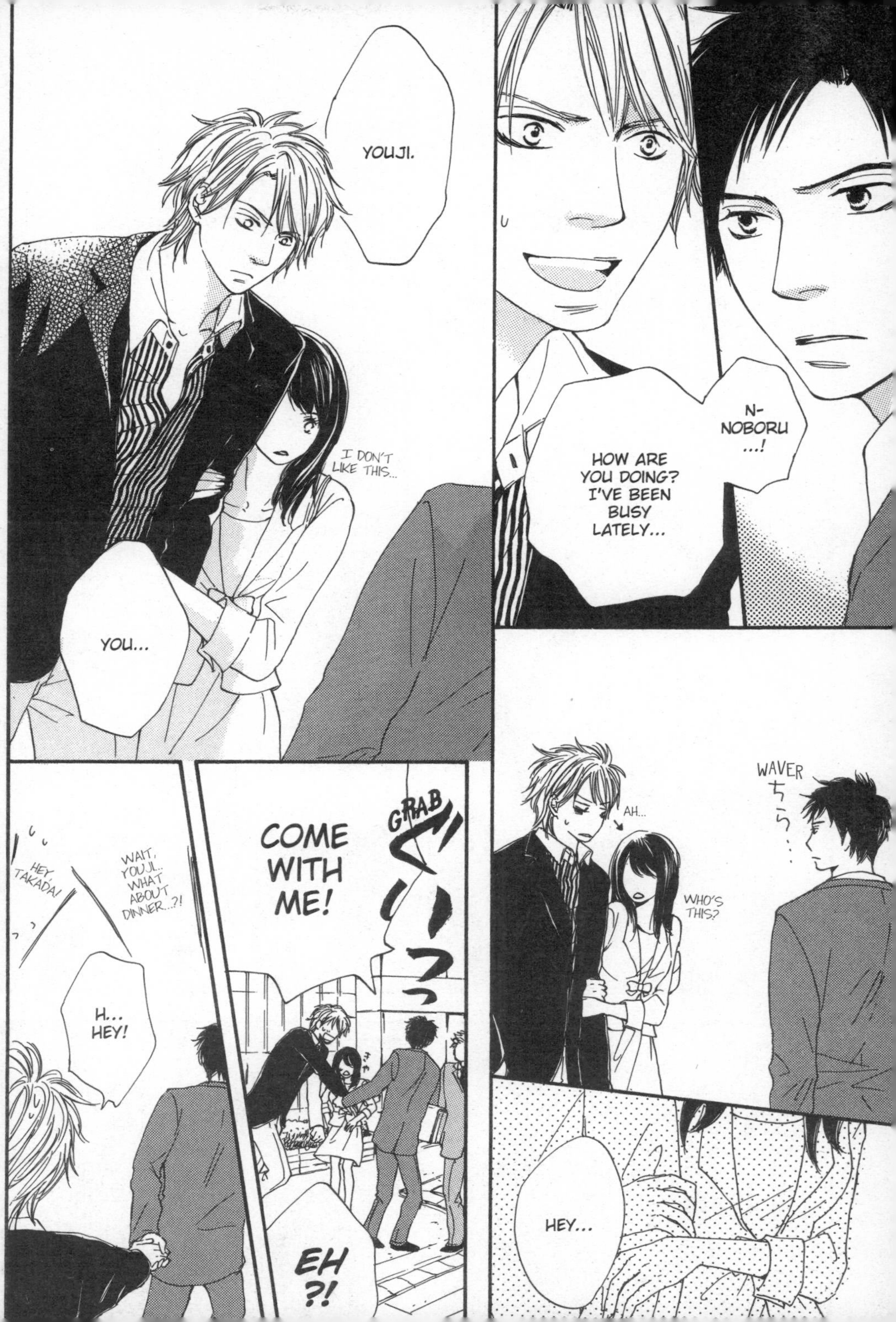
N-NOBORU...!
HOW ARE YOU DOING? I'VE BEEN BUSY LATELY...
YOUJI.
I DON'T LIKE THIS...
YOU...
WAVER
ちら...
AH...
WHO'S THIS?
HEY...
GRAB
COME WITH ME!
EH?!
WAIT, YOUJI.. WHAT ABOUT DINNER...?!
HEY, TAKADA!
H... HEY!

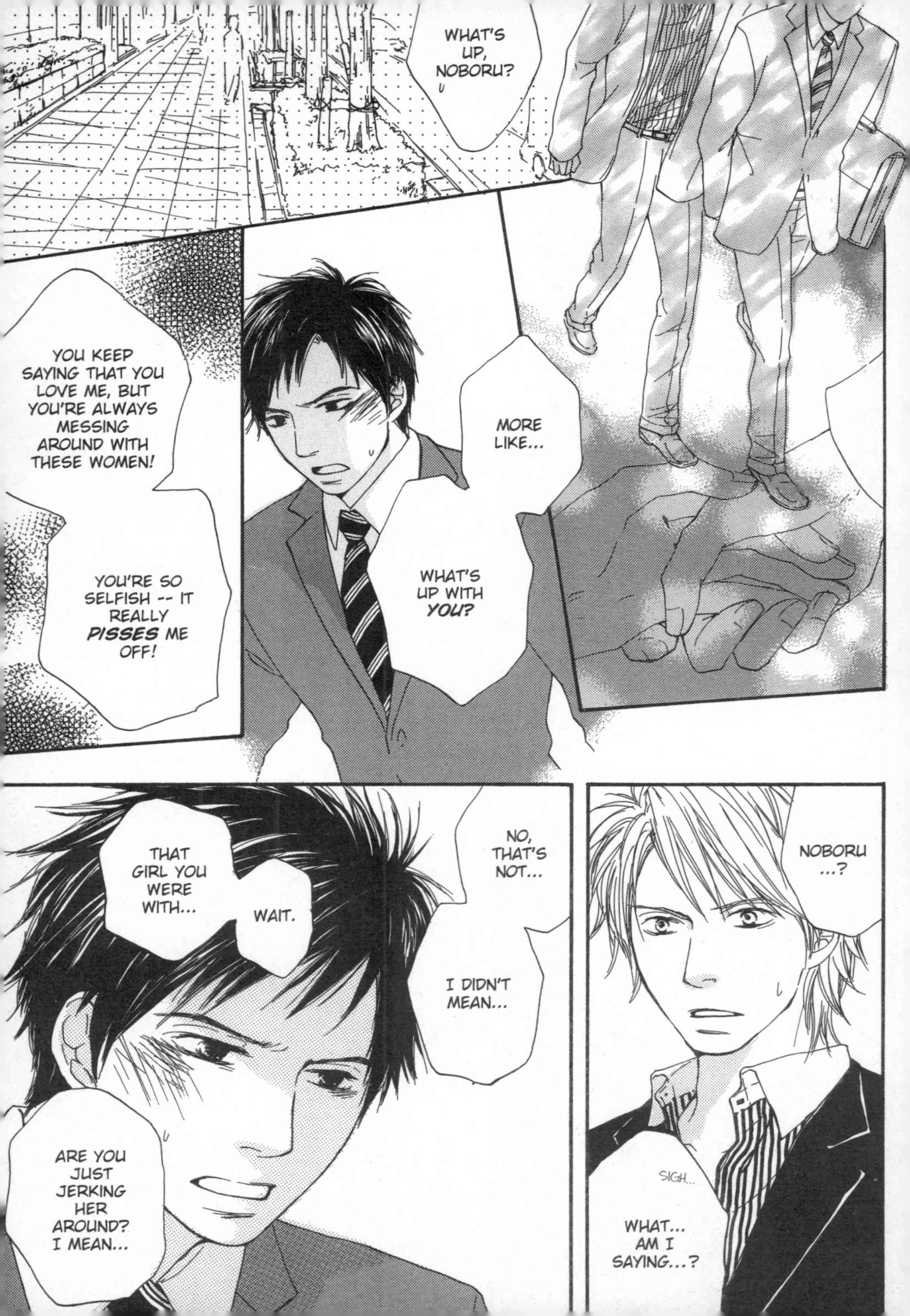
WHAT'S UP, NOBORU?
MORE LIKE...
WHAT'S UP WITH *YOU?*
YOU KEEP SAYING THAT YOU LOVE ME, BUT YOU'RE ALWAYS MESSING AROUND WITH THESE WOMEN!
YOU'RE SO SELFISH -- IT REALLY *PISSES* ME OFF!
NOBORU ...?
SIGH...
WHAT... AM I SAYING...?
NO, THAT'S NOT...
I DIDN'T MEAN...
WAIT.
THAT GIRL YOU WERE WITH...
ARE YOU JUST JERKING HER AROUND? I MEAN...

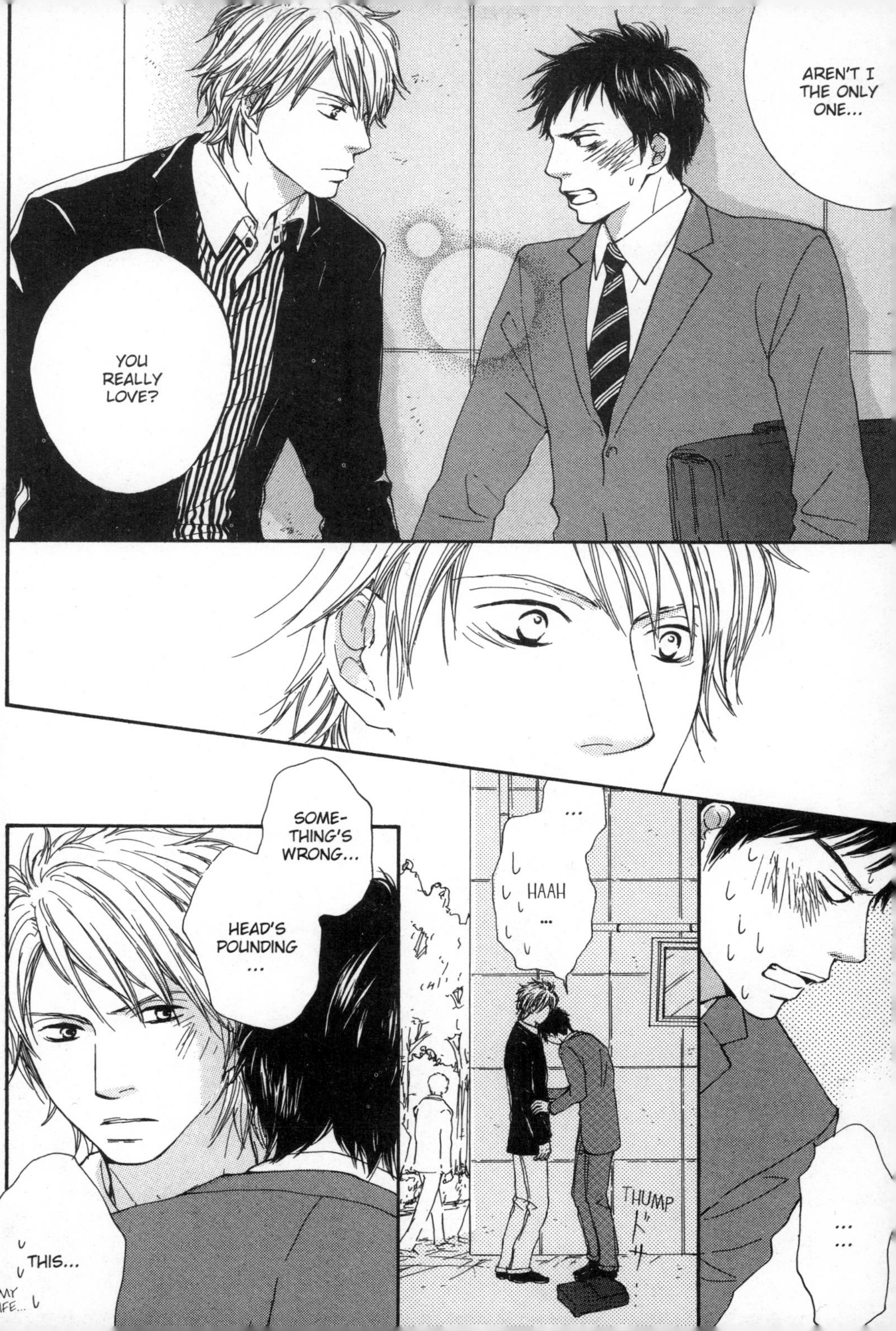
AREN'T I THE ONLY ONE...
YOU REALLY LOVE?
... ...
... HAAH ...
THUMP
SOME-THING'S WRONG...
HEAD'S POUNDING ...
THIS...
MY LIFE...

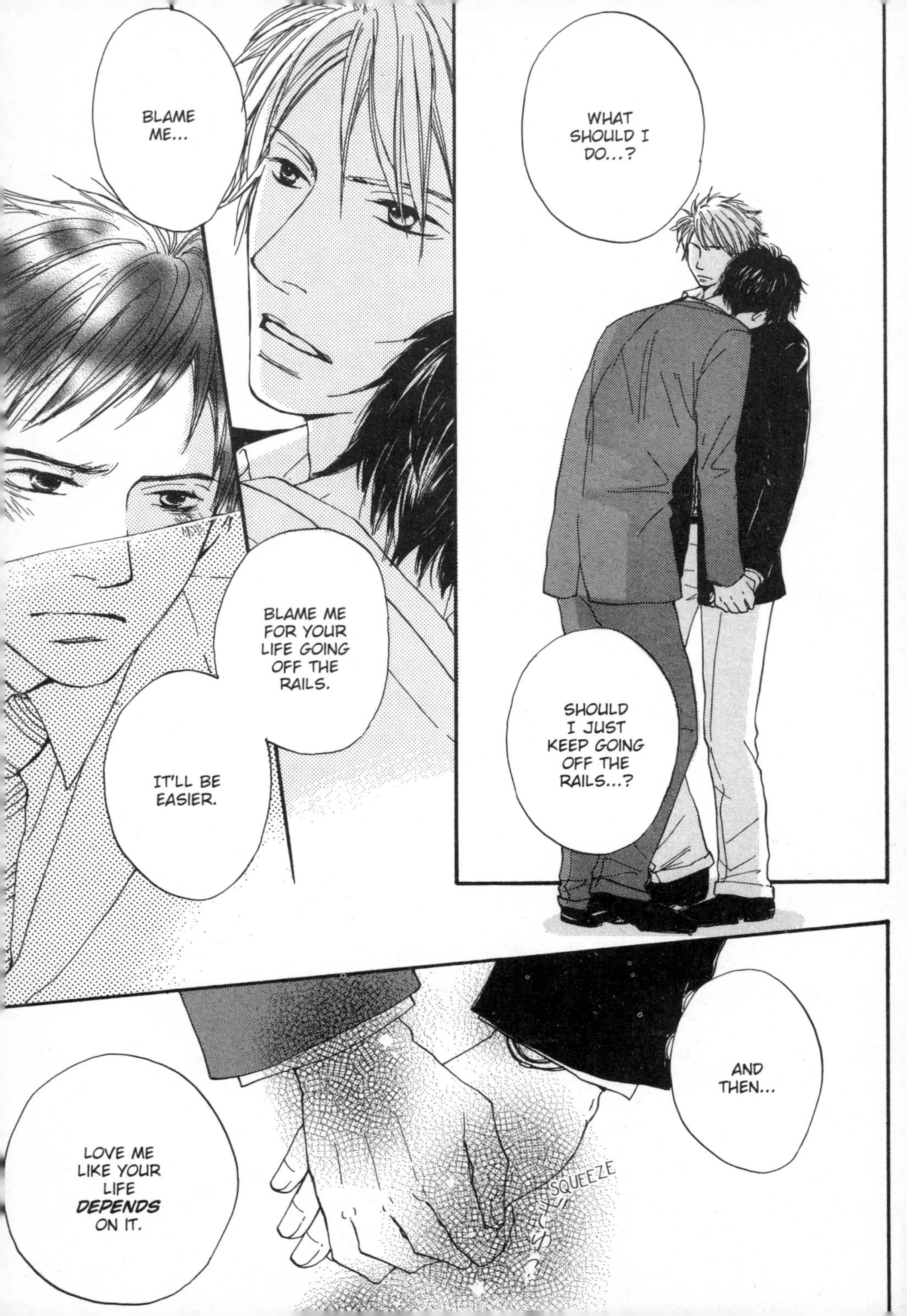
WHAT SHOULD I DO...?
SHOULD I JUST KEEP GOING OFF THE RAILS...?
BLAME ME...
BLAME ME FOR YOUR LIFE GOING OFF THE RAILS.
IT'LL BE EASIER.
AND THEN...
SQUEEZE
LOVE ME LIKE YOUR LIFE DEPENDS ON IT.

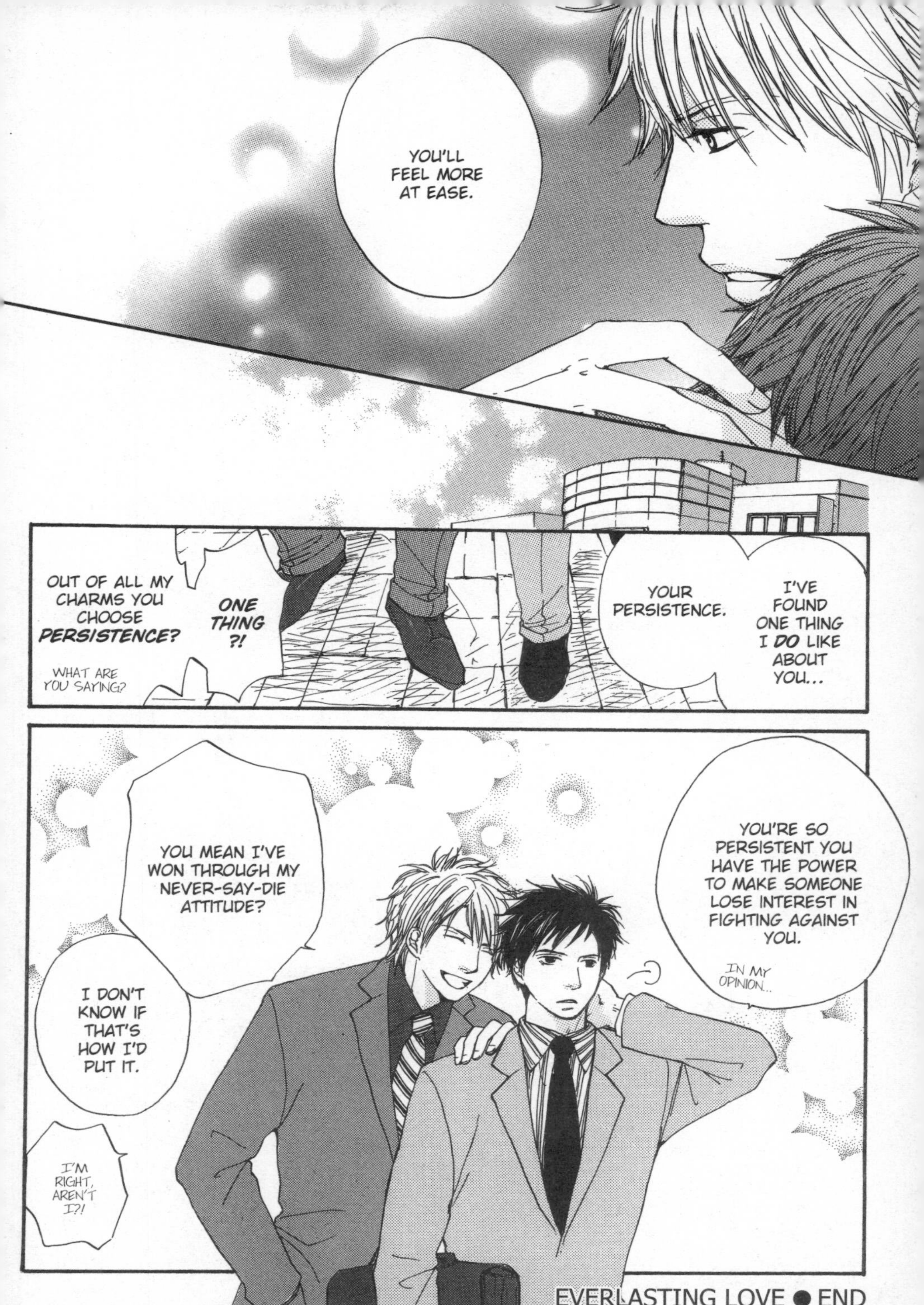
YOU'LL FEEL MORE AT EASE.
I'VE FOUND ONE THING I **DO** LIKE ABOUT YOU...
YOUR PERSISTENCE.
ONE THING ?!
OUT OF ALL MY CHARMS YOU CHOOSE **PERSISTENCE?**
WHAT ARE YOU SAYING?
YOU'RE SO PERSISTENT YOU HAVE THE POWER TO MAKE SOMEONE LOSE INTEREST IN FIGHTING AGAINST YOU.
IN MY OPINION...
YOU MEAN I'VE WON THROUGH MY NEVER-SAY-DIE ATTITUDE?
I DON'T KNOW IF THAT'S HOW I'D PUT IT.
I'M RIGHT, AREN'T I?!

EVERLASTING LOVE ● END

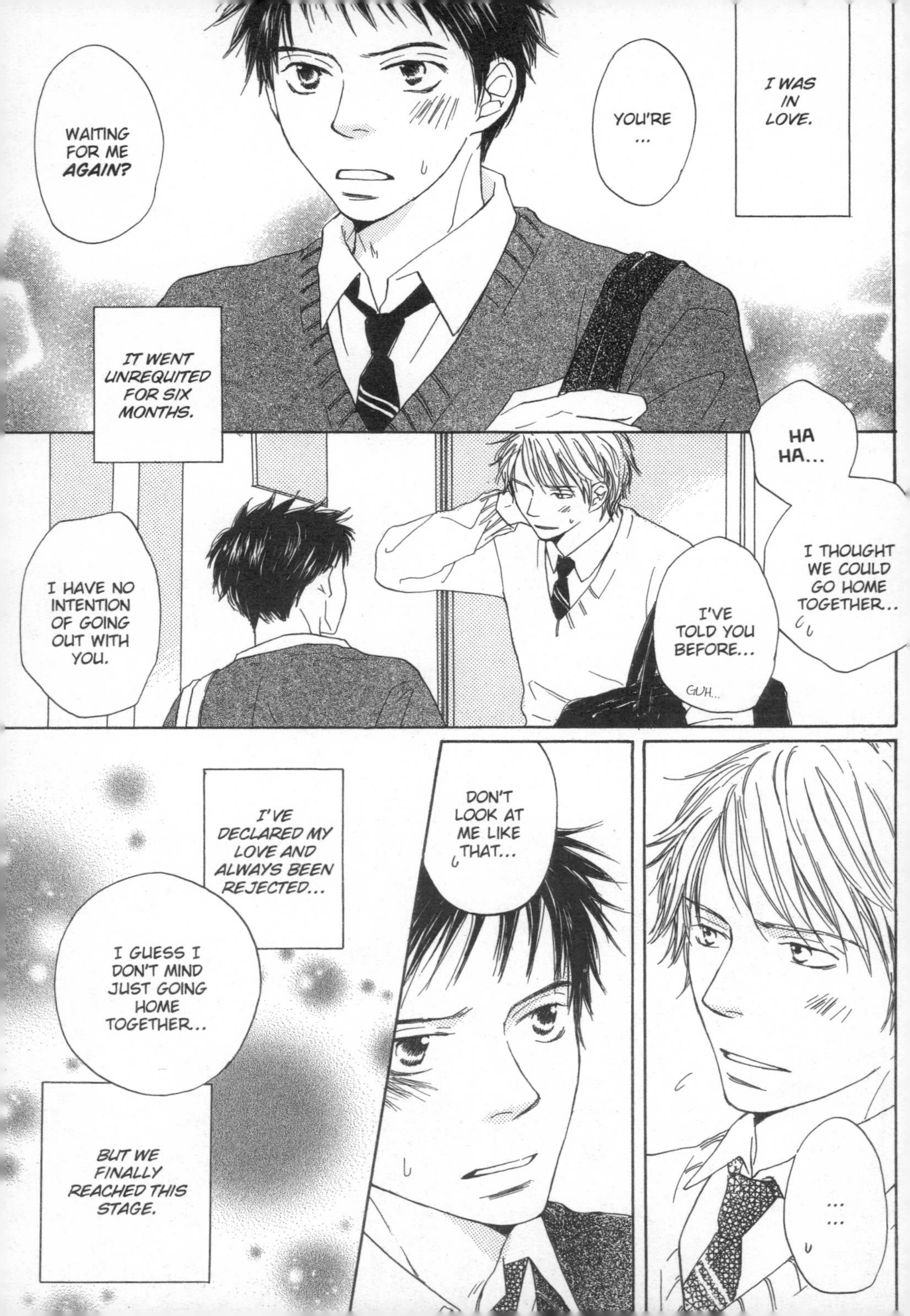
I WAS IN LOVE.
YOU'RE ...
WAITING FOR ME AGAIN?
IT WENT UNREQUITED FOR SIX MONTHS.
HA HA...
I THOUGHT WE COULD GO HOME TOGETHER...
I'VE TOLD YOU BEFORE...
GUH...
I HAVE NO INTENTION OF GOING OUT WITH YOU.
... ...
DON'T LOOK AT ME LIKE THAT...
I'VE DECLARED MY LOVE AND ALWAYS BEEN REJECTED...
I GUESS I DON'T MIND JUST GOING HOME TOGETHER...
BUT WE FINALLY REACHED THIS STAGE.

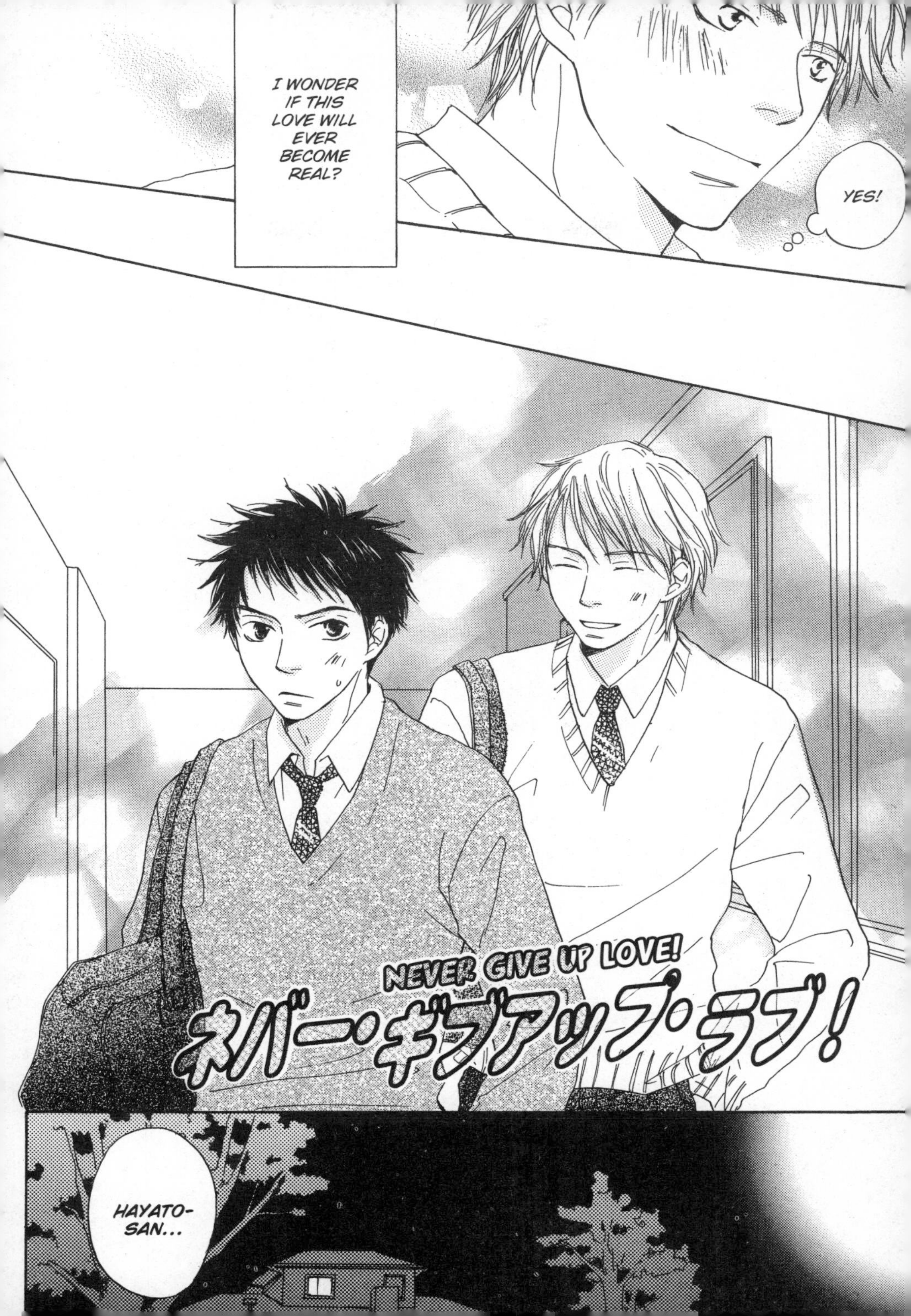
I WONDER IF THIS LOVE WILL EVER BECOME REAL?
YES!
NEVER GIVE UP LOVE!
ネバー・ギブアップ・ラブ!
HAYATO-SAN...

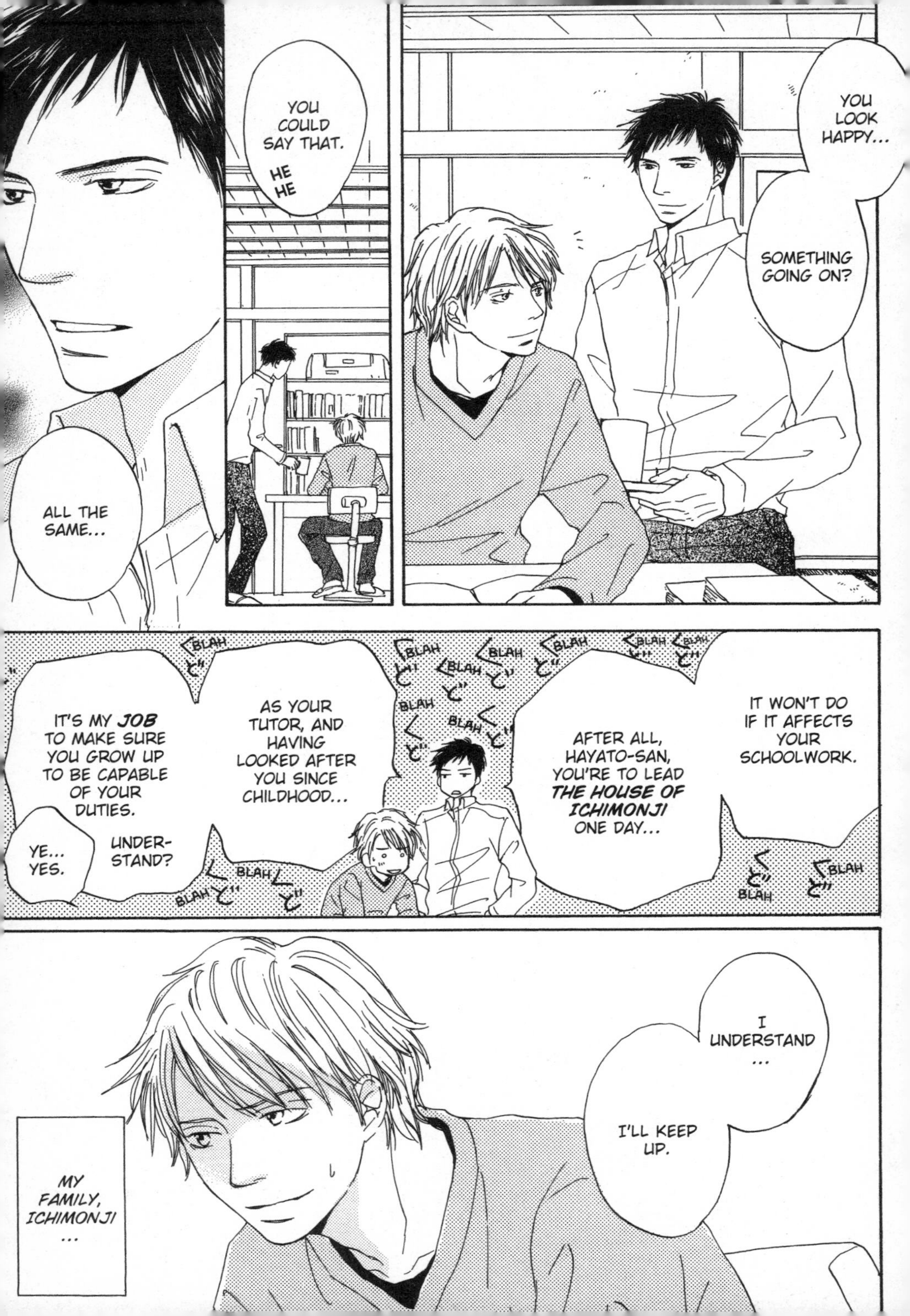
YOU LOOK HAPPY...
SOMETHING GOING ON?
YOU COULD SAY THAT.
HE HE
ALL THE SAME...
BLAH BLAH BLAH BLAH BLAH BLAH BLAH BLAH
IT WON'T DO IF IT AFFECTS YOUR SCHOOLWORK.
AFTER ALL, HAYATO-SAN, YOU'RE TO LEAD ***THE HOUSE OF ICHIMONJI*** ONE DAY...
AS YOUR TUTOR, AND HAVING LOOKED AFTER YOU SINCE CHILDHOOD...
IT'S MY ***JOB*** TO MAKE SURE YOU GROW UP TO BE CAPABLE OF YOUR DUTIES.
UNDER-STAND?
YE... YES.
BLAH BLAH BLAH BLAH
I UNDERSTAND ...
I'LL KEEP UP.
MY FAMILY, ICHIMONJI ...

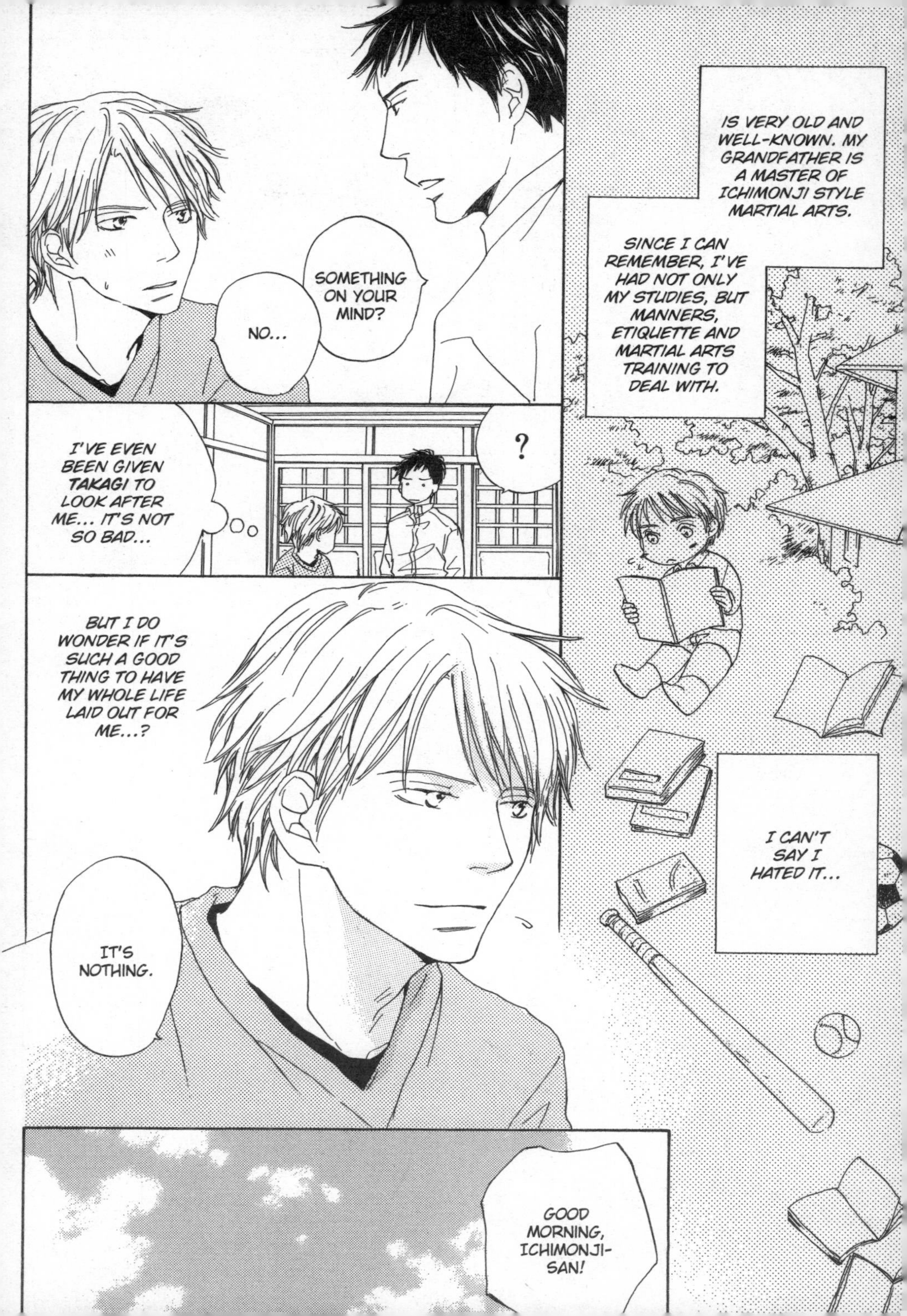
IS VERY OLD AND WELL-KNOWN. MY GRANDFATHER IS A MASTER OF ICHIMONJI STYLE MARTIAL ARTS.
SINCE I CAN REMEMBER, I'VE HAD NOT ONLY MY STUDIES, BUT MANNERS, ETIQUETTE AND MARTIAL ARTS TRAINING TO DEAL WITH.
I CAN'T SAY I HATED IT...
SOMETHING ON YOUR MIND?
NO...
?
I'VE EVEN BEEN GIVEN TAKAGI TO LOOK AFTER ME... IT'S NOT SO BAD...
BUT I DO WONDER IF IT'S SUCH A GOOD THING TO HAVE MY WHOLE LIFE LAID OUT FOR ME...?
IT'S NOTHING.
GOOD MORNING, ICHIMONJI-SAN!

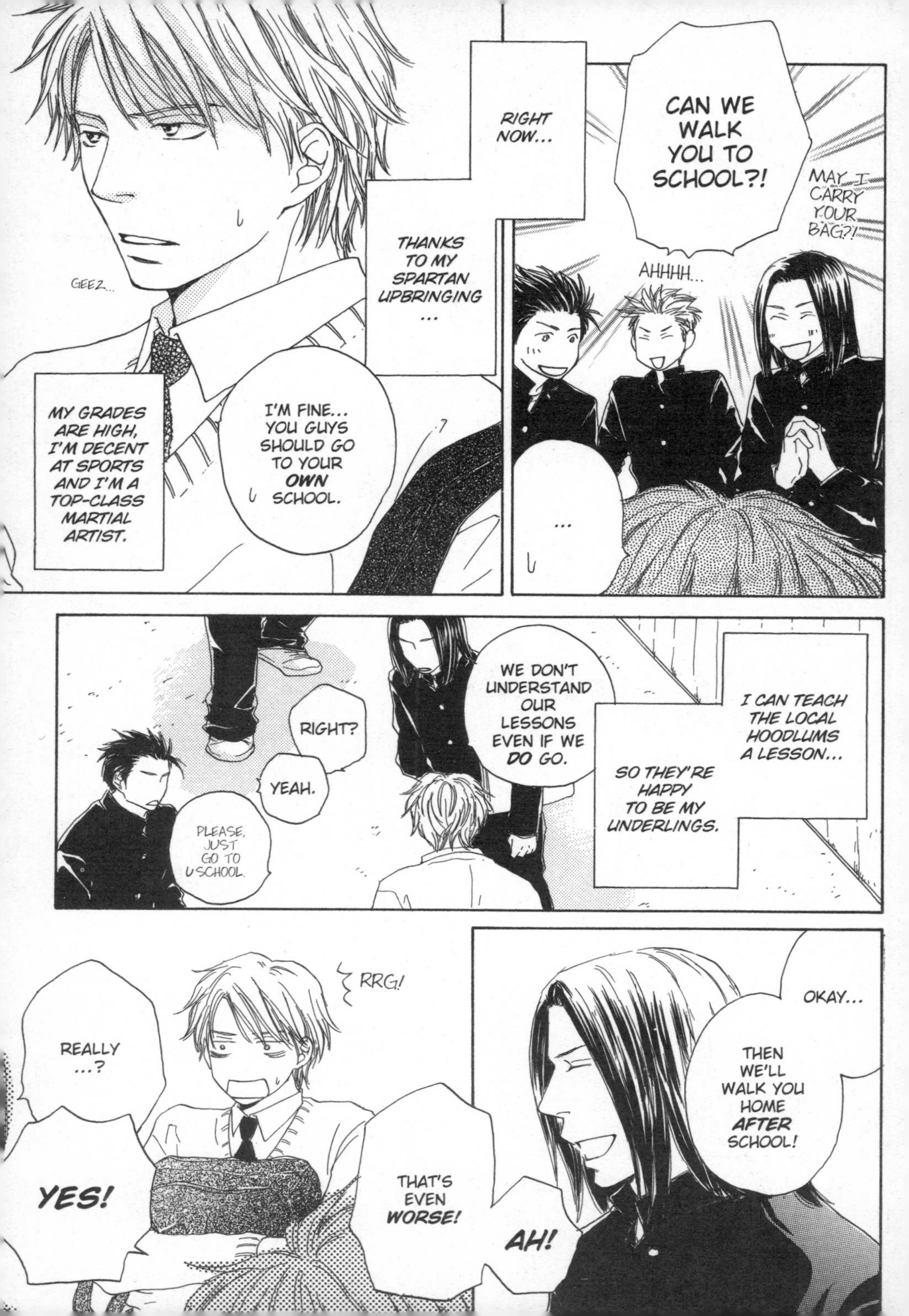
CAN WE WALK YOU TO SCHOOL?!
MAY I CARRY YOUR BAG?!
AHHHH...
...
RIGHT NOW...
THANKS TO MY SPARTAN UPBRINGING...
MY GRADES ARE HIGH, I'M DECENT AT SPORTS AND I'M A TOP-CLASS MARTIAL ARTIST.
I'M FINE... YOU GUYS SHOULD GO TO YOUR **OWN** SCHOOL.
GEEZ...
I CAN TEACH THE LOCAL HOODLUMS A LESSON...
SO THEY'RE HAPPY TO BE MY UNDERLINGS.
WE DON'T UNDERSTAND OUR LESSONS EVEN IF WE **DO** GO.
RIGHT?
YEAH.
PLEASE, JUST GO TO SCHOOL.
OKAY...
THEN WE'LL WALK YOU HOME **AFTER** SCHOOL!
AH!
RRG!
THAT'S EVEN **WORSE**!
REALLY...?
YES!

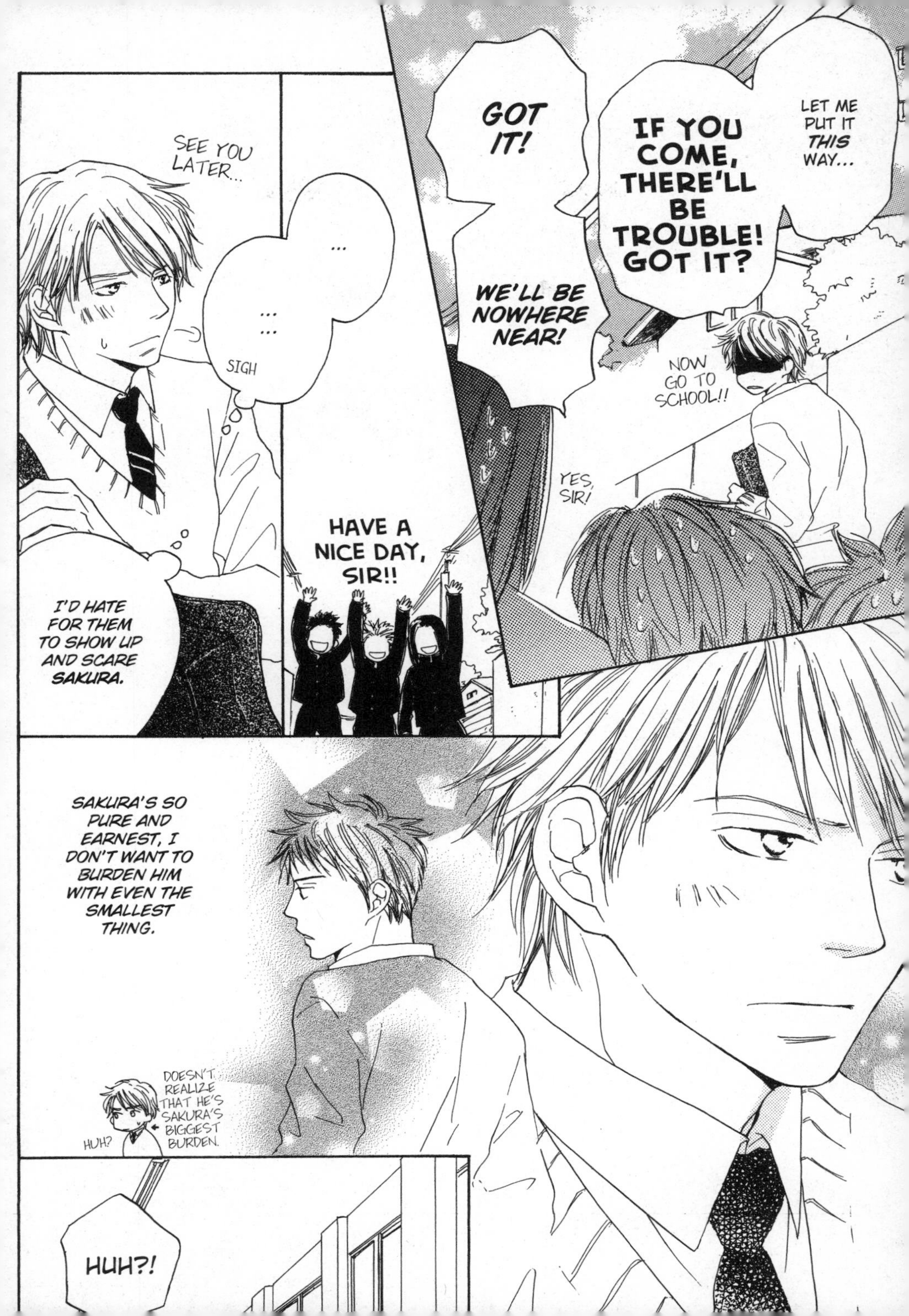
LET ME PUT IT *THIS* WAY...
IF YOU COME, THERE'LL BE TROUBLE! GOT IT?
NOW GO TO SCHOOL!!
GOT IT!
WE'LL BE NOWHERE NEAR!
YES, SIR!
HAVE A NICE DAY, SIR!!
SEE YOU LATER...
...
... ...
SIGH
I'D HATE FOR THEM TO SHOW UP AND SCARE SAKURA.
SAKURA'S SO PURE AND EARNEST, I DON'T WANT TO BURDEN HIM WITH EVEN THE SMALLEST THING.
DOESN'T REALIZE THAT HE'S SAKURA'S BIGGEST BURDEN.
HUH?
HUH?!

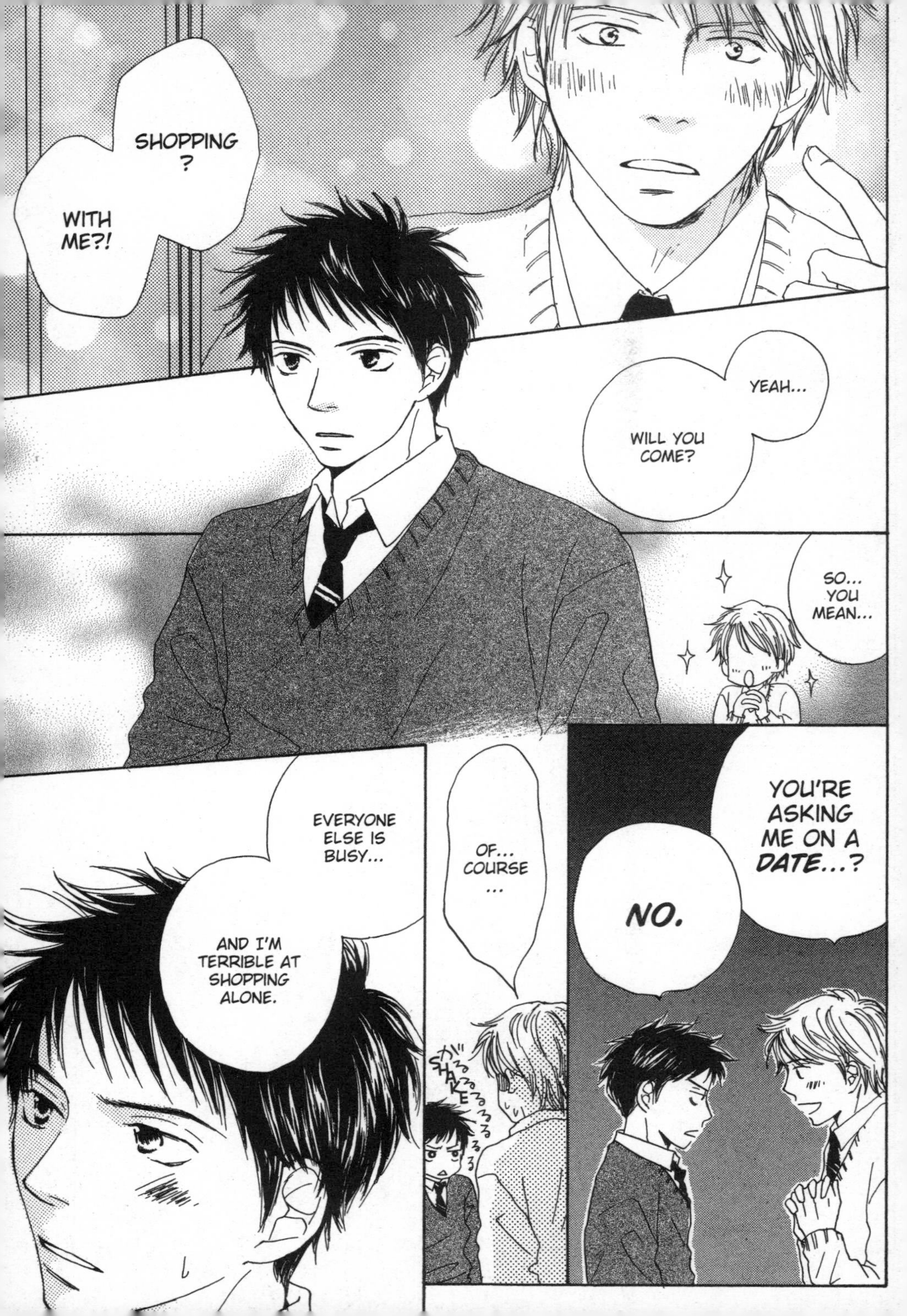
SHOPPING? WITH ME?!
YEAH... WILL YOU COME?
SO... YOU MEAN...
YOU'RE ASKING ME ON A *DATE*...?
NO.
OF... COURSE...
SHAKE
EVERYONE ELSE IS BUSY... AND I'M TERRIBLE AT SHOPPING ALONE.

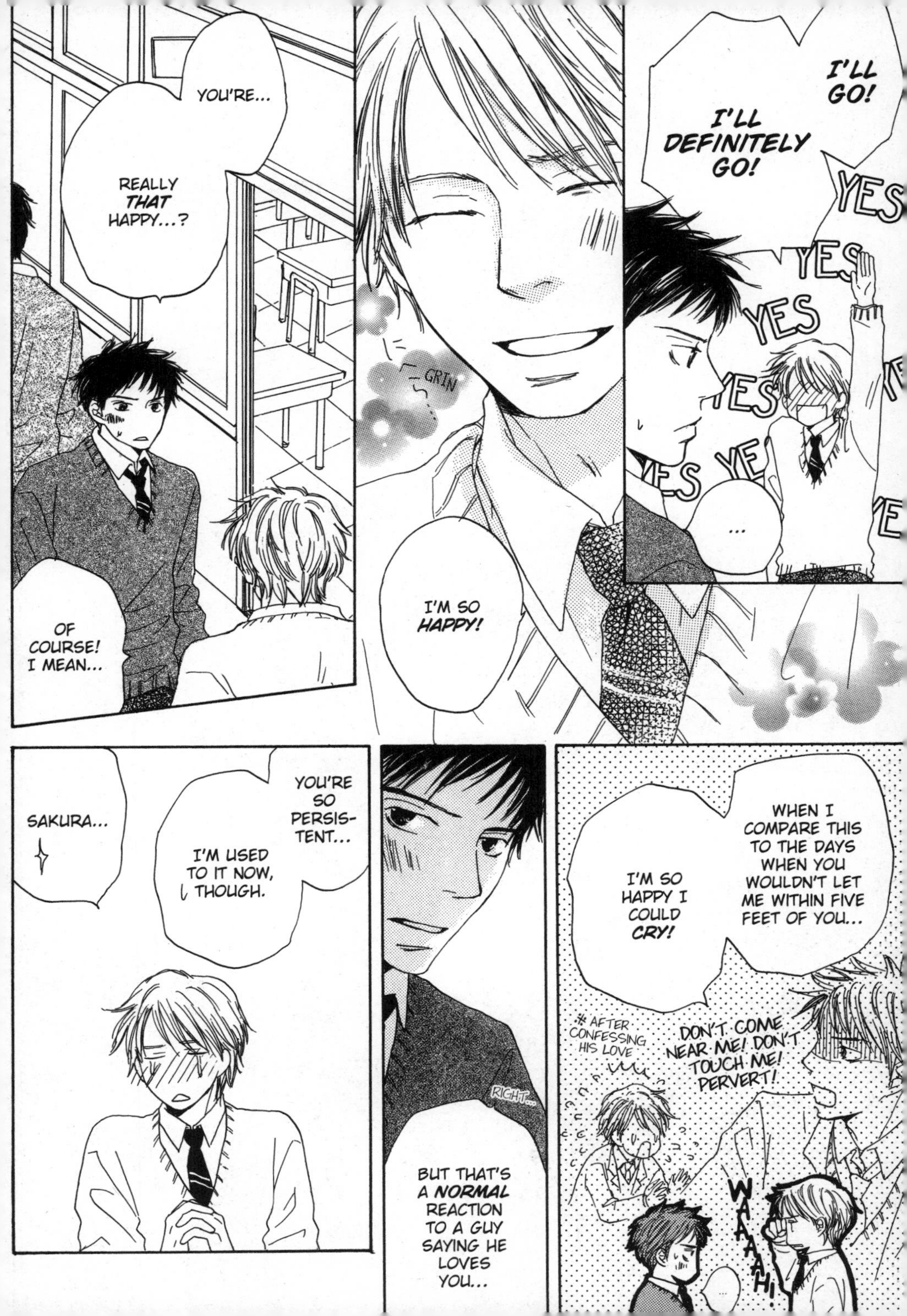
I'LL GO!
I'LL DEFINITELY GO!
YES YES YES YES YES YES YES YES
...
GRIN
I'M SO HAPPY!
YOU'RE...
REALLY THAT HAPPY...?
OF COURSE! I MEAN...
WHEN I COMPARE THIS TO THE DAYS WHEN YOU WOULDN'T LET ME WITHIN FIVE FEET OF YOU...
I'M SO HAPPY I COULD CRY!
※AFTER CONFESSING HIS LOVE
DON'T COME NEAR ME! DON'T TOUCH ME! PERVERT!
WAAAAAH!
...
RIGHT...
BUT THAT'S A NORMAL REACTION TO A GUY SAYING HE LOVES YOU...
YOU'RE SO PERSISTENT...
I'M USED TO IT NOW, THOUGH.
SAKURA...

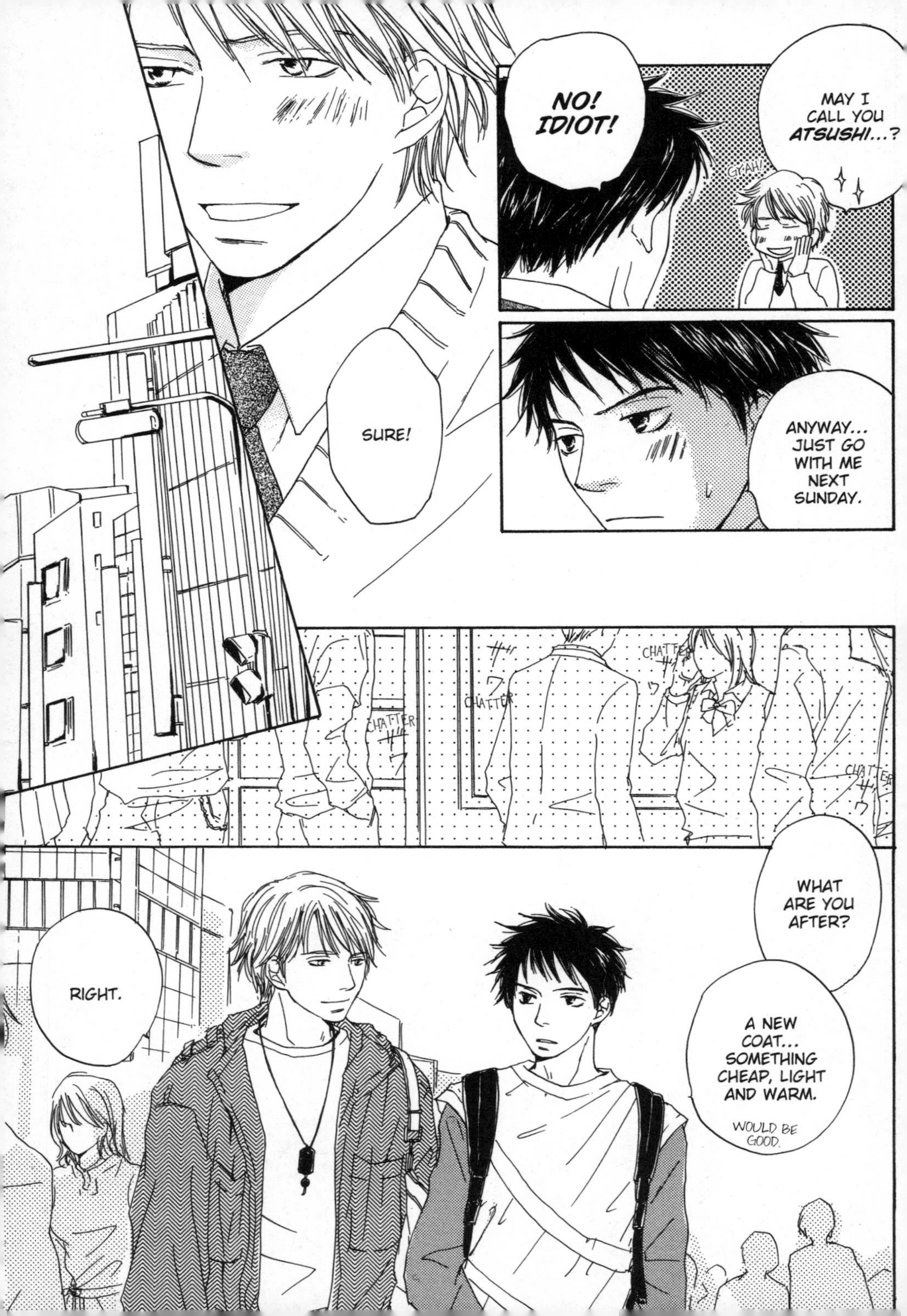
MAY I CALL YOU ATSUSHI...?
GYAH!
NO! IDIOT!
ANYWAY... JUST GO WITH ME NEXT SUNDAY.
SURE!
CHATTER
CHATTER
CHATTER
CHATTER
WHAT ARE YOU AFTER?
A NEW COAT... SOMETHING CHEAP, LIGHT AND WARM.
WOULD BE GOOD.
RIGHT.

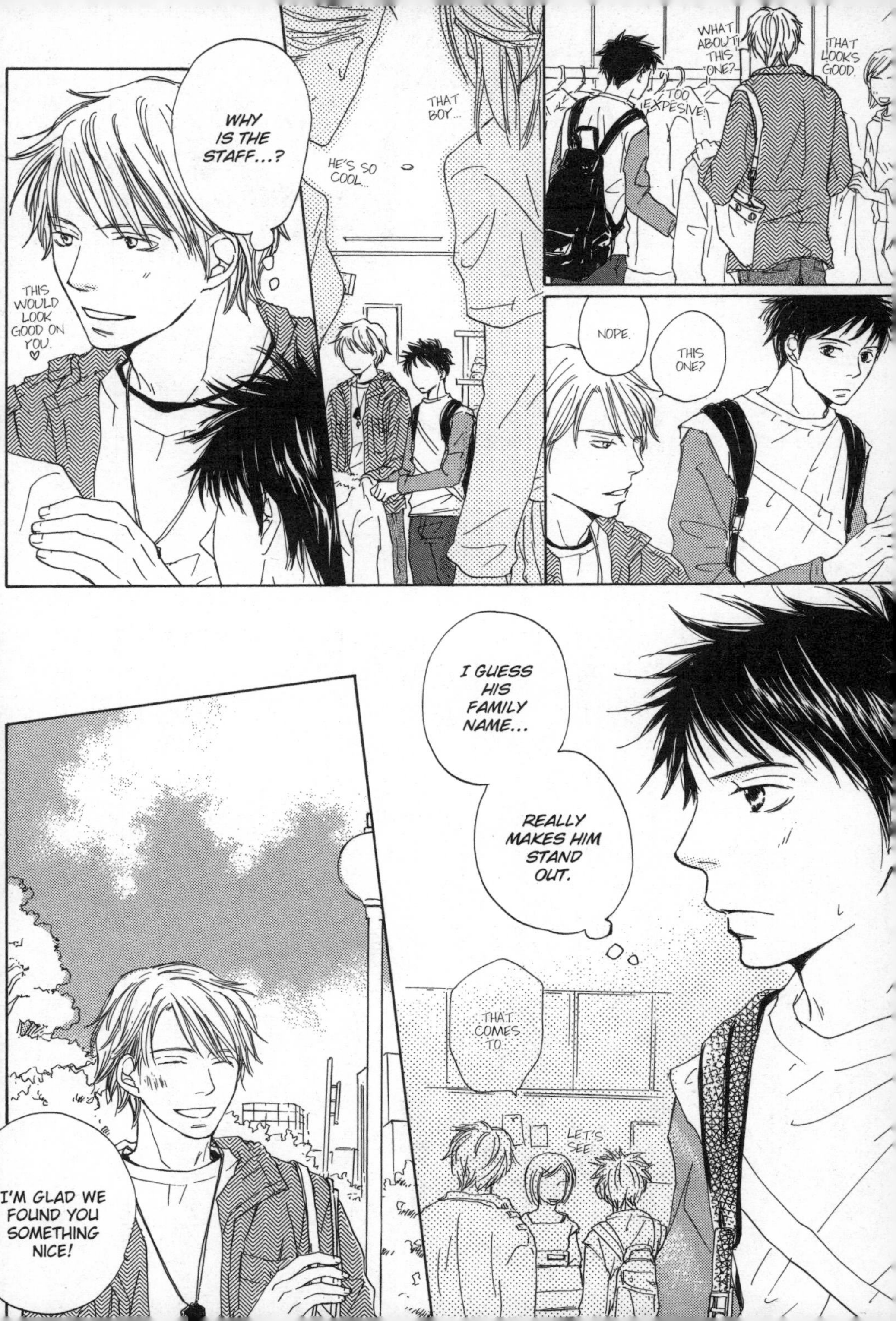
THAT LOOKS GOOD.
WHAT ABOUT THIS ONE?
TOO EXPESIVE!
THIS ONE?
NOPE.
THAT BOY...
HE'S SO COOL...
WHY IS THE STAFF...?
THIS WOULD LOOK GOOD ON YOU. ♥
I GUESS HIS FAMILY NAME...
REALLY MAKES HIM STAND OUT.
THAT COMES TO...
LET'S SEE...
I'M GLAD WE FOUND YOU SOMETHING NICE!

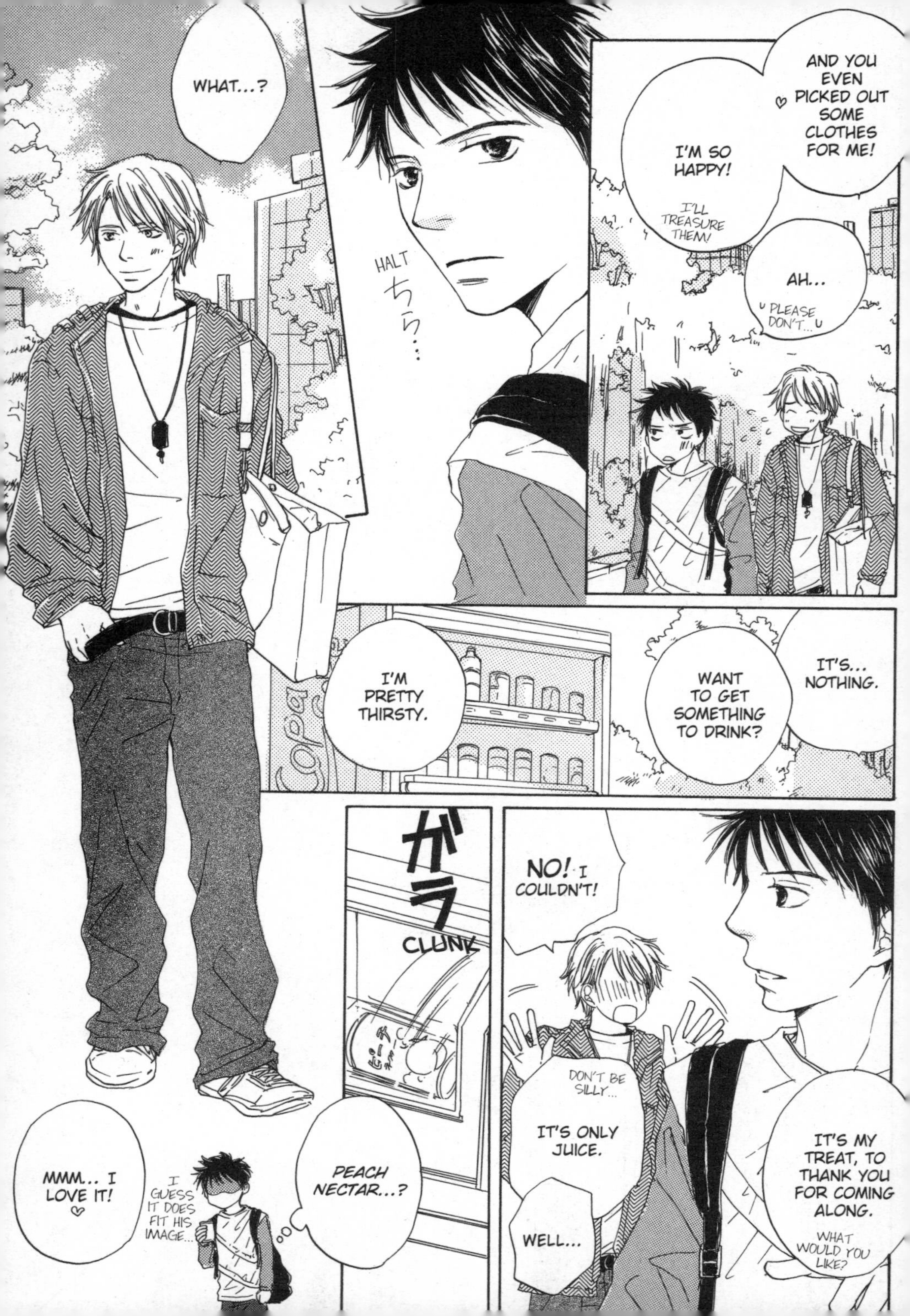
AND YOU EVEN PICKED OUT SOME CLOTHES FOR ME!
I'M SO HAPPY!
I'LL TREASURE THEM!
AH...
PLEASE DON'T...
HALT ちら…
WHAT...?
IT'S... NOTHING.
WANT TO GET SOMETHING TO DRINK?
I'M PRETTY THIRSTY.
IT'S MY TREAT, TO THANK YOU FOR COMING ALONG.
WHAT WOULD YOU LIKE?
NO! I COULDN'T!
DON'T BE SILLY...
IT'S ONLY JUICE.
WELL...
ガラ CLUNK
PEACH NECTAR...?
I GUESS IT DOES FIT HIS IMAGE...
MMM... I LOVE IT!

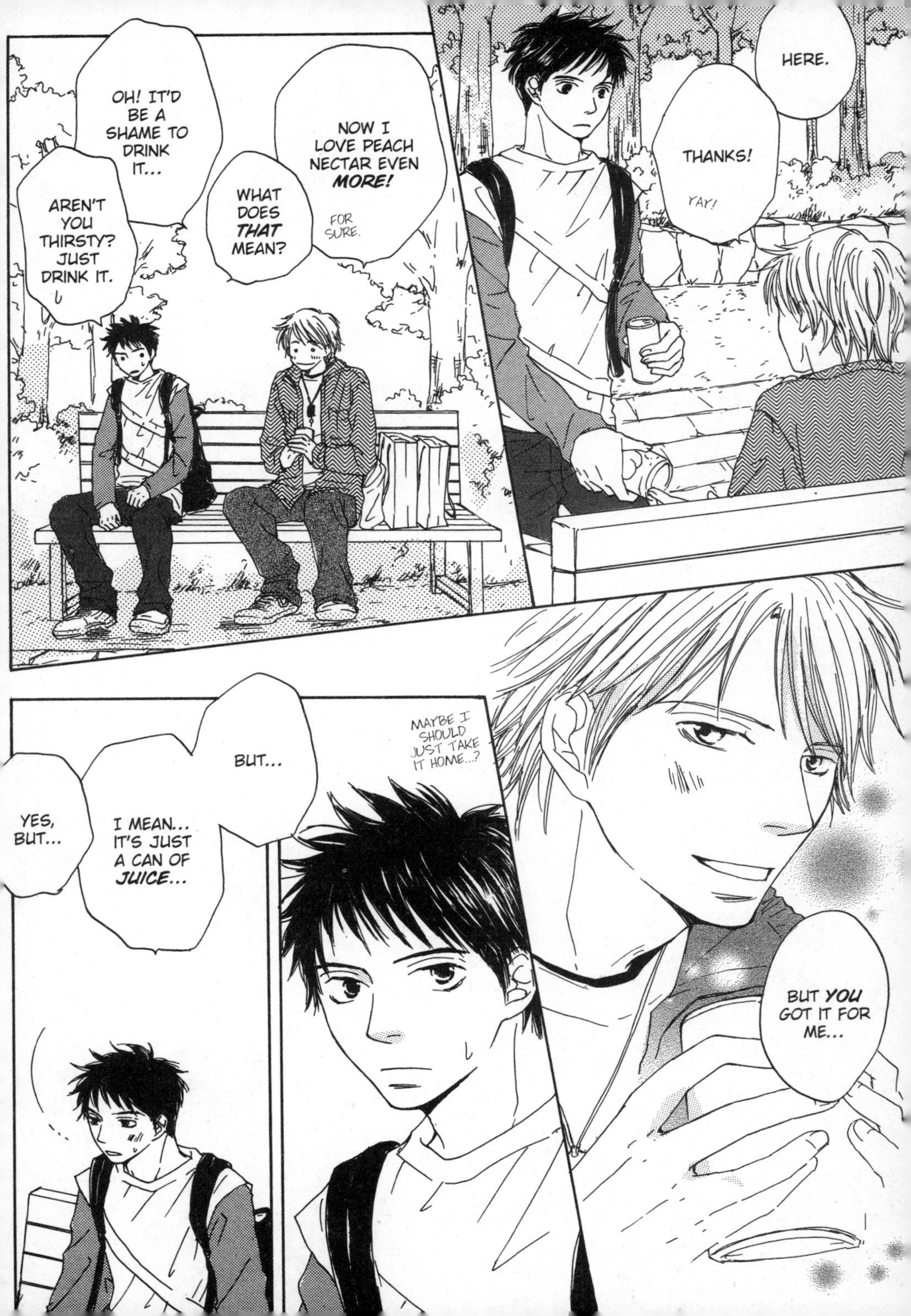
HERE.
THANKS!
YAY!
NOW I LOVE PEACH NECTAR EVEN ***MORE!***
FOR SURE.
WHAT DOES ***THAT*** MEAN?
OH! IT'D BE A SHAME TO DRINK IT...
AREN'T YOU THIRSTY? JUST DRINK IT.
MAYBE I SHOULD JUST TAKE IT HOME...?
BUT ***YOU*** GOT IT FOR ME...
BUT...
I MEAN... IT'S JUST A CAN OF ***JUICE***...
YES, BUT...
...

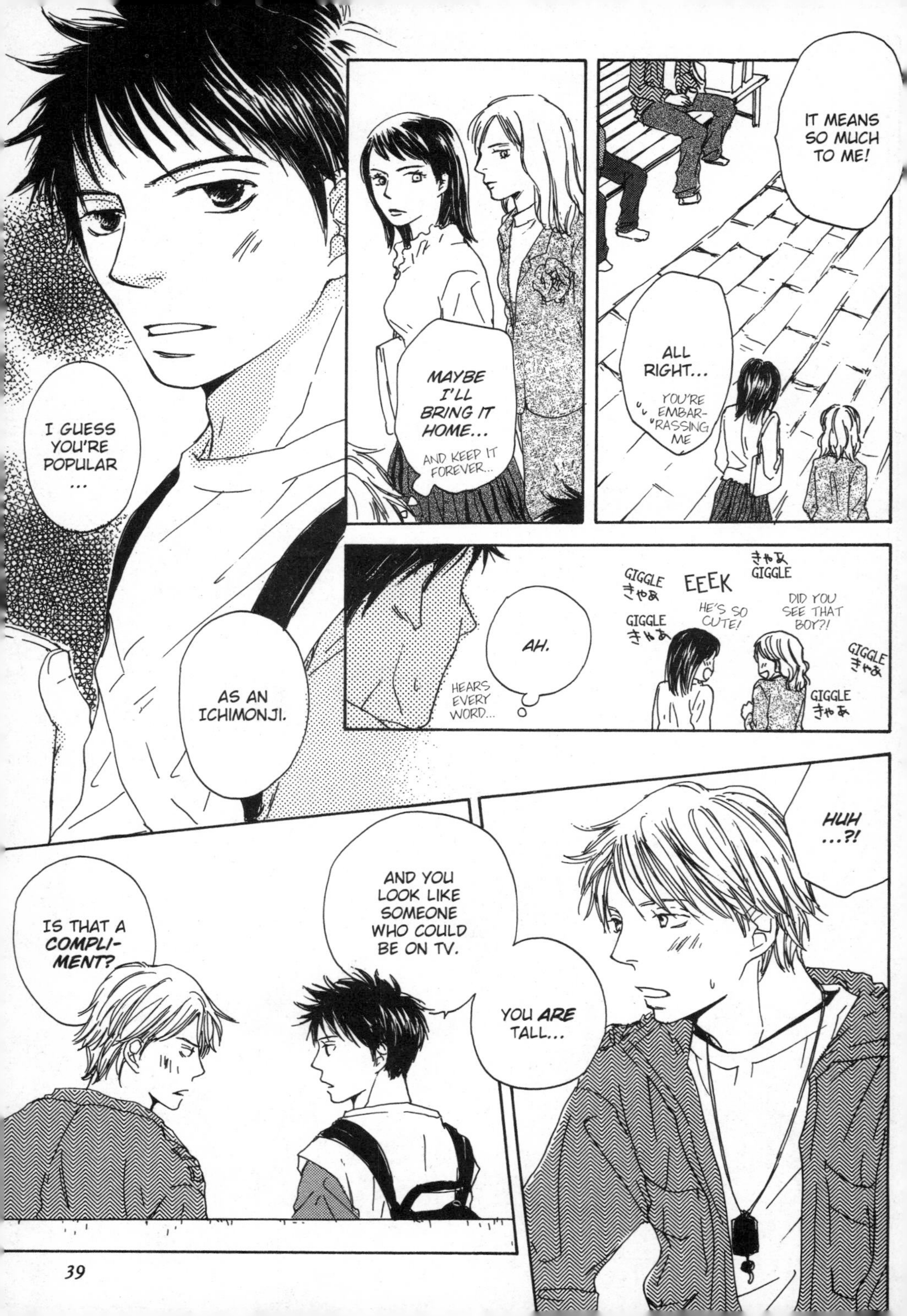
IT MEANS SO MUCH TO ME!
ALL RIGHT...
YOU'RE EMBARRASSING ME
MAYBE I'LL BRING IT HOME...
AND KEEP IT FOREVER...
きゃあ GIGGLE
GIGGLE きゃあ
EEEK
GIGGLE きゃあ
DID YOU SEE THAT BOY?!
HE'S SO CUTE!
GIGGLE きゃあ
GIGGLE きゃあ
GIGGLE きゃあ
AH.
HEARS EVERY WORD...
I GUESS YOU'RE POPULAR...
AS AN ICHIMONJI.
HUH...?!
YOU ARE TALL...
AND YOU LOOK LIKE SOMEONE WHO COULD BE ON TV.
IS THAT A COMPLIMENT?

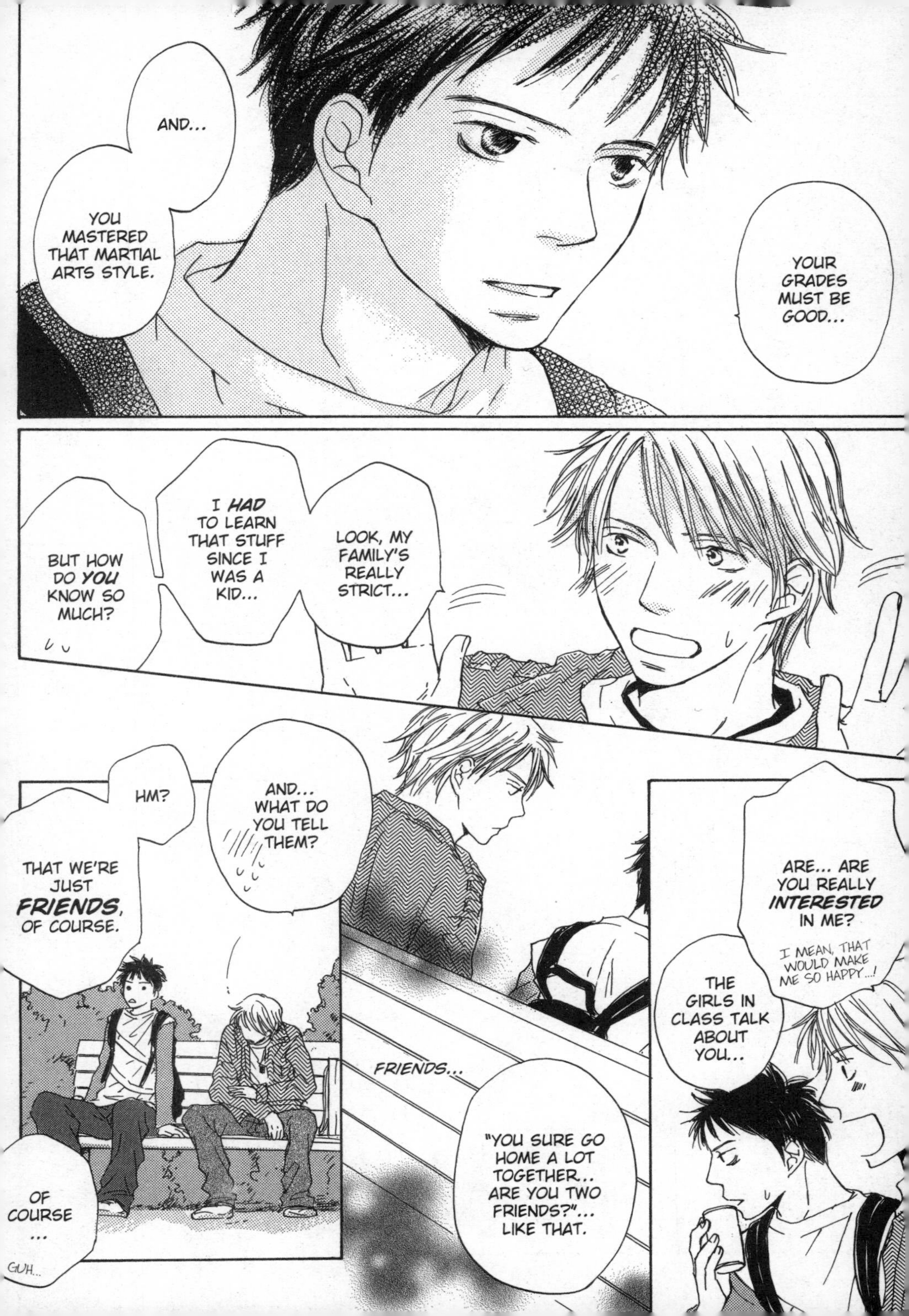
YOUR GRADES MUST BE GOOD...
AND...
YOU MASTERED THAT MARTIAL ARTS STYLE.
LOOK, MY FAMILY'S REALLY STRICT...
I HAD TO LEARN THAT STUFF SINCE I WAS A KID...
BUT HOW DO YOU KNOW SO MUCH?
ARE... ARE YOU REALLY INTERESTED IN ME?
I MEAN, THAT WOULD MAKE ME SO HAPPY...!
THE GIRLS IN CLASS TALK ABOUT YOU...
"YOU SURE GO HOME A LOT TOGETHER.. ARE YOU TWO FRIENDS?"... LIKE THAT.
AND... WHAT DO YOU TELL THEM?
HM?
THAT WE'RE JUST FRIENDS, OF COURSE.
FRIENDS...
OF COURSE ...
GUH...

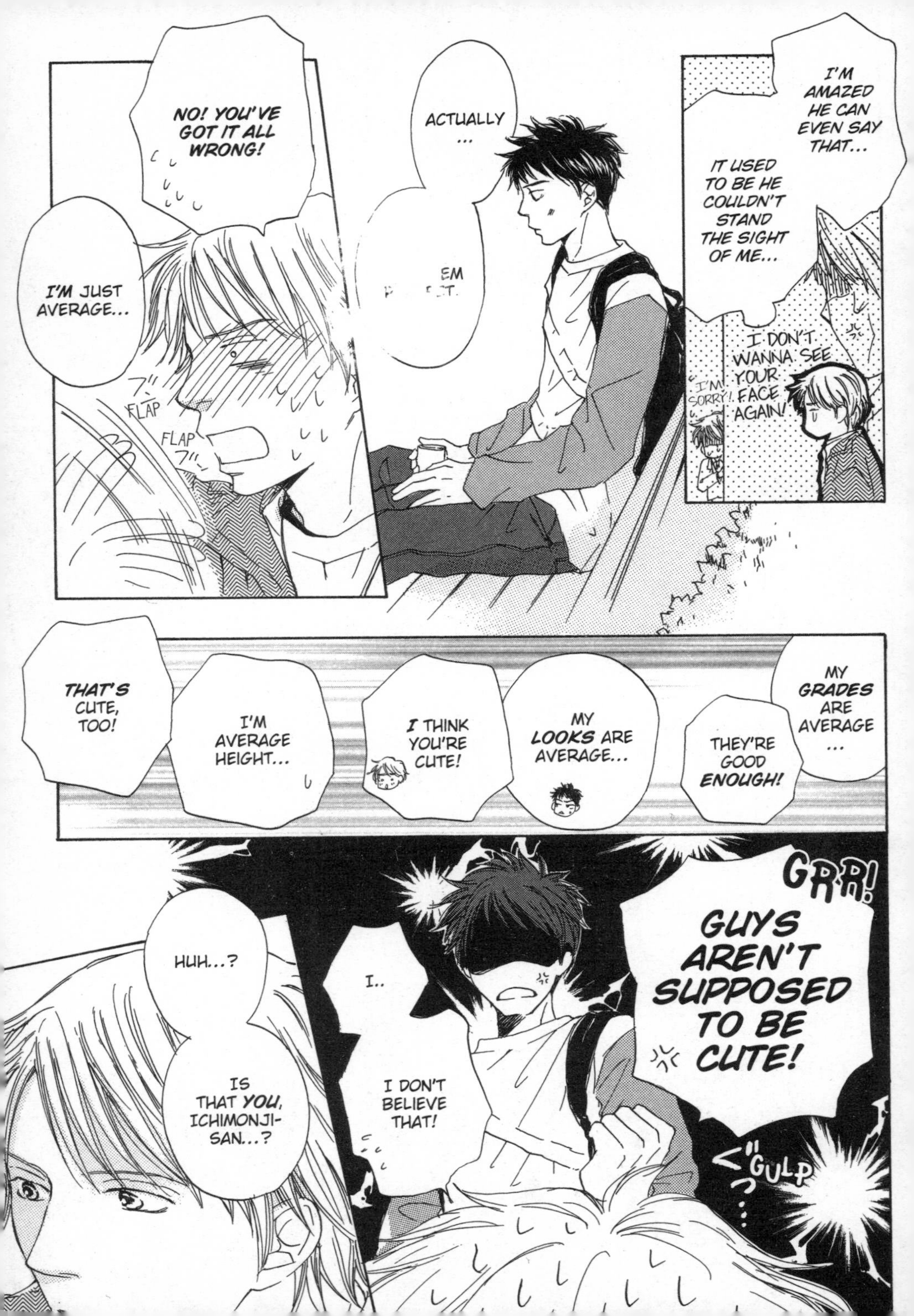
I'M AMAZED HE CAN EVEN SAY THAT...
IT USED TO BE HE COULDN'T STAND THE SIGHT OF ME...
I DON'T WANNA SEE YOUR FACE AGAIN!
I'M SORRY!
ACTUALLY ...
NO! YOU'VE GOT IT ALL WRONG!
I'M JUST AVERAGE...
FLAP
FLAP
MY GRADES ARE AVERAGE ...
THEY'RE GOOD ENOUGH!
MY LOOKS ARE AVERAGE...
I THINK YOU'RE CUTE!
I'M AVERAGE HEIGHT...
THAT'S CUTE, TOO!
GRR!
GUYS AREN'T SUPPOSED TO BE CUTE!
GULP
I..
I DON'T BELIEVE THAT!
HUH...?
IS THAT YOU, ICHIMONJI-SAN...?

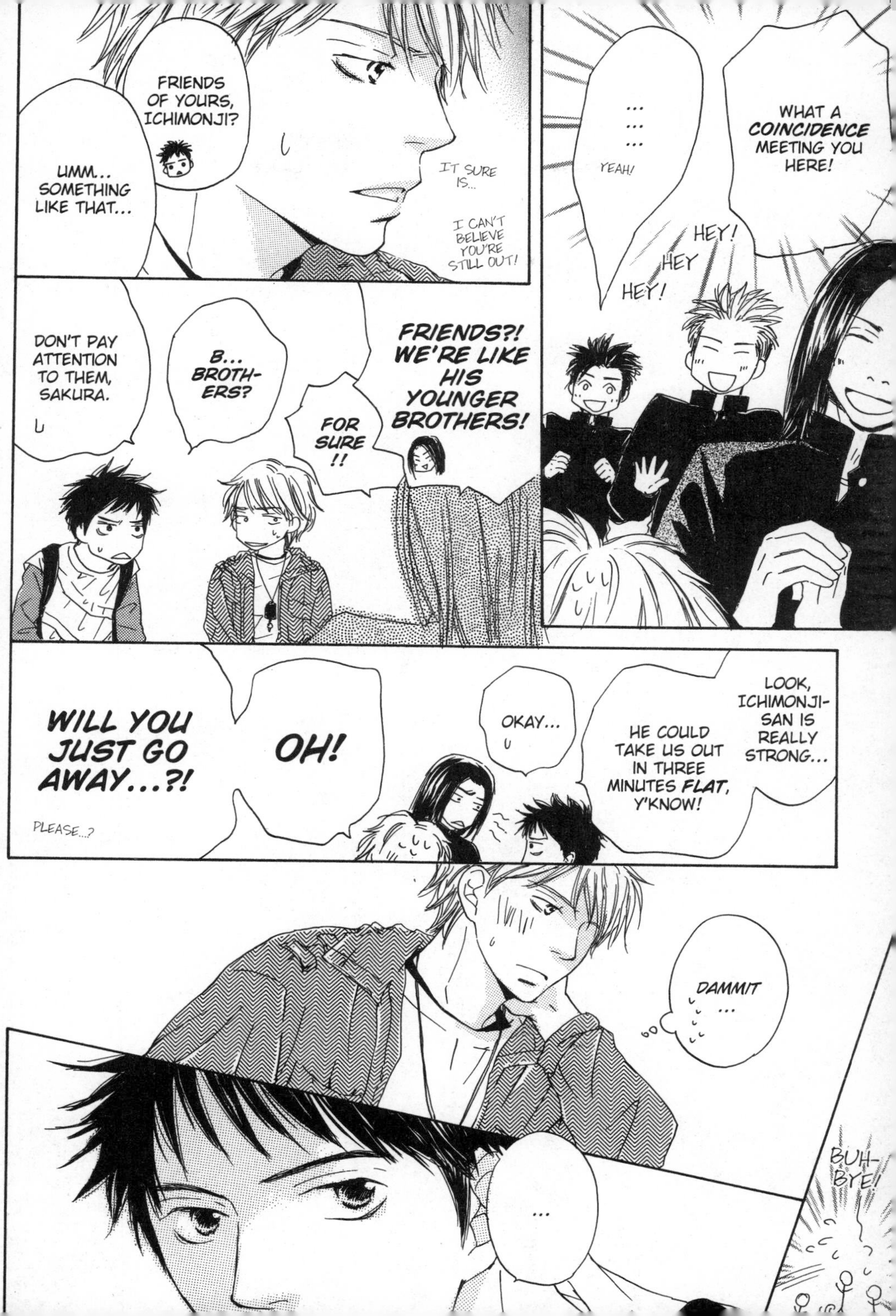
WHAT A COINCIDENCE MEETING YOU HERE!
... ...
YEAH!
HEY!
HEY
HEY!
FRIENDS OF YOURS, ICHIMONJI?
IT SURE IS...
I CAN'T BELIEVE YOU'RE STILL OUT!
UMM... SOMETHING LIKE THAT...
FRIENDS?! WE'RE LIKE HIS YOUNGER BROTHERS!
FOR SURE!!
B... BROTHERS?
DON'T PAY ATTENTION TO THEM, SAKURA.
LOOK, ICHIMONJI-SAN IS REALLY STRONG...
HE COULD TAKE US OUT IN THREE MINUTES FLAT, Y'KNOW!
OKAY...
OH!
WILL YOU JUST GO AWAY...?!
PLEASE...?
DAMMIT ...
BUH-BYE!
...

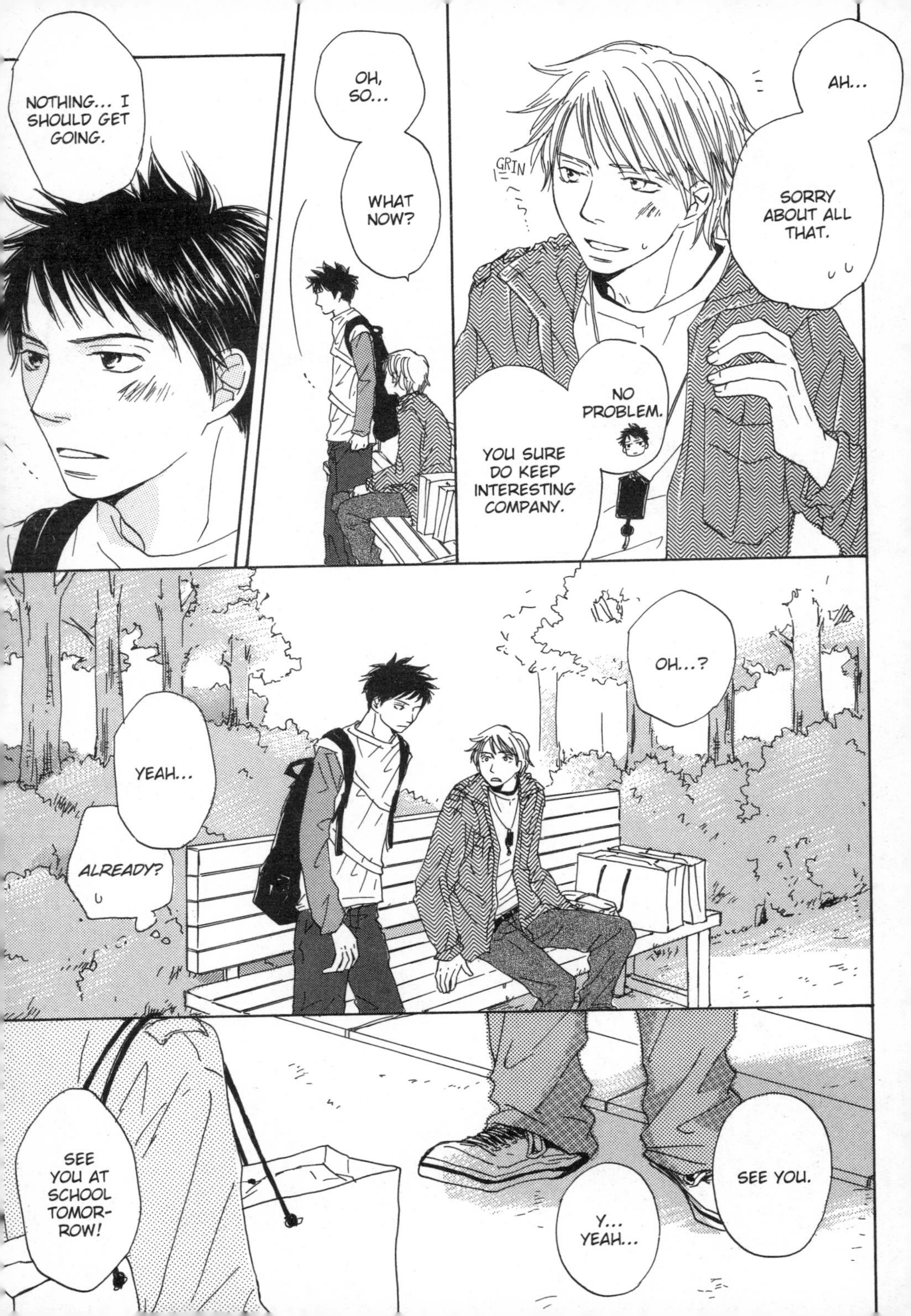
AH...
SORRY ABOUT ALL THAT.
GRIN
NO PROBLEM.
YOU SURE DO KEEP INTERESTING COMPANY.
OH, SO...
WHAT NOW?
NOTHING... I SHOULD GET GOING.
OH...?
YEAH...
ALREADY?
SEE YOU.
Y... YEAH...
SEE YOU AT SCHOOL TOMOR-ROW!

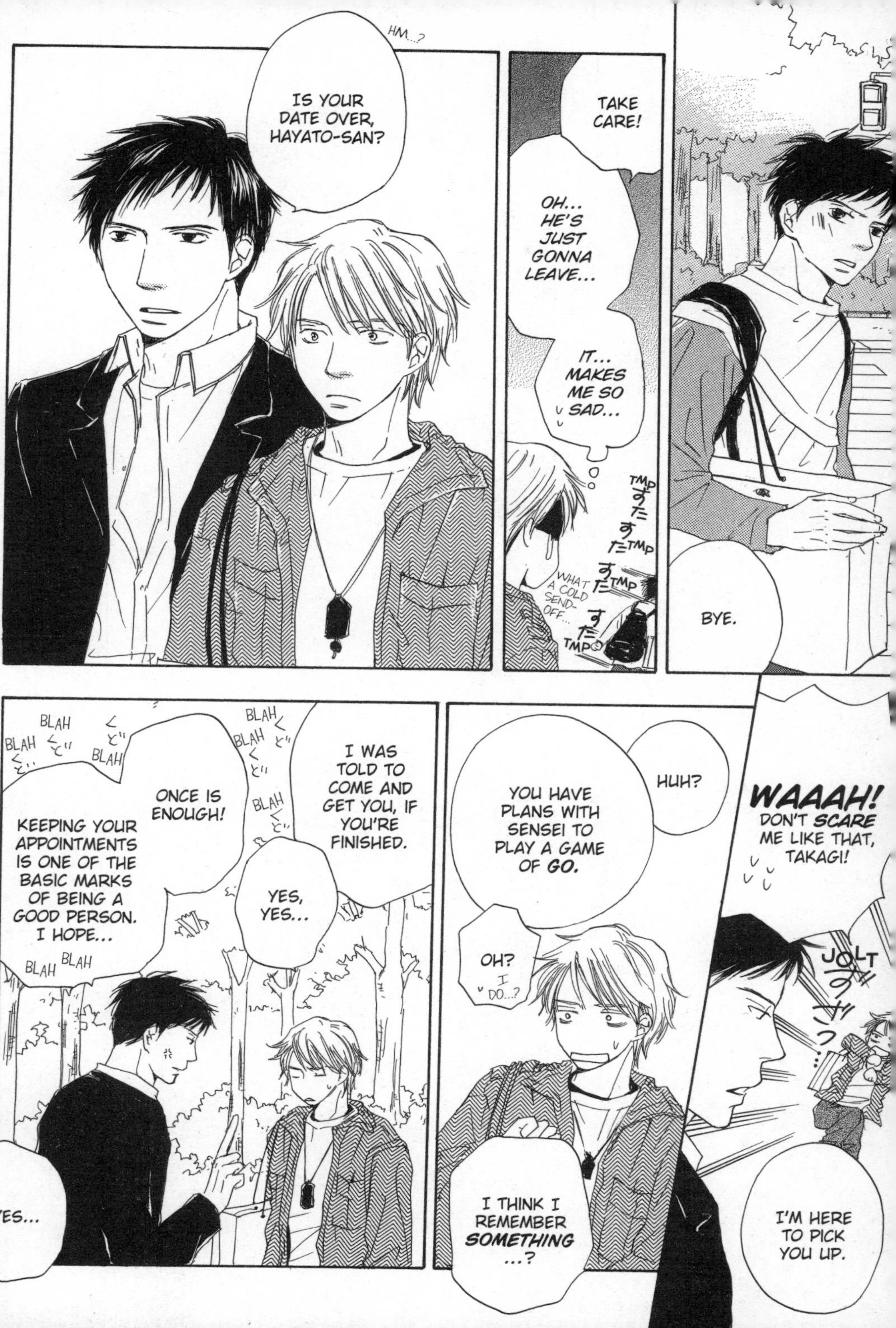
BYE.
TAKE CARE!
OH... HE'S JUST GONNA LEAVE...
IT... MAKES ME SO SAD...
TMP すた
TMP すた
TMP すた
TMP すた
WHAT A COLD SEND-OFF...
HM...?
IS YOUR DATE OVER, HAYATO-SAN?
WAAAH! DON'T SCARE ME LIKE THAT, TAKAGI!
JOLT ずざっ
I'M HERE TO PICK YOU UP.
HUH?
YOU HAVE PLANS WITH SENSEI TO PLAY A GAME OF GO.
OH?
I DO...?
I THINK I REMEMBER SOMETHING...?
I WAS TOLD TO COME AND GET YOU, IF YOU'RE FINISHED.
BLAH くど BLAH くど BLAH くど
ONCE IS ENOUGH!
BLAH くど BLAH くど BLAH くど
KEEPING YOUR APPOINTMENTS IS ONE OF THE BASIC MARKS OF BEING A GOOD PERSON. I HOPE...
BLAH BLAH
YES, YES...
YES...

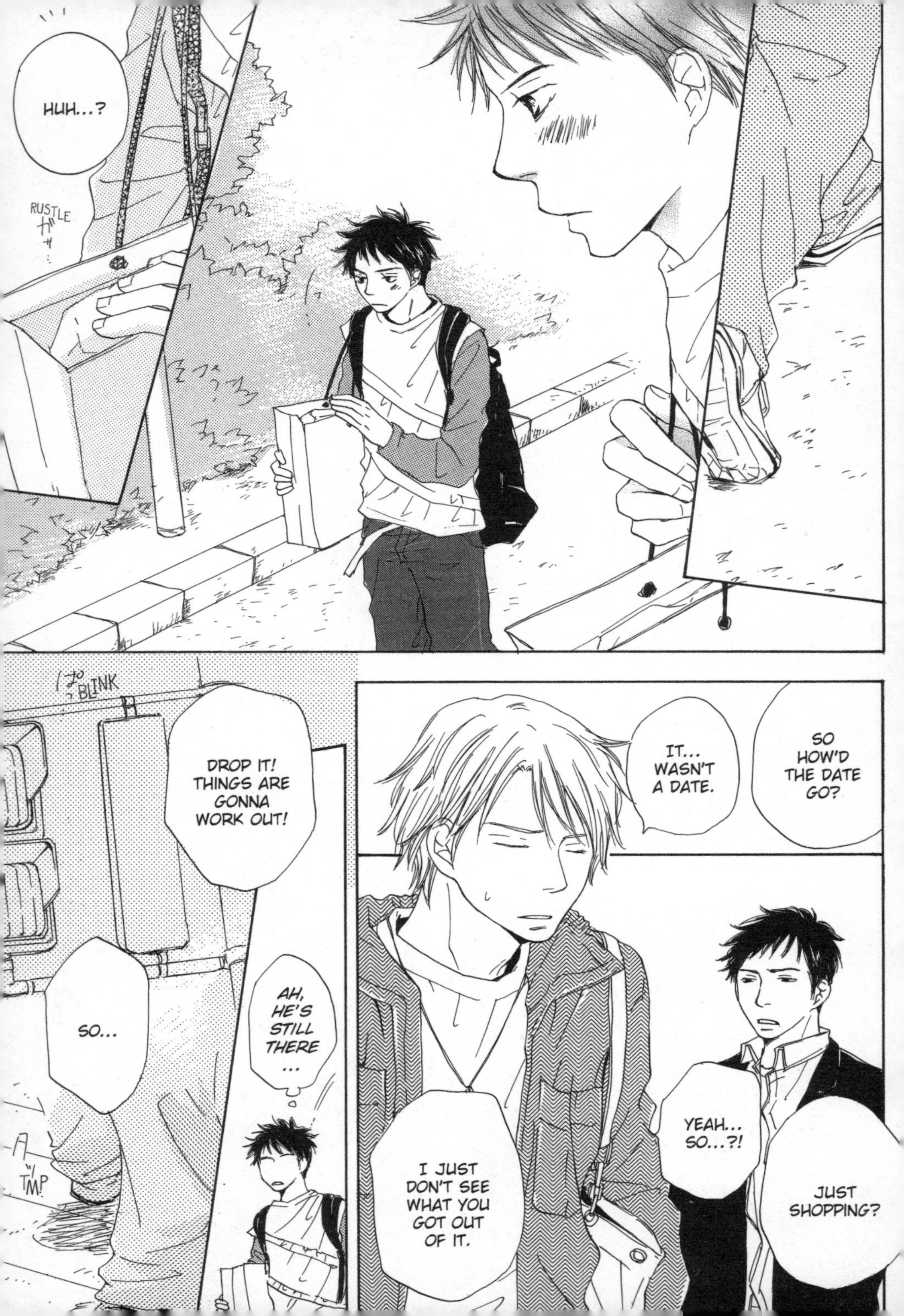
HUH...?
RUSTLE
SO HOW'D THE DATE GO?
IT... WASN'T A DATE.
JUST SHOPPING?
YEAH... SO...?!
I JUST DON'T SEE WHAT YOU GOT OUT OF IT.
BLINK
DROP IT! THINGS ARE GONNA WORK OUT!
AH, HE'S STILL THERE...
SO...
TMP

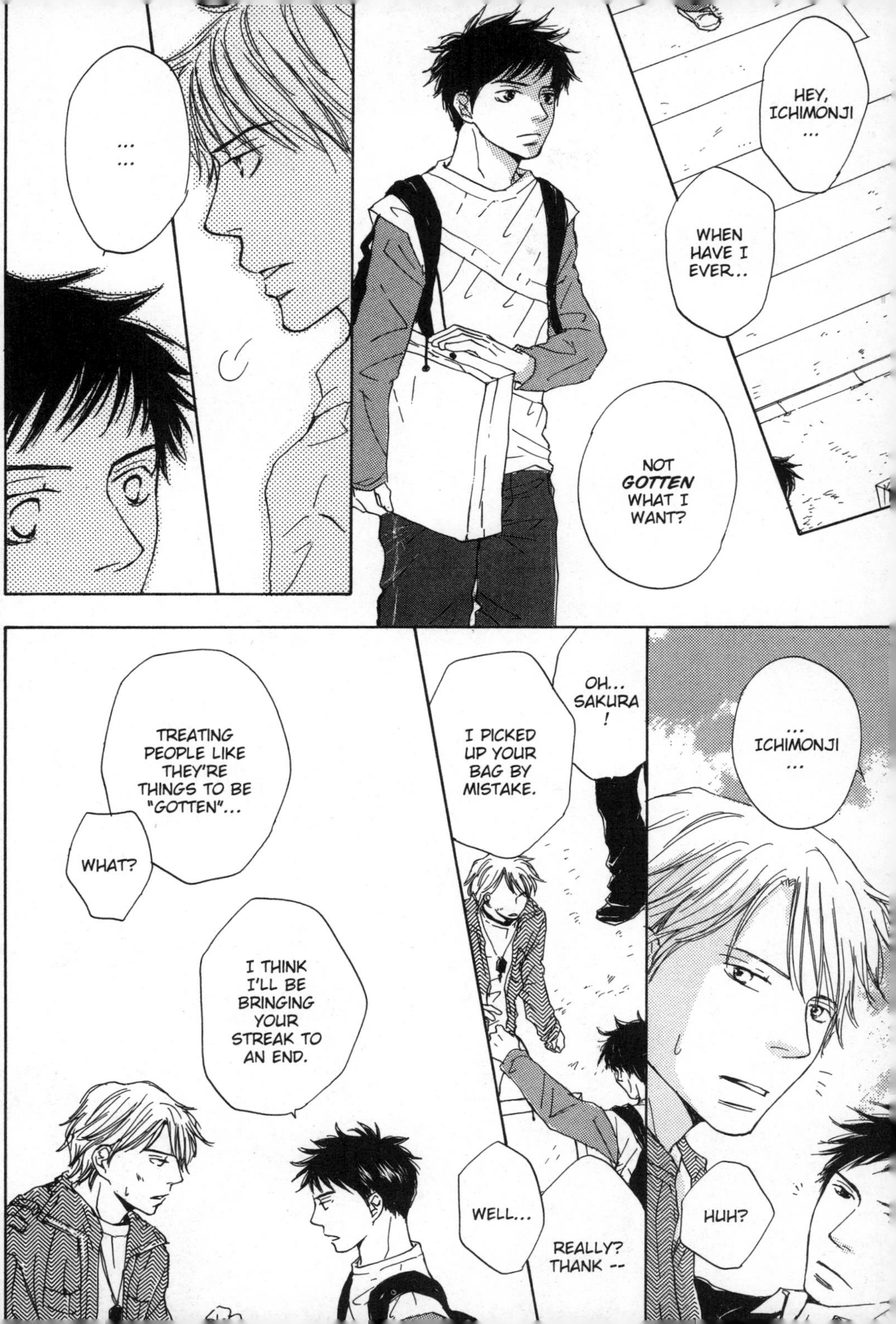
HEY, ICHIMONJI ...
WHEN HAVE I EVER..
NOT *GOTTEN* WHAT I WANT?
... ...
... ICHIMONJI ...
HUH?
OH... SAKURA !
I PICKED UP YOUR BAG BY MISTAKE.
WELL...
REALLY? THANK --
TREATING PEOPLE LIKE THEY'RE THINGS TO BE "GOTTEN"...
WHAT?
I THINK I'LL BE BRINGING YOUR STREAK TO AN END.

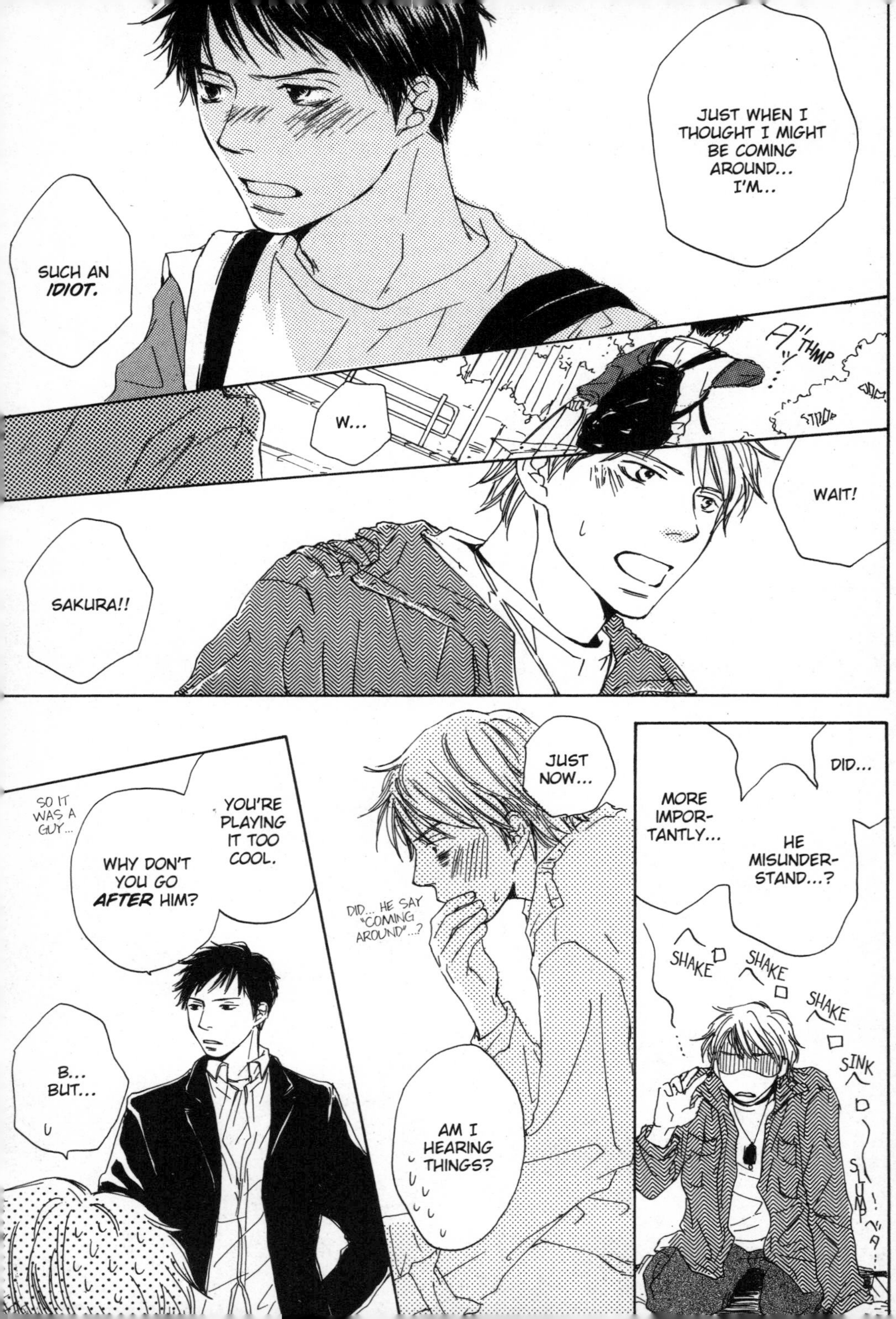
JUST WHEN I THOUGHT I MIGHT BE COMING AROUND... I'M...
SUCH AN *IDIOT.*
THMP
W...
WAIT!
SAKURA!!
DID...
HE MISUNDERSTAND...?
MORE IMPORTANTLY...
SHAKE
SHAKE
SHAKE
SINK
SLUMP
JUST NOW...
DID... HE SAY "COMING AROUND"...?
AM I HEARING THINGS?
YOU'RE PLAYING IT TOO COOL.
SO IT WAS A GUY...
WHY DON'T YOU GO *AFTER* HIM?
B... BUT...

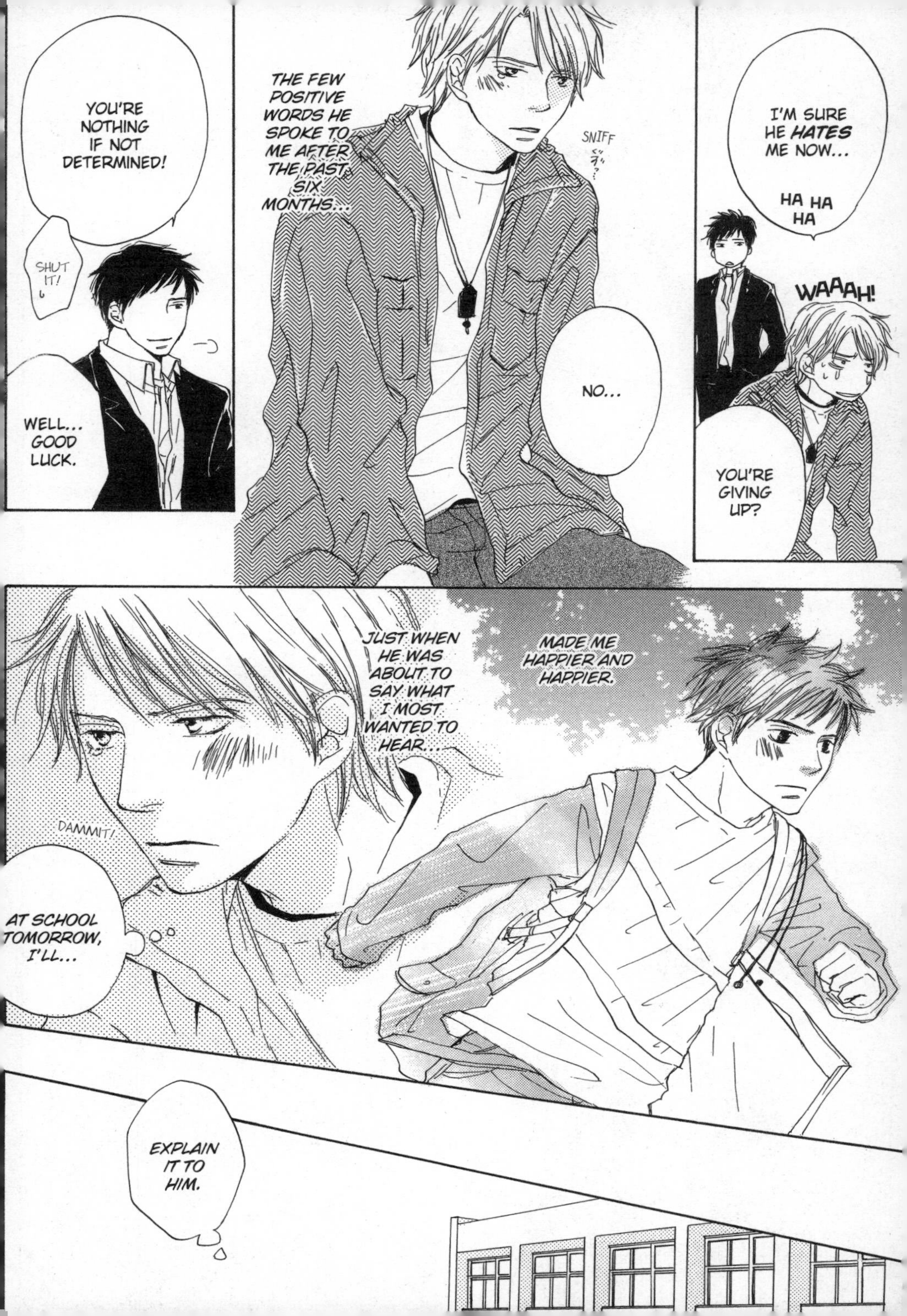
I'M SURE HE HATES ME NOW...
HA HA HA
WAAAH!
YOU'RE GIVING UP?
THE FEW POSITIVE WORDS HE SPOKE TO ME AFTER THE PAST SIX MONTHS...
SNIFF
NO...
YOU'RE NOTHING IF NOT DETERMINED!
SHUT IT!
WELL... GOOD LUCK.
MADE ME HAPPIER AND HAPPIER.
JUST WHEN HE WAS ABOUT TO SAY WHAT I MOST WANTED TO HEAR...
DAMMIT!
AT SCHOOL TOMORROW, I'LL...
EXPLAIN IT TO HIM.

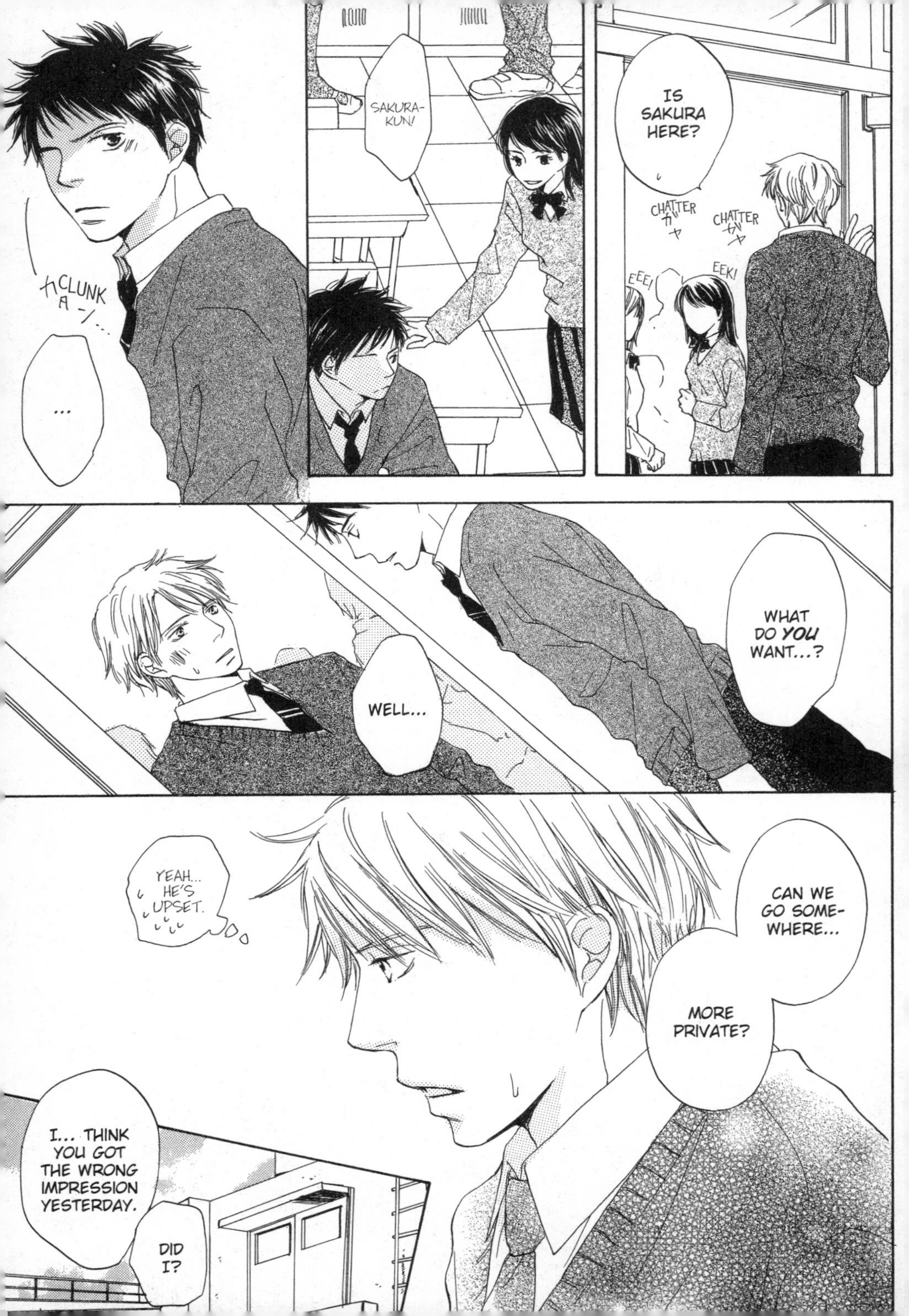
IS SAKURA HERE?
CHATTER
CHATTER
EEK!
EEE!
SAKURA-KUN!
CLUNK
...
WHAT DO *YOU* WANT...?
WELL...
CAN WE GO SOME-WHERE...
MORE PRIVATE?
YEAH... HE'S UPSET.
I... THINK YOU GOT THE WRONG IMPRESSION YESTERDAY.
DID I?

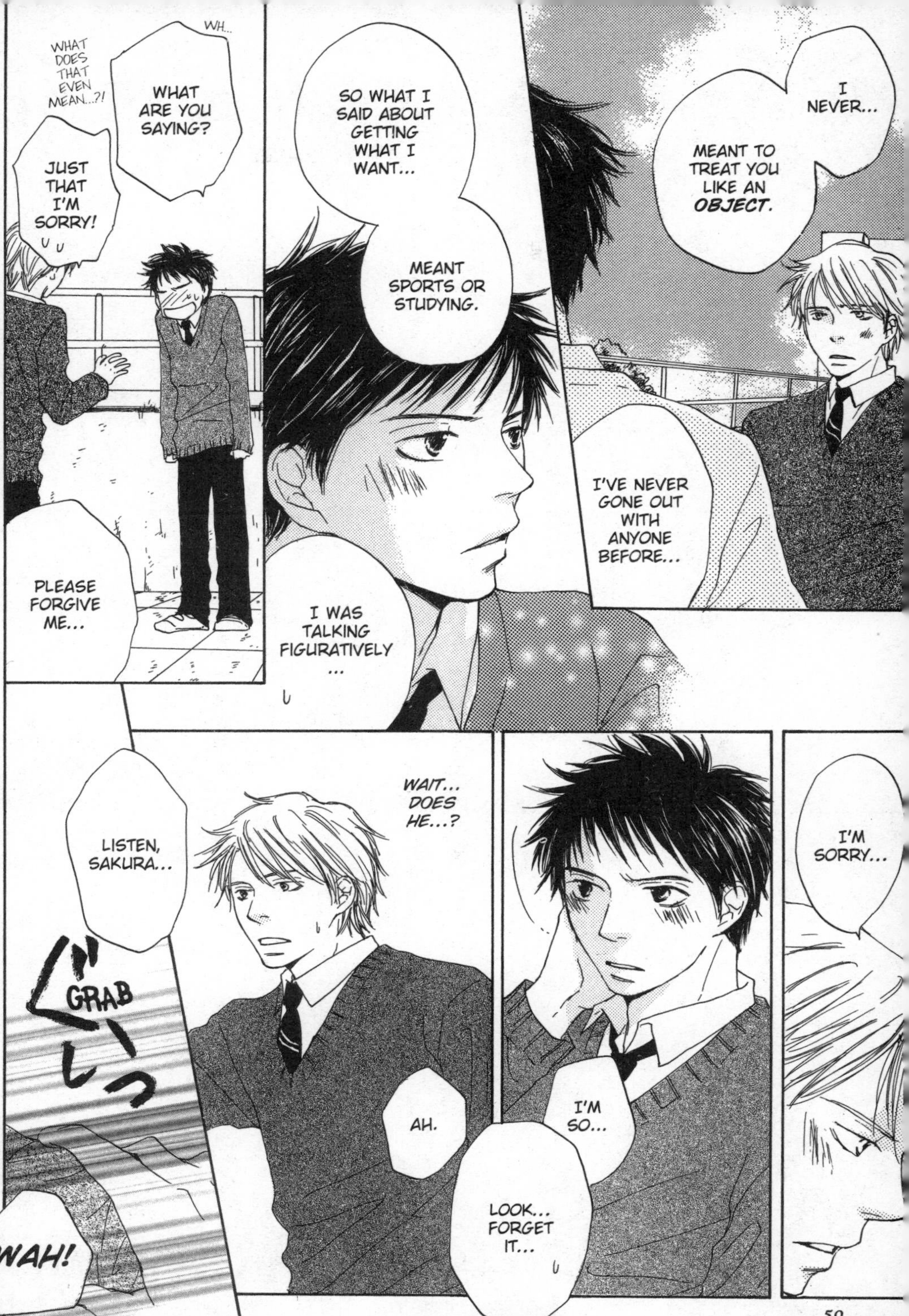
I NEVER...
MEANT TO TREAT YOU LIKE AN *OBJECT*.
I'VE NEVER GONE OUT WITH ANYONE BEFORE...
SO WHAT I SAID ABOUT GETTING WHAT I WANT...
MEANT SPORTS OR STUDYING.
I WAS TALKING FIGURATIVELY...
WH...
WHAT ARE YOU SAYING?
WHAT DOES THAT EVEN MEAN...?!
JUST THAT I'M SORRY!
PLEASE FORGIVE ME...
I'M SORRY...
I'M SO...
LOOK... FORGET IT...
WAIT... DOES HE...?
LISTEN, SAKURA...
AH.
GRAB
WAH!

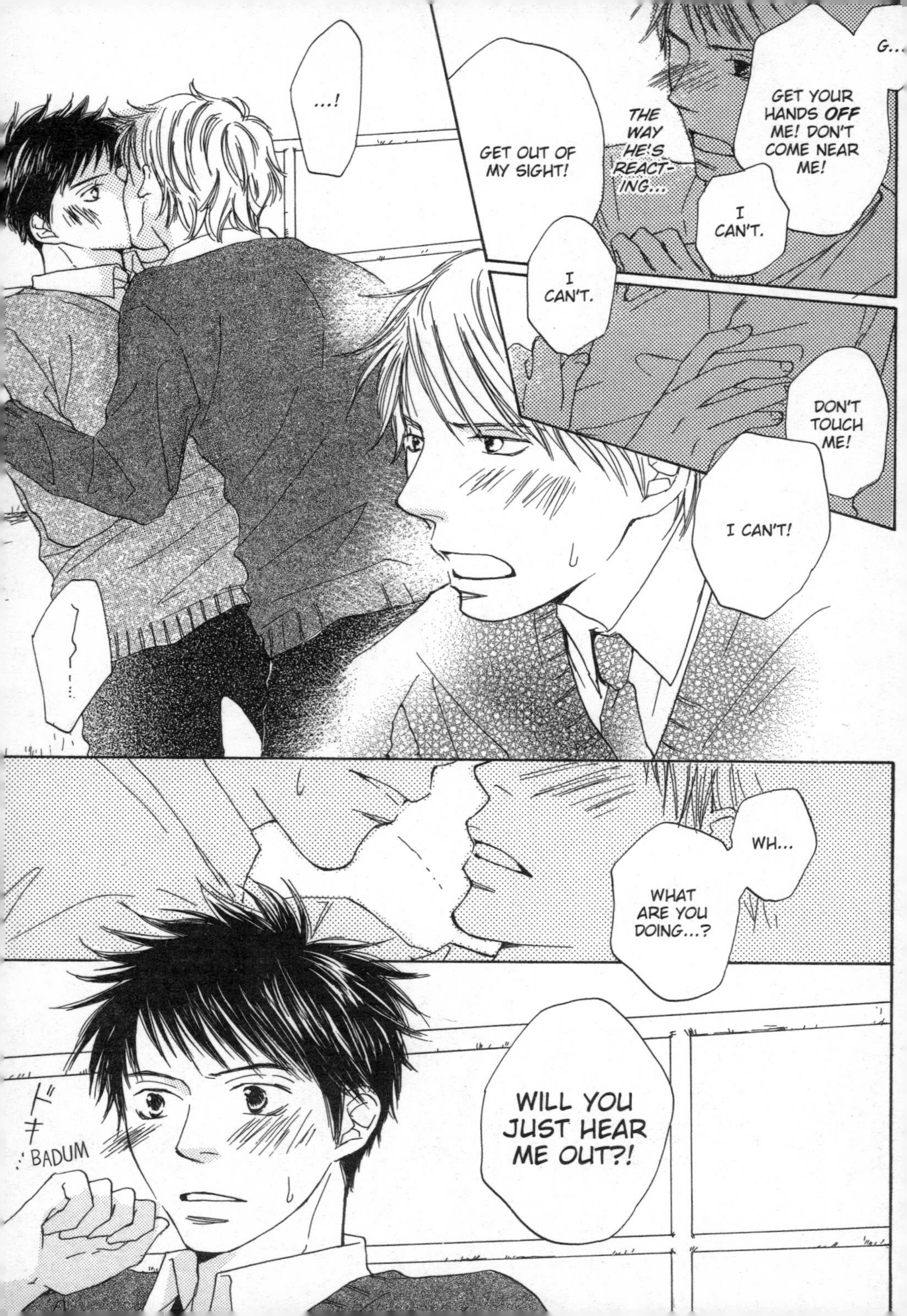
G...
GET YOUR HANDS **OFF** ME! DON'T COME NEAR ME!
I CAN'T.
THE WAY HE'S REACTING...
GET OUT OF MY SIGHT!
...!
I CAN'T.
DON'T TOUCH ME!
I CAN'T!
WH...
WHAT ARE YOU DOING...?
WILL YOU JUST HEAR ME OUT?!
ドキ
BADUM

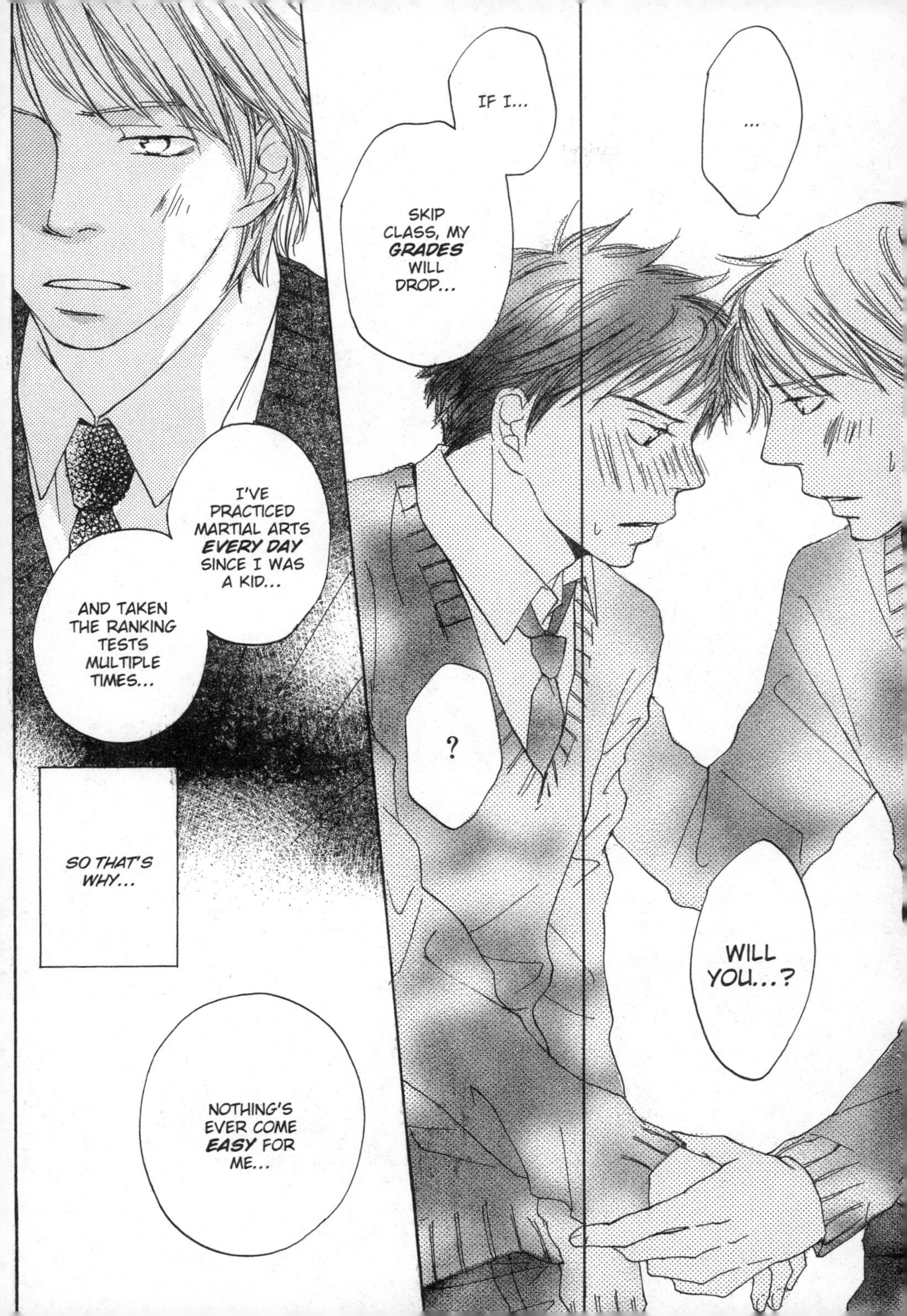
...
WILL YOU...?
IF I...
SKIP CLASS, MY GRADES WILL DROP...
?
I'VE PRACTICED MARTIAL ARTS EVERY DAY SINCE I WAS A KID...
AND TAKEN THE RANKING TESTS MULTIPLE TIMES...
SO THAT'S WHY...
NOTHING'S EVER COME EASY FOR ME...

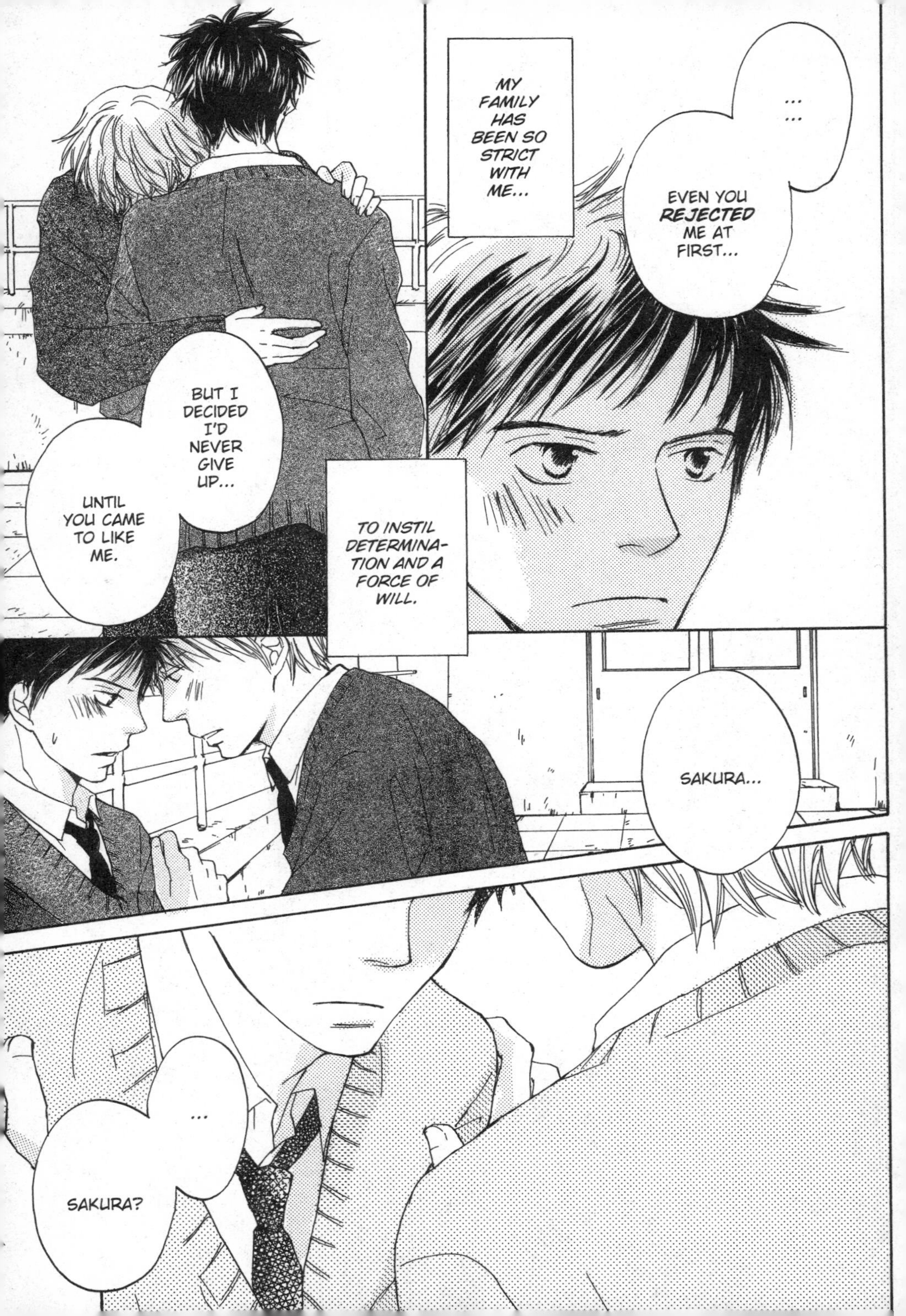
... ...
EVEN YOU REJECTED ME AT FIRST...
MY FAMILY HAS BEEN SO STRICT WITH ME...
TO INSTIL DETERMINATION AND A FORCE OF WILL.
BUT I DECIDED I'D NEVER GIVE UP...
UNTIL YOU CAME TO LIKE ME.
SAKURA...
...
SAKURA?

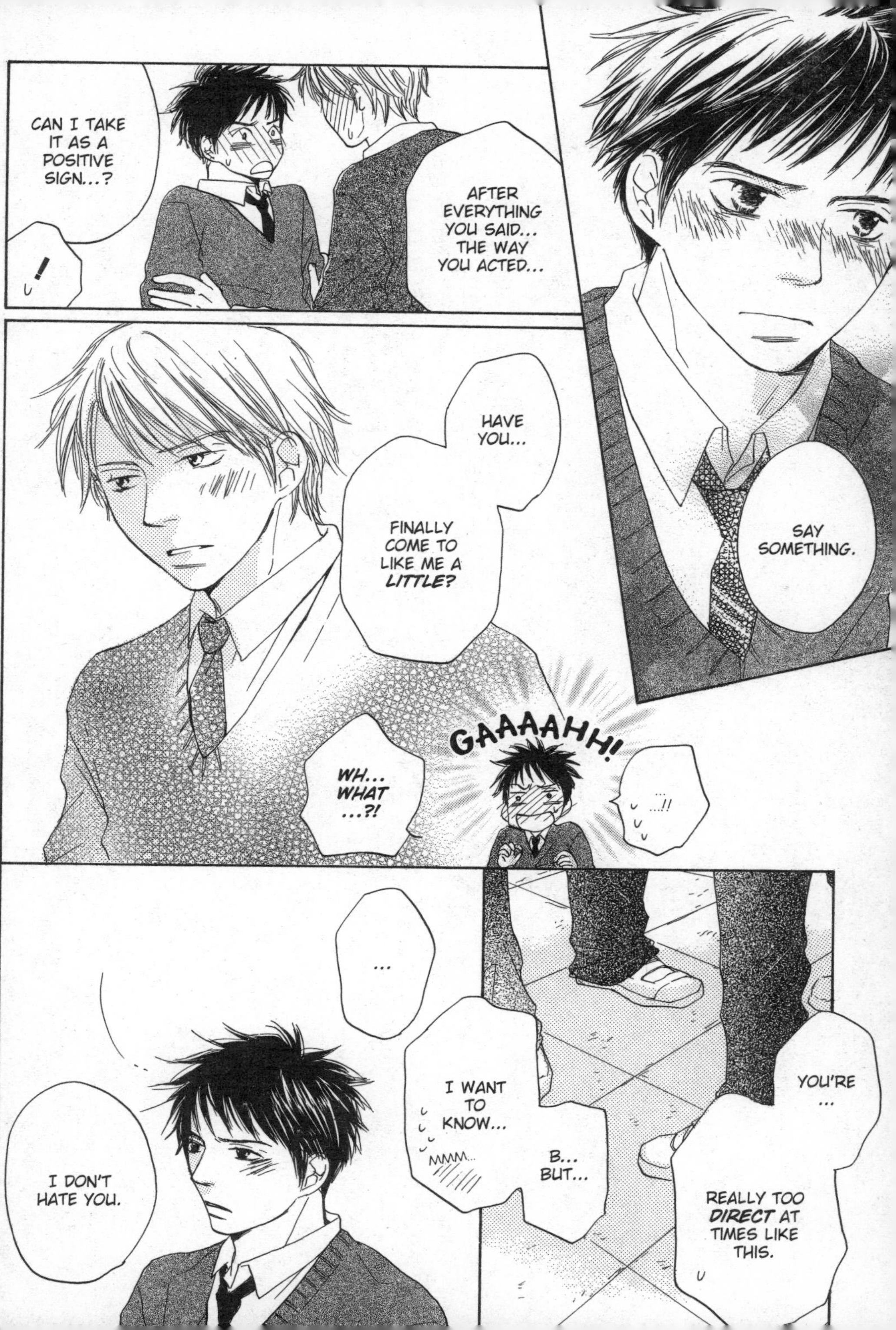
SAY SOMETHING.
AFTER EVERYTHING YOU SAID... THE WAY YOU ACTED...
CAN I TAKE IT AS A POSITIVE SIGN...?
!
HAVE YOU...
FINALLY COME TO LIKE ME A *LITTLE?*
GAAAAHH!
... ...!!
WH... WHAT ...?!
YOU'RE ...
REALLY TOO *DIRECT* AT TIMES LIKE THIS.
B... BUT...
I WANT TO KNOW...
...
I DON'T HATE YOU.

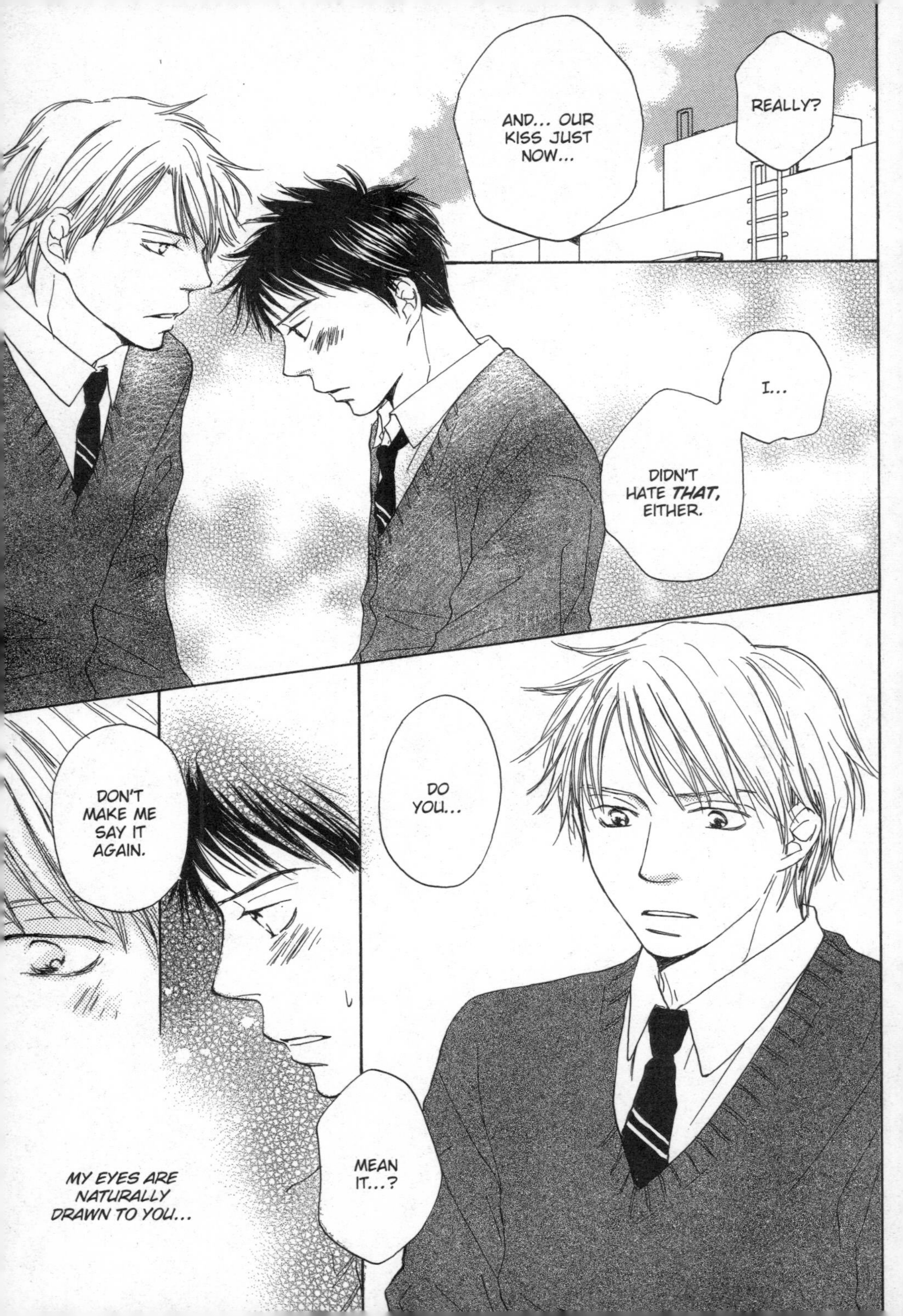
REALLY?
AND... OUR KISS JUST NOW...
I...
DIDN'T HATE *THAT*, EITHER.
DO YOU...
MEAN IT...?
DON'T MAKE ME SAY IT AGAIN.
MY EYES ARE NATURALLY DRAWN TO YOU...

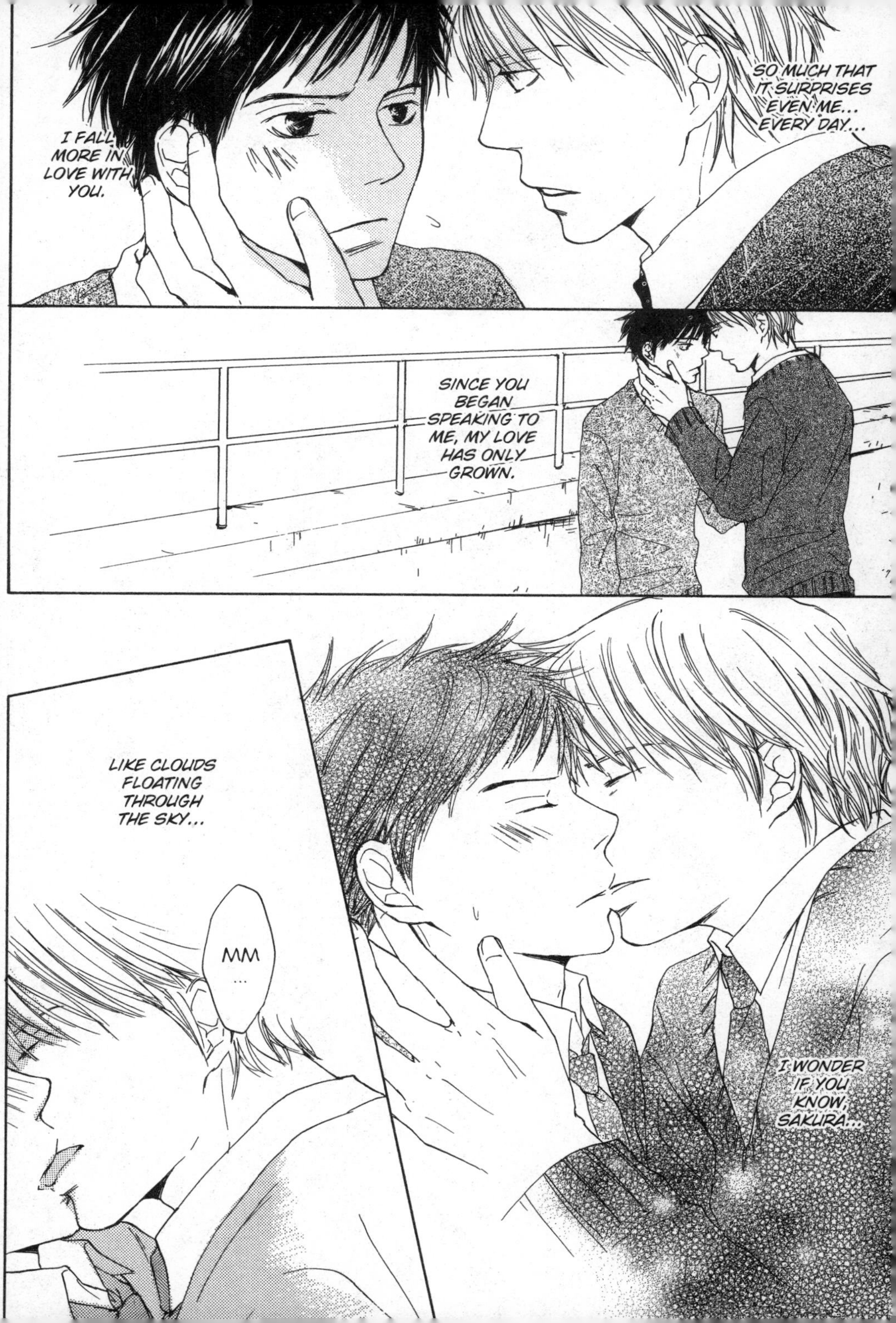
SO MUCH THAT IT SURPRISES EVEN ME... EVERY DAY...
I FALL MORE IN LOVE WITH YOU.
SINCE YOU BEGAN SPEAKING TO ME, MY LOVE HAS ONLY GROWN.
LIKE CLOUDS FLOATING THROUGH THE SKY...
MM...
I WONDER IF YOU KNOW, SAKURA...

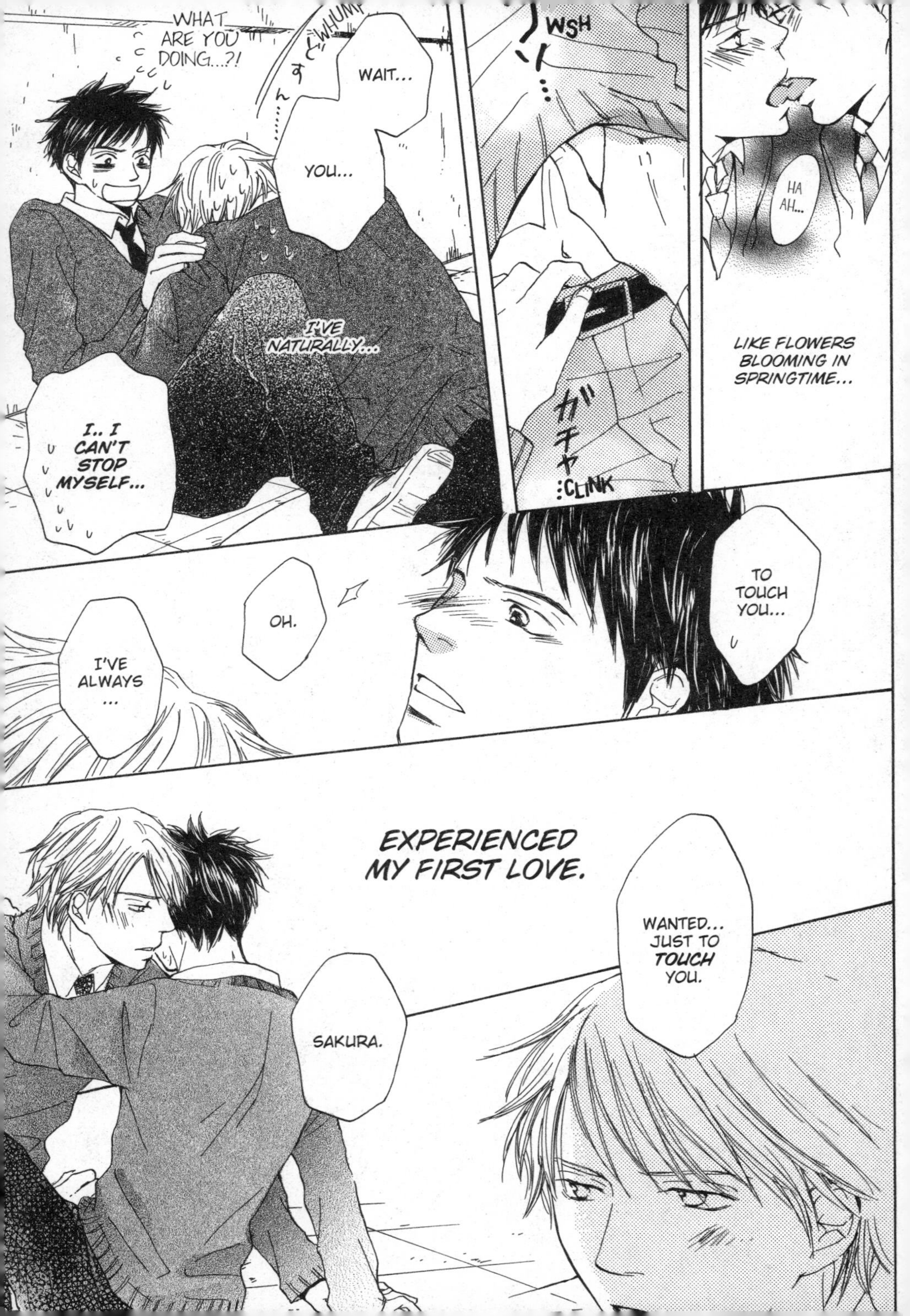
HA AH...
LIKE FLOWERS BLOOMING IN SPRINGTIME...
WSH
ガチャ
CLINK
WHAT ARE YOU DOING...?!
WHUMP
WAIT...
YOU...
I'VE NATURALLY...
I.. I CAN'T STOP MYSELF...
TO TOUCH YOU...
OH.
I'VE ALWAYS ...
EXPERIENCED MY FIRST LOVE.
WANTED... JUST TO TOUCH YOU.
SAKURA.

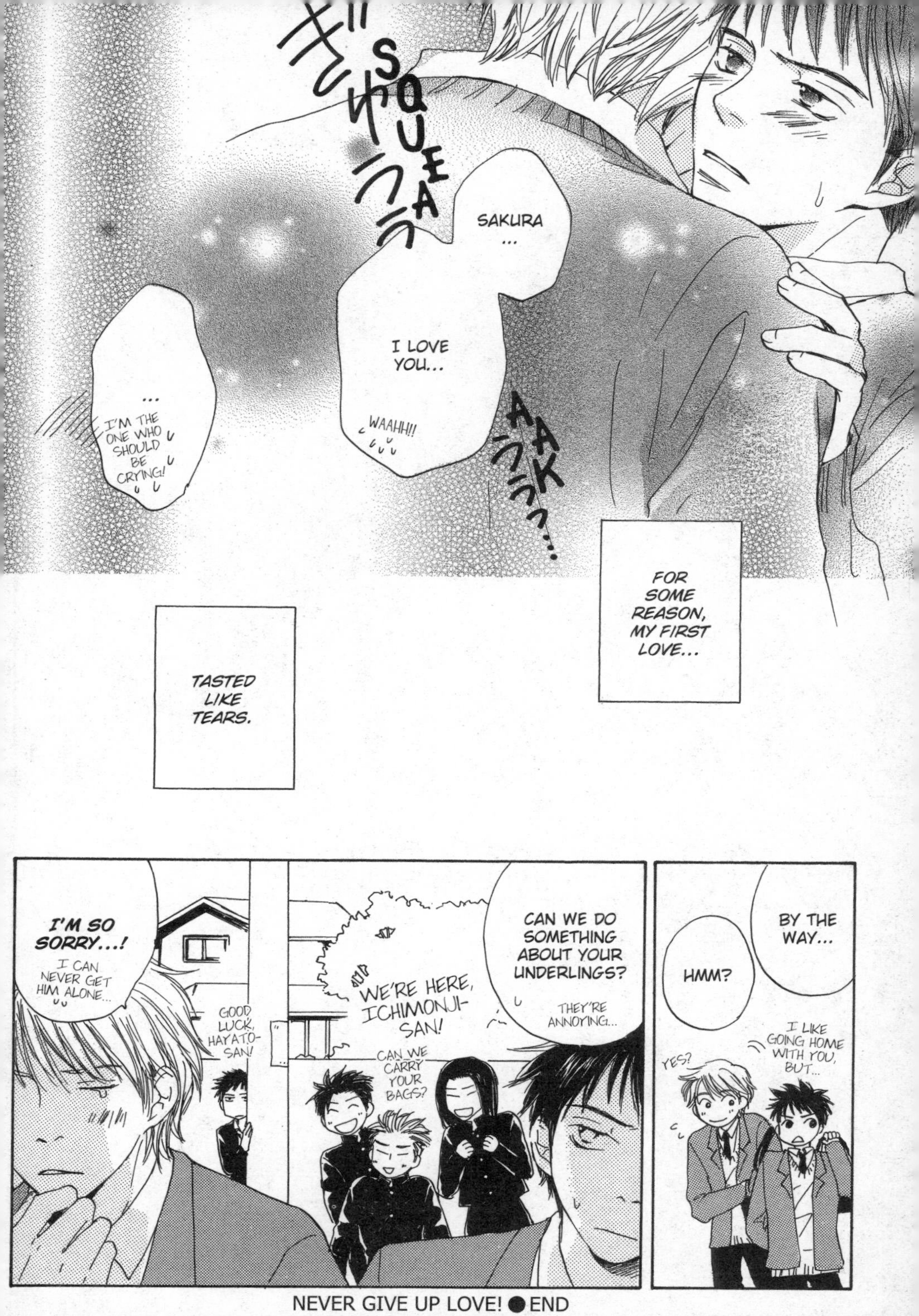
SQUEA
SAKURA ...
I LOVE YOU...
WAAHH!!
AAK
... I'M THE ONE WHO SHOULD BE CRYING!
FOR SOME REASON, MY FIRST LOVE...
TASTED LIKE TEARS.
BY THE WAY...
HMM?
I LIKE GOING HOME WITH YOU, BUT...
YES?
CAN WE DO SOMETHING ABOUT YOUR UNDERLINGS?
THEY'RE ANNOYING...
WE'RE HERE, ICHIMONJI-SAN!
CAN WE CARRY YOUR BAGS?
I'M SO SORRY...!
I CAN NEVER GET HIM ALONE...
GOOD LUCK, HAYATO-SAN!

NEVER GIVE UP LOVE! ● END

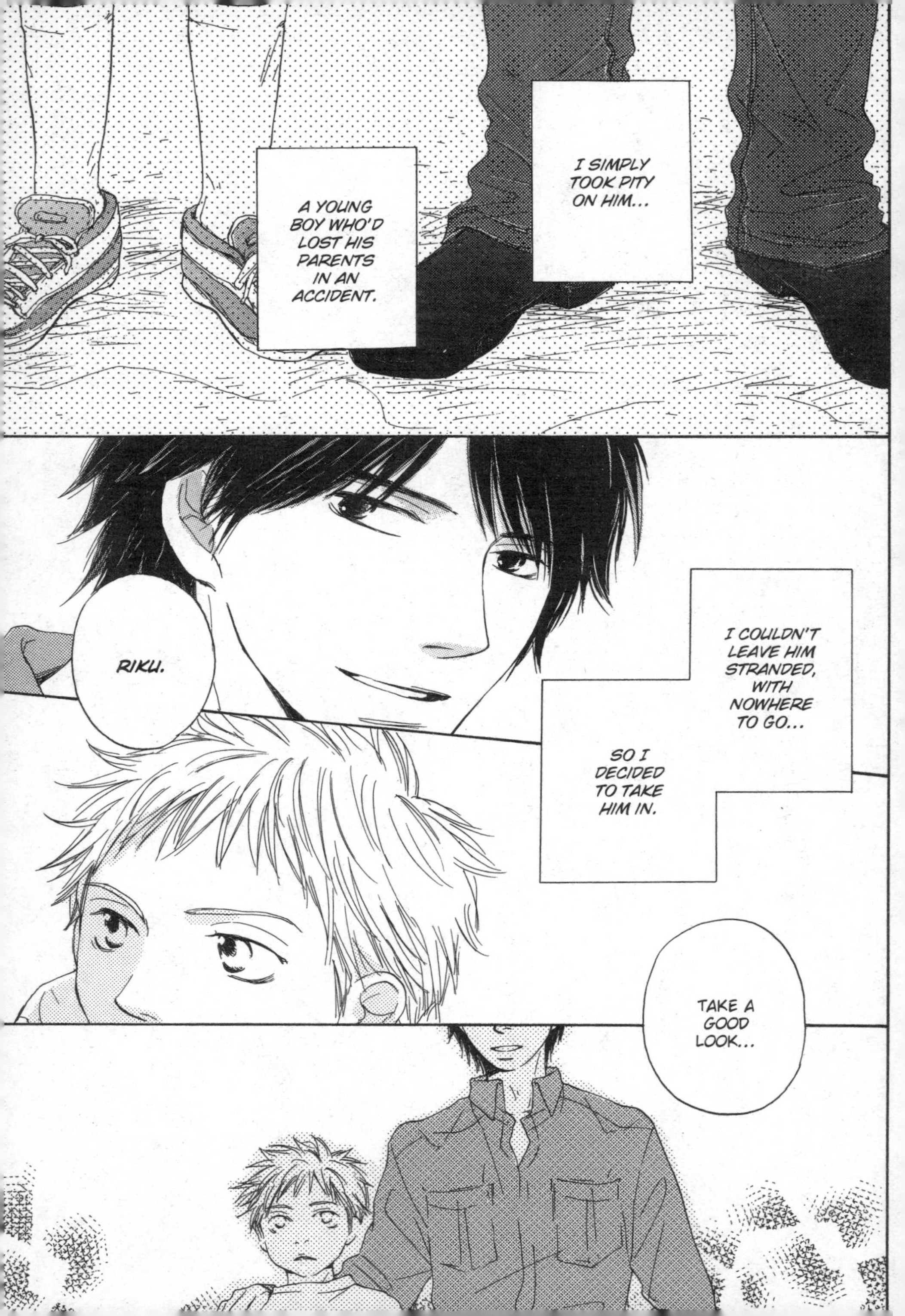
I SIMPLY TOOK PITY ON HIM...
A YOUNG BOY WHO'D LOST HIS PARENTS IN AN ACCIDENT.
I COULDN'T LEAVE HIM STRANDED, WITH NOWHERE TO GO...
SO I DECIDED TO TAKE HIM IN.
RIKU.
TAKE A GOOD LOOK...

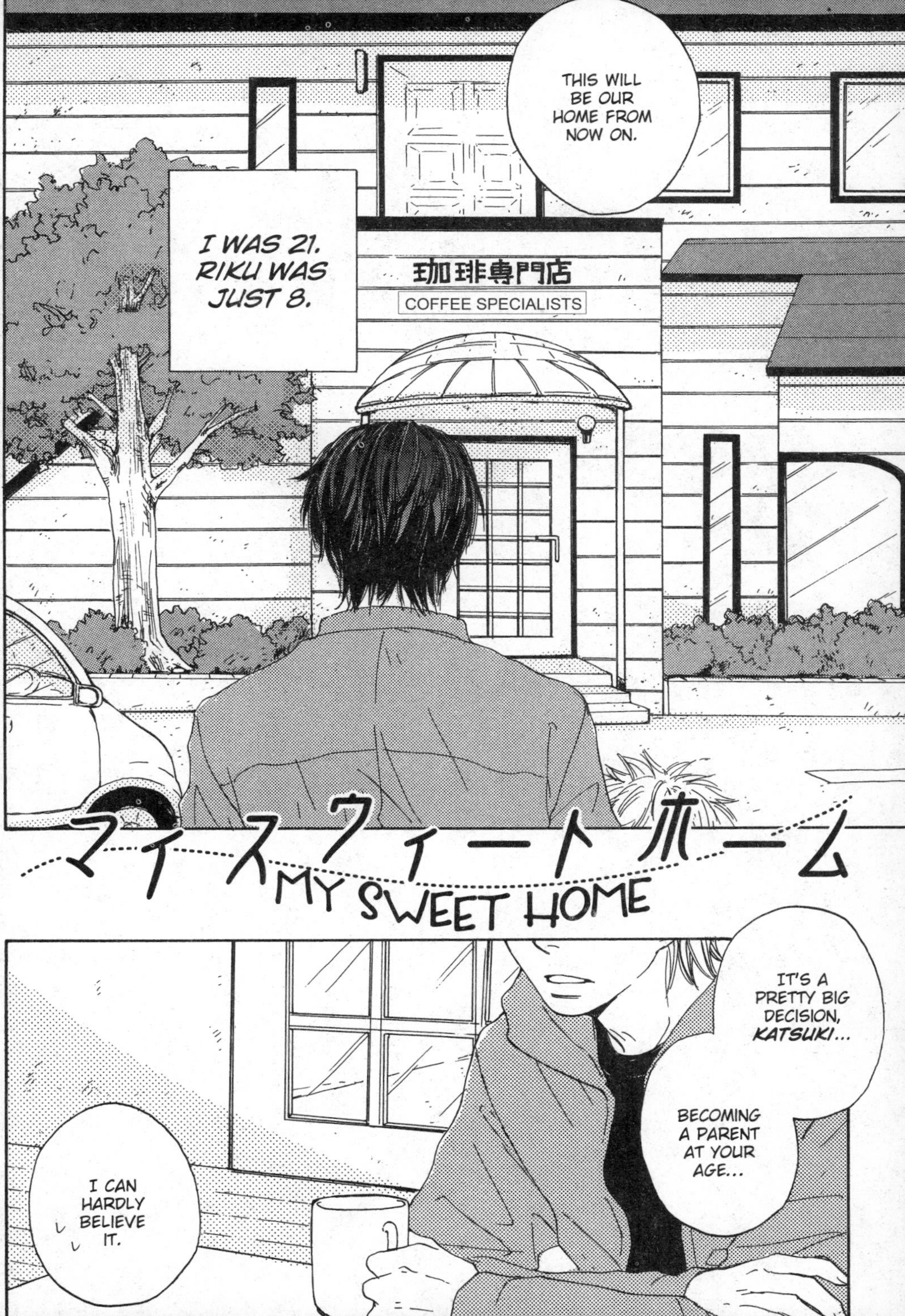
THIS WILL BE OUR HOME FROM NOW ON.
I WAS 21. RIKU WAS JUST 8.
珈琲専門店
COFFEE SPECIALISTS
マイスウィートホーム
MY SWEET HOME
IT'S A PRETTY BIG DECISION, KATSUKI...
BECOMING A PARENT AT YOUR AGE...
I CAN HARDLY BELIEVE IT.

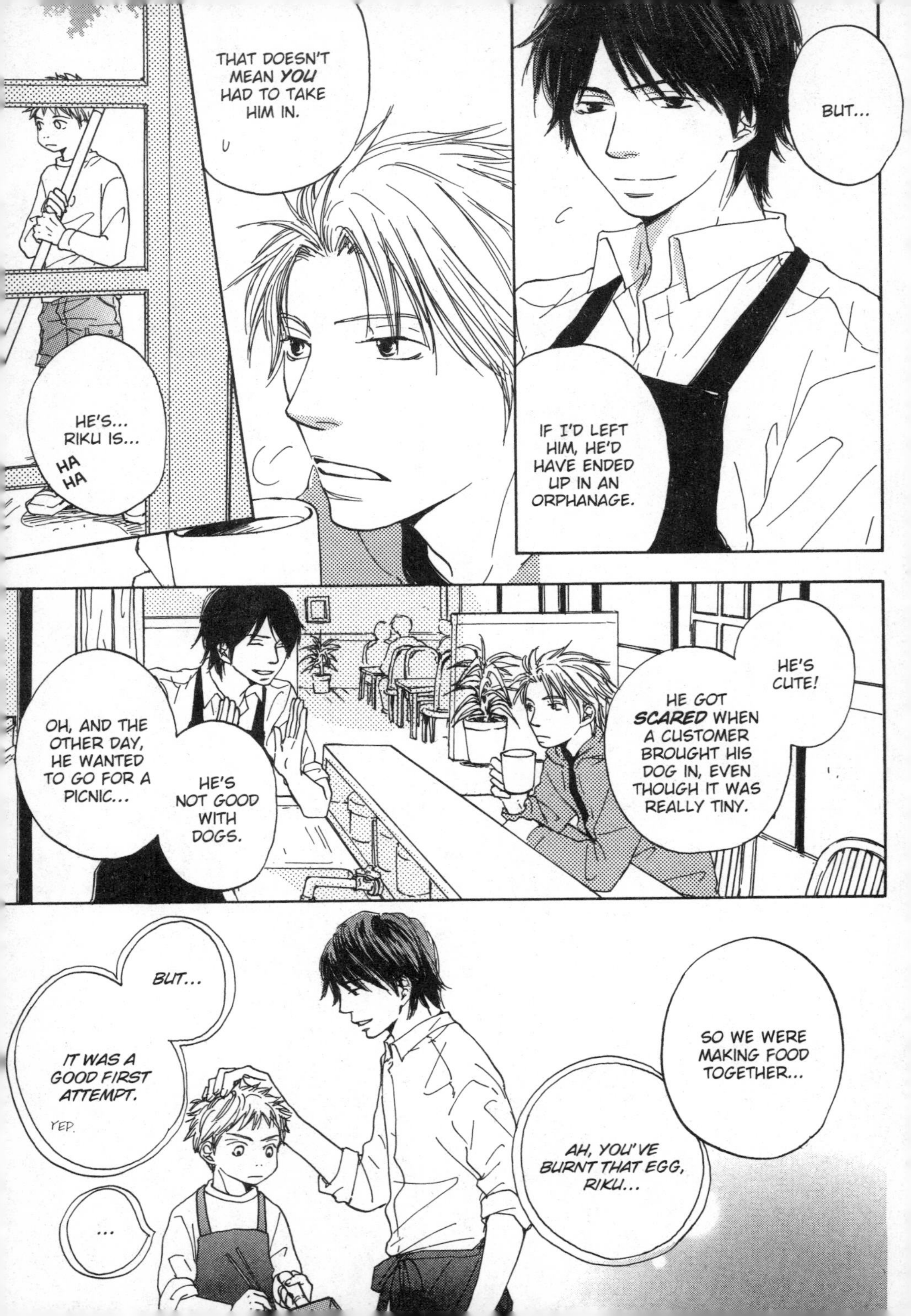
BUT...
IF I'D LEFT HIM, HE'D HAVE ENDED UP IN AN ORPHANAGE.
THAT DOESN'T MEAN YOU HAD TO TAKE HIM IN.
HE'S... RIKU IS...
HA HA
HE'S CUTE!
HE GOT SCARED WHEN A CUSTOMER BROUGHT HIS DOG IN, EVEN THOUGH IT WAS REALLY TINY.
HE'S NOT GOOD WITH DOGS.
OH, AND THE OTHER DAY, HE WANTED TO GO FOR A PICNIC...
SO WE WERE MAKING FOOD TOGETHER...
AH, YOU'VE BURNT THAT EGG, RIKU...
BUT...
IT WAS A GOOD FIRST ATTEMPT.
YEP.
...

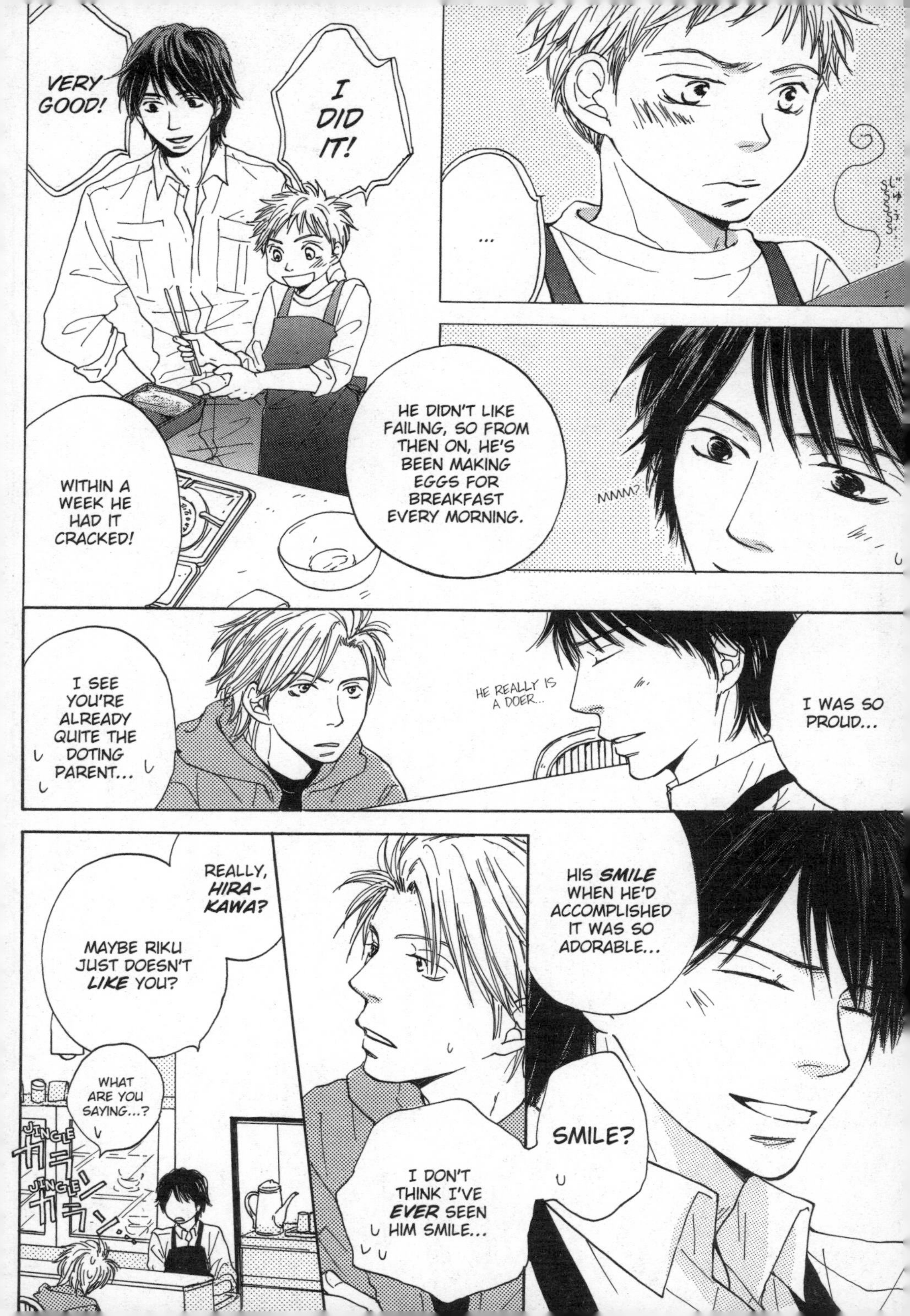
...
MMM?
HE DIDN'T LIKE FAILING, SO FROM THEN ON, HE'S BEEN MAKING EGGS FOR BREAKFAST EVERY MORNING.
VERY GOOD!
I DID IT!
WITHIN A WEEK HE HAD IT CRACKED!
I WAS SO PROUD...
HE REALLY IS A DOER...
I SEE YOU'RE ALREADY QUITE THE DOTING PARENT...
HIS SMILE WHEN HE'D ACCOMPLISHED IT WAS SO ADORABLE...
SMILE?
I DON'T THINK I'VE EVER SEEN HIM SMILE...
REALLY, HIRAKAWA?
MAYBE RIKU JUST DOESN'T LIKE YOU?
WHAT ARE YOU SAYING...?
JINGLE
JINGLE

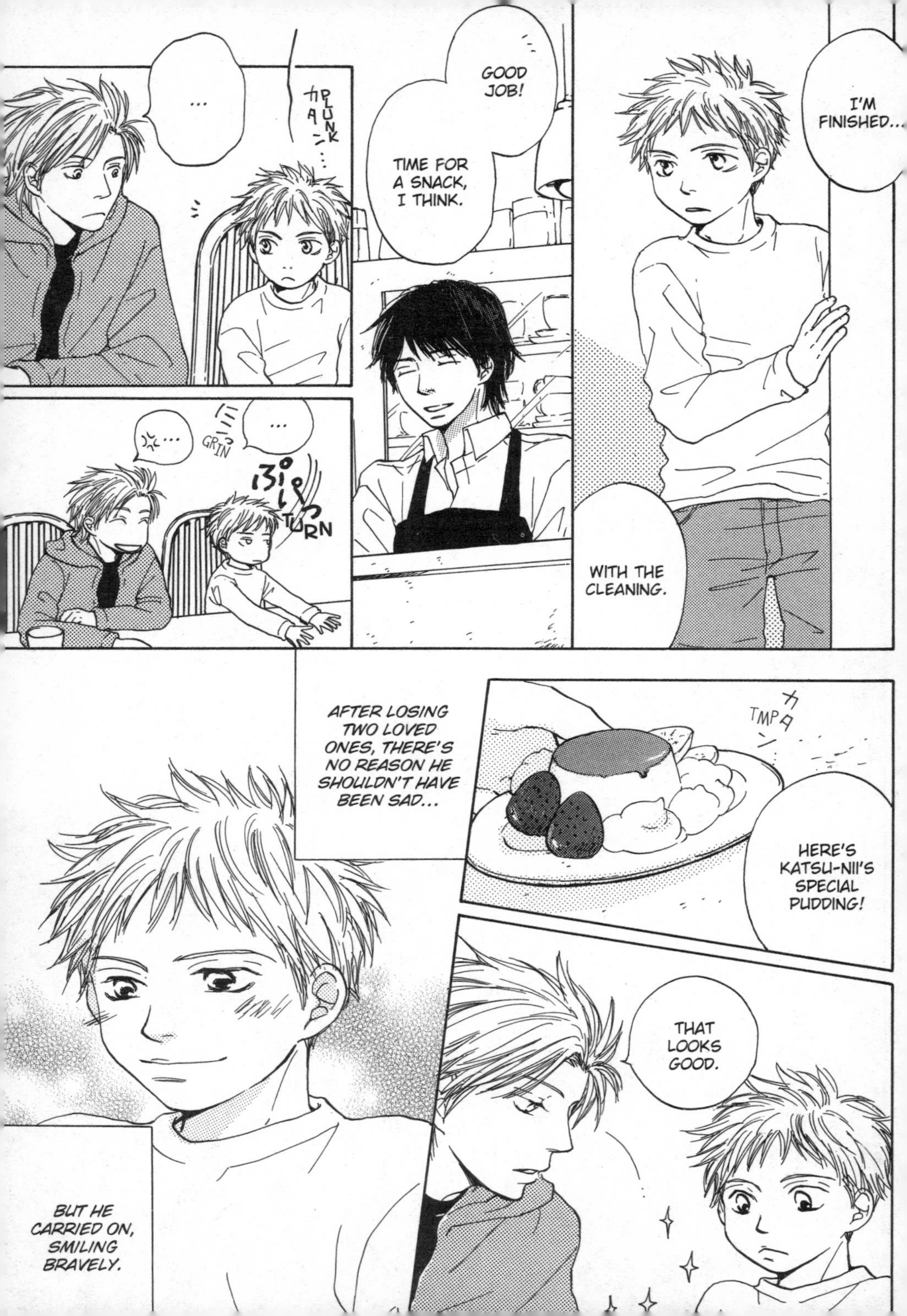
I'M FINISHED...
WITH THE CLEANING.
GOOD JOB!
TIME FOR A SNACK, I THINK.
...
PLUNK
...
...
GRIN
TURN
TMP
HERE'S KATSU-NII'S SPECIAL PUDDING!
THAT LOOKS GOOD.
AFTER LOSING TWO LOVED ONES, THERE'S NO REASON HE SHOULDN'T HAVE BEEN SAD...
BUT HE CARRIED ON, SMILING BRAVELY.

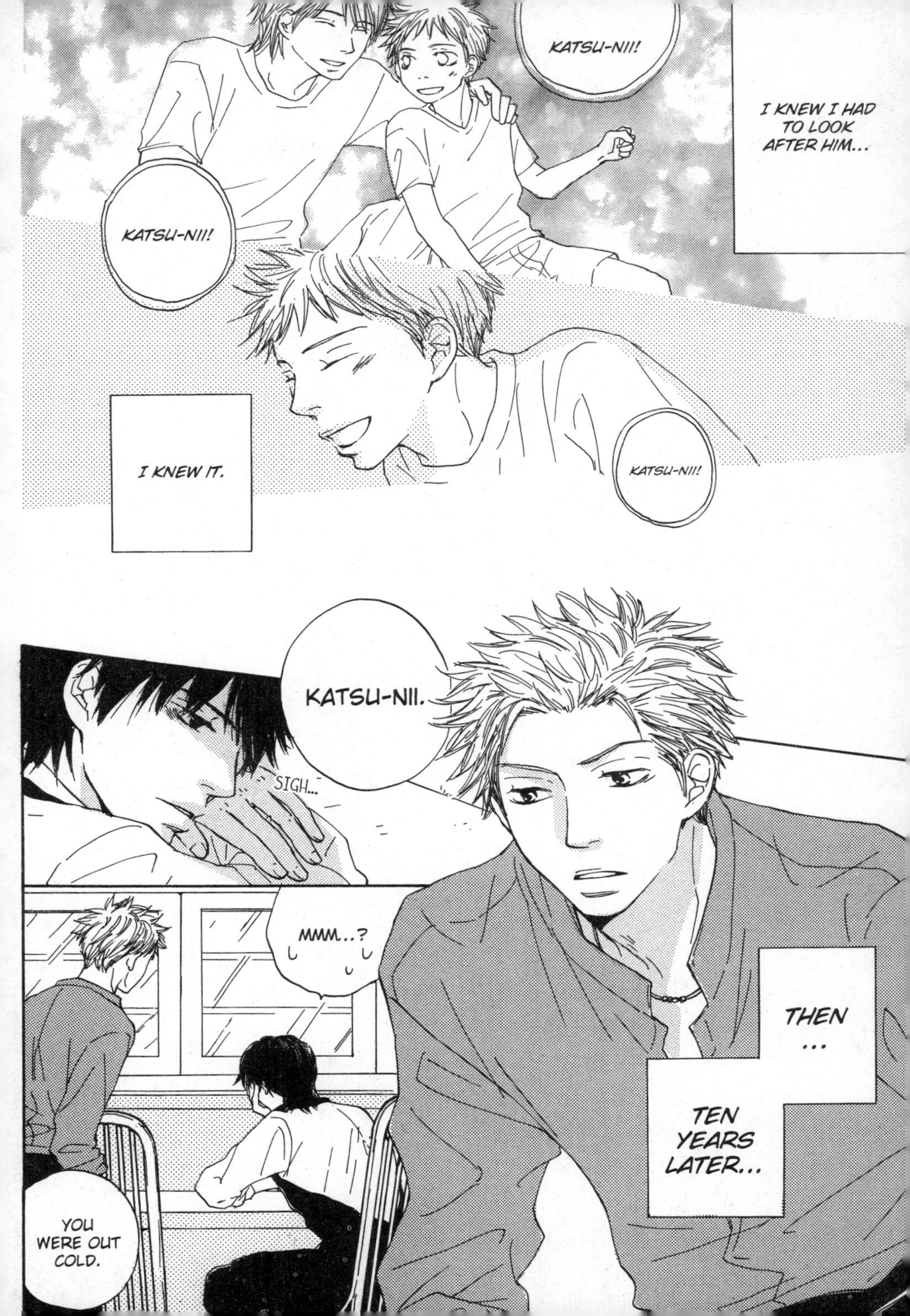
I KNEW I HAD TO LOOK AFTER HIM...
KATSU-NII!
KATSU-NII!
KATSU-NII!
I KNEW IT.
THEN ...
TEN YEARS LATER...
KATSU-NII.
SIGH...
MMM...?
YOU WERE OUT COLD.

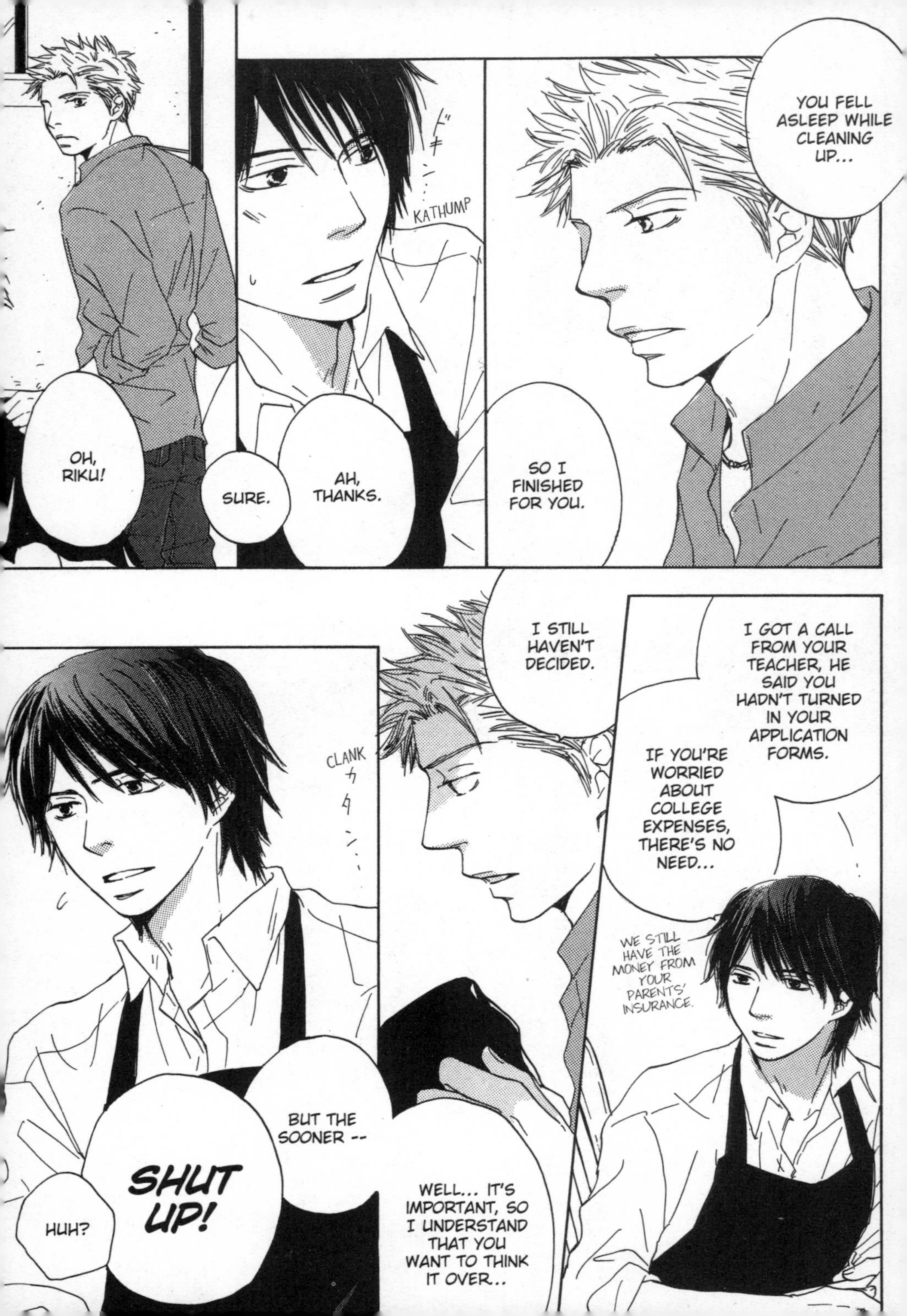
YOU FELL ASLEEP WHILE CLEANING UP...
SO I FINISHED FOR YOU.
KATHUMP
AH, THANKS.
SURE.
OH, RIKU!
I GOT A CALL FROM YOUR TEACHER, HE SAID YOU HADN'T TURNED IN YOUR APPLICATION FORMS.
IF YOU'RE WORRIED ABOUT COLLEGE EXPENSES, THERE'S NO NEED...
WE STILL HAVE THE MONEY FROM YOUR PARENTS' INSURANCE.
I STILL HAVEN'T DECIDED.
WELL... IT'S IMPORTANT, SO I UNDERSTAND THAT YOU WANT TO THINK IT OVER..
CLANK
BUT THE SOONER --
SHUT UP!
HUH?

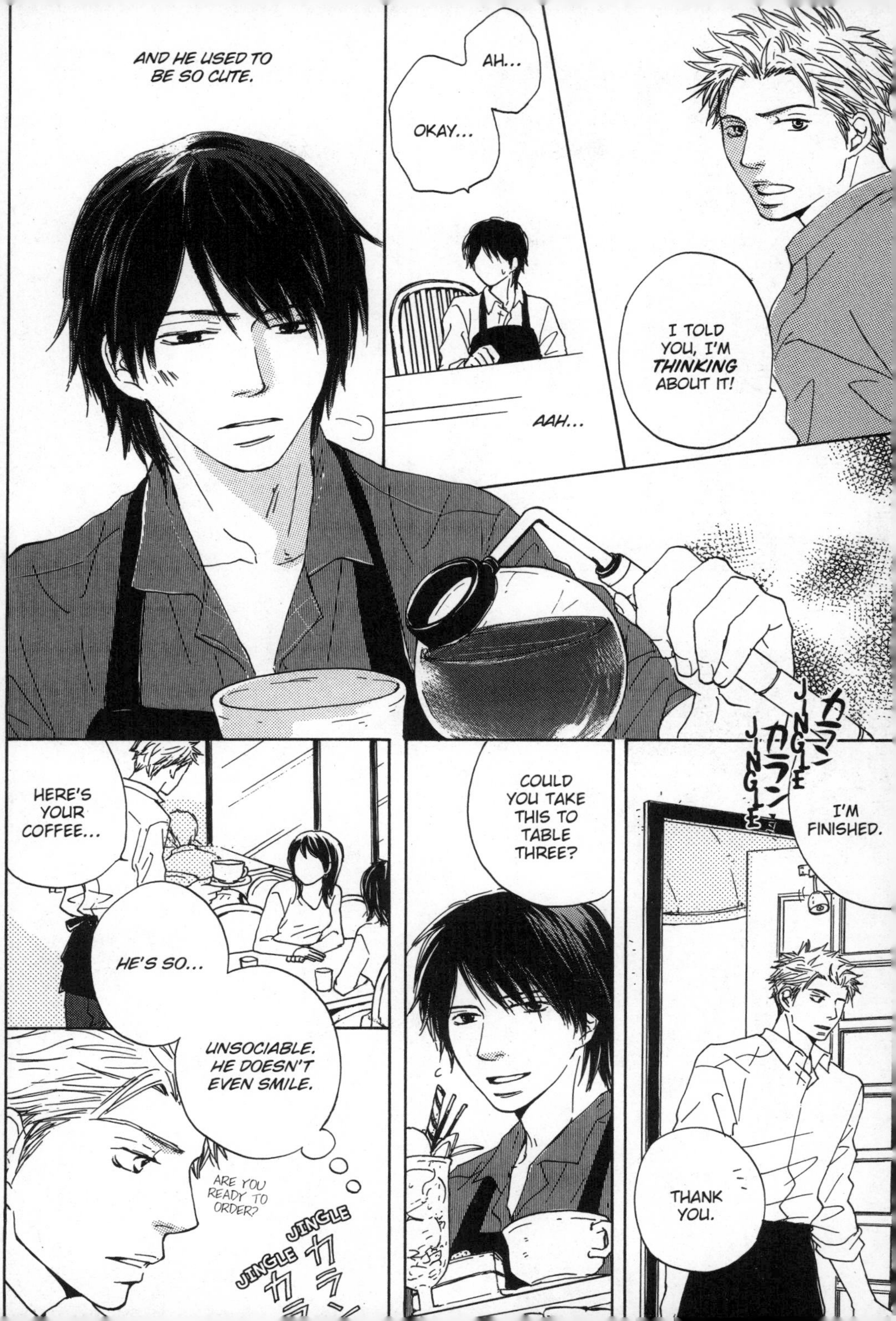
I TOLD YOU, I'M *THINKING* ABOUT IT!
AH... OKAY...
AAH...
AND HE USED TO BE SO CUTE.
カラン JINGLE カラン JINGLE
I'M FINISHED.
THANK YOU.
COULD YOU TAKE THIS TO TABLE THREE?
HERE'S YOUR COFFEE...
HE'S SO...
UNSOCIABLE. HE DOESN'T EVEN SMILE.
ARE YOU READY TO ORDER?
JINGLE カラ JINGLE カラ

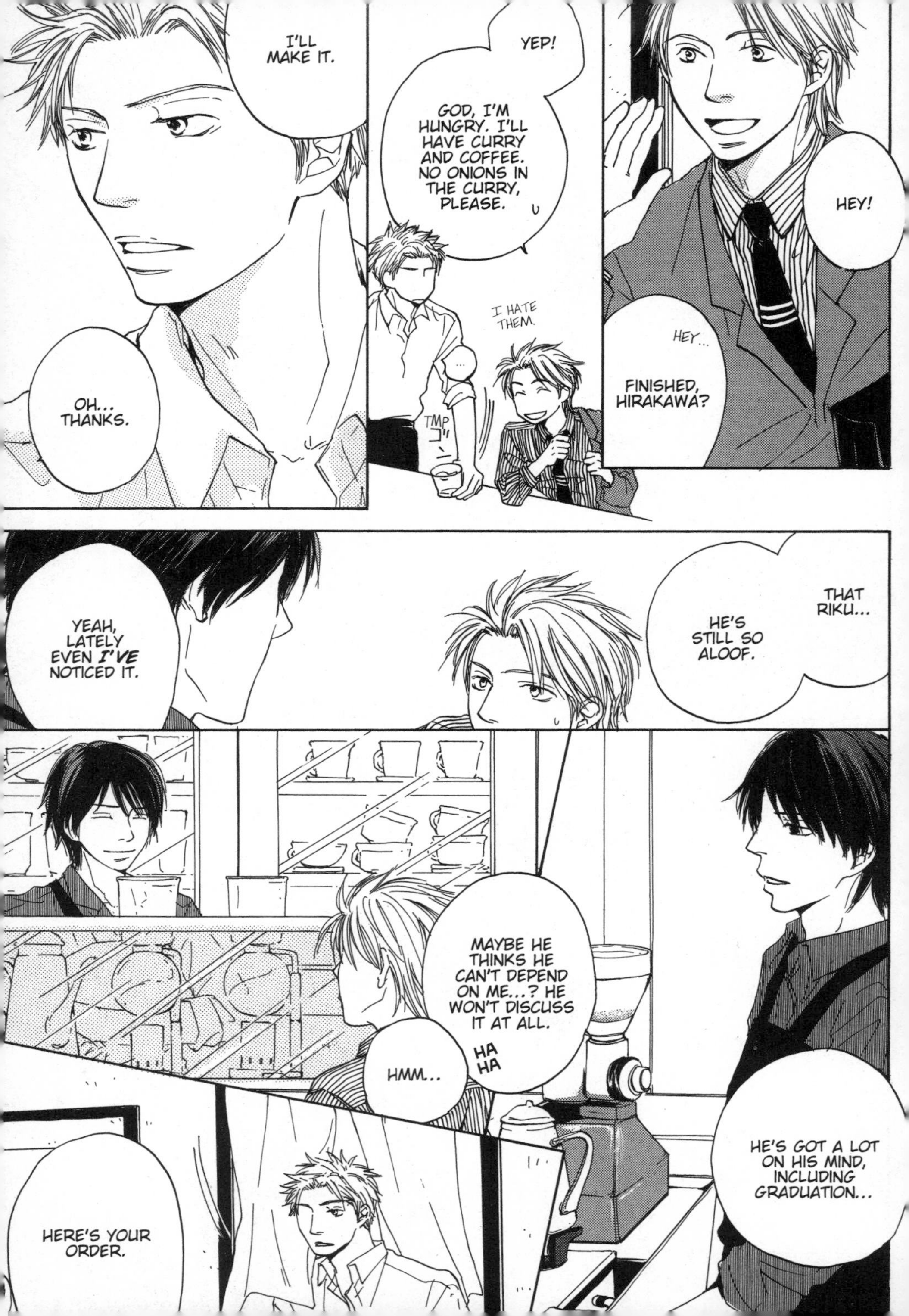
HEY!
HEY...
FINISHED, HIRAKAWA?
YEP!
GOD, I'M HUNGRY. I'LL HAVE CURRY AND COFFEE. NO ONIONS IN THE CURRY, PLEASE.
I HATE THEM.
...
TMP
I'LL MAKE IT.
OH... THANKS.
THAT RIKU...
HE'S STILL SO ALOOF.
YEAH, LATELY EVEN *I'VE* NOTICED IT.
HE'S GOT A LOT ON HIS MIND, INCLUDING GRADUATION...
MAYBE HE THINKS HE CAN'T DEPEND ON ME...? HE WON'T DISCUSS IT AT ALL.
HA HA
HMM...
HERE'S YOUR ORDER.

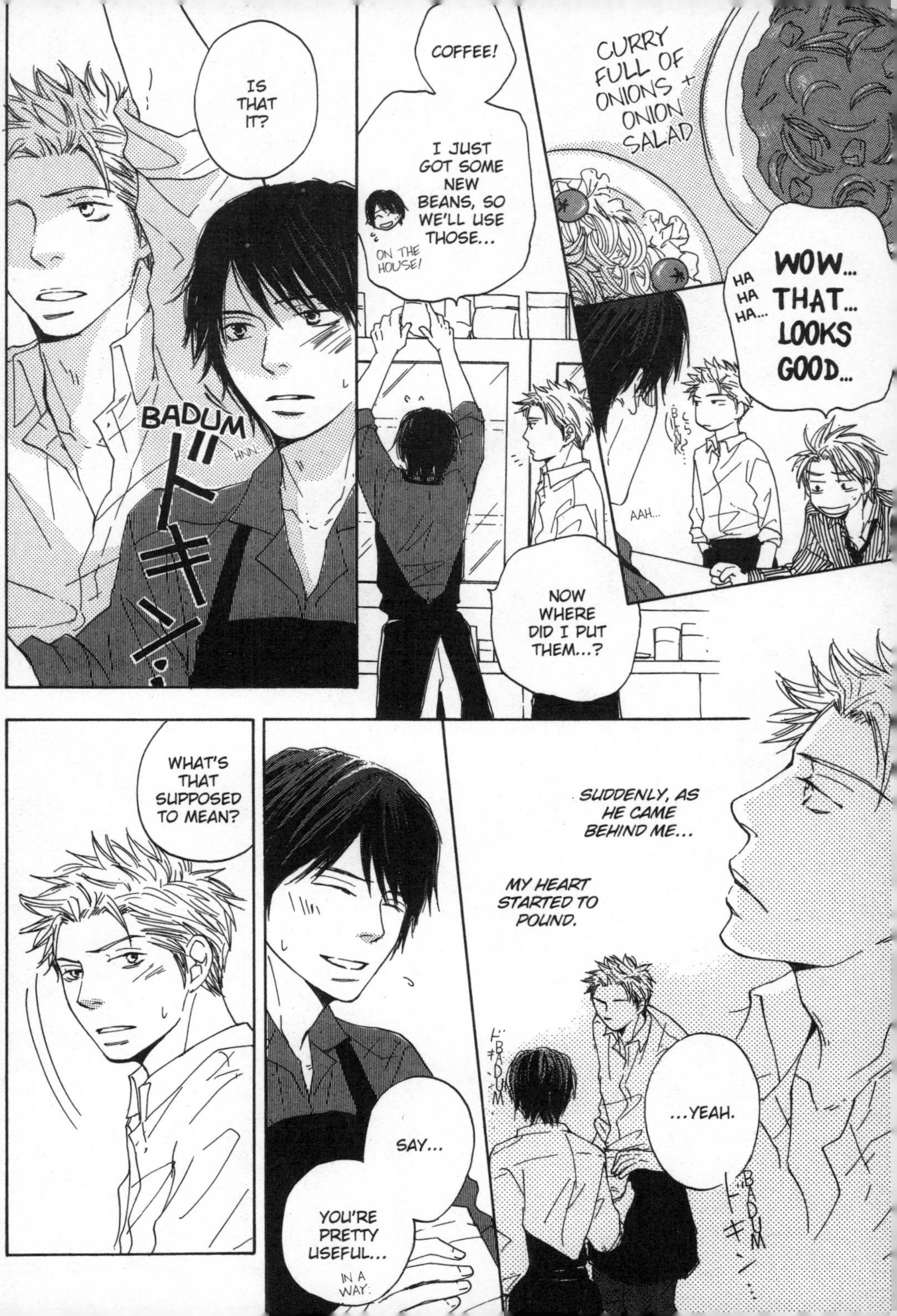
CURRY FULL OF ONIONS + ONION SALAD
HA HA HA...
WOW... THAT... LOOKS GOOD...
BLINK
AAH...
COFFEE!
I JUST GOT SOME NEW BEANS, SO WE'LL USE THOSE...
ON THE HOUSE!
NOW WHERE DID I PUT THEM...?
IS THAT IT?
BADUM
HNN.
SUDDENLY, AS HE CAME BEHIND ME...
MY HEART STARTED TO POUND.
...YEAH.
BADUM
BADUM
SAY...
YOU'RE PRETTY USEFUL...
IN A WAY.
WHAT'S THAT SUPPOSED TO MEAN?

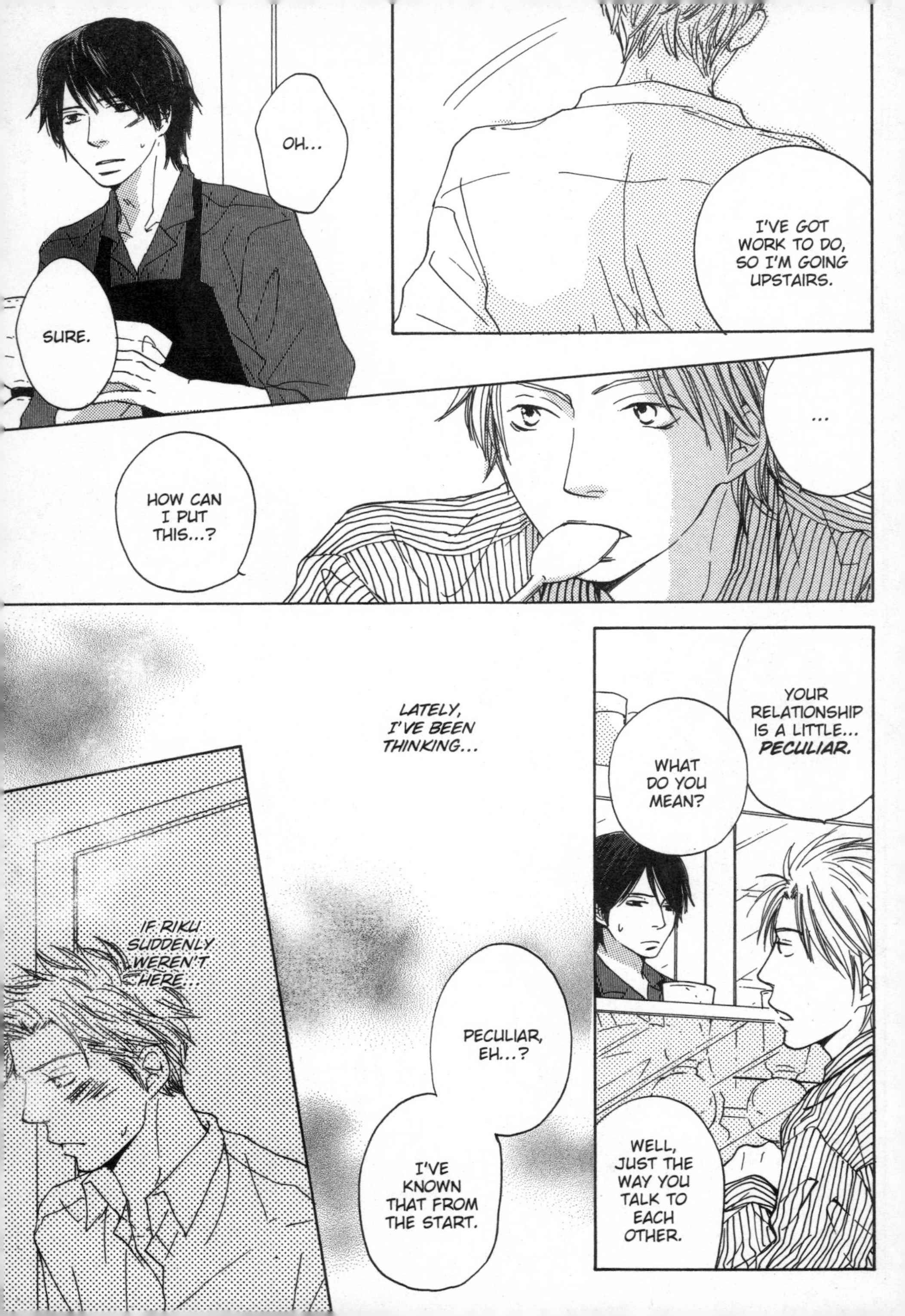
I'VE GOT WORK TO DO, SO I'M GOING UPSTAIRS.
OH...
SURE.
...
HOW CAN I PUT THIS...?
YOUR RELATIONSHIP IS A LITTLE... PECULIAR.
WHAT DO YOU MEAN?
WELL, JUST THE WAY YOU TALK TO EACH OTHER.
PECULIAR, EH...?
I'VE KNOWN THAT FROM THE START.
LATELY, I'VE BEEN THINKING...
IF RIKU SUDDENLY WEREN'T HERE...

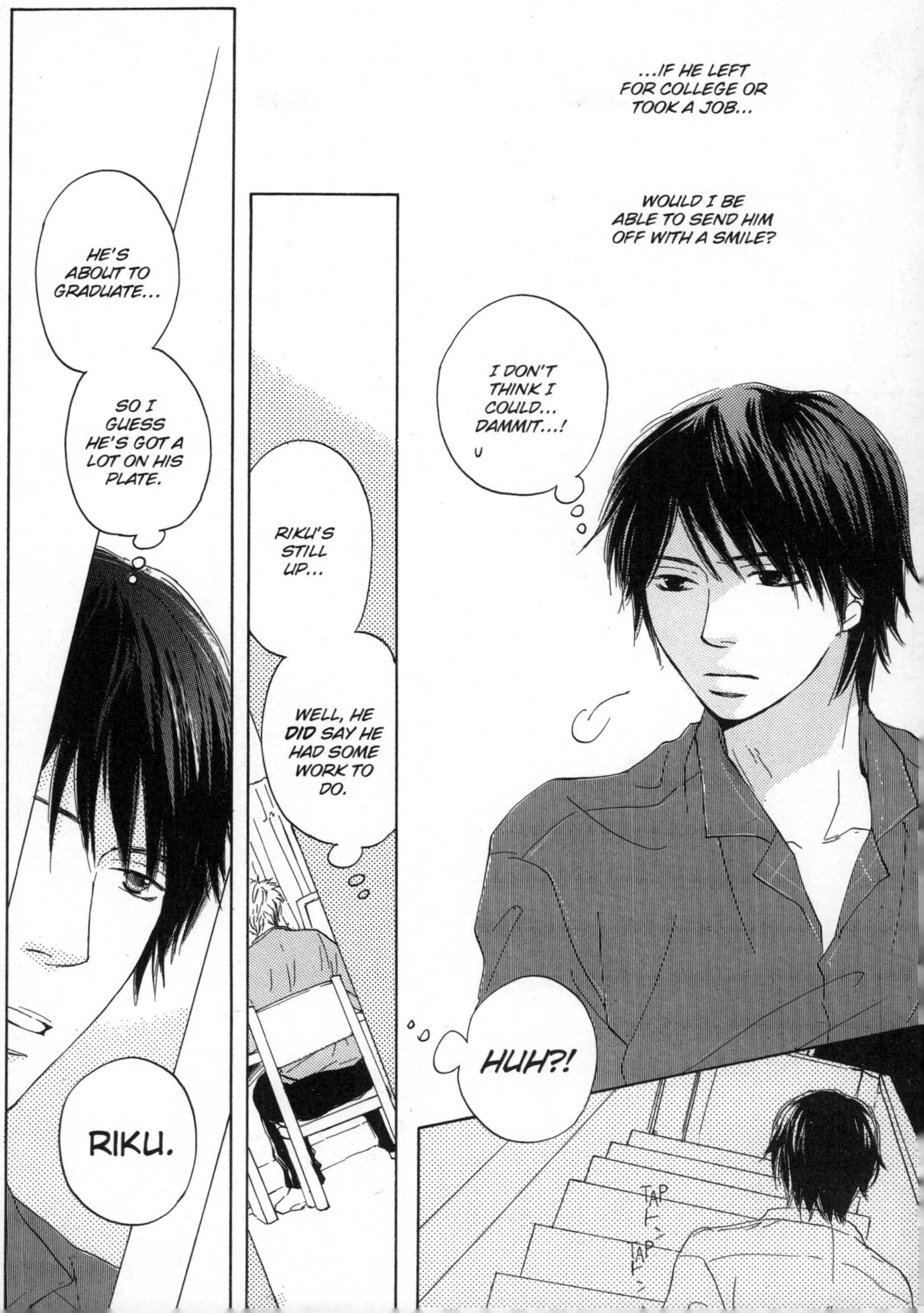
...IF HE LEFT FOR COLLEGE OR TOOK A JOB...
WOULD I BE ABLE TO SEND HIM OFF WITH A SMILE?
I DON'T THINK I COULD... DAMMIT...!
HUH?!
TAP TAP
RIKU'S STILL UP...
WELL, HE DID SAY HE HAD SOME WORK TO DO.
HE'S ABOUT TO GRADUATE...
SO I GUESS HE'S GOT A LOT ON HIS PLATE.
RIKU.

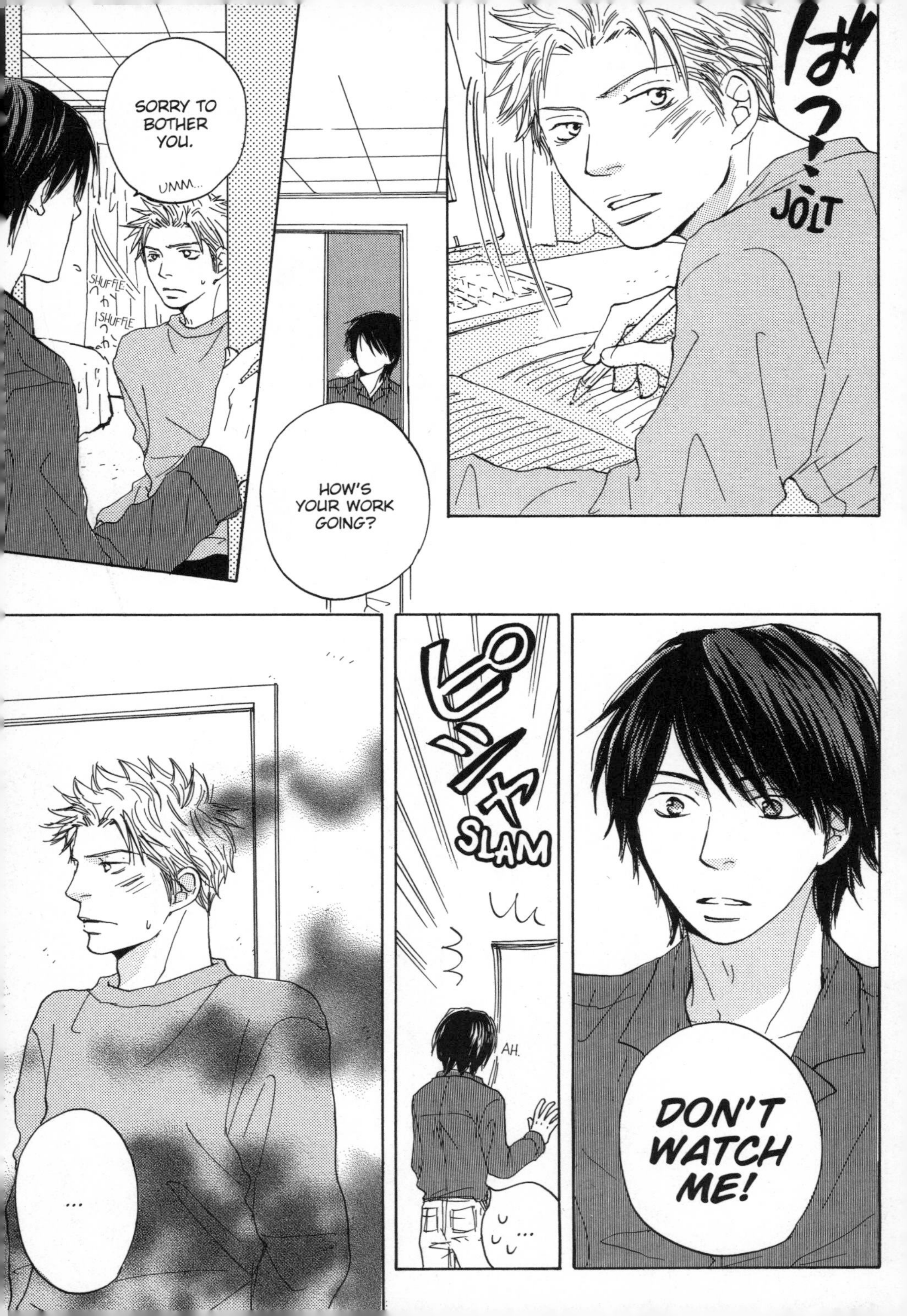
ぱっ!
JOLT
SORRY TO BOTHER YOU.
UMM...
SHUFFLE
SHUFFLE
HOW'S YOUR WORK GOING?
DON'T WATCH ME!
ピシャ
SLAM
AH.
...
...

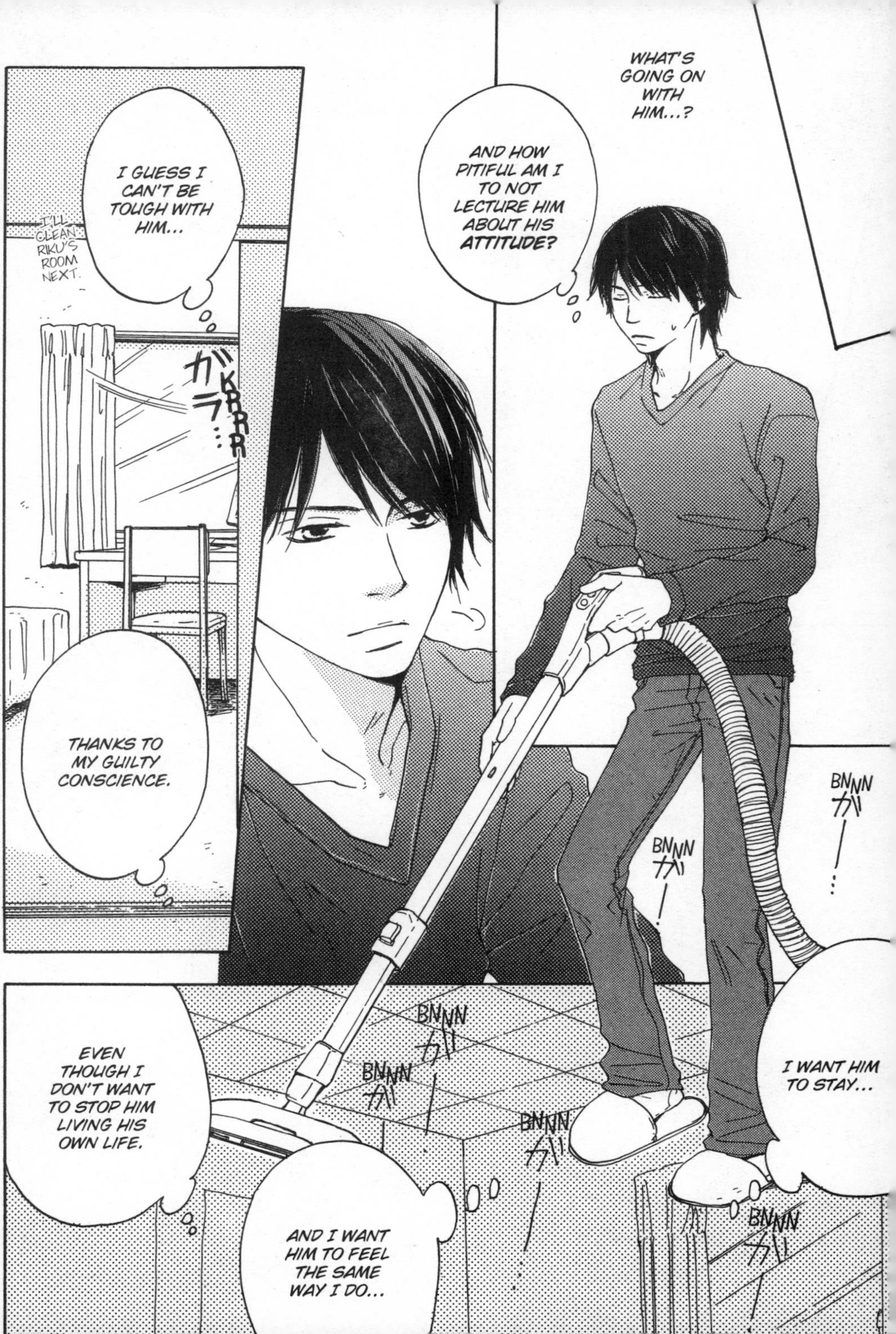
WHAT'S GOING ON WITH HIM...?
AND HOW PITIFUL AM I TO NOT LECTURE HIM ABOUT HIS ATTITUDE?
BNNN
BNNN
I GUESS I CAN'T BE TOUGH WITH HIM...
I'LL CLEAN RIKU'S ROOM NEXT.
ガラ
KRRR
THANKS TO MY GUILTY CONSCIENCE.
I WANT HIM TO STAY...
BNNN
BNNN
BNNN
BNNN
AND I WANT HIM TO FEEL THE SAME WAY I DO...
EVEN THOUGH I DON'T WANT TO STOP HIM LIVING HIS OWN LIFE.

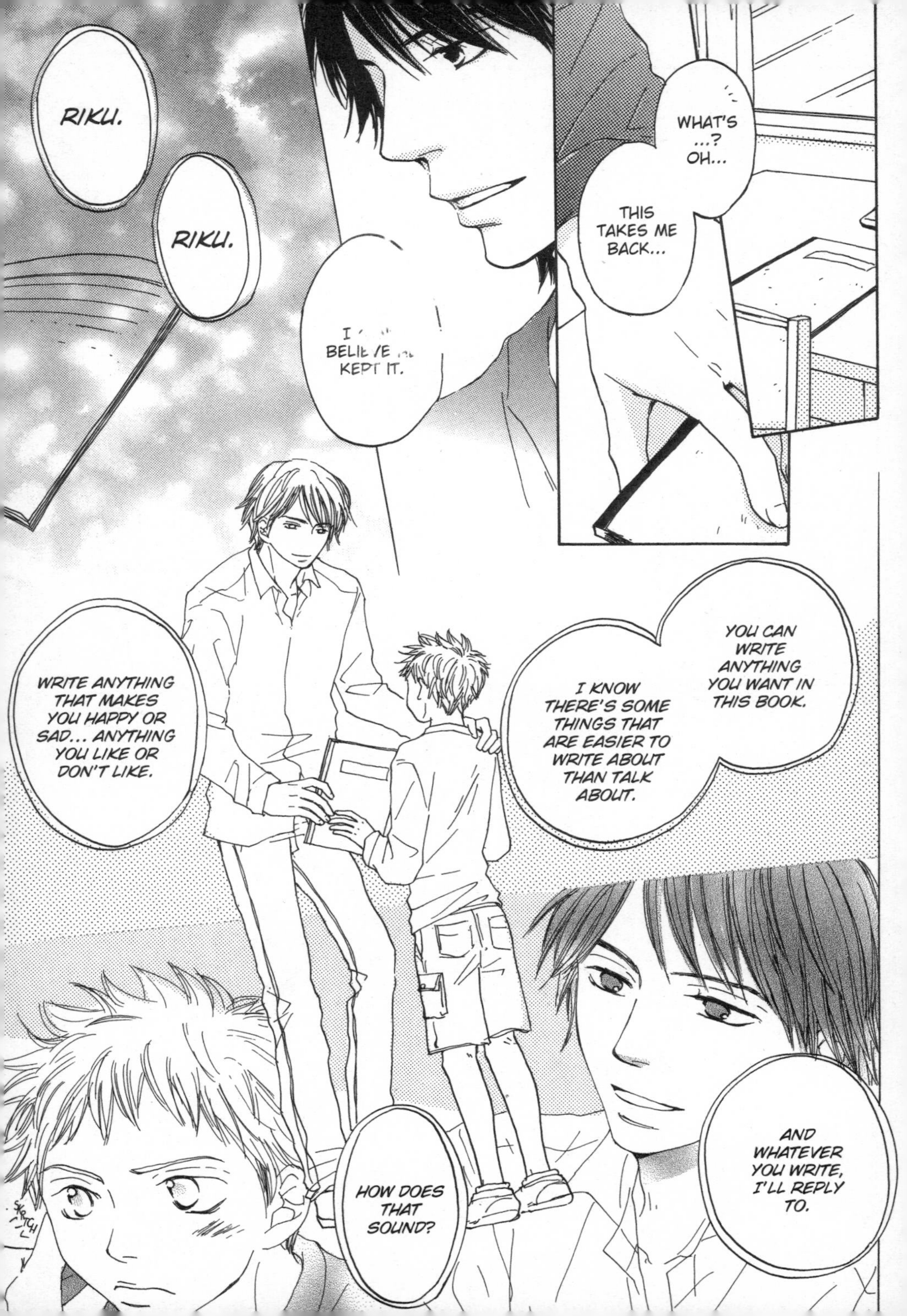
WHAT'S ...? OH...
THIS TAKES ME BACK...
I BELIEVE KEPT IT.
RIKU.
RIKU.
YOU CAN WRITE ANYTHING YOU WANT IN THIS BOOK.
I KNOW THERE'S SOME THINGS THAT ARE EASIER TO WRITE ABOUT THAN TALK ABOUT.
WRITE ANYTHING THAT MAKES YOU HAPPY OR SAD... ANYTHING YOU LIKE OR DON'T LIKE.
AND WHATEVER YOU WRITE, I'LL REPLY TO.
HOW DOES THAT SOUND?

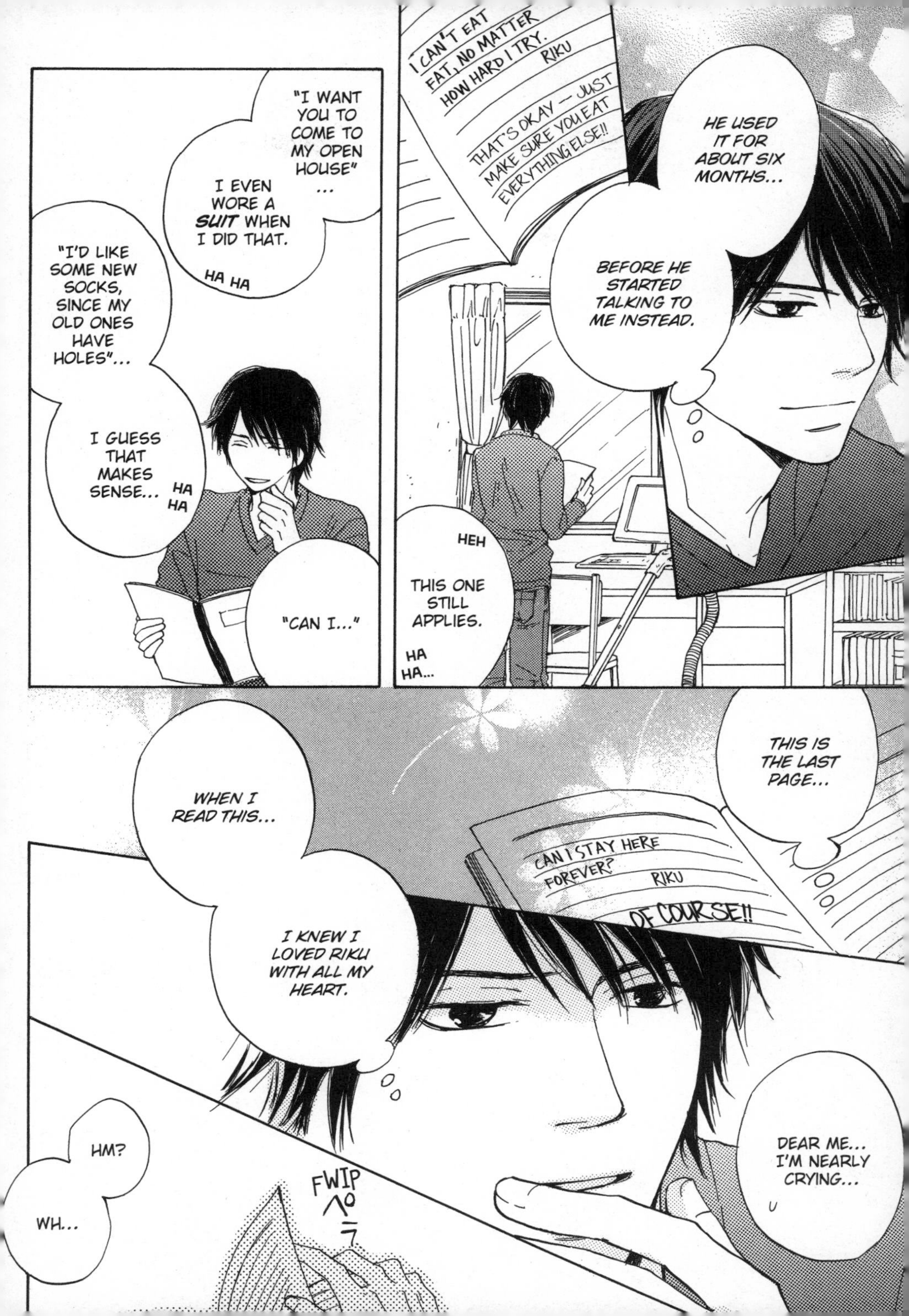
I CAN'T EAT FAT, NO MATTER HOW HARD I TRY. RIKU
THAT'S OKAY — JUST MAKE SURE YOU EAT EVERYTHING ELSE!!
HE USED IT FOR ABOUT SIX MONTHS...
BEFORE HE STARTED TALKING TO ME INSTEAD.
HEH
THIS ONE STILL APPLIES.
HA HA...
"I WANT YOU TO COME TO MY OPEN HOUSE"...
I EVEN WORE A SUIT WHEN I DID THAT.
HA HA
"I'D LIKE SOME NEW SOCKS, SINCE MY OLD ONES HAVE HOLES"...
I GUESS THAT MAKES SENSE...
HA HA
"CAN I..."
THIS IS THE LAST PAGE...
CAN I STAY HERE FOREVER? RIKU
OF COURSE!!
WHEN I READ THIS...
I KNEW I LOVED RIKU WITH ALL MY HEART.
DEAR ME... I'M NEARLY CRYING...
FWIP
HM?
WH...

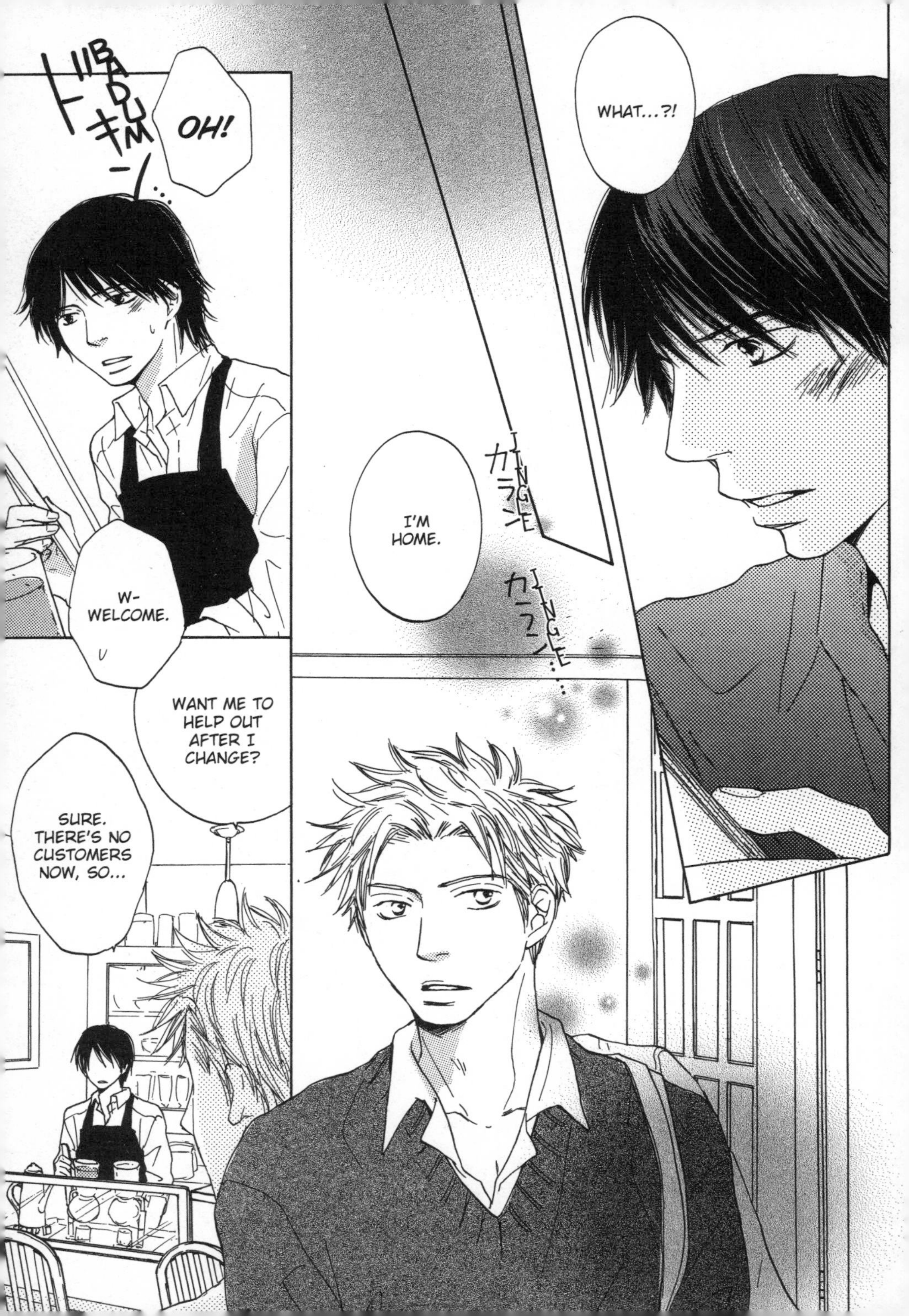
WHAT...?!
JINGLE
I'M HOME.
JINGLE...
BADUM
OH!
W-WELCOME.
WANT ME TO HELP OUT AFTER I CHANGE?
SURE. THERE'S NO CUSTOMERS NOW, SO...

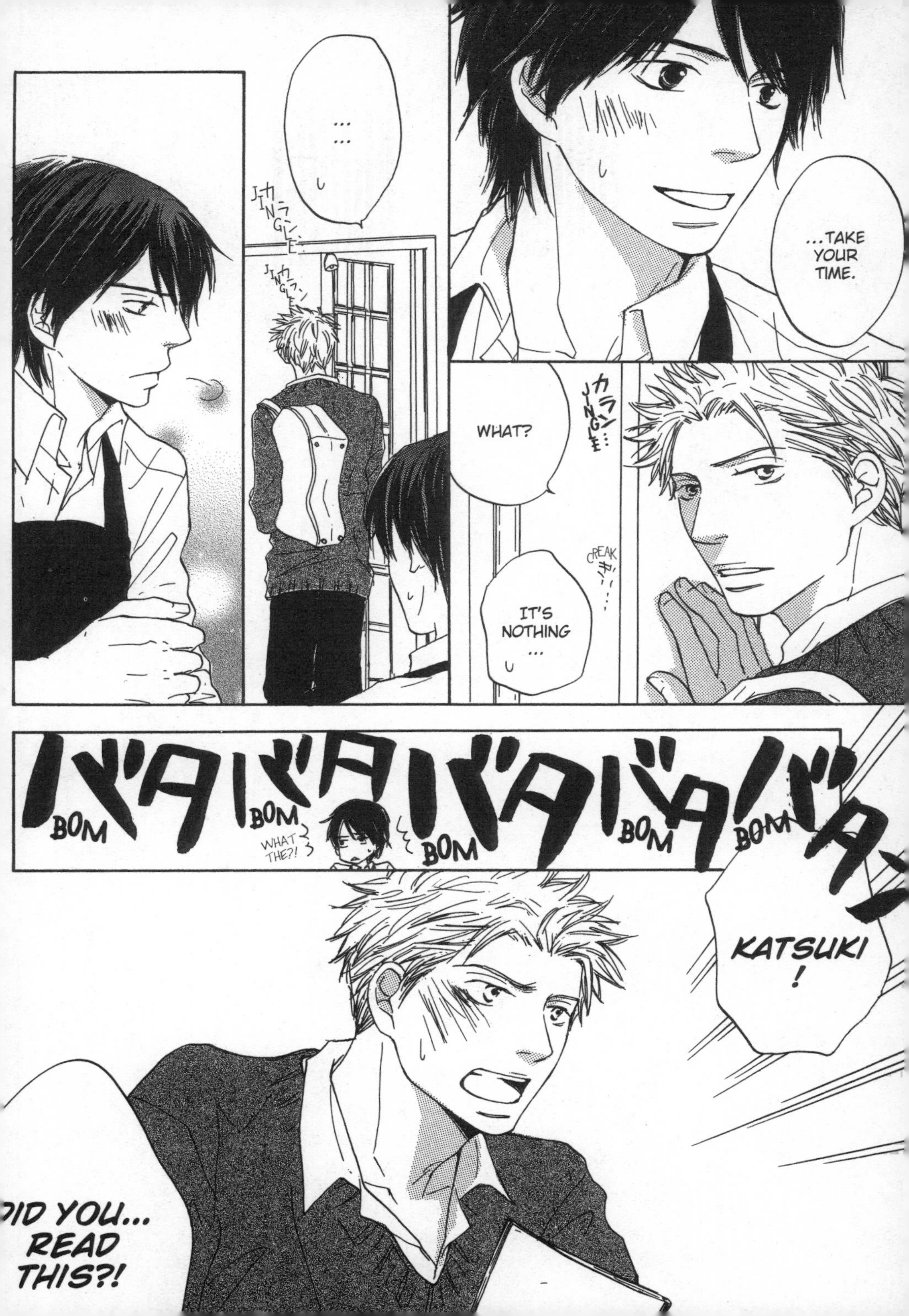
...TAKE YOUR TIME.
JINGLE...
WHAT?
CREAK
IT'S NOTHING ...
... ...
JINGLE
JINGLE
BOM
BOM
BOM
BOM
BOM
WHAT THE?!
KATSUKI!
DID YOU... READ THIS?!

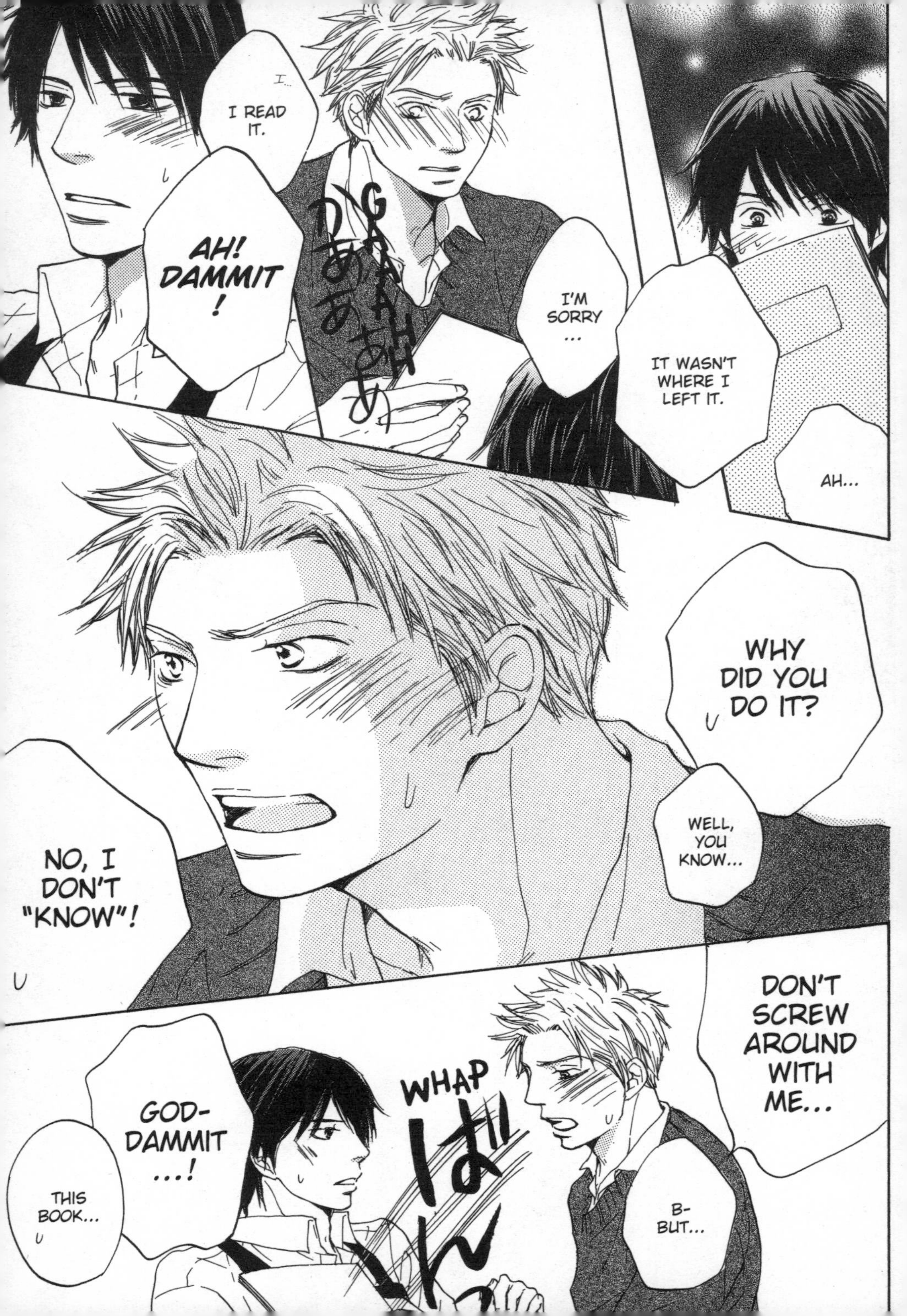
I'M SORRY...
IT WASN'T WHERE I LEFT IT.
AH...
I...
I READ IT.
GAAHH
AH! DAMMIT!
WHY DID YOU DO IT?
WELL, YOU KNOW...
NO, I DON'T "KNOW"!
DON'T SCREW AROUND WITH ME...
B-BUT...
WHAP
GOD-DAMMIT...!
THIS BOOK...

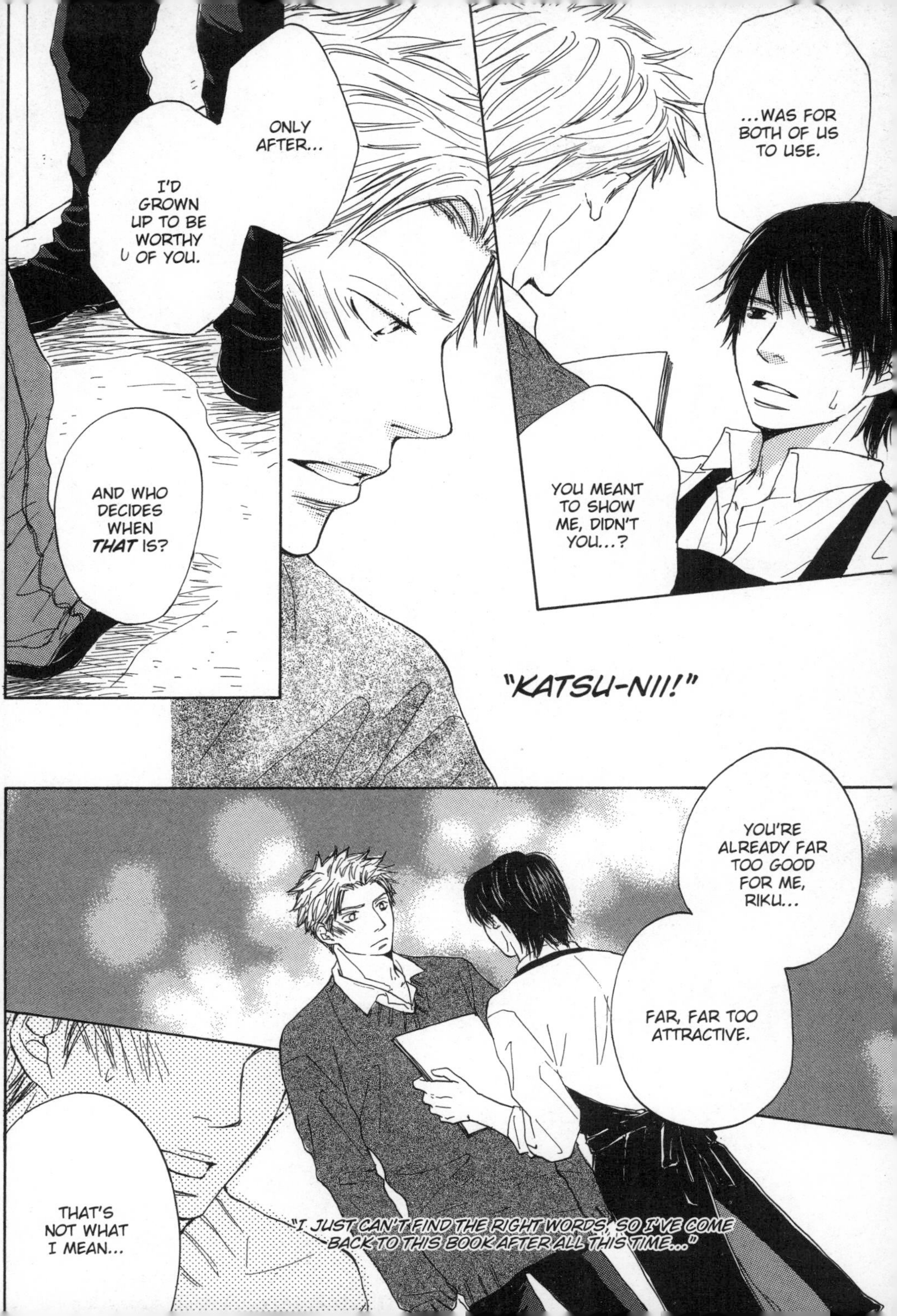
...WAS FOR BOTH OF US TO USE.
YOU MEANT TO SHOW ME, DIDN'T YOU...?
ONLY AFTER...
I'D GROWN UP TO BE WORTHY OF YOU.
AND WHO DECIDES WHEN *THAT* IS?
"KATSU-NII!"
YOU'RE ALREADY FAR TOO GOOD FOR ME, RIKU...
FAR, FAR TOO ATTRACTIVE.
"I JUST CAN'T FIND THE RIGHT WORDS, SO I'VE COME BACK TO THIS BOOK AFTER ALL THIS TIME..."
THAT'S NOT WHAT I MEAN...

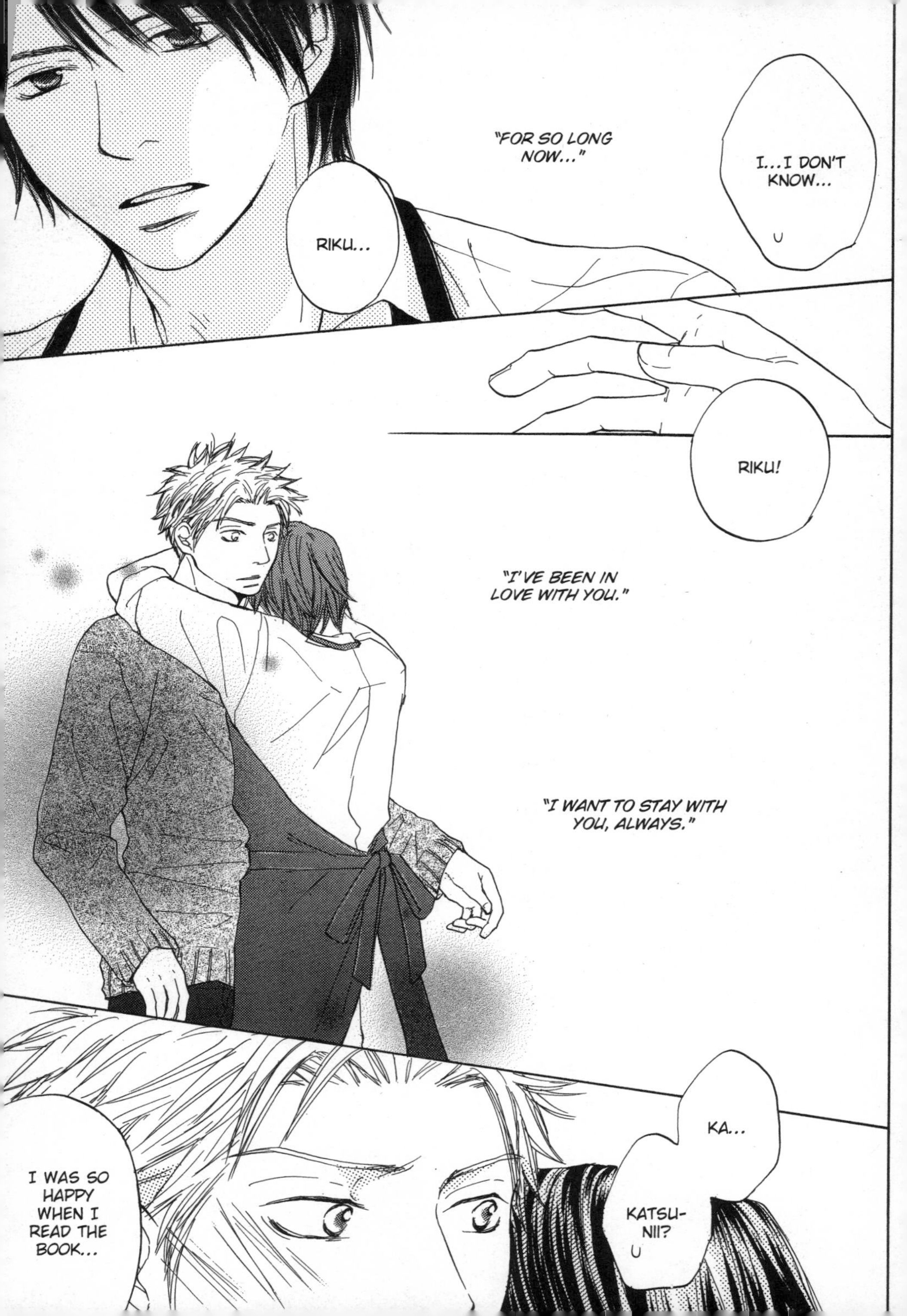
I...I DON'T KNOW...
"FOR SO LONG NOW..."
RIKU...
RIKU!
"I'VE BEEN IN LOVE WITH YOU."
"I WANT TO STAY WITH YOU, ALWAYS."
KA...
KATSU-NII?
I WAS SO HAPPY WHEN I READ THE BOOK...

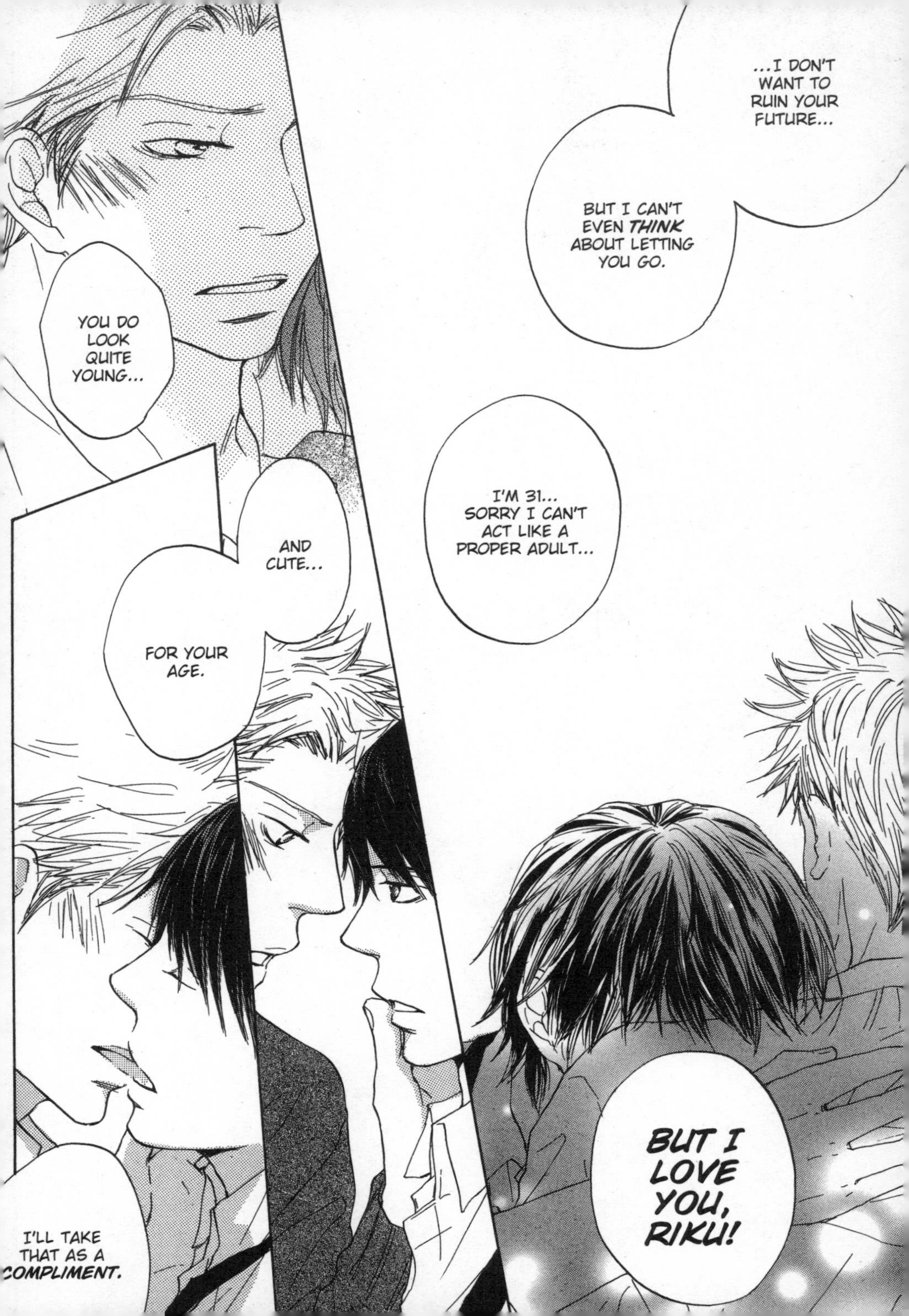
...I DON'T WANT TO RUIN YOUR FUTURE...
BUT I CAN'T EVEN THINK ABOUT LETTING YOU GO.
I'M 31... SORRY I CAN'T ACT LIKE A PROPER ADULT...
BUT I LOVE YOU, RIKU!
YOU DO LOOK QUITE YOUNG...
AND CUTE...
FOR YOUR AGE.
I'LL TAKE THAT AS A COMPLIMENT.

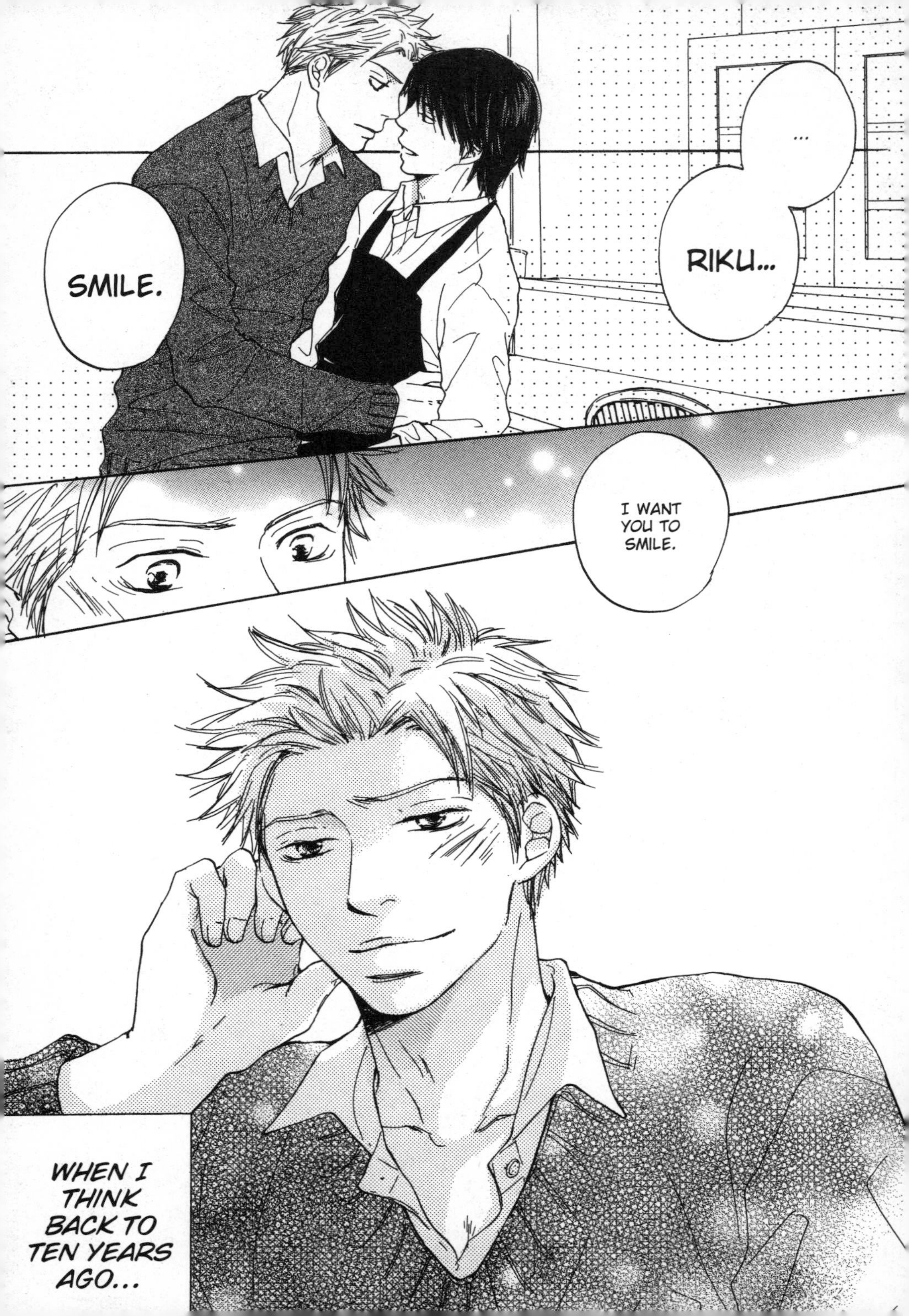
...
RIKU...
SMILE.
I WANT YOU TO SMILE.
WHEN I THINK BACK TO TEN YEARS AGO...

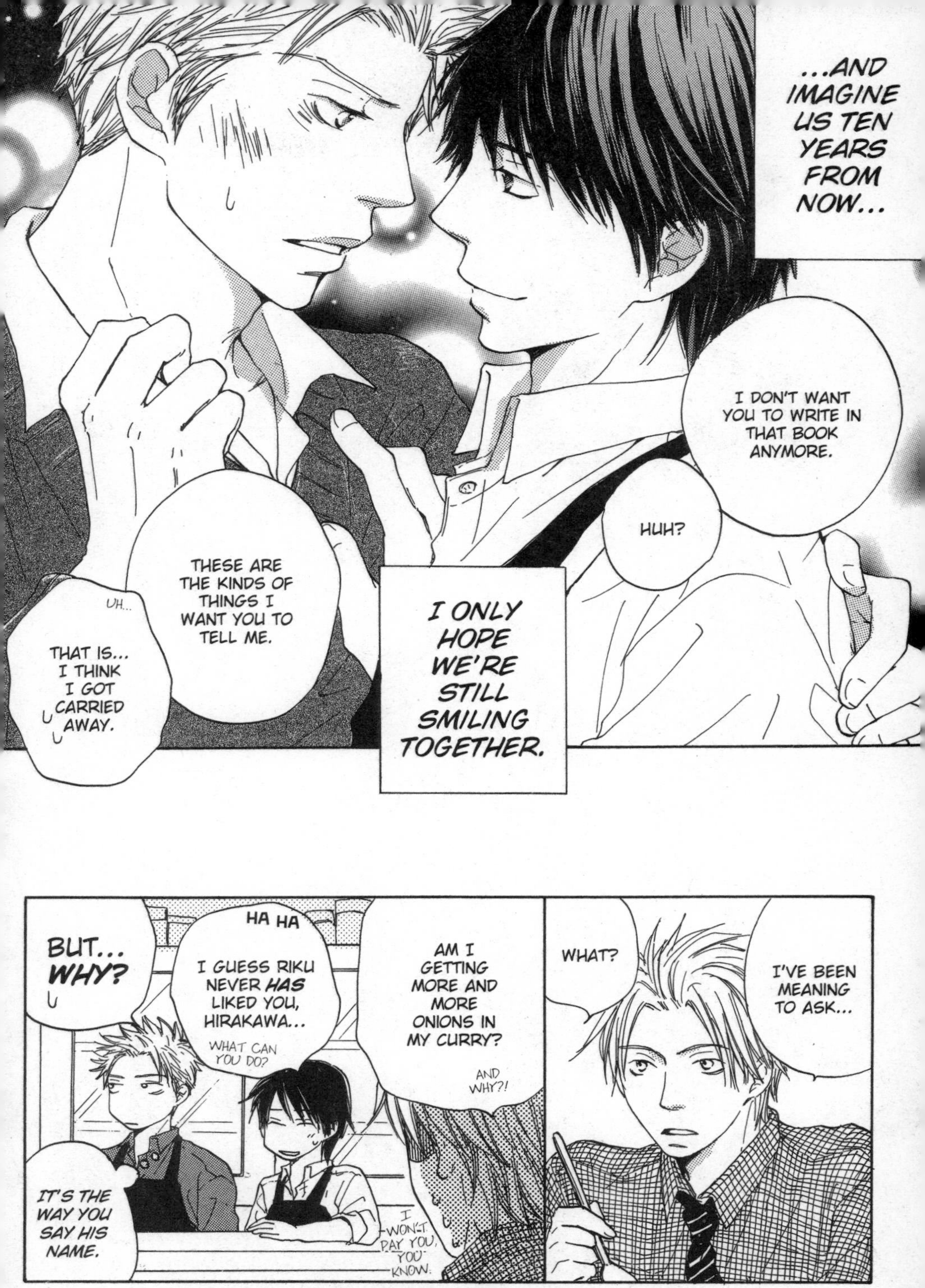
...AND IMAGINE US TEN YEARS FROM NOW...
I DON'T WANT YOU TO WRITE IN THAT BOOK ANYMORE.
HUH?
I ONLY HOPE WE'RE STILL SMILING TOGETHER.
THESE ARE THE KINDS OF THINGS I WANT YOU TO TELL ME.
UH...
THAT IS... I THINK I GOT CARRIED AWAY.
I'VE BEEN MEANING TO ASK...
WHAT?
AM I GETTING MORE AND MORE ONIONS IN MY CURRY?
AND WHY?!
HA HA
I GUESS RIKU NEVER HAS LIKED YOU, HIRAKAWA...
WHAT CAN YOU DO?
I WON'T PAY YOU, YOU KNOW.
BUT... WHY?
IT'S THE WAY YOU SAY HIS NAME.

MY SWEET HOME ● END

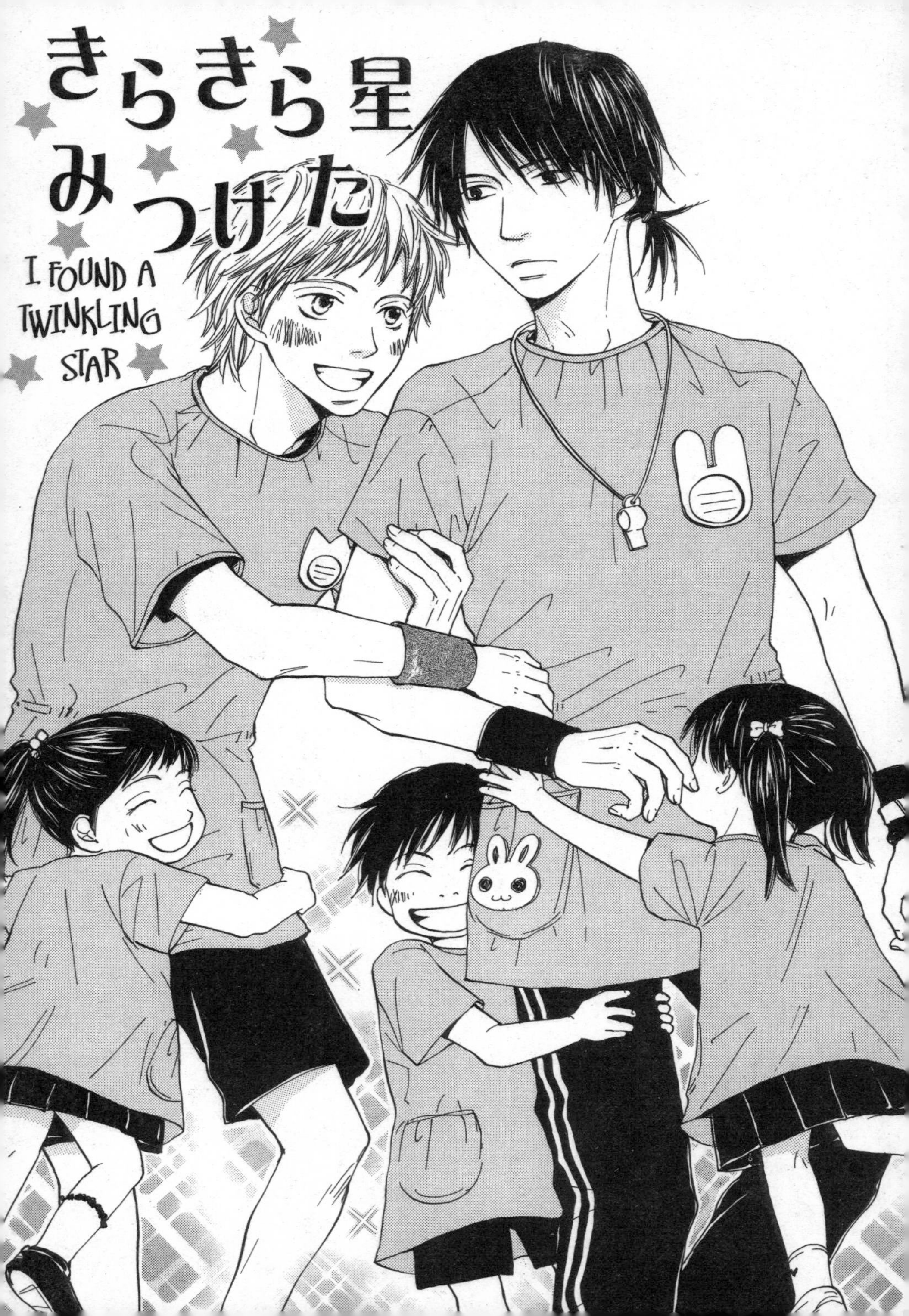
きらきら星みつけた
I FOUND A TWINKLING STAR

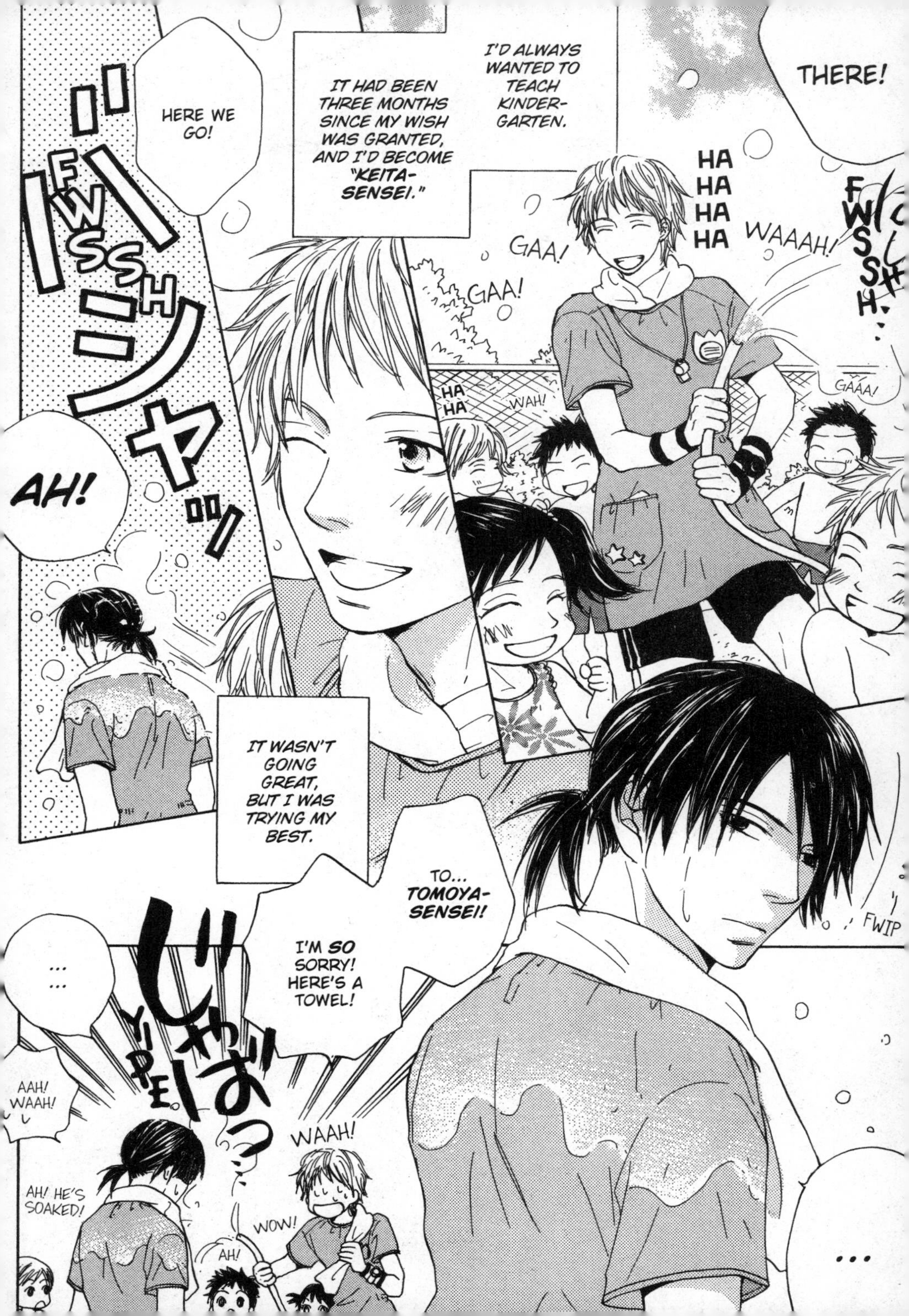
THERE!
I'D ALWAYS WANTED TO TEACH KINDER-GARTEN.
IT HAD BEEN THREE MONTHS SINCE MY WISH WAS GRANTED, AND I'D BECOME "KEITA-SENSEI."
FWSSH
HA HA HA HA
WAAAH!
GAA!
GAA!
GAAA!
WAH!
HA HA
HERE WE GO!
FWSSH
AH!
IT WASN'T GOING GREAT, BUT I WAS TRYING MY BEST.
FWIP
TO... TOMOYA-SENSEI!
...
I'M SO SORRY! HERE'S A TOWEL!
... ...
YIPE!
WAAH!
AAH! WAAH!
AH! HE'S SOAKED!
WOW!
AH!

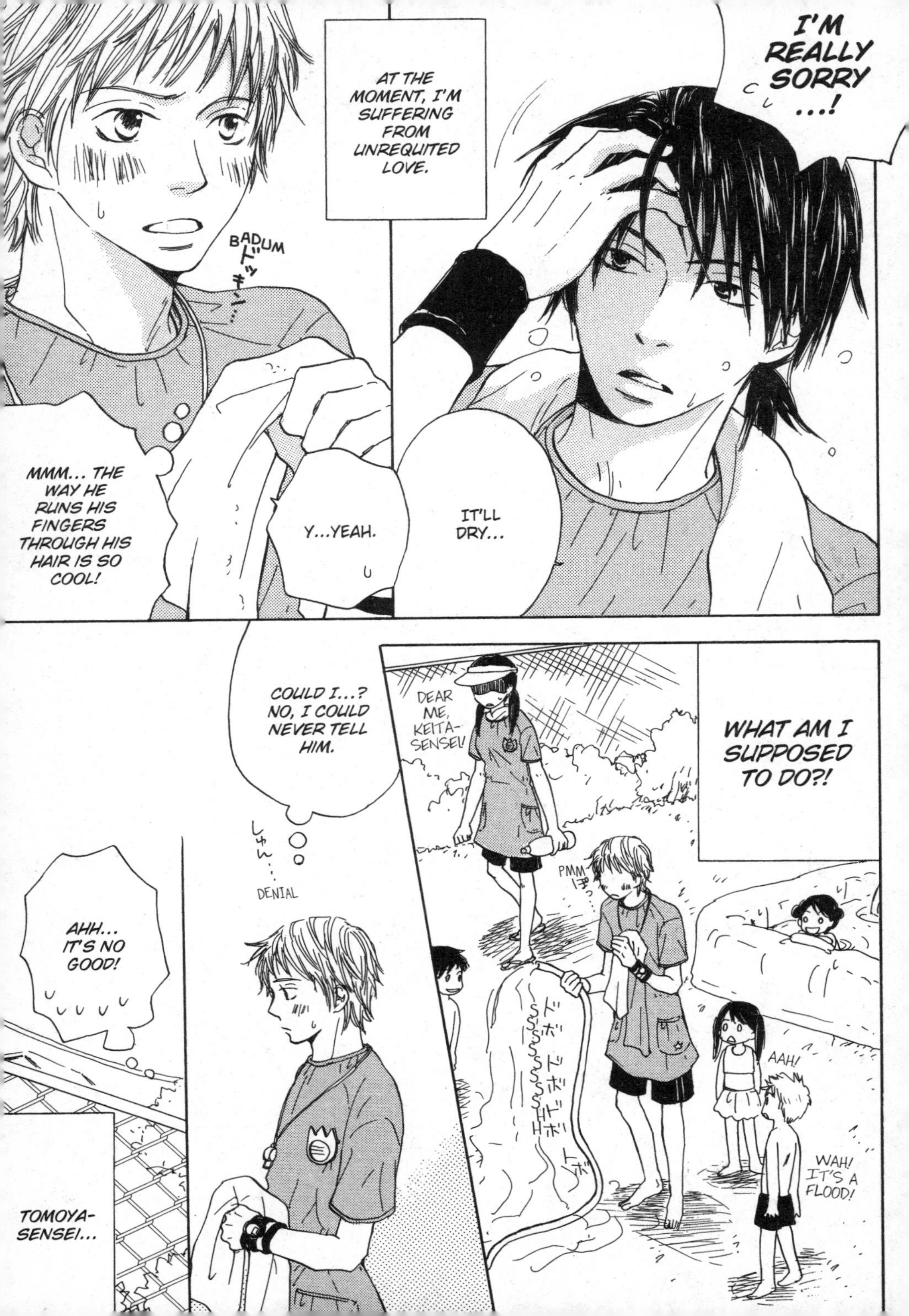
I'M REALLY SORRY ...!
IT'LL DRY...
AT THE MOMENT, I'M SUFFERING FROM UNREQUITED LOVE.
BADUM
Y...YEAH.
MMM... THE WAY HE RUNS HIS FINGERS THROUGH HIS HAIR IS SO COOL!
WHAT AM I SUPPOSED TO DO?!
DEAR ME, KEITA-SENSEI!
PMM
SSSSSSHH
AAH!
WAH! IT'S A FLOOD!
COULD I...? NO, I COULD NEVER TELL HIM.
DENIAL
AHH... IT'S NO GOOD!
TOMOYA-SENSEI...

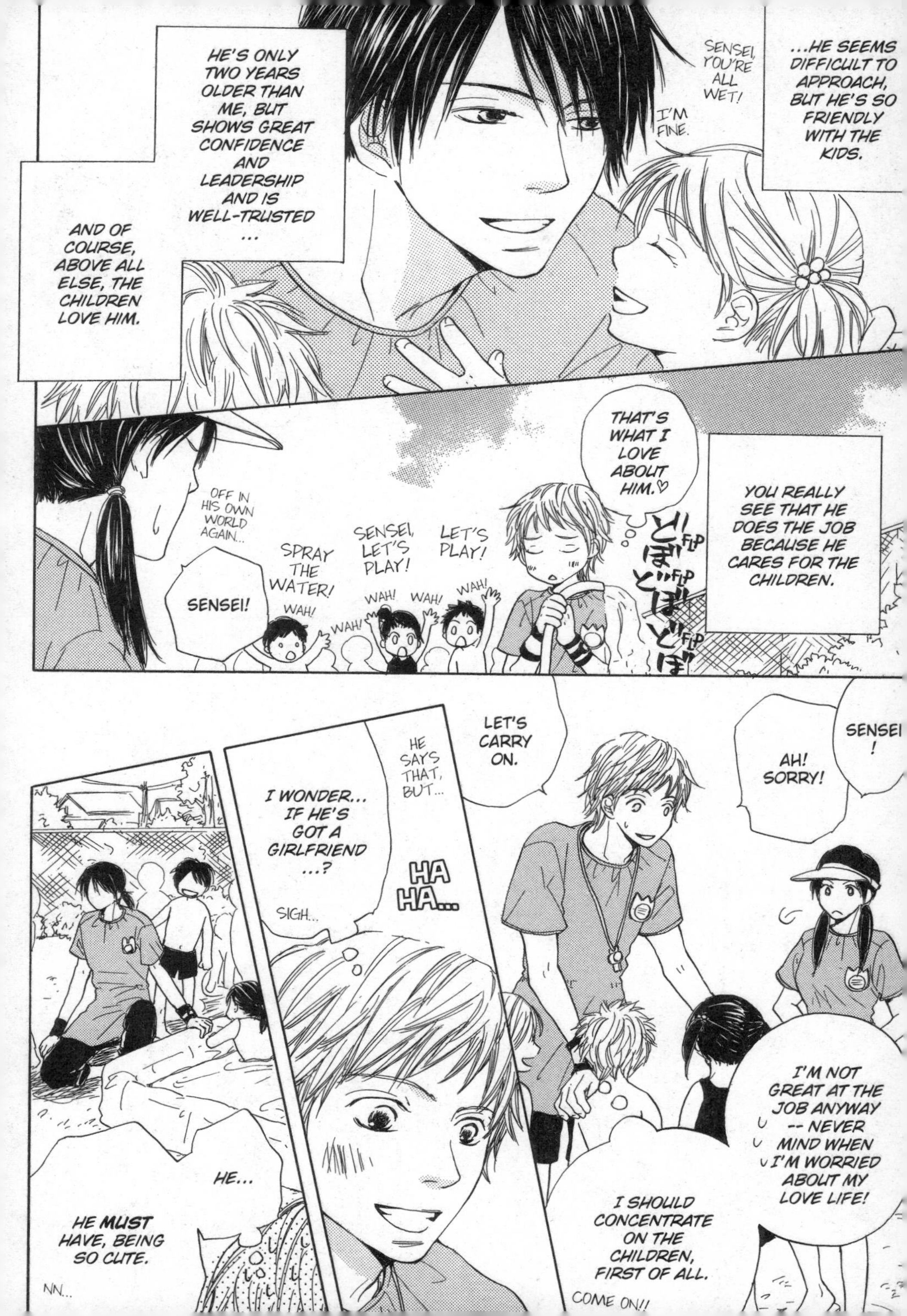
...HE SEEMS DIFFICULT TO APPROACH, BUT HE'S SO FRIENDLY WITH THE KIDS.
SENSEI, YOU'RE ALL WET!
I'M FINE.
HE'S ONLY TWO YEARS OLDER THAN ME, BUT SHOWS GREAT CONFIDENCE AND LEADERSHIP AND IS WELL-TRUSTED ...
AND OF COURSE, ABOVE ALL ELSE, THE CHILDREN LOVE HIM.
YOU REALLY SEE THAT HE DOES THE JOB BECAUSE HE CARES FOR THE CHILDREN.
THAT'S WHAT I LOVE ABOUT HIM.♡
どぼ FLIP どぼ FLIP どぼ FLIP
LET'S PLAY!
WAH!
SENSEI, LET'S PLAY!
WAH!
WAH!
SPRAY THE WATER!
WAH!
WAH!
OFF IN HIS OWN WORLD AGAIN...
SENSEI!
SENSEI!
AH! SORRY!
LET'S CARRY ON.
I'M NOT GREAT AT THE JOB ANYWAY -- NEVER MIND WHEN I'M WORRIED ABOUT MY LOVE LIFE!
I SHOULD CONCENTRATE ON THE CHILDREN, FIRST OF ALL.
COME ON!!
HE SAYS THAT, BUT...
HA HA...
I WONDER... IF HE'S GOT A GIRLFRIEND ...?
SIGH...
HE...
HE MUST HAVE, BEING SO CUTE.
NN...

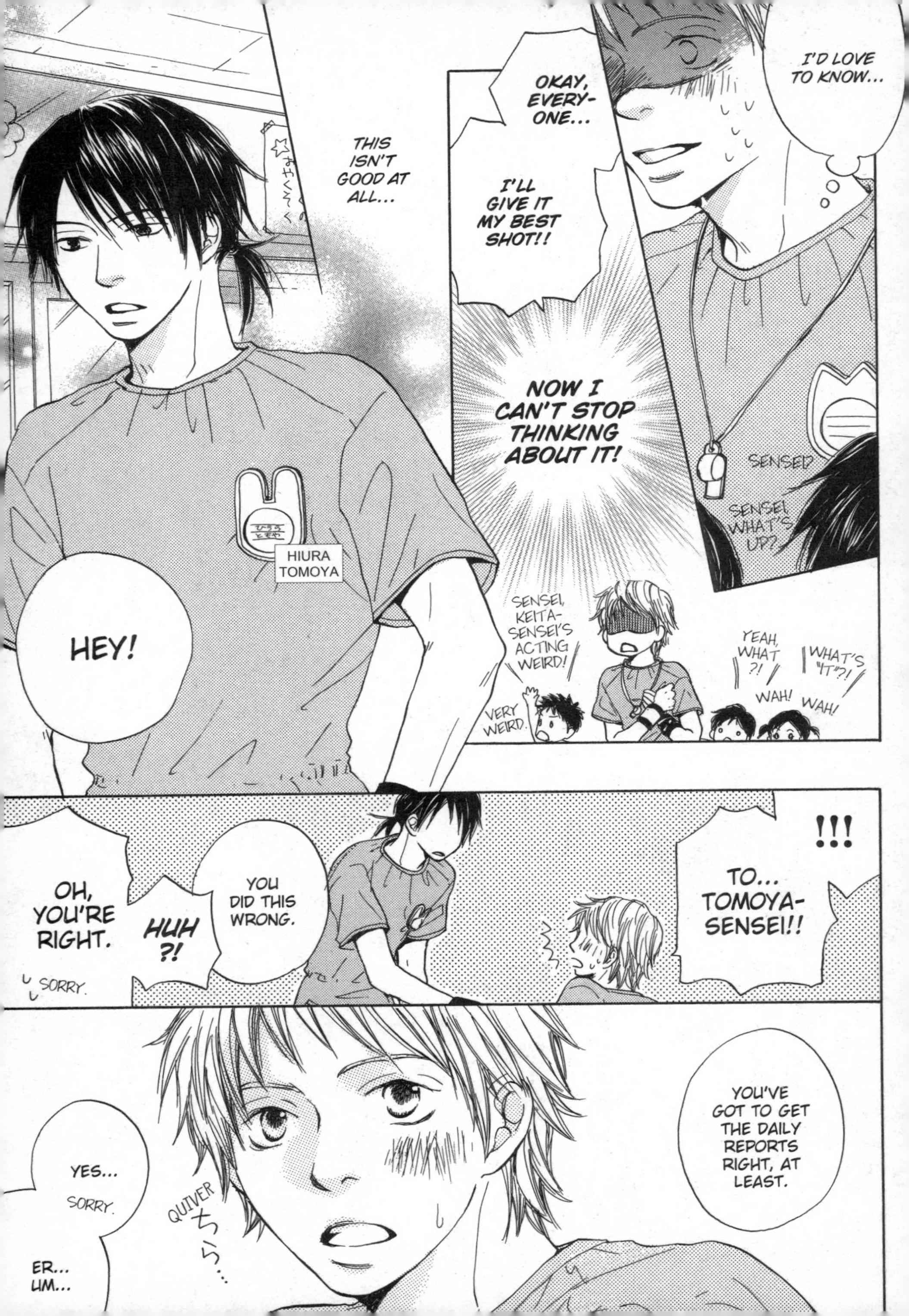
I'D LOVE TO KNOW...
OKAY, EVERY-ONE...
I'LL GIVE IT MY BEST SHOT!!
THIS ISN'T GOOD AT ALL...
NOW I CAN'T STOP THINKING ABOUT IT!
SENSEI?
SENSEI, WHAT'S UP?
WHAT'S "IT"?!
WAH!
YEAH, WHAT?!
WAH!
SENSEI, KEITA-SENSEI'S ACTING WEIRD!
VERY WEIRD.
HIURA TOMOYA
HEY!
!!!
TO... TOMOYA-SENSEI!!
YOU DID THIS WRONG.
HUH?!
OH, YOU'RE RIGHT.
SORRY.
YOU'VE GOT TO GET THE DAILY REPORTS RIGHT, AT LEAST.
QUIVER
YES...
SORRY.
ER... UM...

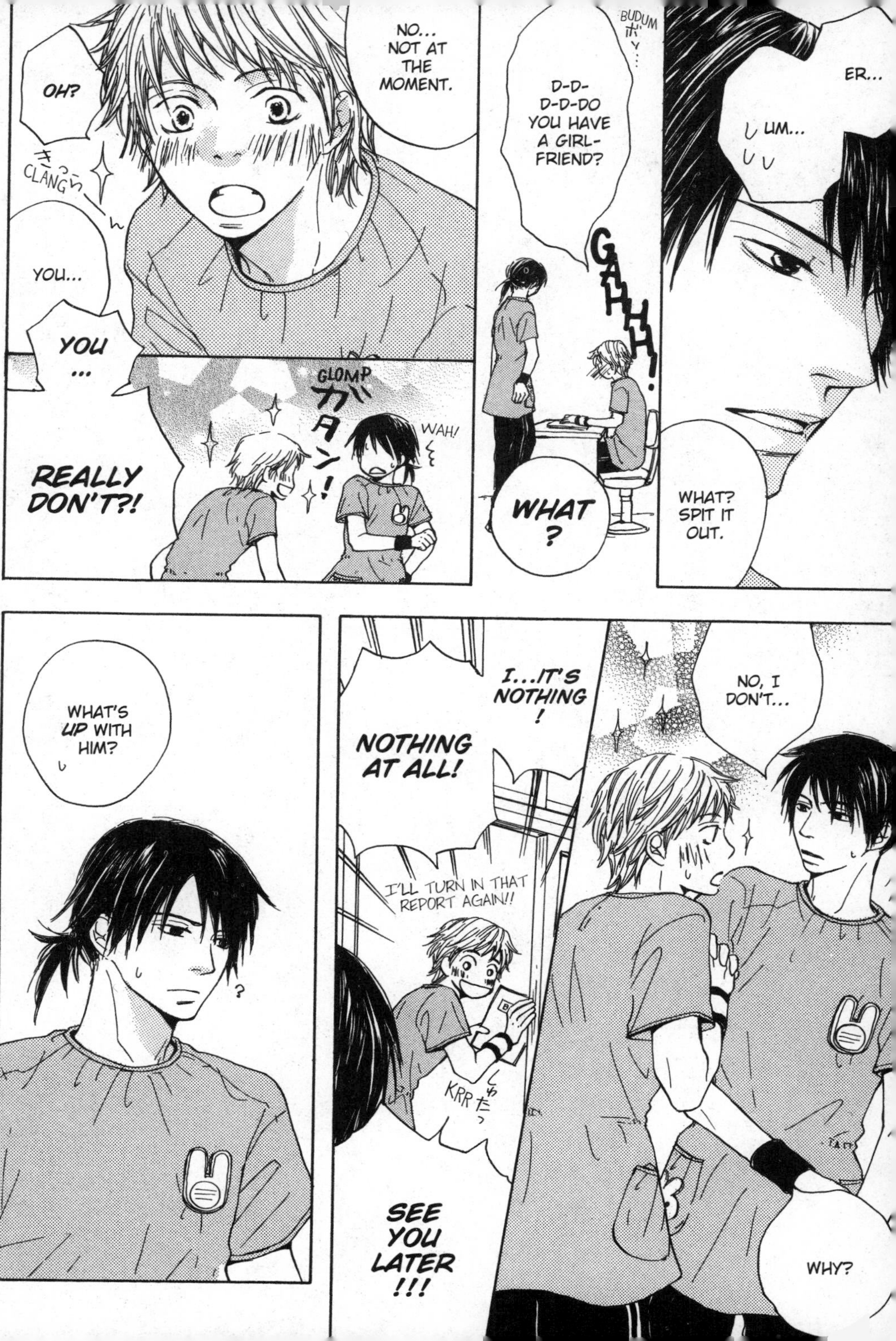
ER...
UM...
WHAT? SPIT IT OUT.
BUDUM
D-D-D-D-DO YOU HAVE A GIRL-FRIEND?
GAHHH!
WHAT?
NO... NOT AT THE MOMENT.
OH?
CLANG
YOU...
YOU...
GLOMP
WAH!
REALLY DON'T?!
NO, I DON'T...
WHY?
I...IT'S NOTHING!
NOTHING AT ALL!
I'LL TURN IN THAT REPORT AGAIN!!
KRR
SEE YOU LATER!!!
WHAT'S UP WITH HIM?

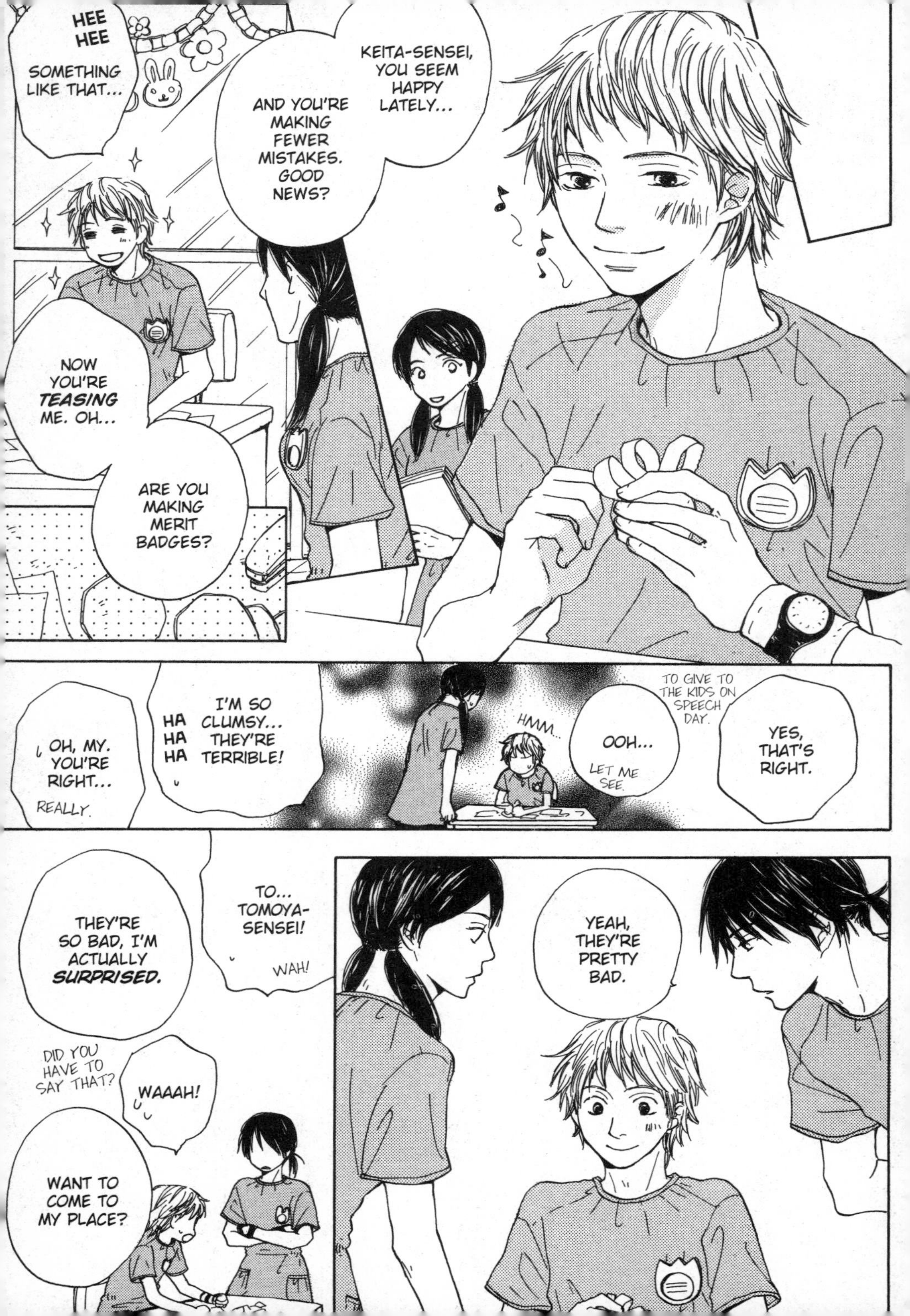
KEITA-SENSEI, YOU SEEM HAPPY LATELY...
AND YOU'RE MAKING FEWER MISTAKES. GOOD NEWS?
HEE HEE
SOMETHING LIKE THAT...
NOW YOU'RE *TEASING* ME. OH...
ARE YOU MAKING MERIT BADGES?
YES, THAT'S RIGHT.
TO GIVE TO THE KIDS ON SPEECH DAY.
OOH...
LET ME SEE.
HMM...
I'M SO CLUMSY... THEY'RE TERRIBLE!
HA HA HA
OH, MY. YOU'RE RIGHT...
REALLY.
YEAH, THEY'RE PRETTY BAD.
TO... TOMOYA-SENSEI!
WAH!
THEY'RE SO BAD, I'M ACTUALLY **SURPRISED.**
WAAAH!
DID YOU HAVE TO SAY THAT?
WANT TO COME TO MY PLACE?

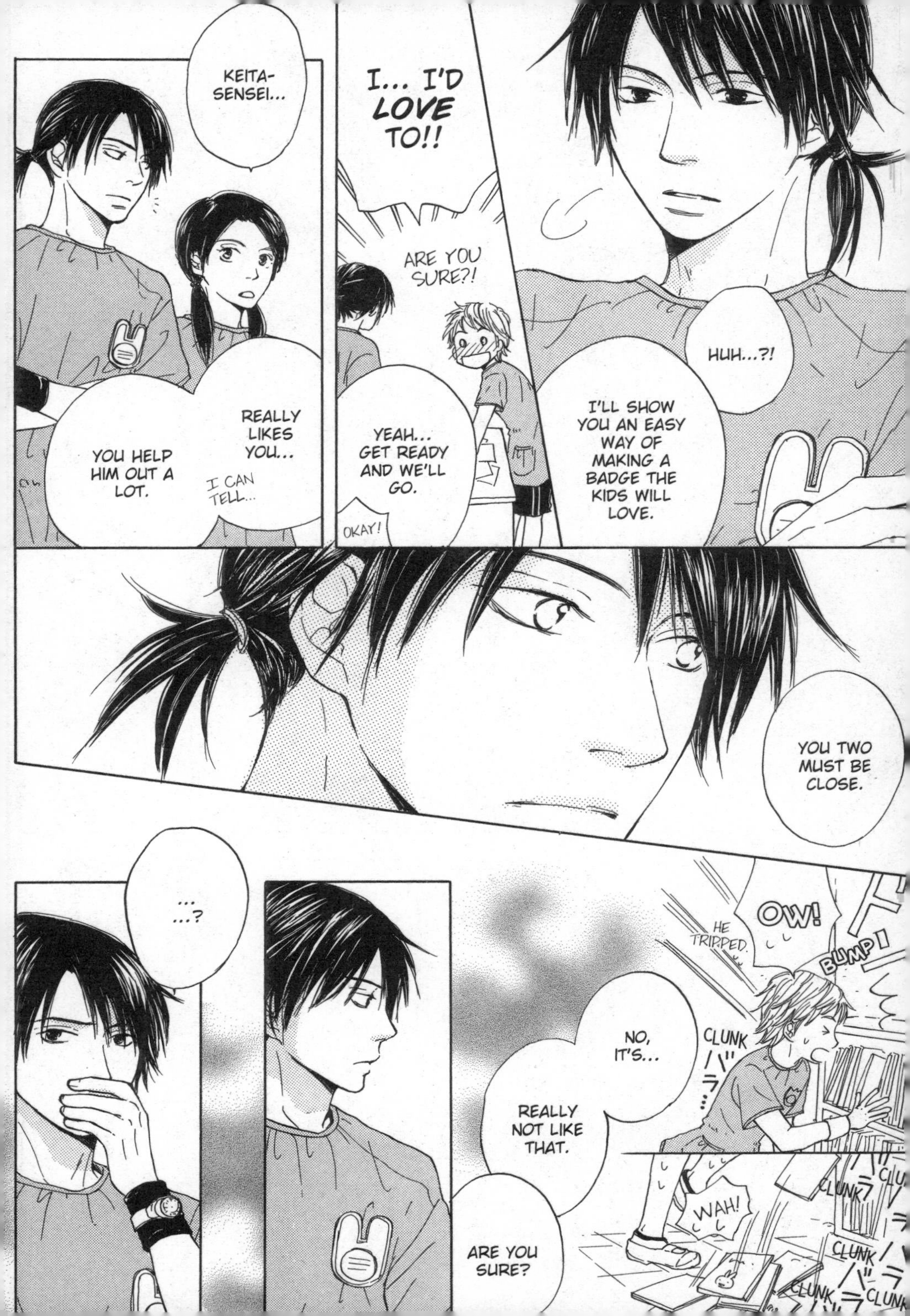
HUH...?!
I'LL SHOW YOU AN EASY WAY OF MAKING A BADGE THE KIDS WILL LOVE.
I... I'D LOVE TO!!
ARE YOU SURE?!
YEAH... GET READY AND WE'LL GO.
OKAY!
KEITA-SENSEI...
REALLY LIKES YOU...
I CAN TELL...
YOU HELP HIM OUT A LOT.
YOU TWO MUST BE CLOSE.
OW!
HE TRIPPED.
BUMP!
CLUNK
NO, IT'S...
REALLY NOT LIKE THAT.
WAH!
CLUNK
CLUNK
CLUNK
CLUNK
ARE YOU SURE?
...
...?

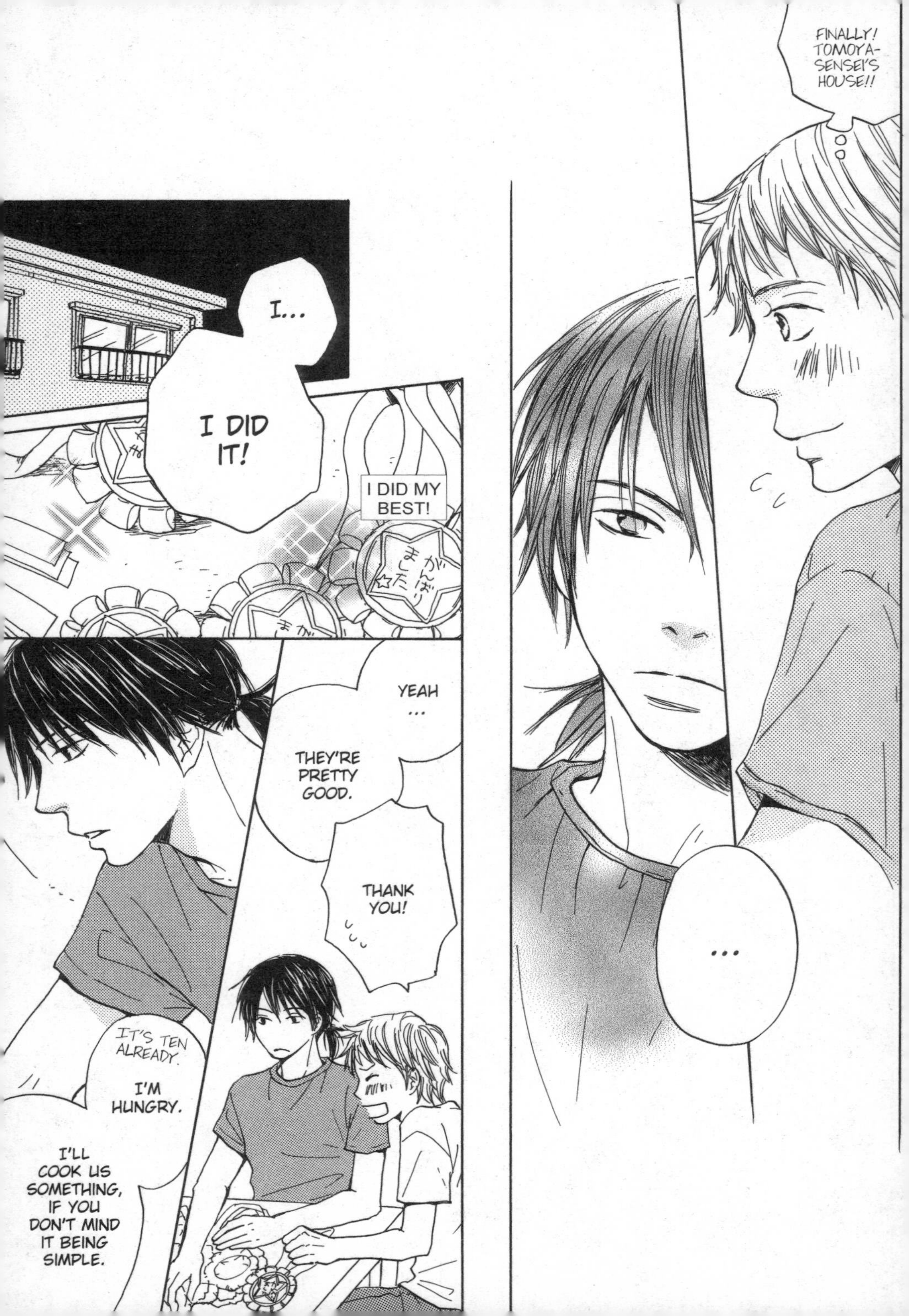
FINALLY! TOMOYA-SENSEI'S HOUSE!!
...
I...
I DID IT!
I DID MY BEST!
がんばりました
YEAH ...
THEY'RE PRETTY GOOD.
THANK YOU!
IT'S TEN ALREADY.
I'M HUNGRY.
I'LL COOK US SOMETHING, IF YOU DON'T MIND IT BEING SIMPLE.

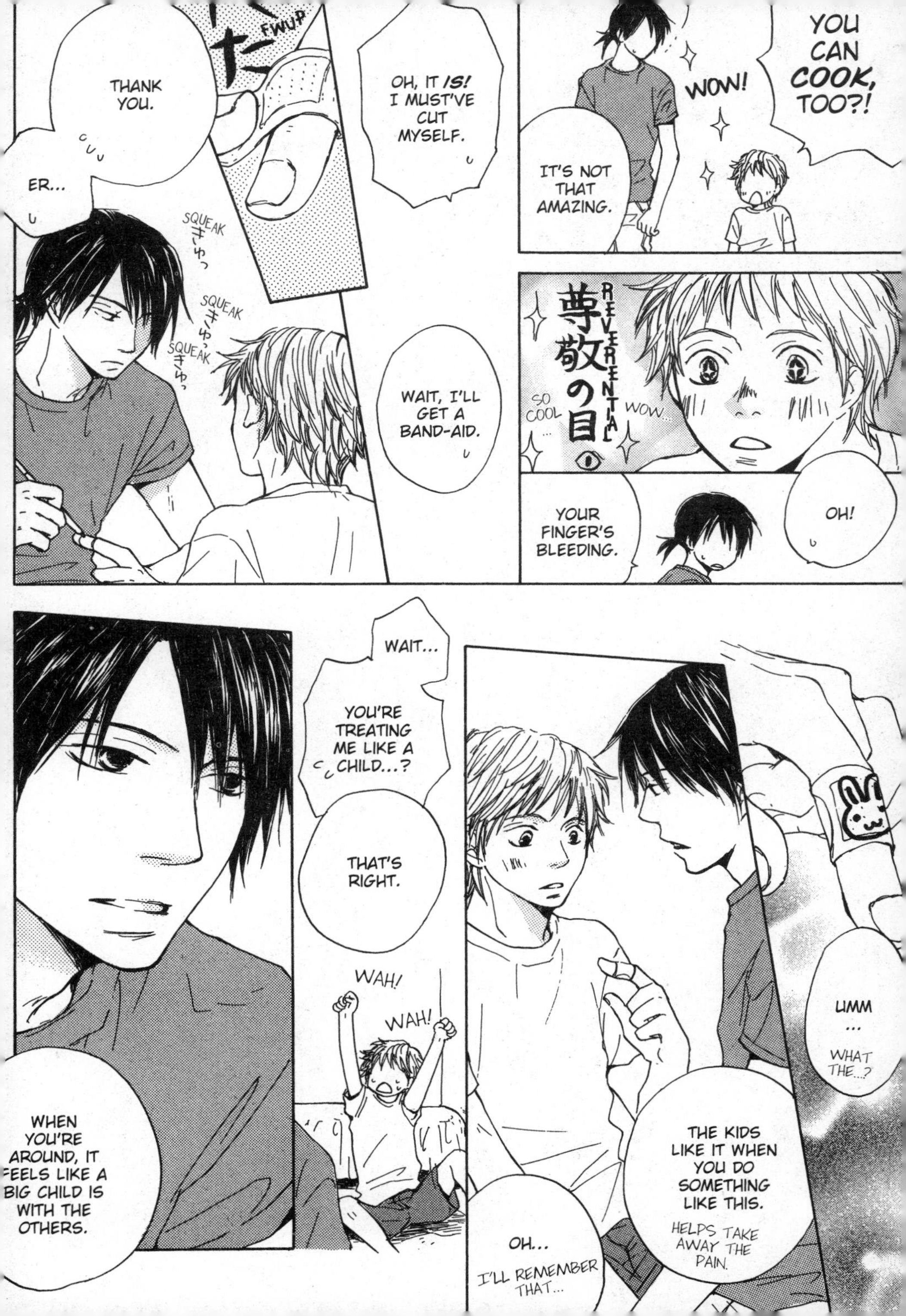
YOU CAN COOK, TOO?!
WOW!
IT'S NOT THAT AMAZING.
尊敬の目
REVERENTIAL
SO COOL...
WOW...
OH!
YOUR FINGER'S BLEEDING.
OH, IT IS! I MUST'VE CUT MYSELF.
WAIT, I'LL GET A BAND-AID.
FWUP
THANK YOU.
ER...
SQUEAK
きゅっ
SQUEAK
きゅっ
SQUEAK
きゅっ
UMM...
WHAT THE...?
THE KIDS LIKE IT WHEN YOU DO SOMETHING LIKE THIS.
HELPS TAKE AWAY THE PAIN.
OH...
I'LL REMEMBER THAT...
WAIT...
YOU'RE TREATING ME LIKE A CHILD...?
THAT'S RIGHT.
WAH!
WAH!
WHEN YOU'RE AROUND, IT FEELS LIKE A BIG CHILD IS WITH THE OTHERS.

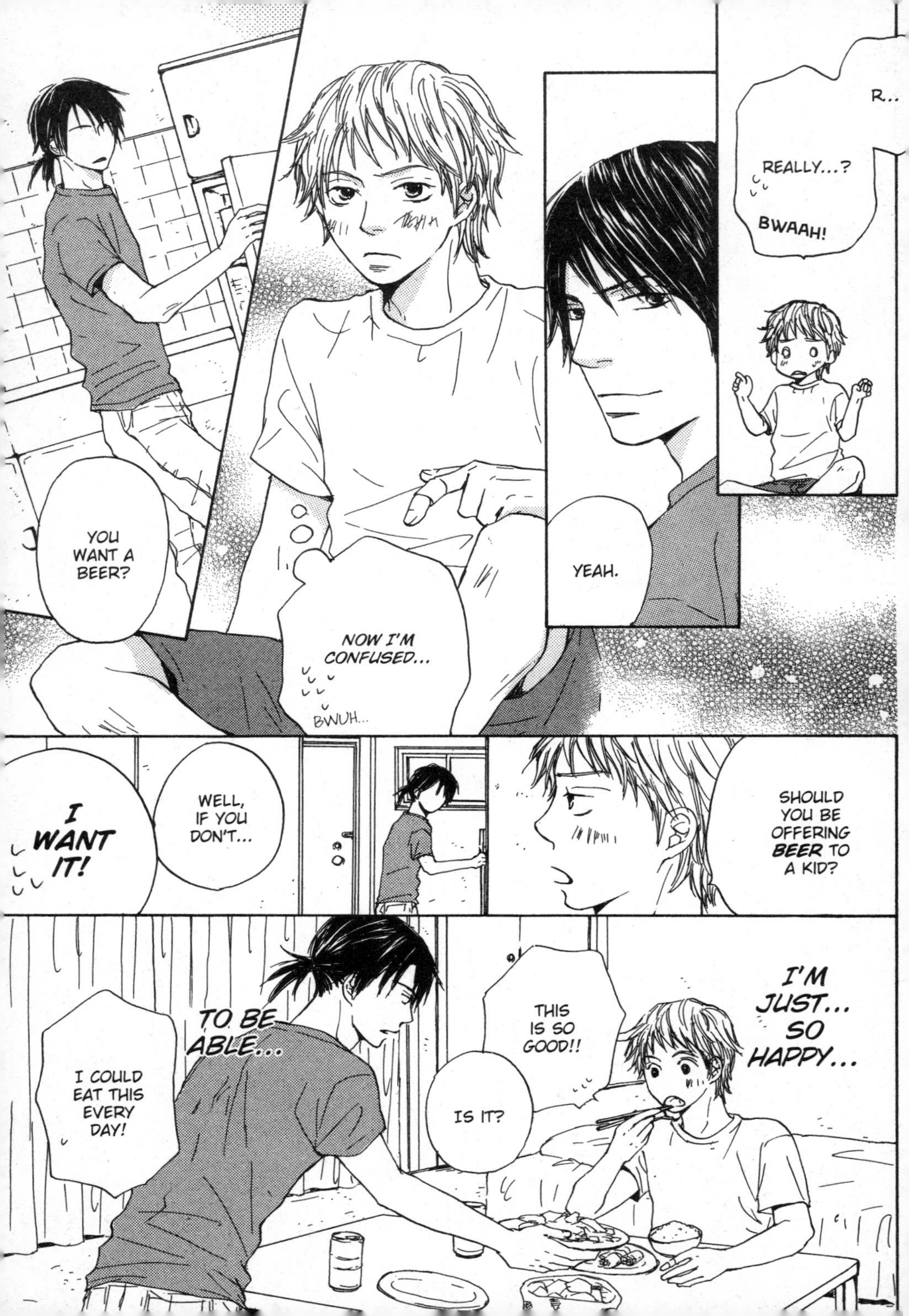
R...
REALLY...?
BWAAH!
YEAH.
NOW I'M CONFUSED...
BWUH...
YOU WANT A BEER?
SHOULD YOU BE OFFERING BEER TO A KID?
WELL, IF YOU DON'T...
I WANT IT!
I'M JUST... SO HAPPY...
THIS IS SO GOOD!!
IS IT?
TO BE ABLE...
I COULD EAT THIS EVERY DAY!

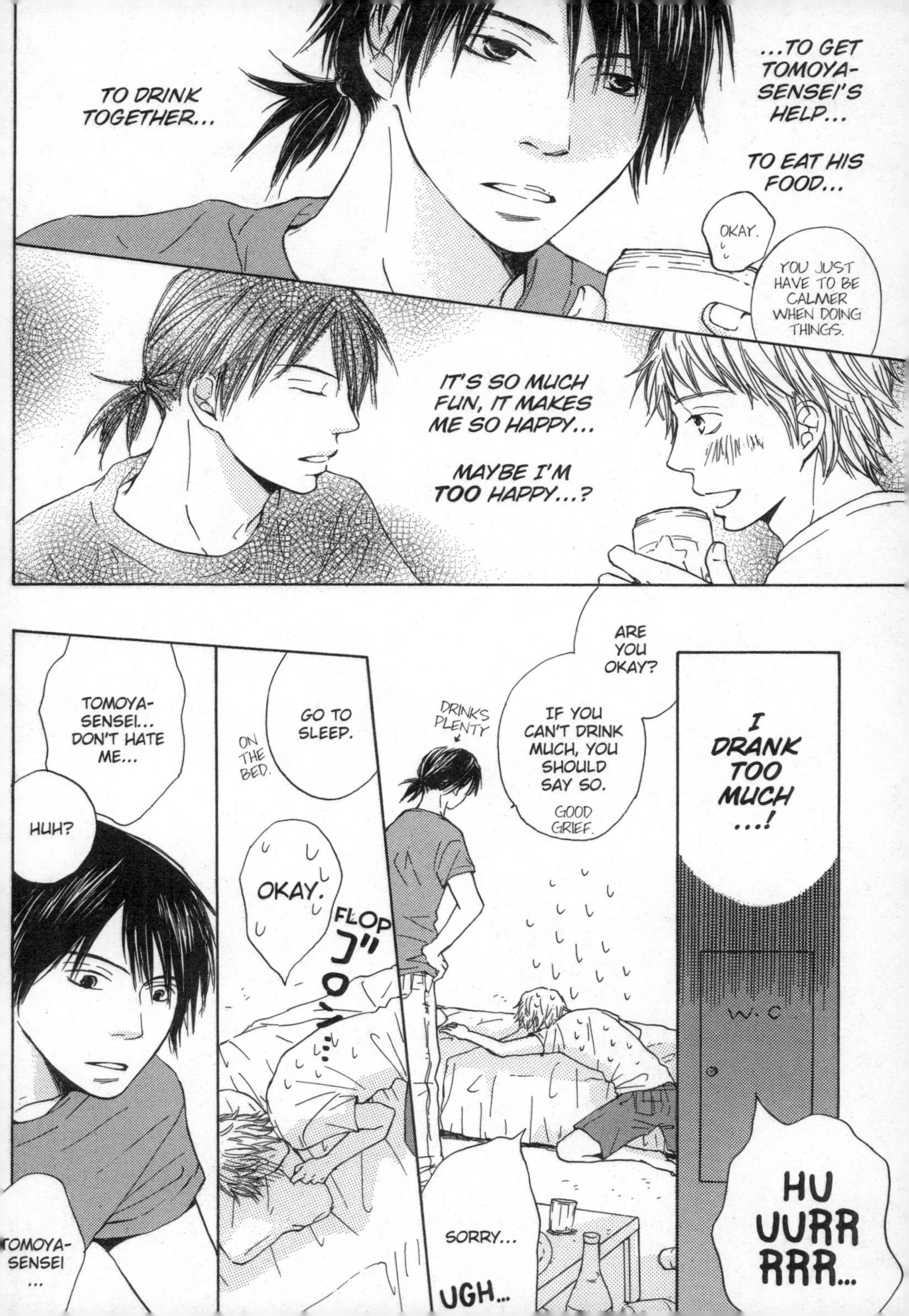
...TO GET TOMOYA-SENSEI'S HELP...
TO EAT HIS FOOD...
TO DRINK TOGETHER...
OKAY.
YOU JUST HAVE TO BE CALMER WHEN DOING THINGS.
IT'S SO MUCH FUN, IT MAKES ME SO HAPPY...
MAYBE I'M TOO HAPPY...?
I DRANK TOO MUCH...!
HU UURR RRR...
ARE YOU OKAY?
IF YOU CAN'T DRINK MUCH, YOU SHOULD SAY SO.
GOOD GRIEF.
DRINKS PLENTY
SORRY...
UGH...
GO TO SLEEP.
ON THE BED.
OKAY.
FLOP
ゴロン...
TOMOYA-SENSEI... DON'T HATE ME...
HUH?
TOMOYA-SENSEI ...

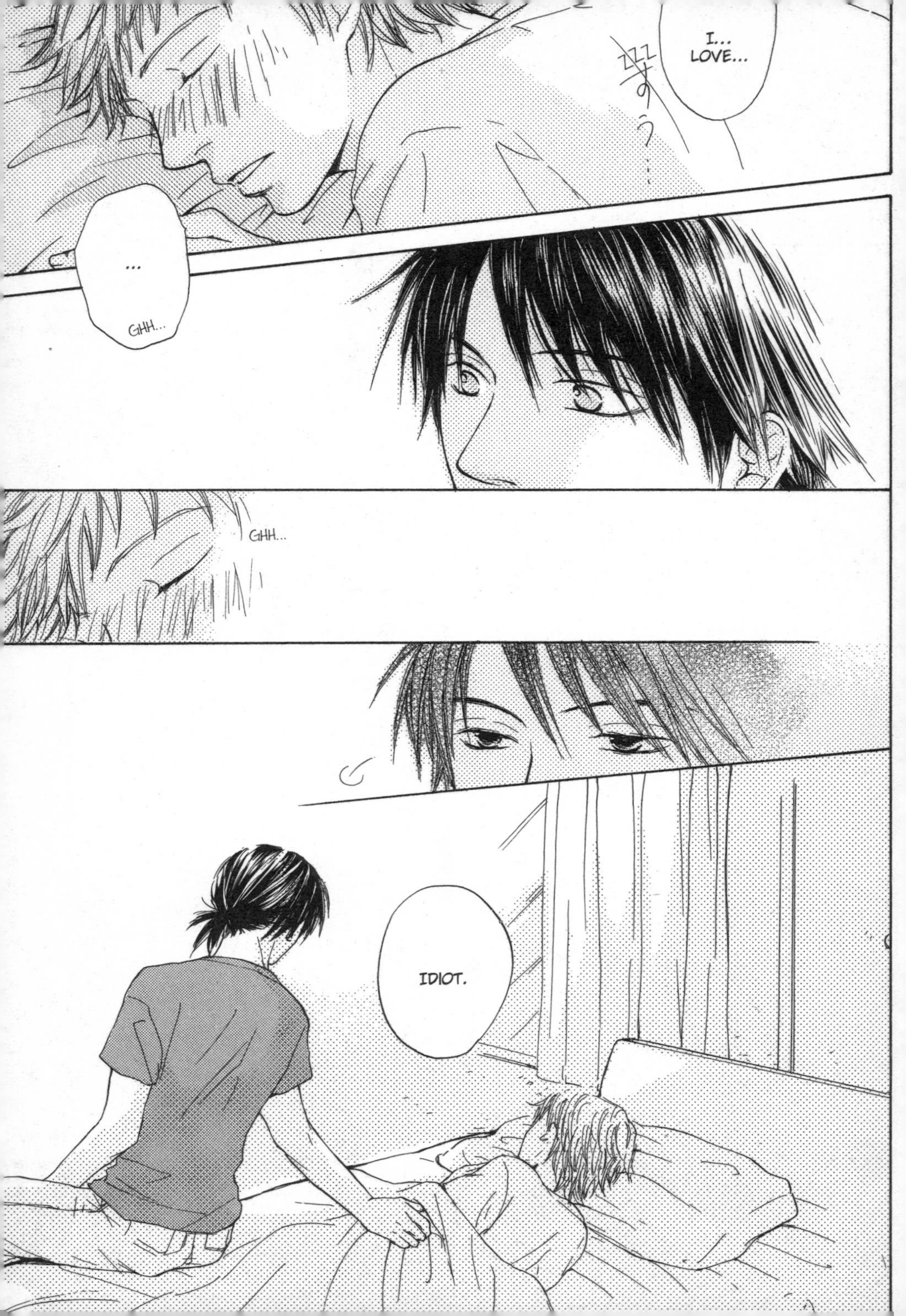
I... LOVE...
ZZZ
...
GHH...
GHH...
IDIOT.

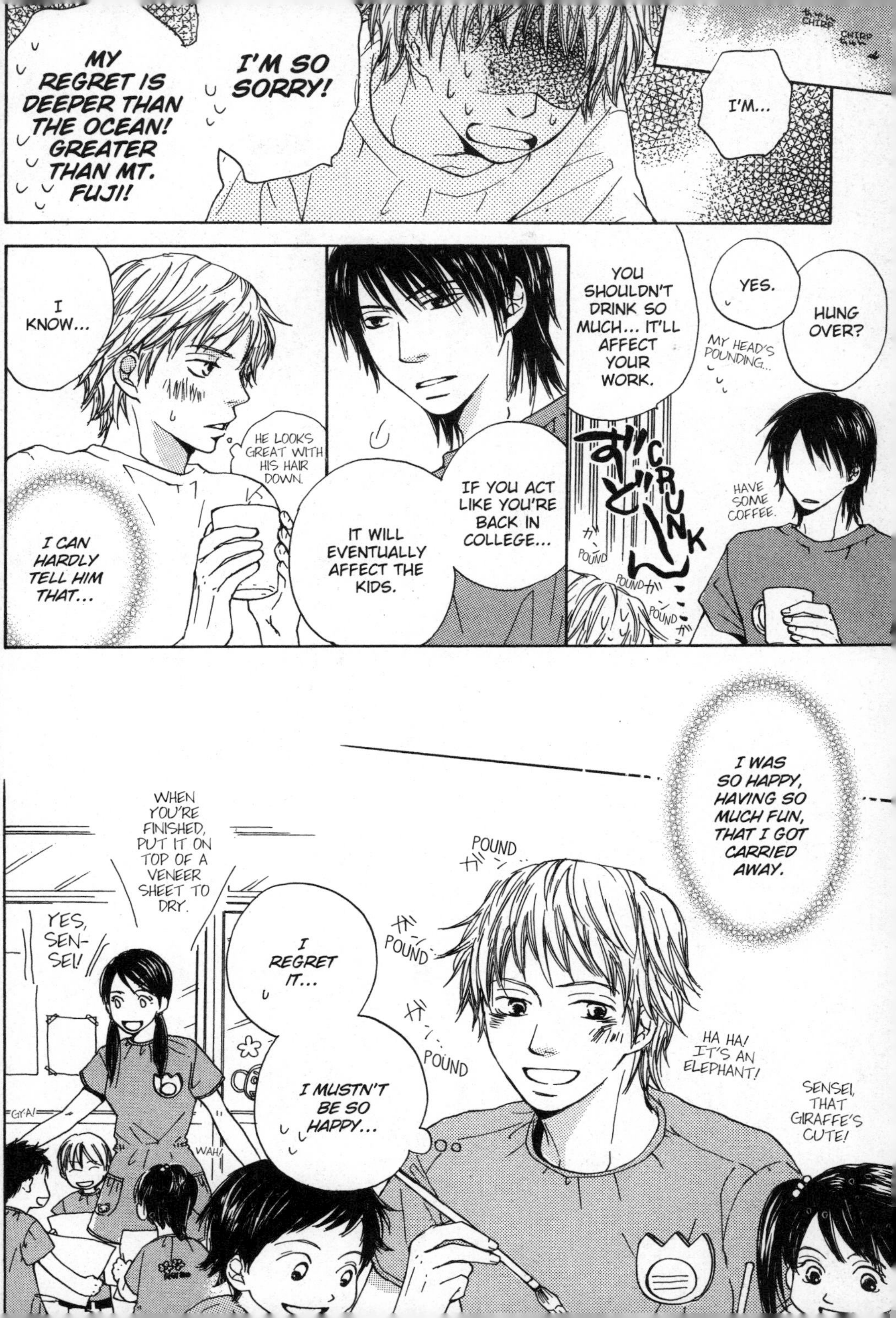
CHIRP
CHIRP
I'M...
I'M SO SORRY!
MY REGRET IS DEEPER THAN THE OCEAN! GREATER THAN MT. FUJI!
YES.
HUNG OVER?
MY HEAD'S POUNDING...
HAVE SOME COFFEE.
YOU SHOULDN'T DRINK SO MUCH... IT'LL AFFECT YOUR WORK.
CRUNK
POUND
POUND
POUND
IF YOU ACT LIKE YOU'RE BACK IN COLLEGE...
IT WILL EVENTUALLY AFFECT THE KIDS.
I KNOW...
HE LOOKS GREAT WITH HIS HAIR DOWN.
I CAN HARDLY TELL HIM THAT...
I WAS SO HAPPY, HAVING SO MUCH FUN, THAT I GOT CARRIED AWAY.
SENSEI, THAT GIRAFFE'S CUTE!
HA HA! IT'S AN ELEPHANT!
POUND
POUND
POUND
I REGRET IT...
I MUSTN'T BE SO HAPPY...
WHEN YOU'RE FINISHED, PUT IT ON TOP OF A VENEER SHEET TO DRY.
YES, SENSEI!
WAH!
GYA!

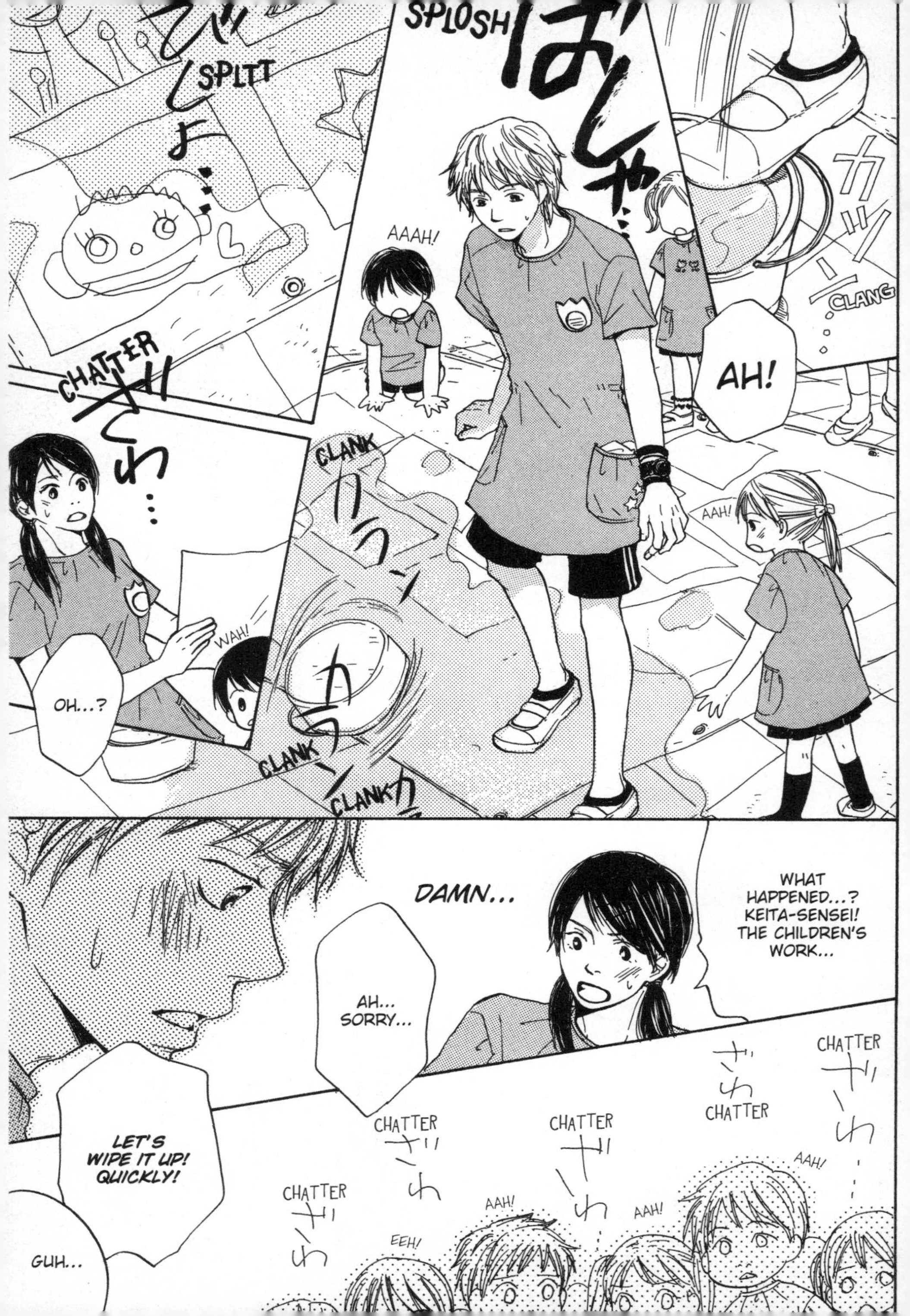
CLANG
AH!
SPLOSH
AAAH!
CLANK
AAH!
CLANK
CLANK
SPLTT
CHATTER
OH...?
WAH!
WHAT HAPPENED...? KEITA-SENSEI! THE CHILDREN'S WORK...
DAMN...
AH... SORRY...
LET'S WIPE IT UP! QUICKLY!
GUH...
CHATTER
CHATTER
AAH!
CHATTER
AAH!
CHATTER
AAH!
EEH!
CHATTER

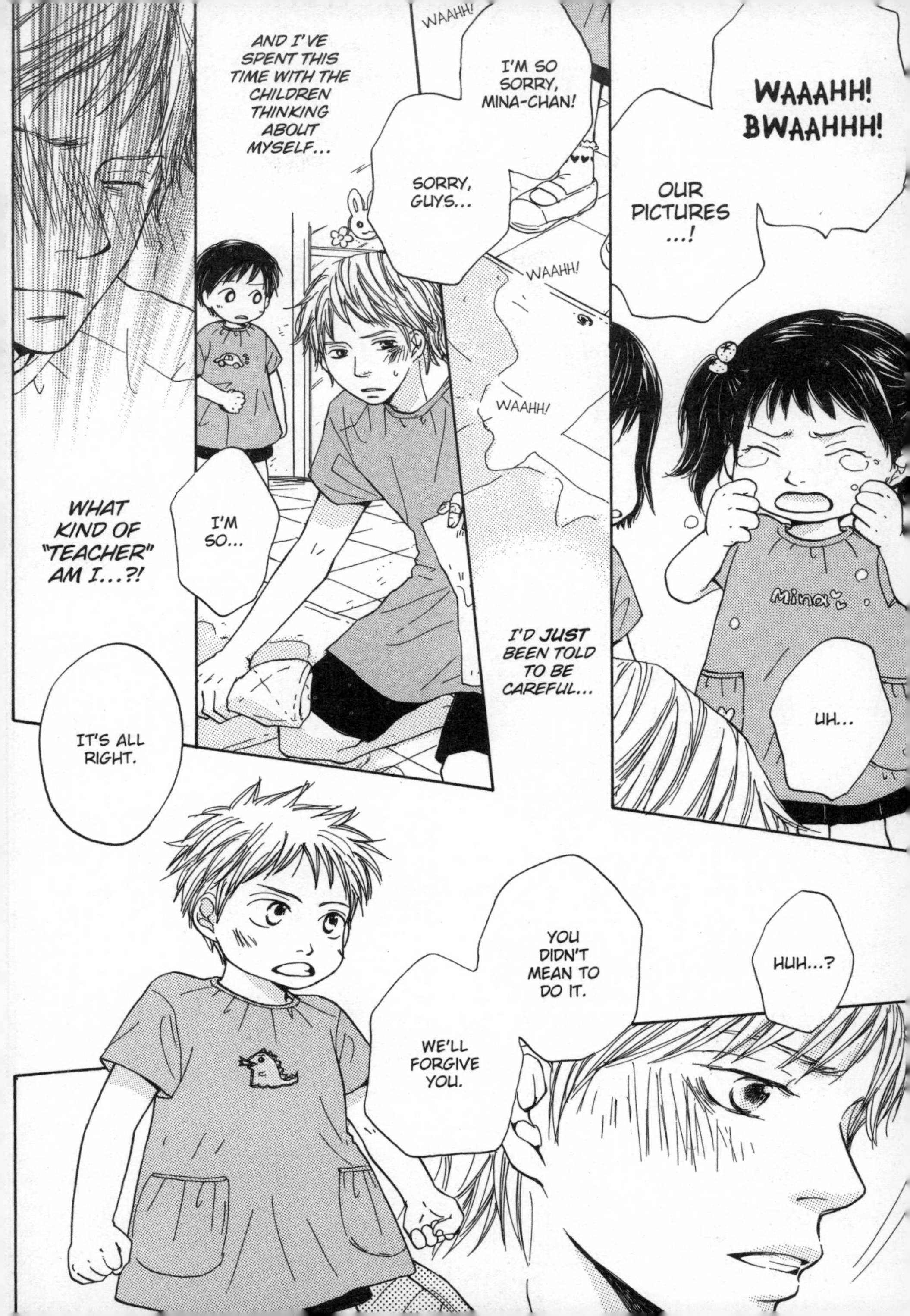
WAAAHH! BWAAHHH!
OUR PICTURES ...!
UH...
WAAHH!
I'M SO SORRY, MINA-CHAN!
SORRY, GUYS...
WAAHH!
WAAHH!
I'D JUST BEEN TOLD TO BE CAREFUL...
I'M SO...
AND I'VE SPENT THIS TIME WITH THE CHILDREN THINKING ABOUT MYSELF...
WHAT KIND OF "TEACHER" AM I...?!
HUH...?
YOU DIDN'T MEAN TO DO IT.
WE'LL FORGIVE YOU.
IT'S ALL RIGHT.

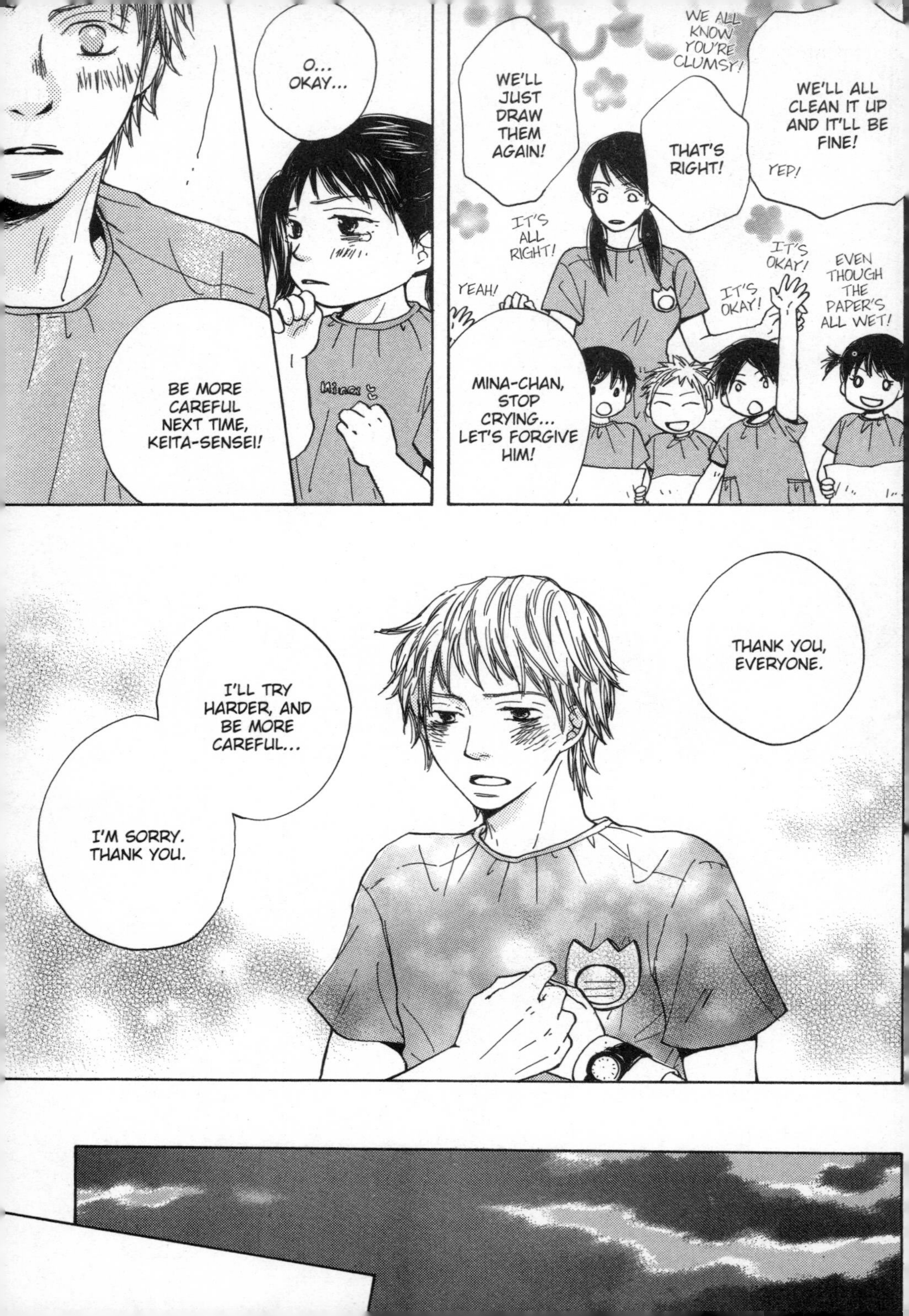
WE ALL KNOW YOU'RE CLUMSY!
WE'LL ALL CLEAN IT UP AND IT'LL BE FINE!
THAT'S RIGHT!
YEP!
WE'LL JUST DRAW THEM AGAIN!
EVEN THOUGH THE PAPER'S ALL WET!
IT'S OKAY!
IT'S OKAY!
IT'S ALL RIGHT!
YEAH!
MINA-CHAN, STOP CRYING... LET'S FORGIVE HIM!
O... OKAY...
BE MORE CAREFUL NEXT TIME, KEITA-SENSEI!
THANK YOU, EVERYONE.
I'LL TRY HARDER, AND BE MORE CAREFUL...
I'M SORRY. THANK YOU.

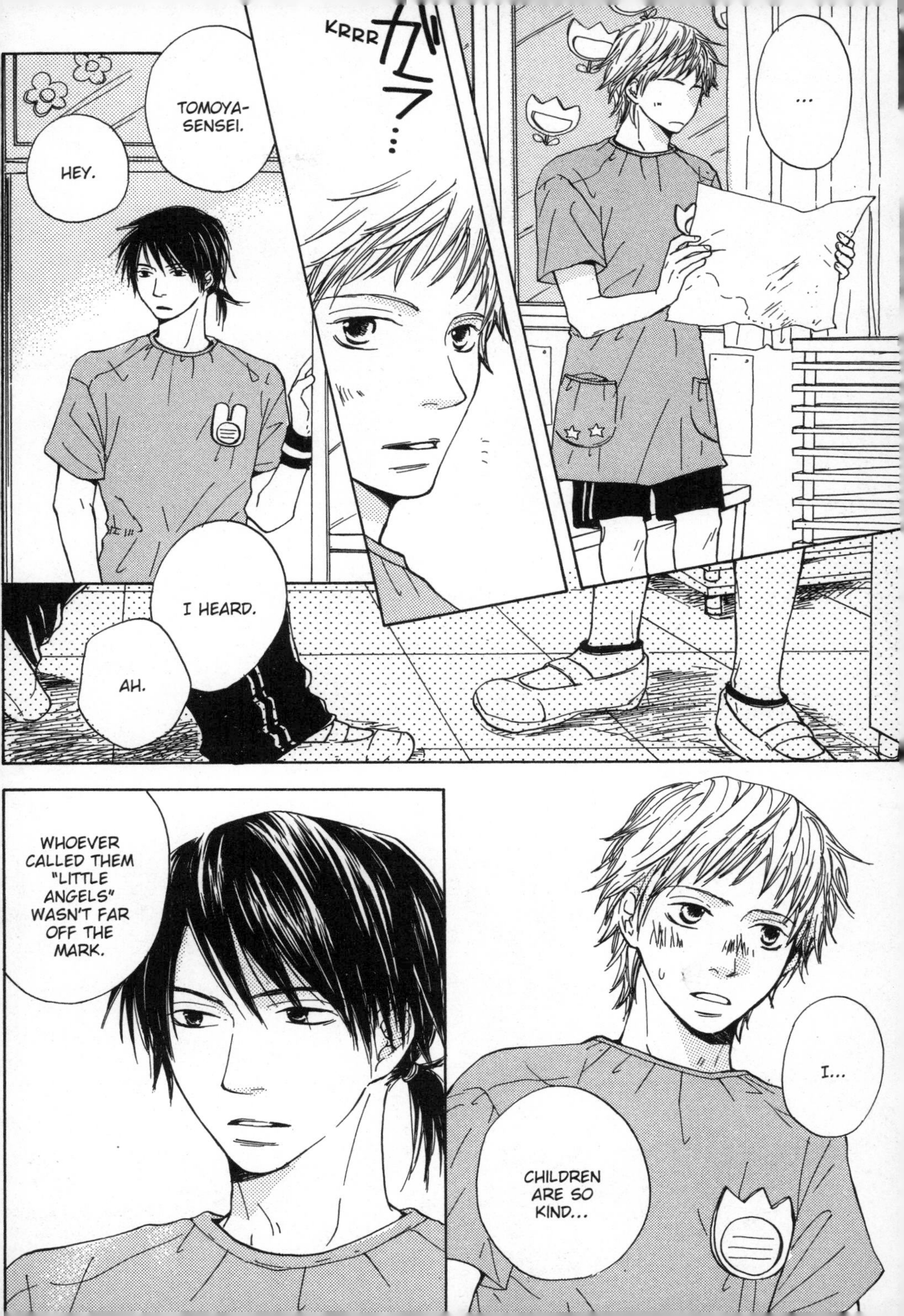
...
KRRR
ガラ…
TOMOYA-SENSEI.
HEY.
I HEARD.
AH.
I...
CHILDREN ARE SO KIND...
WHOEVER CALLED THEM "LITTLE ANGELS" WASN'T FAR OFF THE MARK.

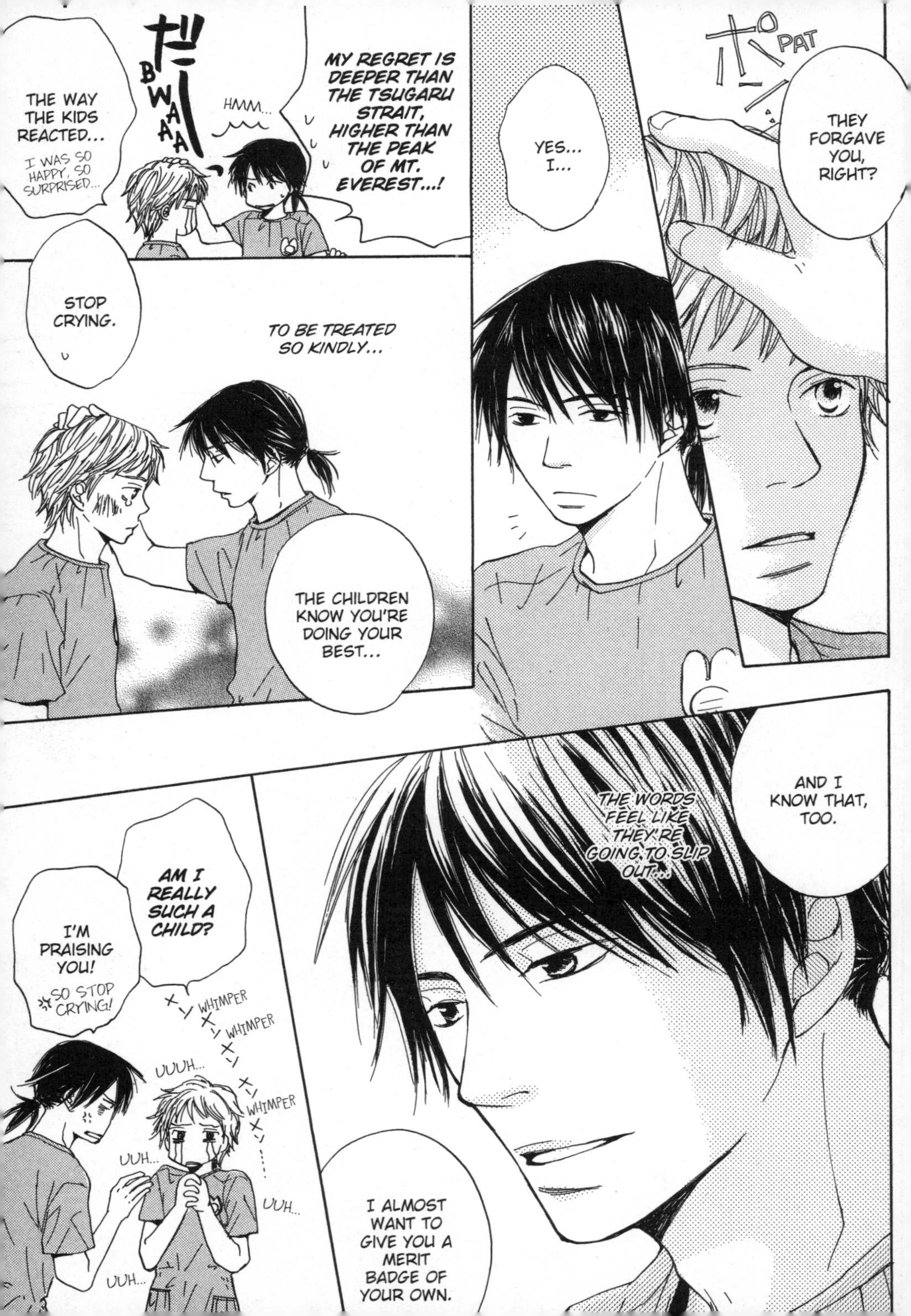
PAT
THEY FORGAVE YOU, RIGHT?
YES... I...
MY REGRET IS DEEPER THAN THE TSUGARU STRAIT, HIGHER THAN THE PEAK OF MT. EVEREST...!
HMM...
BWAAA
THE WAY THE KIDS REACTED...
I WAS SO HAPPY, SO SURPRISED...
TO BE TREATED SO KINDLY...
STOP CRYING.
THE CHILDREN KNOW YOU'RE DOING YOUR BEST...
AND I KNOW THAT, TOO.
THE WORDS FEEL LIKE THEY'RE GOING TO SLIP OUT...
I ALMOST WANT TO GIVE YOU A MERIT BADGE OF YOUR OWN.
AM I REALLY SUCH A CHILD?
I'M PRAISING YOU!
SO STOP CRYING!
WHIMPER
WHIMPER
WHIMPER
UUUH...
UUH...
UUH...
UUH...

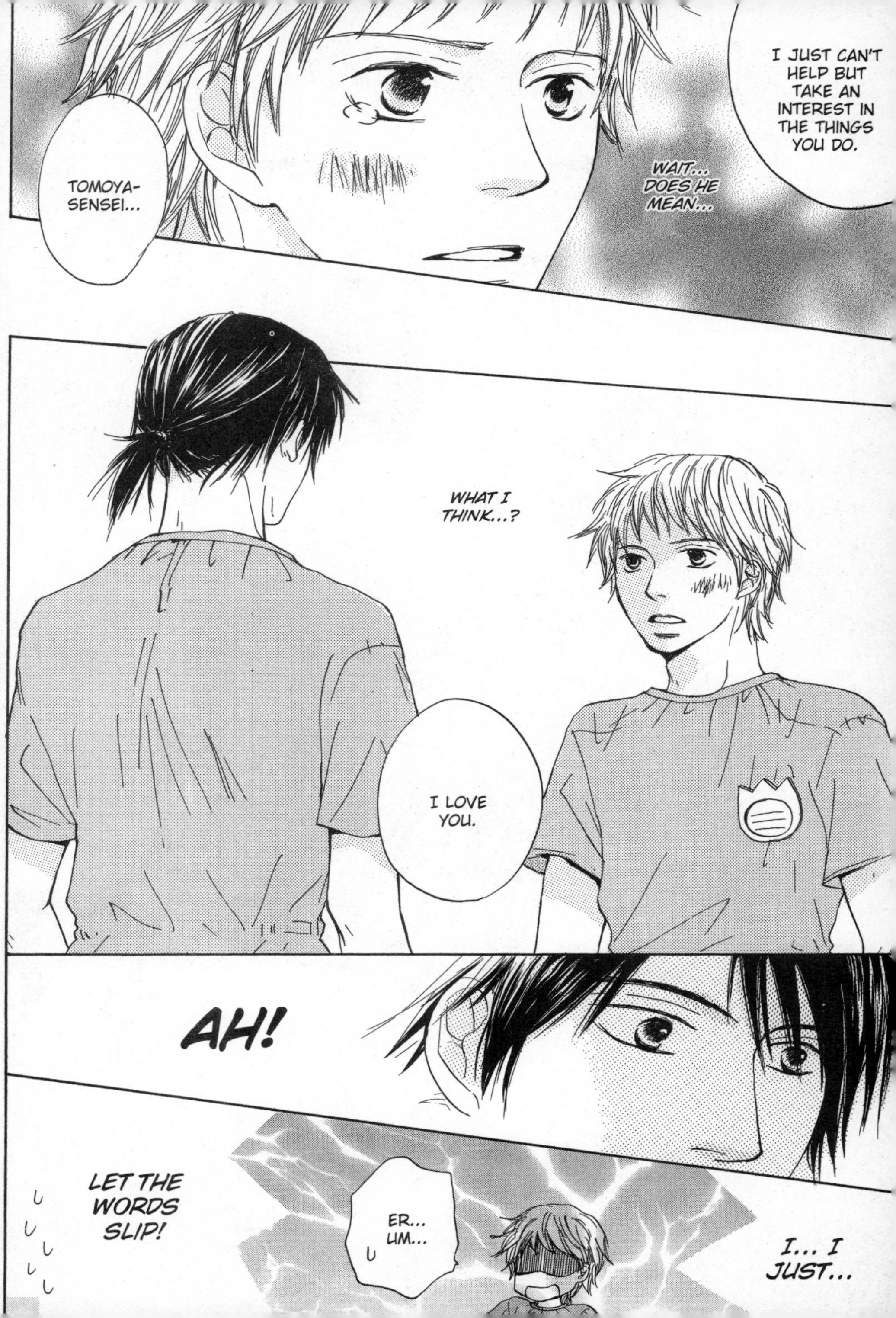
I JUST CAN'T HELP BUT TAKE AN INTEREST IN THE THINGS YOU DO.
WAIT... DOES HE MEAN...
TOMOYA-SENSEI...
WHAT I THINK...?
I LOVE YOU.
AH!
I... I JUST...
ER... UM...
LET THE WORDS SLIP!

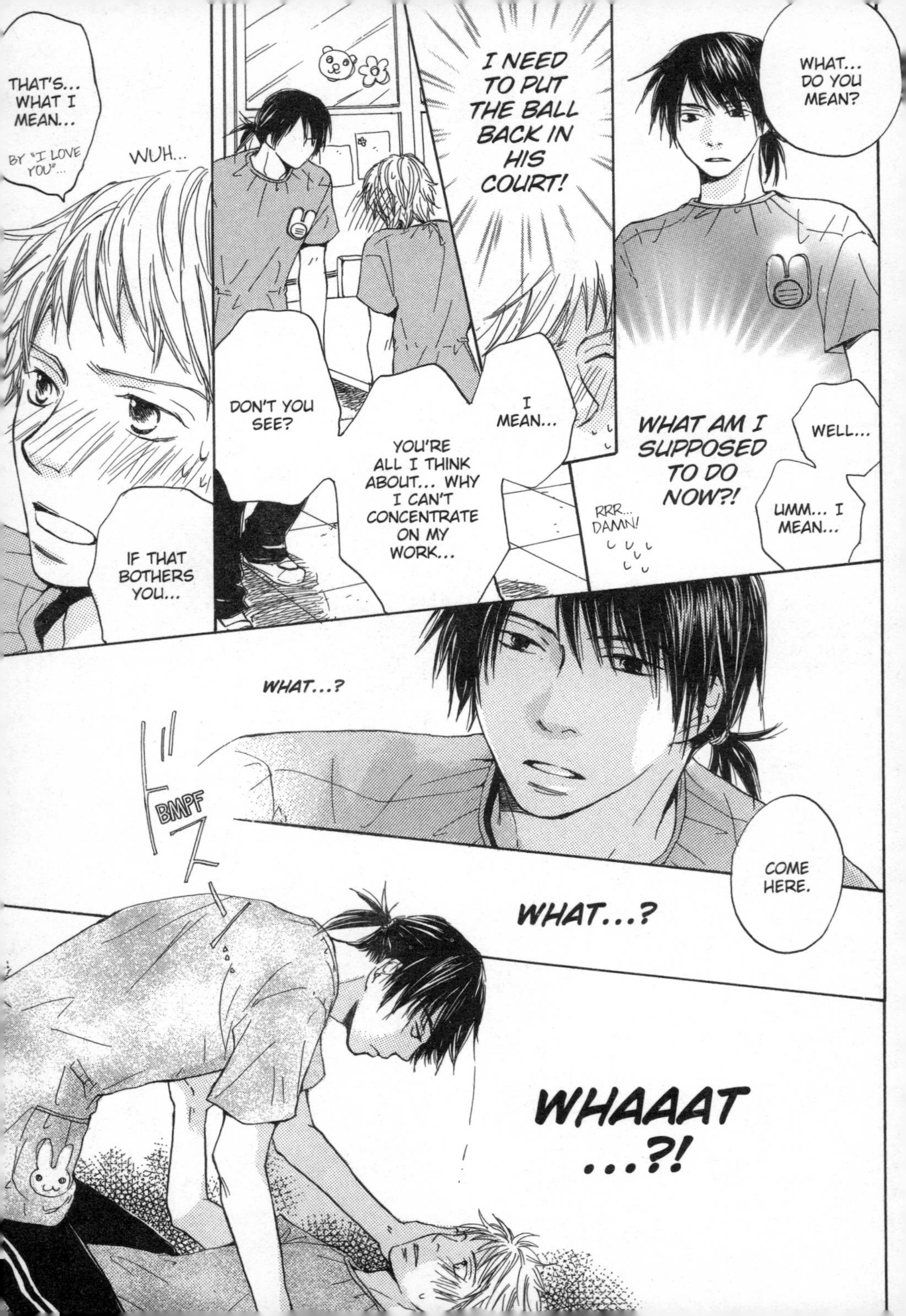
WHAT... DO YOU MEAN?
WELL...
UMM... I MEAN...
WHAT AM I SUPPOSED TO DO NOW?!
RRR... DAMN!
I NEED TO PUT THE BALL BACK IN HIS COURT!
I MEAN...
YOU'RE ALL I THINK ABOUT... WHY I CAN'T CONCENTRATE ON MY WORK...
DON'T YOU SEE?
THAT'S... WHAT I MEAN...
BY "I LOVE YOU"...
WUH...
IF THAT BOTHERS YOU...
COME HERE.
WHAT...?
BMPF
WHAT...?
WHAAAT ...?!

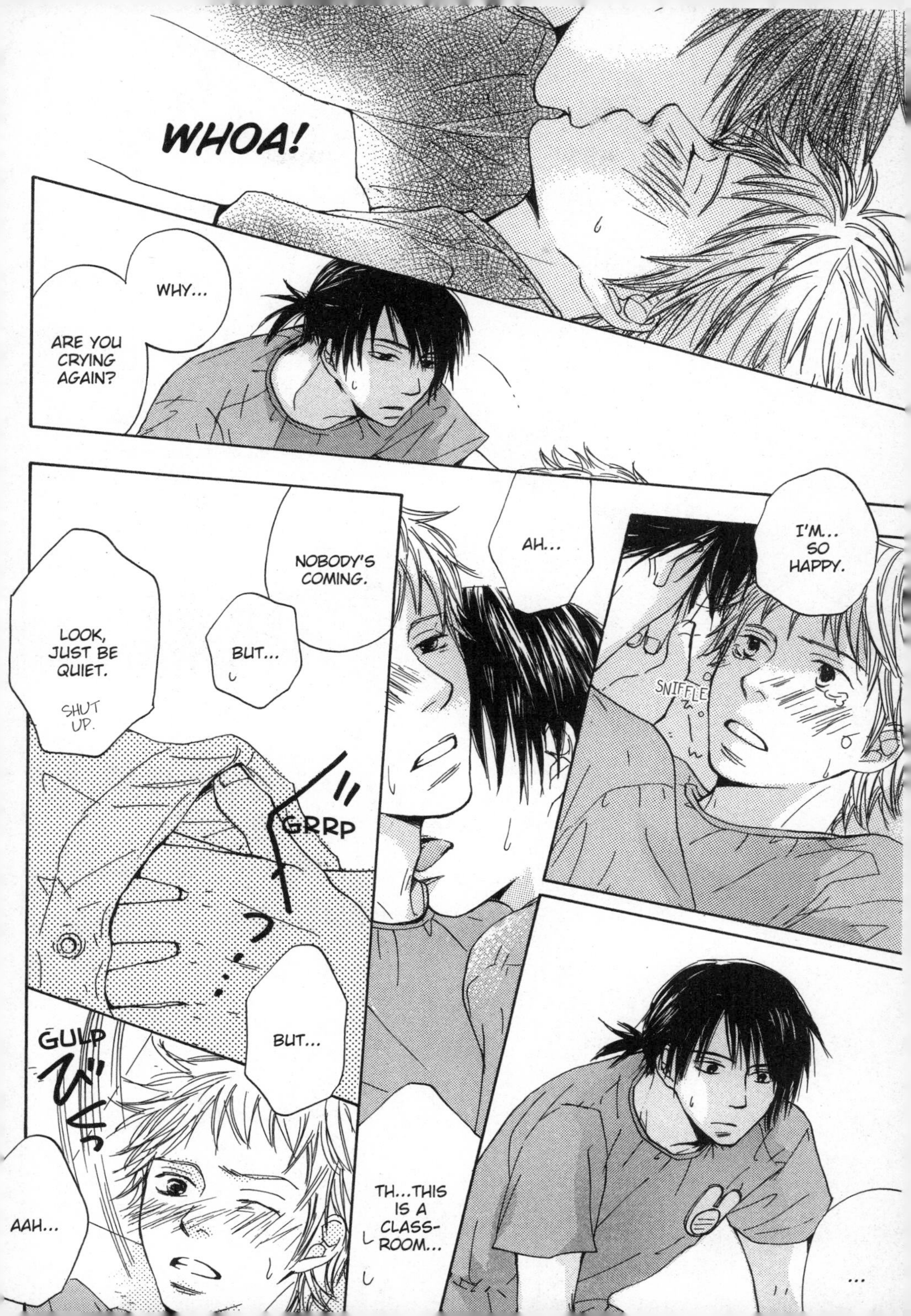
WHOA!
WHY...
ARE YOU CRYING AGAIN?
I'M... SO HAPPY.
SNIFFLE
AH...
NOBODY'S COMING.
BUT...
LOOK, JUST BE QUIET.
SHUT UP.
GRRP
...
TH...THIS IS A CLASS-ROOM...
BUT...
GULP
AAH...

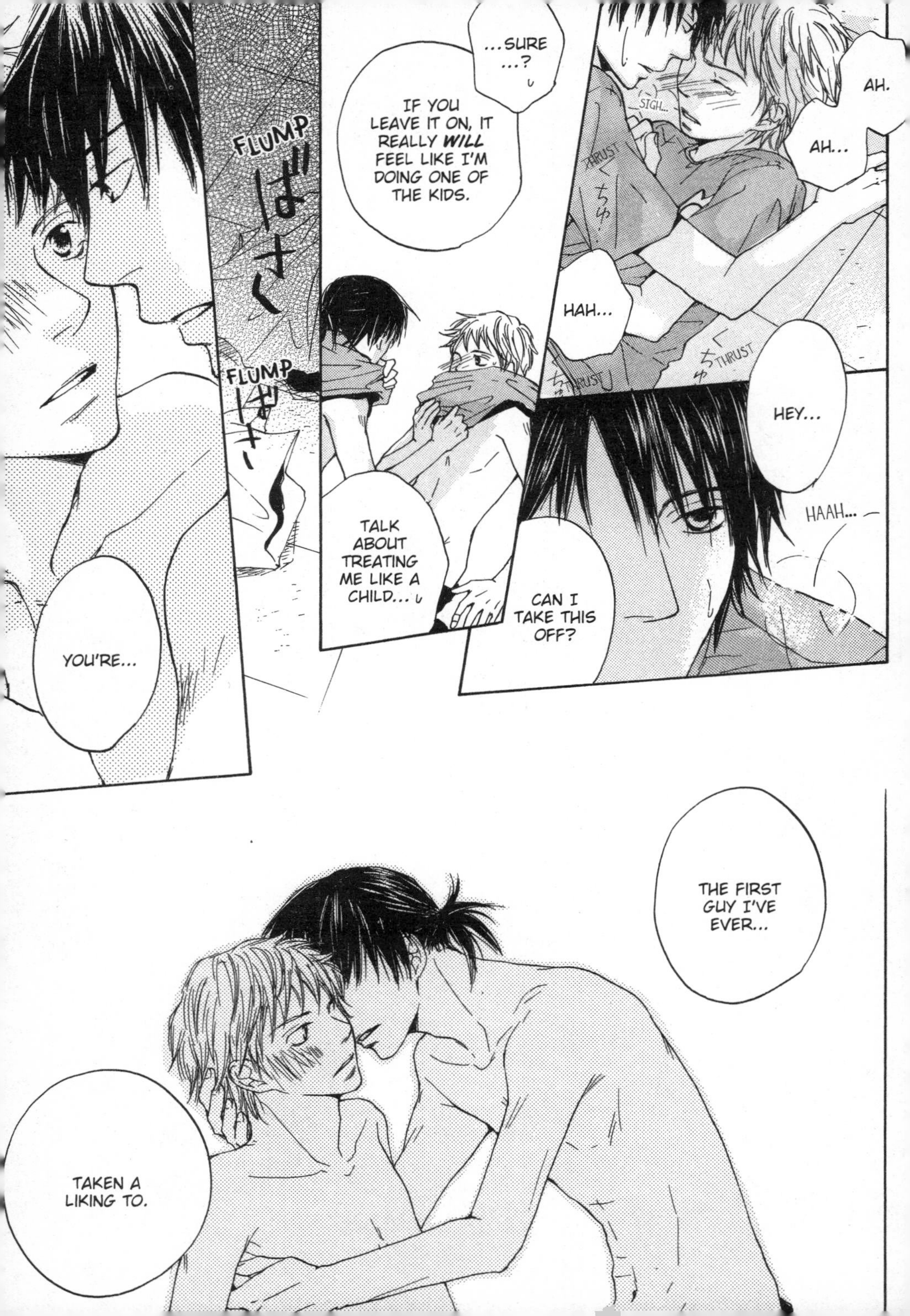
AH.
AH...
SIGH...
THRUST
THRUST
THRUST
HAH...
HEY...
HAAH...
CAN I TAKE THIS OFF?
...SURE ...?
IF YOU LEAVE IT ON, IT REALLY WILL FEEL LIKE I'M DOING ONE OF THE KIDS.
FLUMP
FLUMP
TALK ABOUT TREATING ME LIKE A CHILD...
YOU'RE...
THE FIRST GUY I'VE EVER...
TAKEN A LIKING TO.

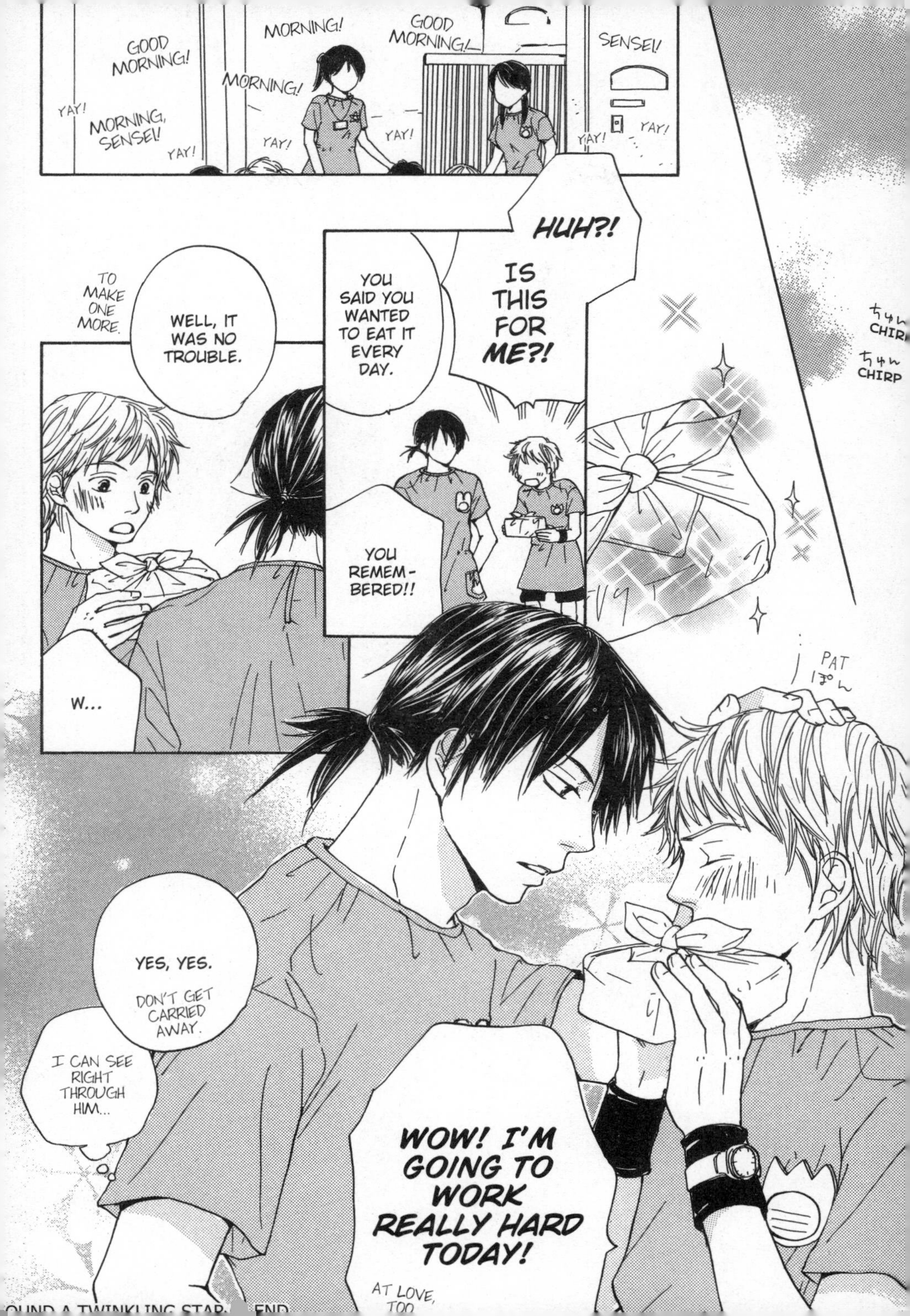
SENSEI!
YAY!
YAY!
GOOD MORNING!
MORNING!
MORNING!
YAY!
YAY!
GOOD MORNING!
YAY!
MORNING, SENSEI!
YAY!
ちゅん
CHIRP
ちゅん
CHIRP
HUH?!
IS THIS FOR ME?!
YOU SAID YOU WANTED TO EAT IT EVERY DAY.
YOU REMEMBERED!!
WELL, IT WAS NO TROUBLE.
TO MAKE ONE MORE.
W...
PAT
ぽん
YES, YES.
DON'T GET CARRIED AWAY.
I CAN SEE RIGHT THROUGH HIM...
WOW! I'M GOING TO WORK REALLY HARD TODAY!
AT LOVE, TOO
OUND A TWINKLING STAR
END

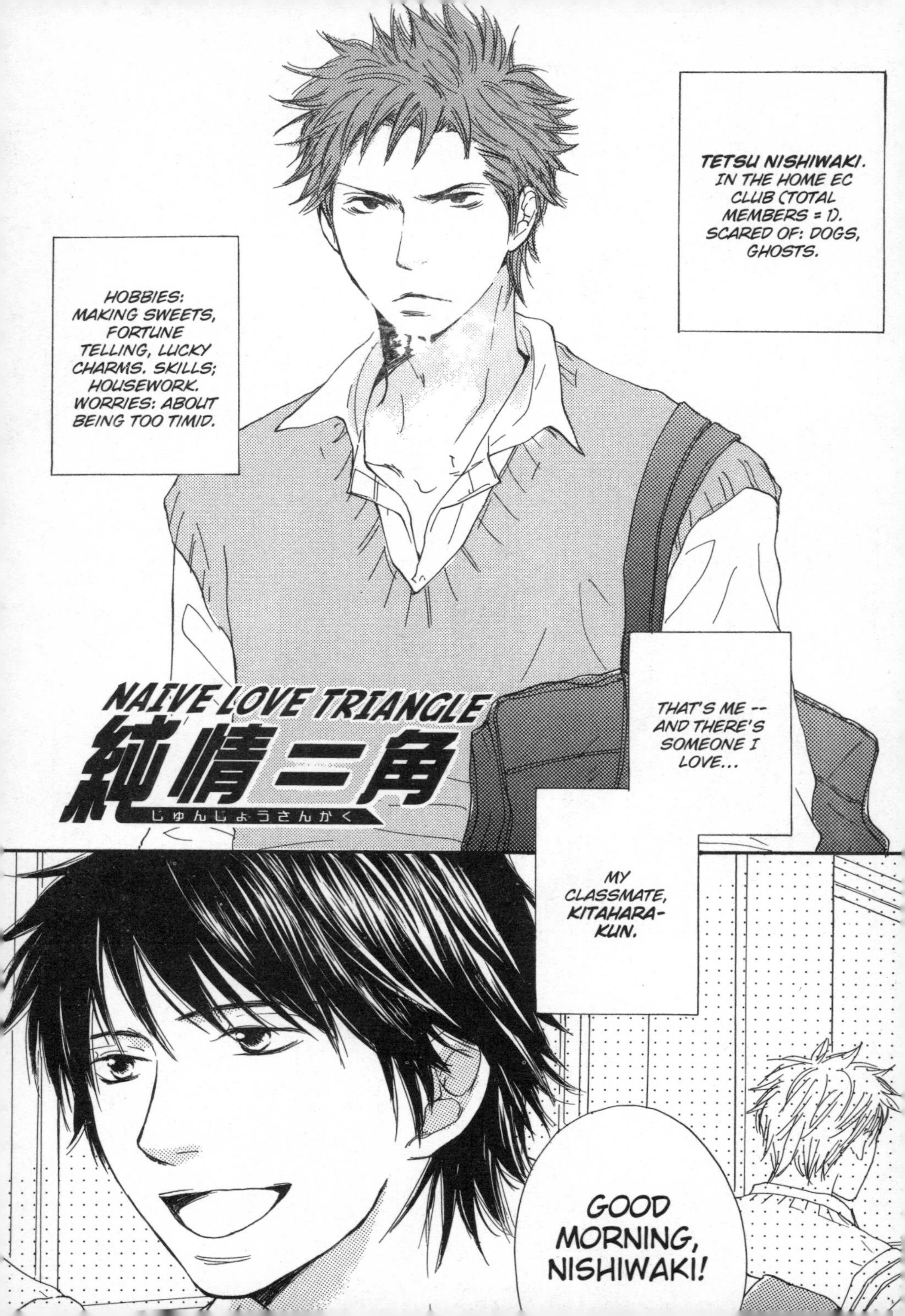
TETSU NISHIWAKI. IN THE HOME EC CLUB (TOTAL MEMBERS = 1). SCARED OF: DOGS, GHOSTS.
HOBBIES: MAKING SWEETS, FORTUNE TELLING, LUCKY CHARMS. SKILLS; HOUSEWORK. WORRIES: ABOUT BEING TOO TIMID.
NAIVE LOVE TRIANGLE
純情三角
じゅんじょうさんかく
THAT'S ME -- AND THERE'S SOMEONE I LOVE...
MY CLASSMATE, KITAHARA-KUN.
GOOD MORNING, NISHIWAKI!

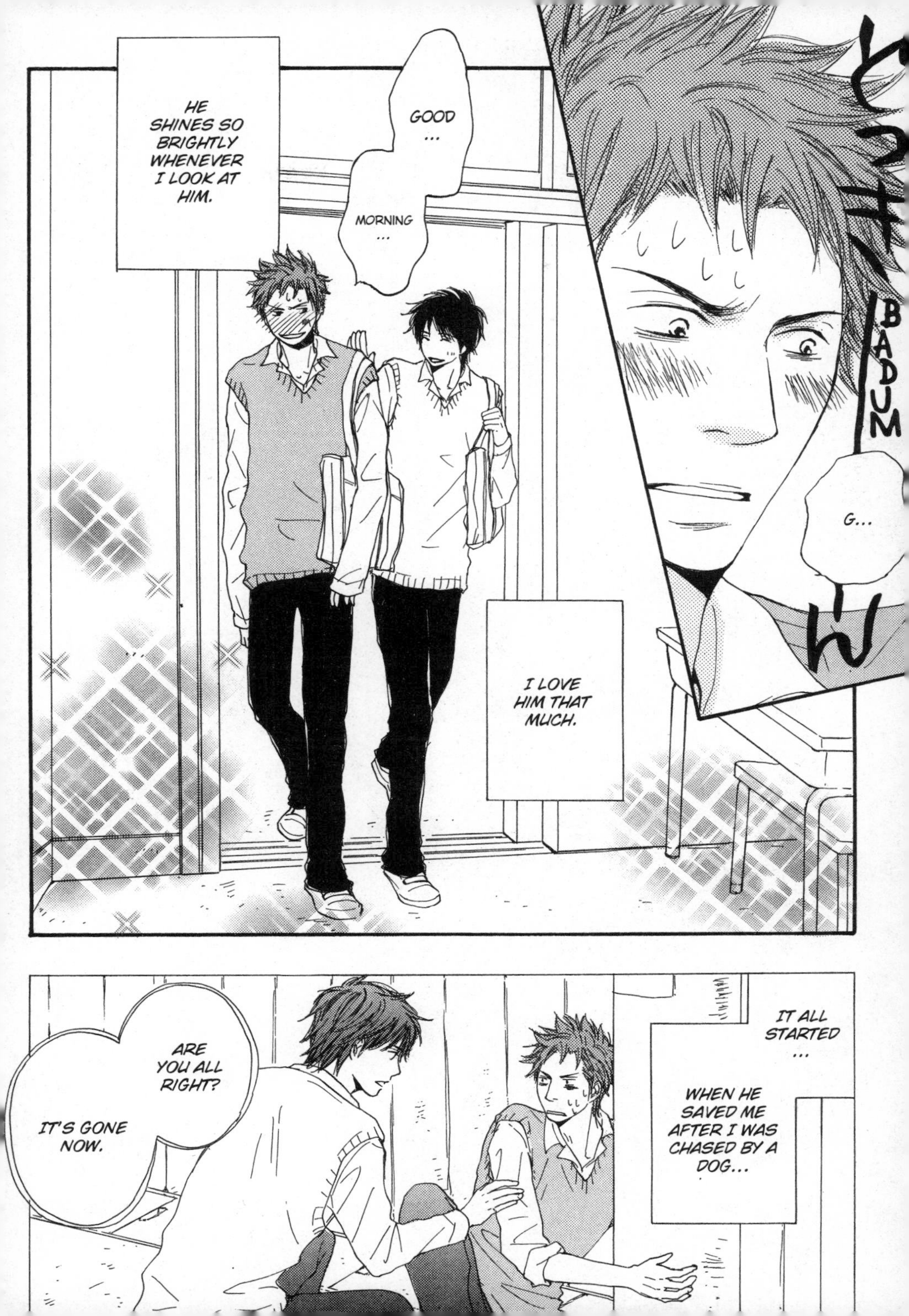
BADUM
G...
GOOD ... MORNING ...
HE SHINES SO BRIGHTLY WHENEVER I LOOK AT HIM.
I LOVE HIM THAT MUCH.
IT ALL STARTED ...
WHEN HE SAVED ME AFTER I WAS CHASED BY A DOG...
ARE YOU ALL RIGHT?
IT'S GONE NOW.

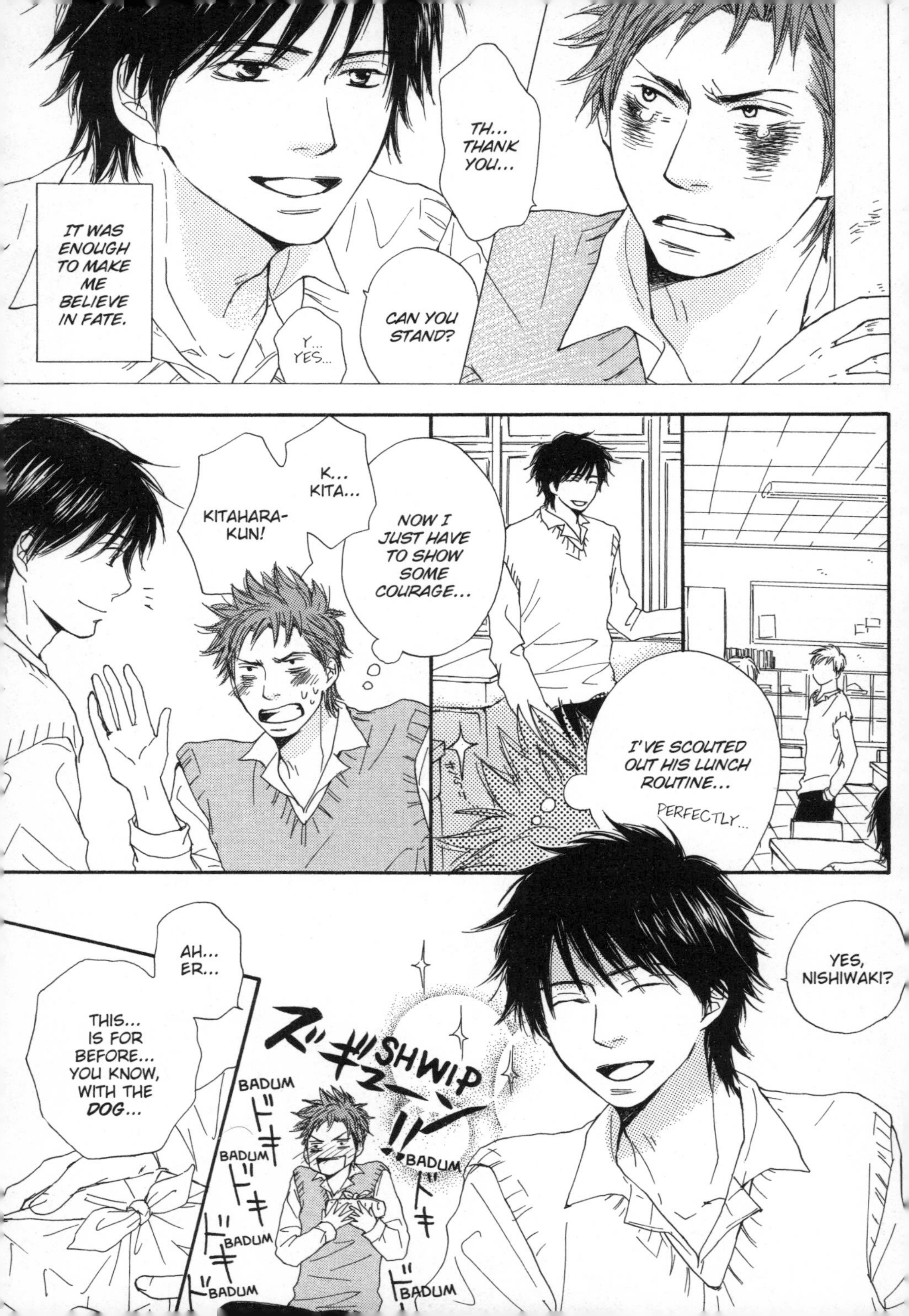
TH... THANK YOU...
CAN YOU STAND?
Y... YES...
IT WAS ENOUGH TO MAKE ME BELIEVE IN FATE.
I'VE SCOUTED OUT HIS LUNCH ROUTINE...
PERFECTLY...
NOW I JUST HAVE TO SHOW SOME COURAGE...
K... KITA...
KITAHARA-KUN!
YES, NISHIWAKI?
SHWIP
BADUM
BADUM
BADUM
BADUM
BADUM
BADUM
AH... ER...
THIS... IS FOR BEFORE... YOU KNOW, WITH THE *DOG*...

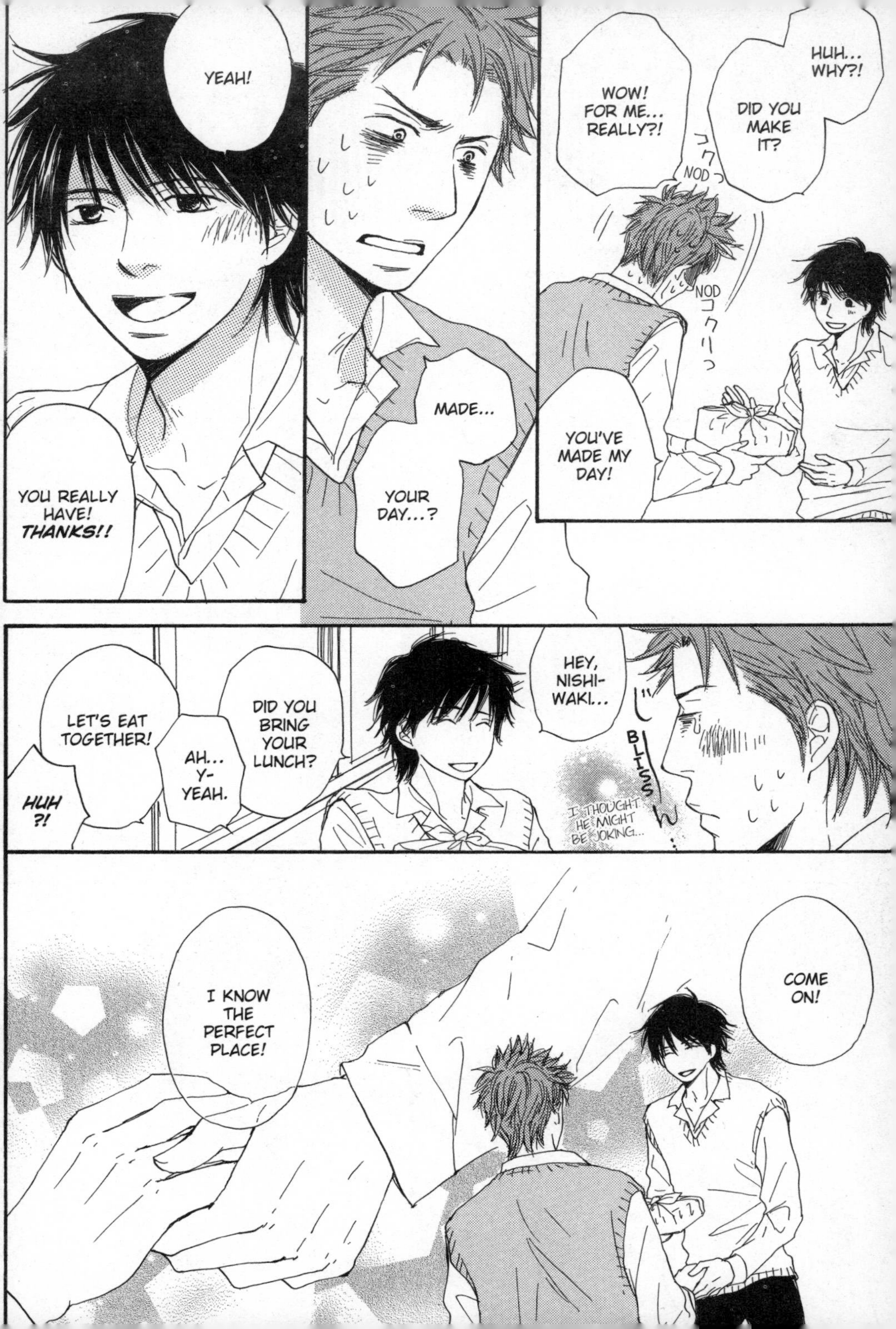
HUH... WHY?!
DID YOU MAKE IT?
WOW! FOR ME... REALLY?!
NOD コクっ
NOD コクリっ
YOU'VE MADE MY DAY!
MADE...
YOUR DAY...?
YEAH!
YOU REALLY HAVE! THANKS!!
HEY, NISHI-WAKI...
BLISS
I THOUGHT HE MIGHT BE JOKING...
DID YOU BRING YOUR LUNCH?
AH... Y-YEAH.
LET'S EAT TOGETHER!
HUH?!
COME ON!
I KNOW THE PERFECT PLACE!

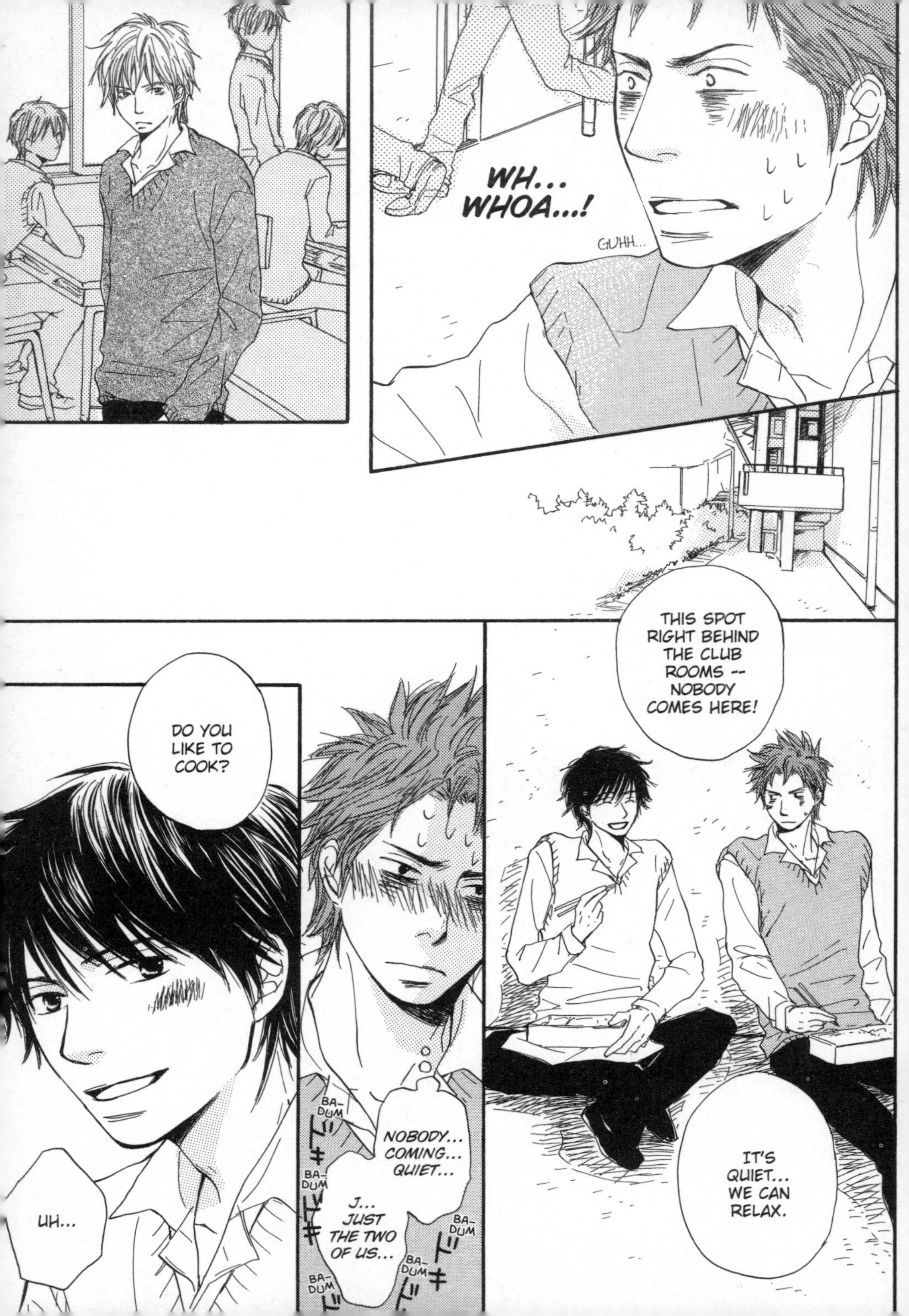
WH... WHOA...!
GUHH...
THIS SPOT RIGHT BEHIND THE CLUB ROOMS -- NOBODY COMES HERE!
IT'S QUIET... WE CAN RELAX.
BA-DUM
BA-DUM
NOBODY... COMING... QUIET...
J... JUST THE TWO OF US...
BA-DUM
BA-DUM
BA-DUM
DO YOU LIKE TO COOK?
UH...

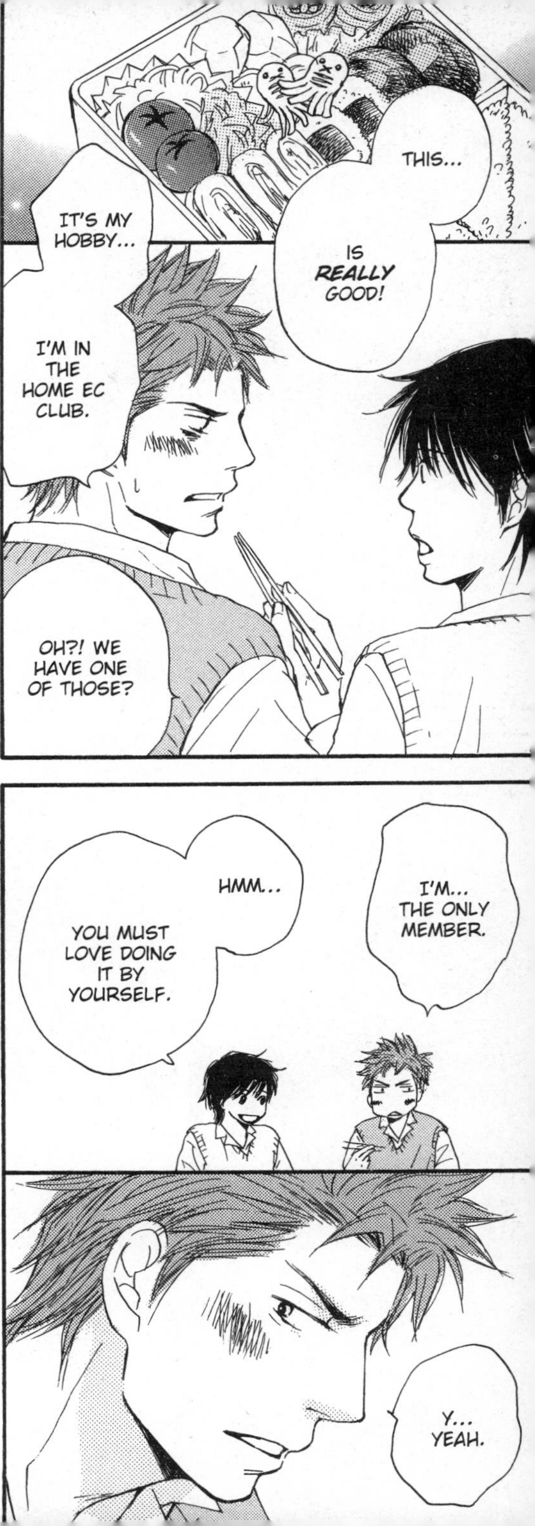
THIS... IS **REALLY** GOOD!
IT'S MY HOBBY...
I'M IN THE HOME EC CLUB.
OH?! WE HAVE ONE OF THOSE?
I'M... THE ONLY MEMBER.
HMM... YOU MUST LOVE DOING IT BY YOURSELF.
Y... YEAH.
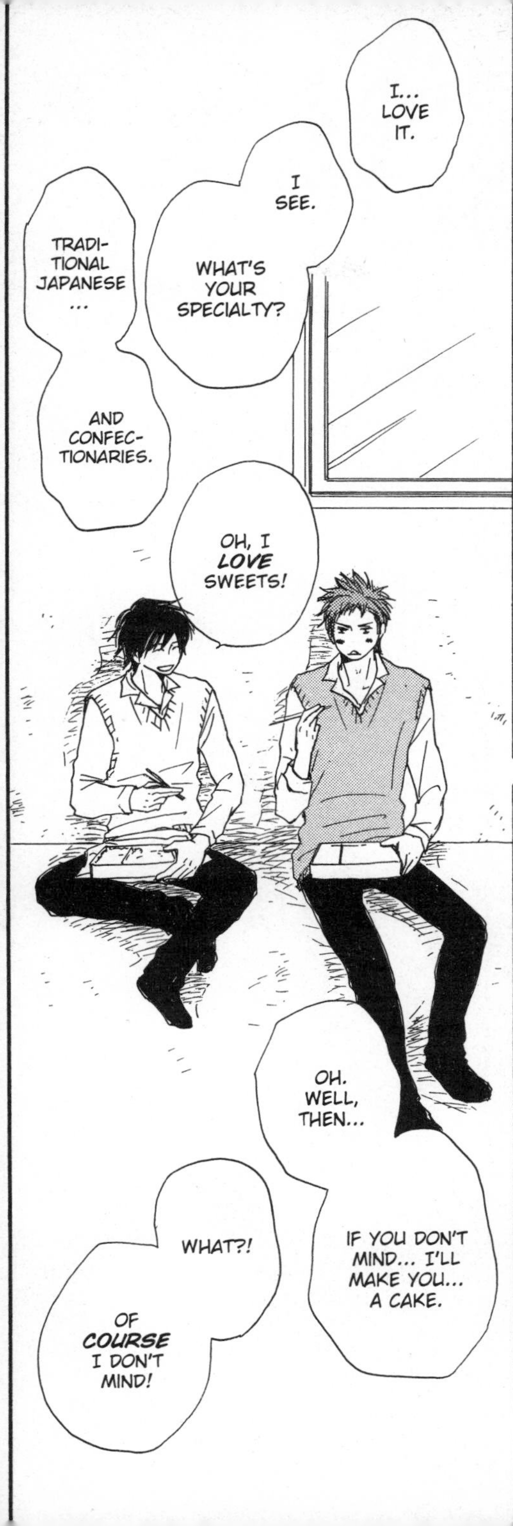
I... LOVE IT.
I SEE. WHAT'S YOUR SPECIALTY?
TRADI-TIONAL JAPANESE ... AND CONFEC-TIONARIES.
OH, I **LOVE** SWEETS!
OH. WELL, THEN... IF YOU DON'T MIND... I'LL MAKE YOU... A CAKE.
WHAT?! OF **COURSE** I DON'T MIND!

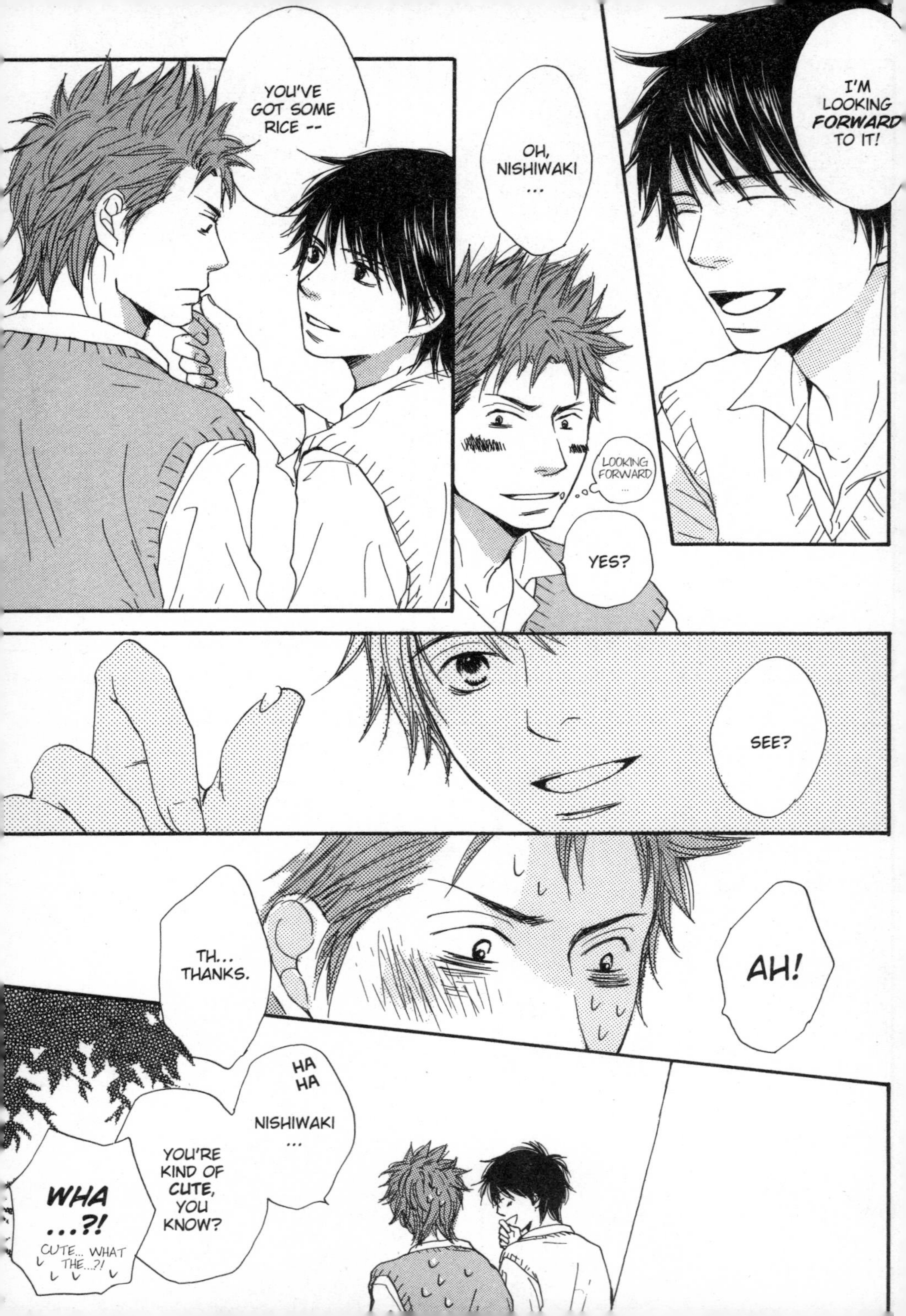
I'M LOOKING FORWARD TO IT!
OH, NISHIWAKI ...
LOOKING FORWARD ...
YES?
YOU'VE GOT SOME RICE --
SEE?
AH!
TH... THANKS.
HA HA
NISHIWAKI ...
YOU'RE KIND OF CUTE, YOU KNOW?
WHA ...?!
CUTE... WHAT THE...?!

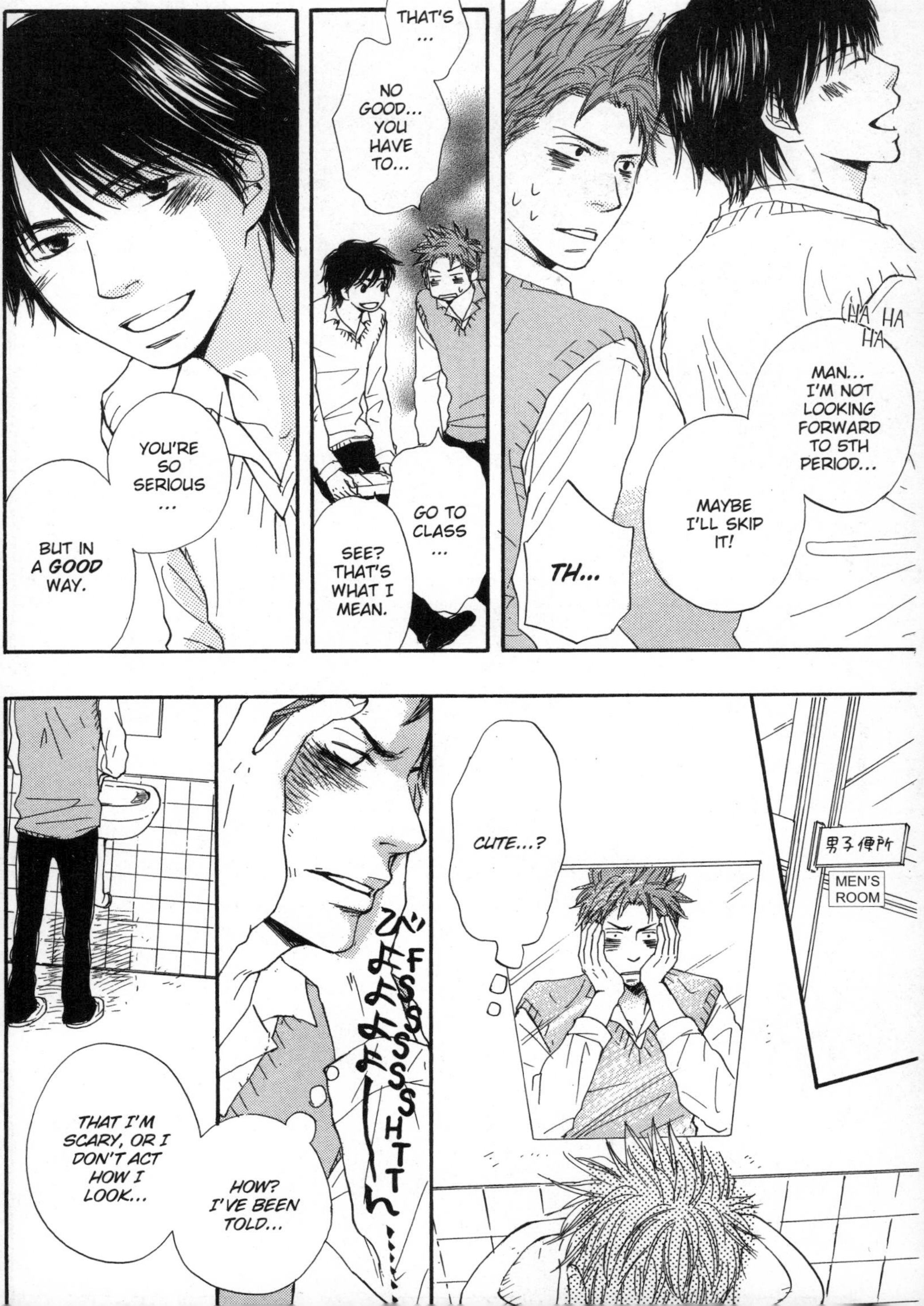
HA HA HA
MAN... I'M NOT LOOKING FORWARD TO 5TH PERIOD...
MAYBE I'LL SKIP IT!
TH...
THAT'S ...
NO GOOD... YOU HAVE TO...
GO TO CLASS ...
SEE? THAT'S WHAT I MEAN.
YOU'RE SO SERIOUS ...
BUT IN A GOOD WAY.
男子便所
MEN'S ROOM
CUTE...?
びよよよよーん…
FSSSSSHTTT
HOW? I'VE BEEN TOLD...
THAT I'M SCARY, OR I DON'T ACT HOW I LOOK...

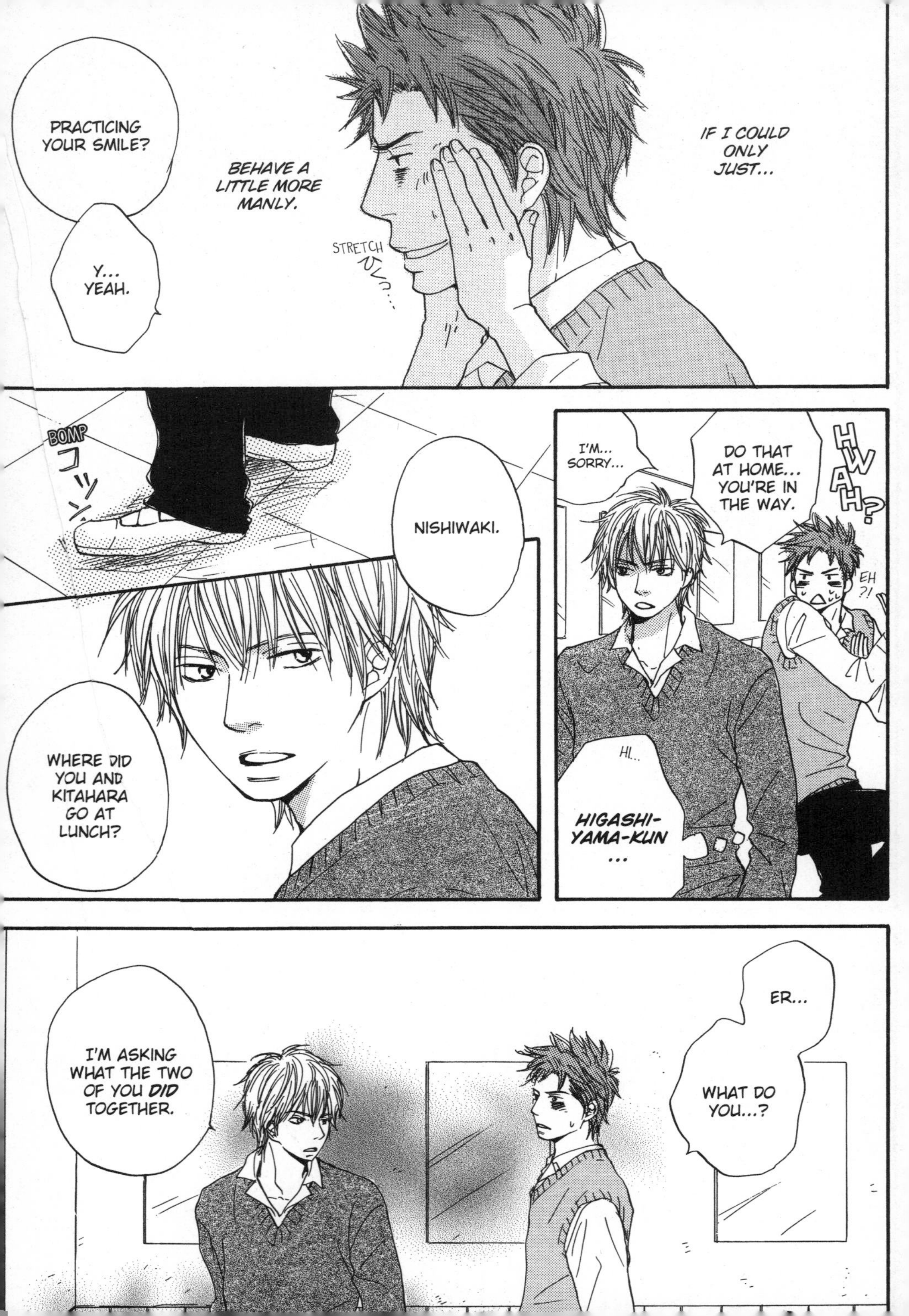
IF I COULD ONLY JUST...
BEHAVE A LITTLE MORE MANLY.
STRETCH
PRACTICING YOUR SMILE?
Y... YEAH.
HWAH?
DO THAT AT HOME... YOU'RE IN THE WAY.
I'M... SORRY...
EH ?!
HI...
HIGASHI-YAMA-KUN ...
BOMP
NISHIWAKI.
WHERE DID YOU AND KITAHARA GO AT LUNCH?
ER...
WHAT DO YOU...?
I'M ASKING WHAT THE TWO OF YOU *DID* TOGETHER.

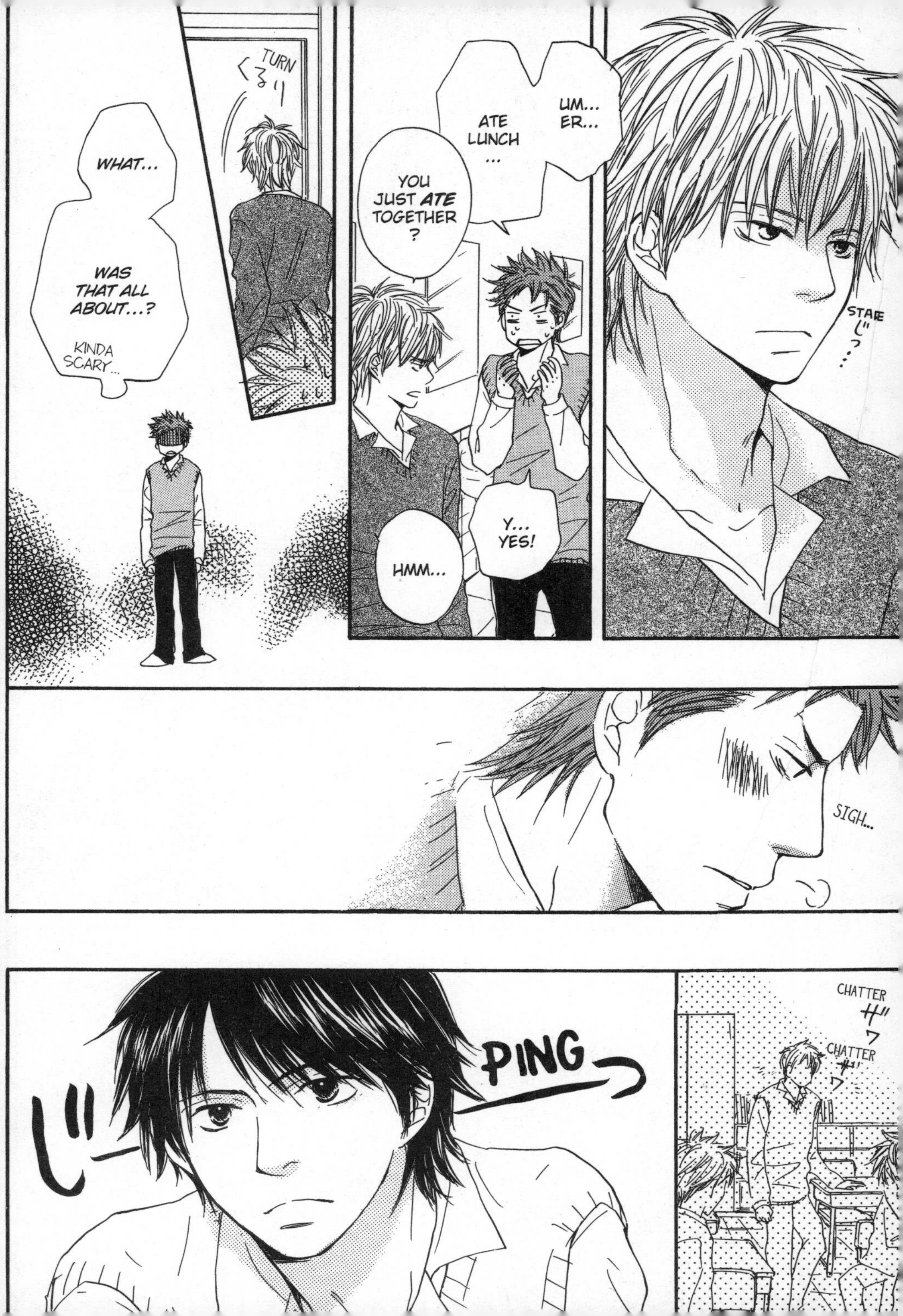
STARE
じ〜…
UM... ER...
ATE LUNCH ...
YOU JUST ATE TOGETHER ?
Y... YES!
HMM...
TURN
くるり
WHAT...
WAS THAT ALL ABOUT...?
KINDA SCARY...
SIGH...
CHATTER
ザワ
CHATTER
ザワ
PING
じー

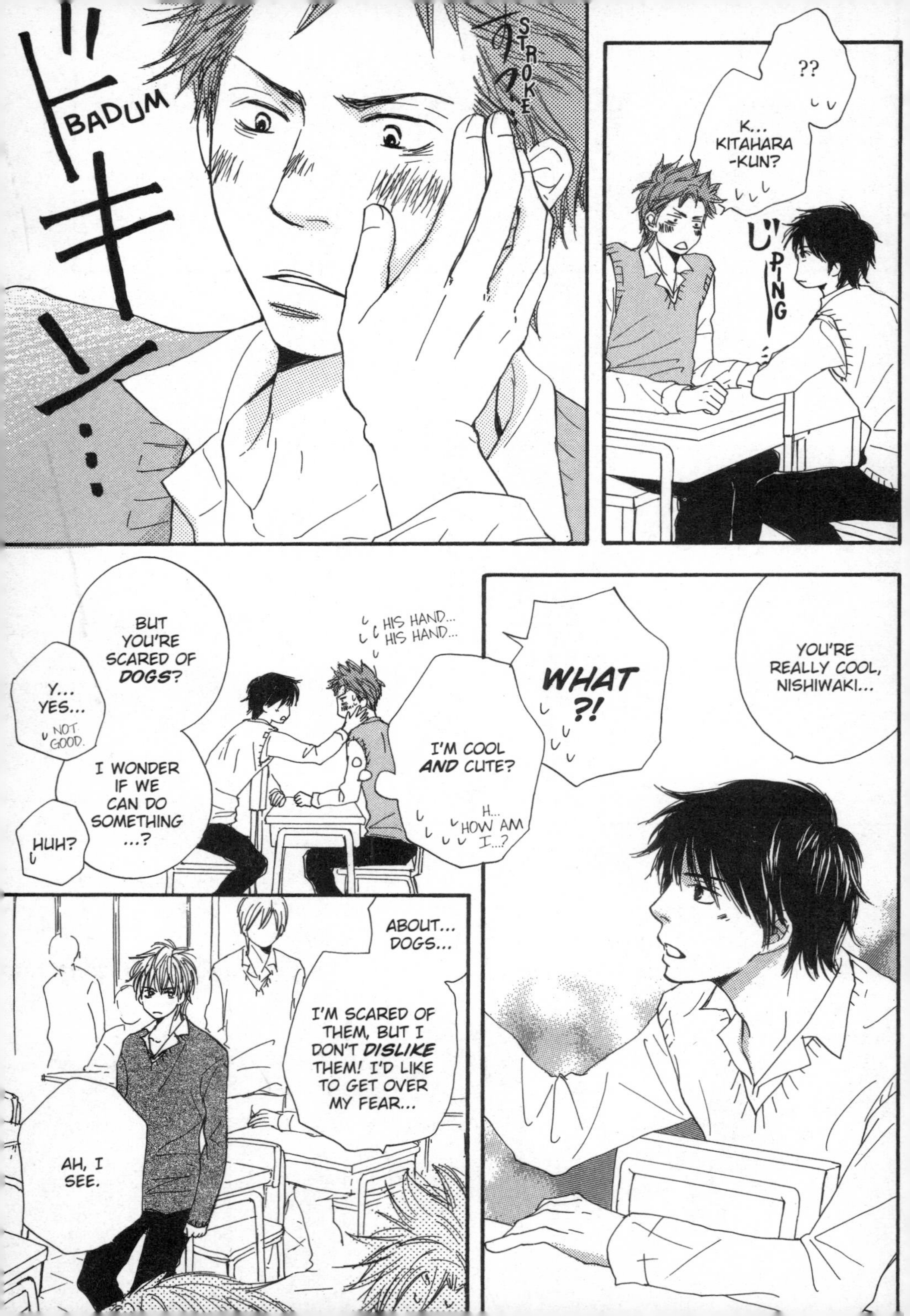
??
K... KITAHARA -KUN?
PING
STROKE
BADUM
YOU'RE REALLY COOL, NISHIWAKI...
WHAT ?!
I'M COOL AND CUTE?
H... HOW AM I...?
HIS HAND... HIS HAND...
BUT YOU'RE SCARED OF DOGS?
Y... YES...
NOT GOOD.
I WONDER IF WE CAN DO SOMETHING ...?
HUH?
ABOUT... DOGS...
I'M SCARED OF THEM, BUT I DON'T DISLIKE THEM! I'D LIKE TO GET OVER MY FEAR...
AH, I SEE.

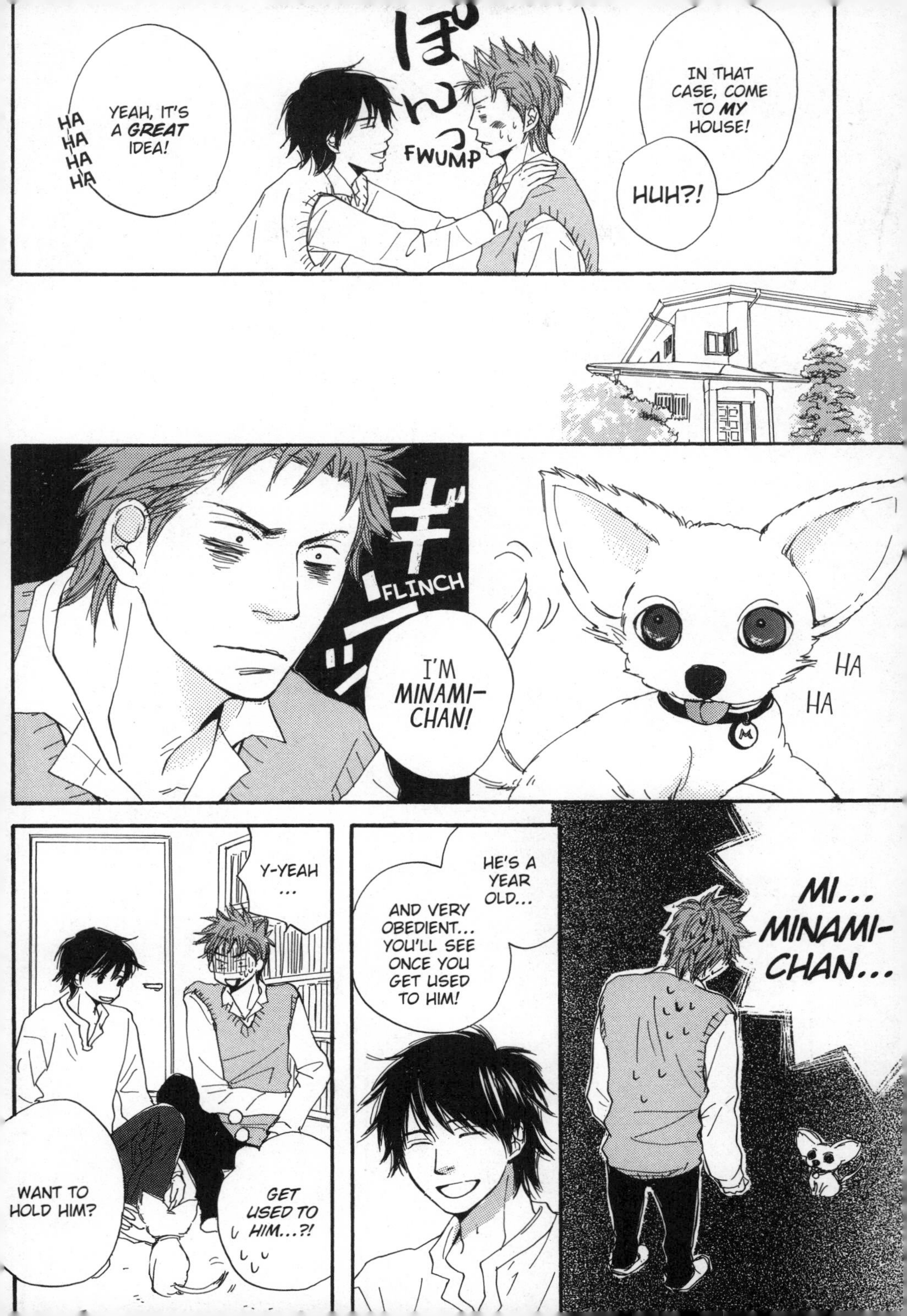
IN THAT CASE, COME TO MY HOUSE!
HUH?!
ぽんっ
FWUMP
YEAH, IT'S A GREAT IDEA!
HA HA HA HA
HA
HA
I'M MINAMI-CHAN!
ギッ
FLINCH
MI... MINAMI-CHAN...
HE'S A YEAR OLD...
AND VERY OBEDIENT... YOU'LL SEE ONCE YOU GET USED TO HIM!
Y-YEAH ...
GET USED TO HIM...?!
WANT TO HOLD HIM?

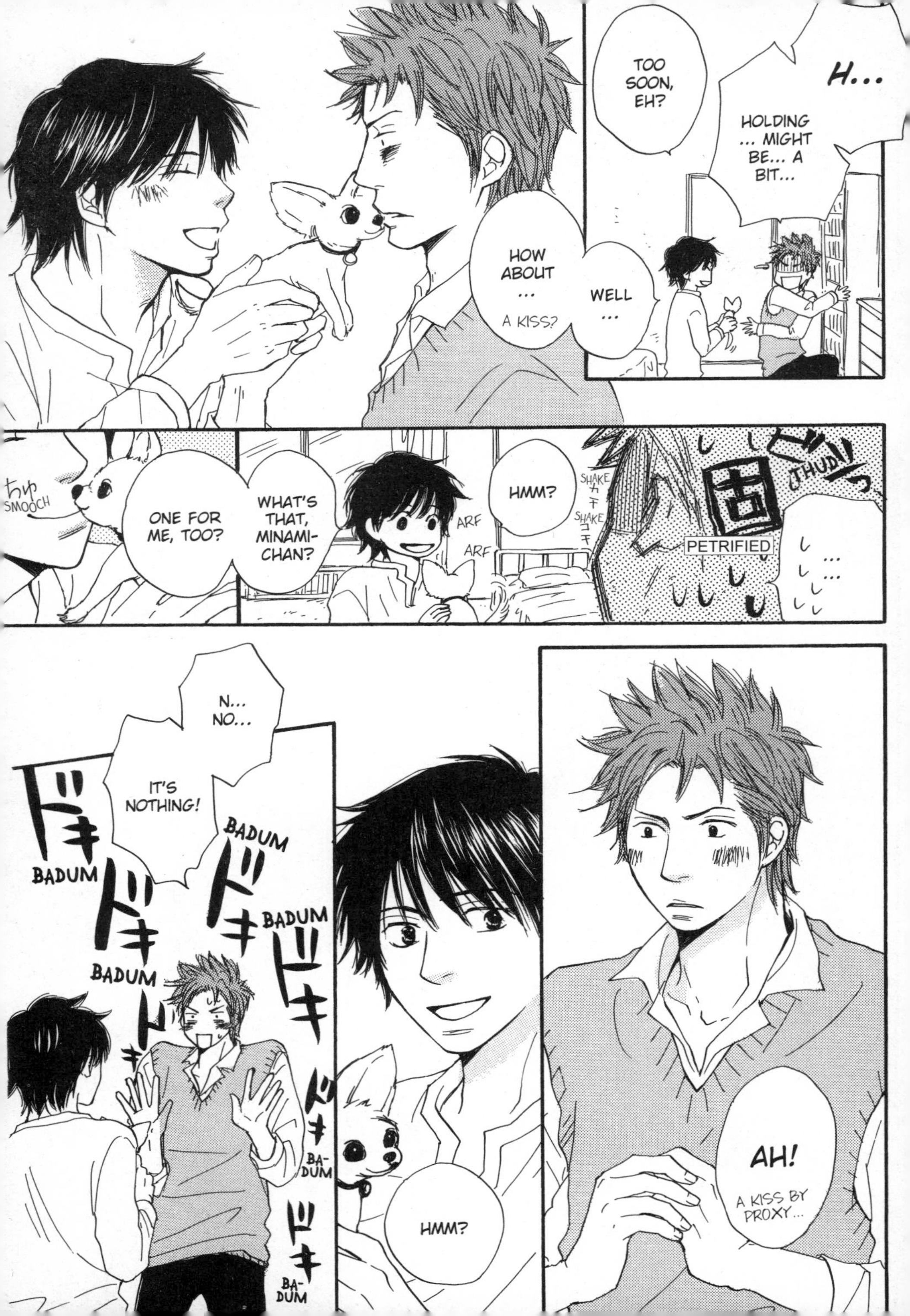
H...
HOLDING ... MIGHT BE... A BIT...
TOO SOON, EH?
WELL ...
HOW ABOUT ... A KISS?
THUD!
PETRIFIED
... ...
SHAKE
SHAKE
HMM?
ARF
ARF
WHAT'S THAT, MINAMI-CHAN?
ONE FOR ME, TOO?
ちゅ
SMOOCH
AH!
A KISS BY PROXY...
HMM?
N... NO...
IT'S NOTHING!
BADUM
BADUM
BADUM
BADUM
BA-DUM
BA-DUM

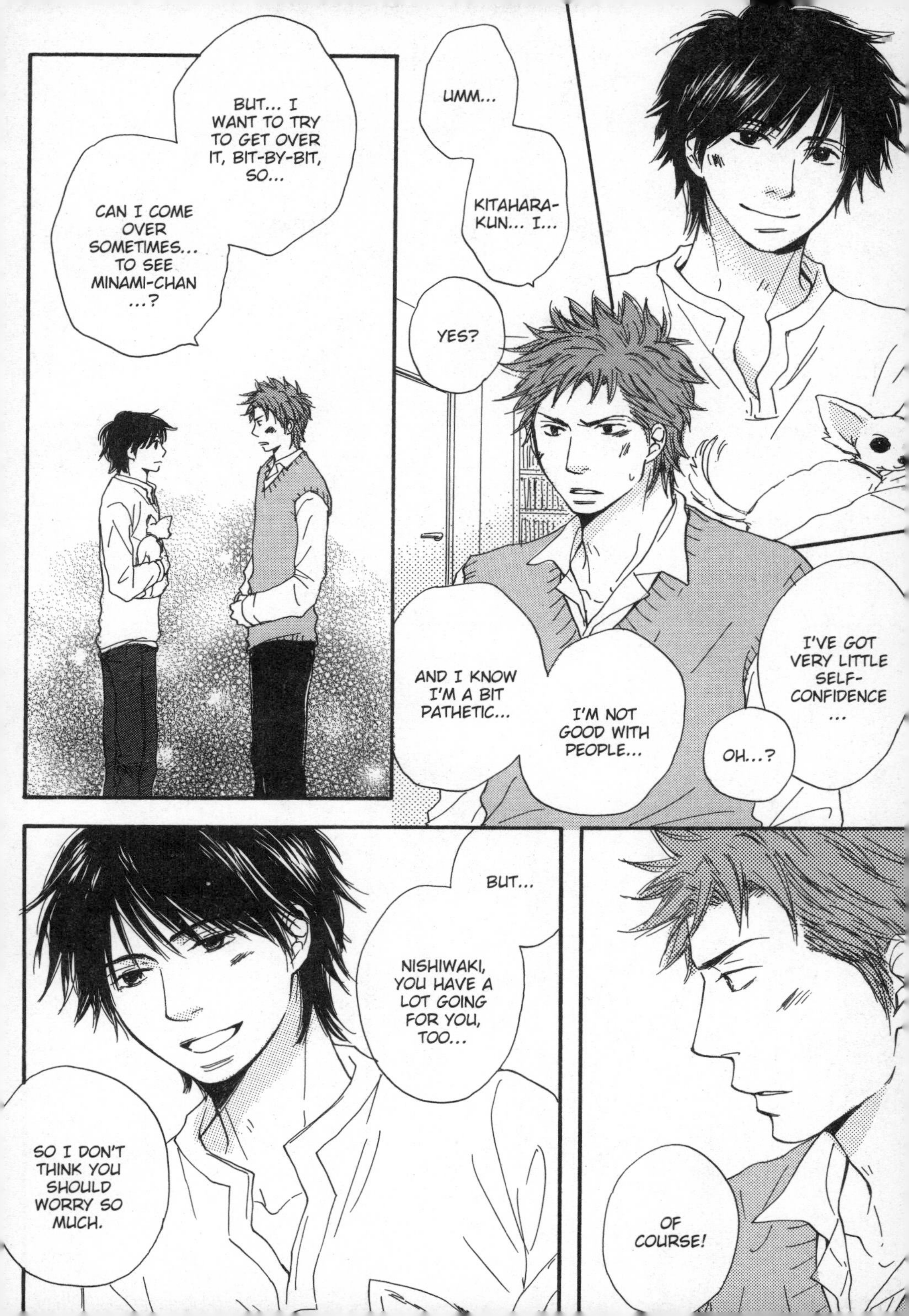
UMM...
KITAHARA-KUN... I...
YES?
I'VE GOT VERY LITTLE SELF-CONFIDENCE...
OH...?
I'M NOT GOOD WITH PEOPLE...
AND I KNOW I'M A BIT PATHETIC...
BUT... I WANT TO TRY TO GET OVER IT, BIT-BY-BIT, SO...
CAN I COME OVER SOMETIMES... TO SEE MINAMI-CHAN...?
OF COURSE!
BUT...
NISHIWAKI, YOU HAVE A LOT GOING FOR YOU, TOO...
SO I DON'T THINK YOU SHOULD WORRY SO MUCH.

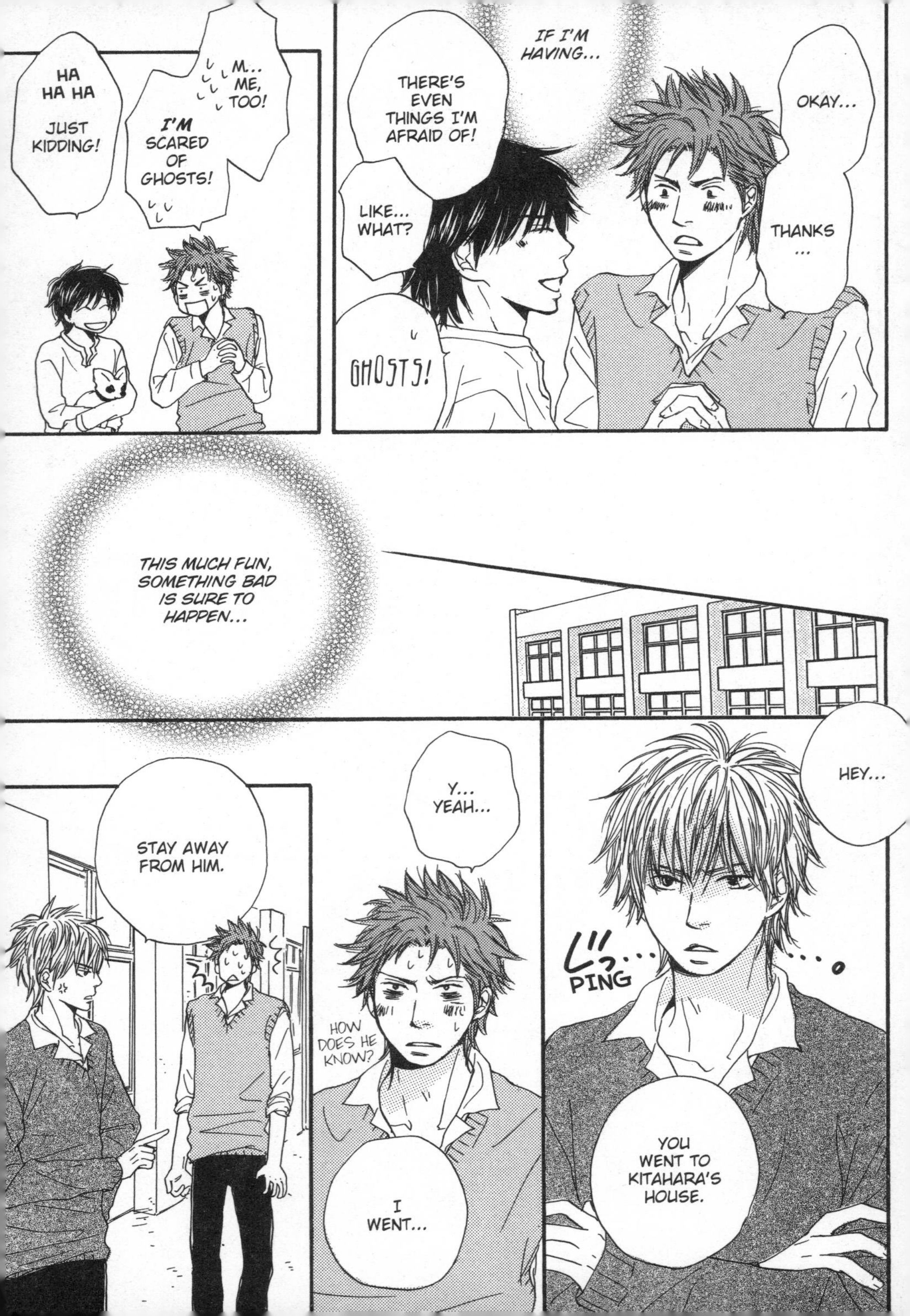
OKAY...
THANKS ...
IF I'M HAVING...
THERE'S EVEN THINGS I'M AFRAID OF!
LIKE... WHAT?
GHOSTS!
M... ME, TOO!
I'M SCARED OF GHOSTS!
HA HA HA
JUST KIDDING!
THIS MUCH FUN, SOMETHING BAD IS SURE TO HAPPEN...
HEY...
じっ...
PING
YOU WENT TO KITAHARA'S HOUSE.
Y... YEAH...
HOW DOES HE KNOW?
I WENT...
STAY AWAY FROM HIM.

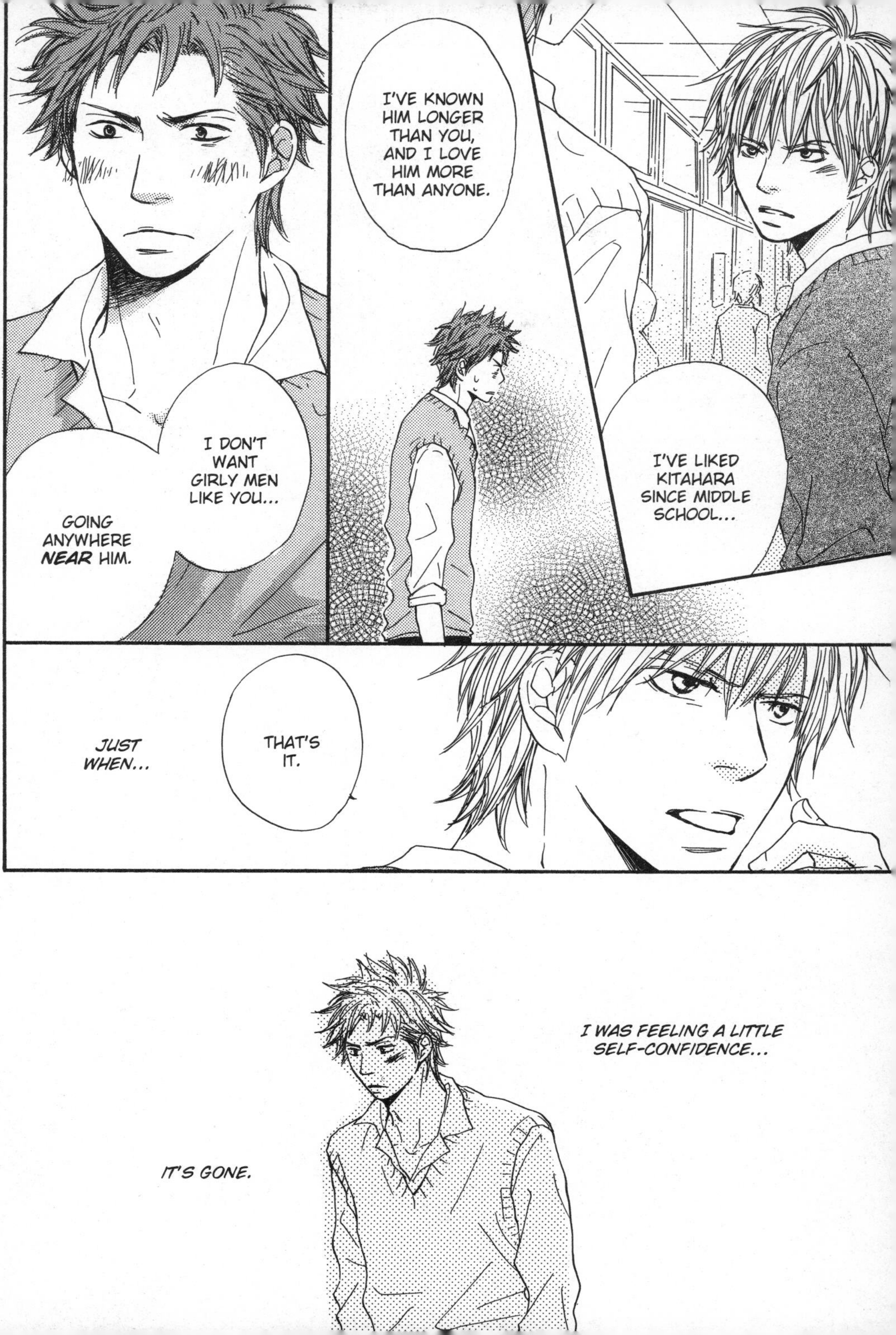
I'VE LIKED KITAHARA SINCE MIDDLE SCHOOL...
I'VE KNOWN HIM LONGER THAN YOU, AND I LOVE HIM MORE THAN ANYONE.
I DON'T WANT GIRLY MEN LIKE YOU...
GOING ANYWHERE **NEAR** HIM.
THAT'S IT.
JUST WHEN...
I WAS FEELING A LITTLE SELF-CONFIDENCE...
IT'S GONE.

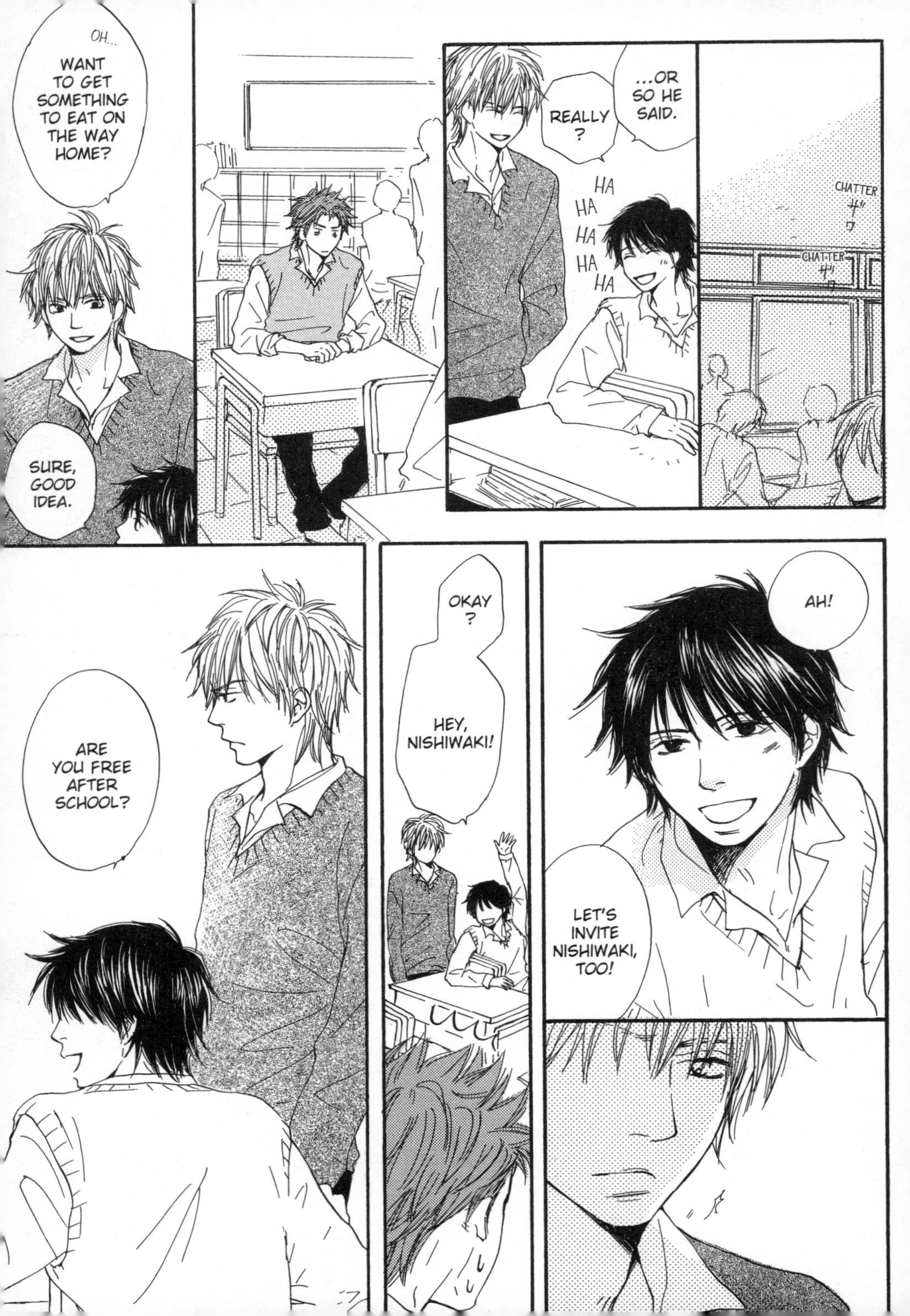

CHATTER ザワ
CHATTER ザワ
...OR SO HE SAID.
REALLY?
HA HA HA HA HA
OH...
WANT TO GET SOMETHING TO EAT ON THE WAY HOME?
SURE, GOOD IDEA.
AH!
LET'S INVITE NISHIWAKI, TOO!
OKAY?
HEY, NISHIWAKI!
ARE YOU FREE AFTER SCHOOL?

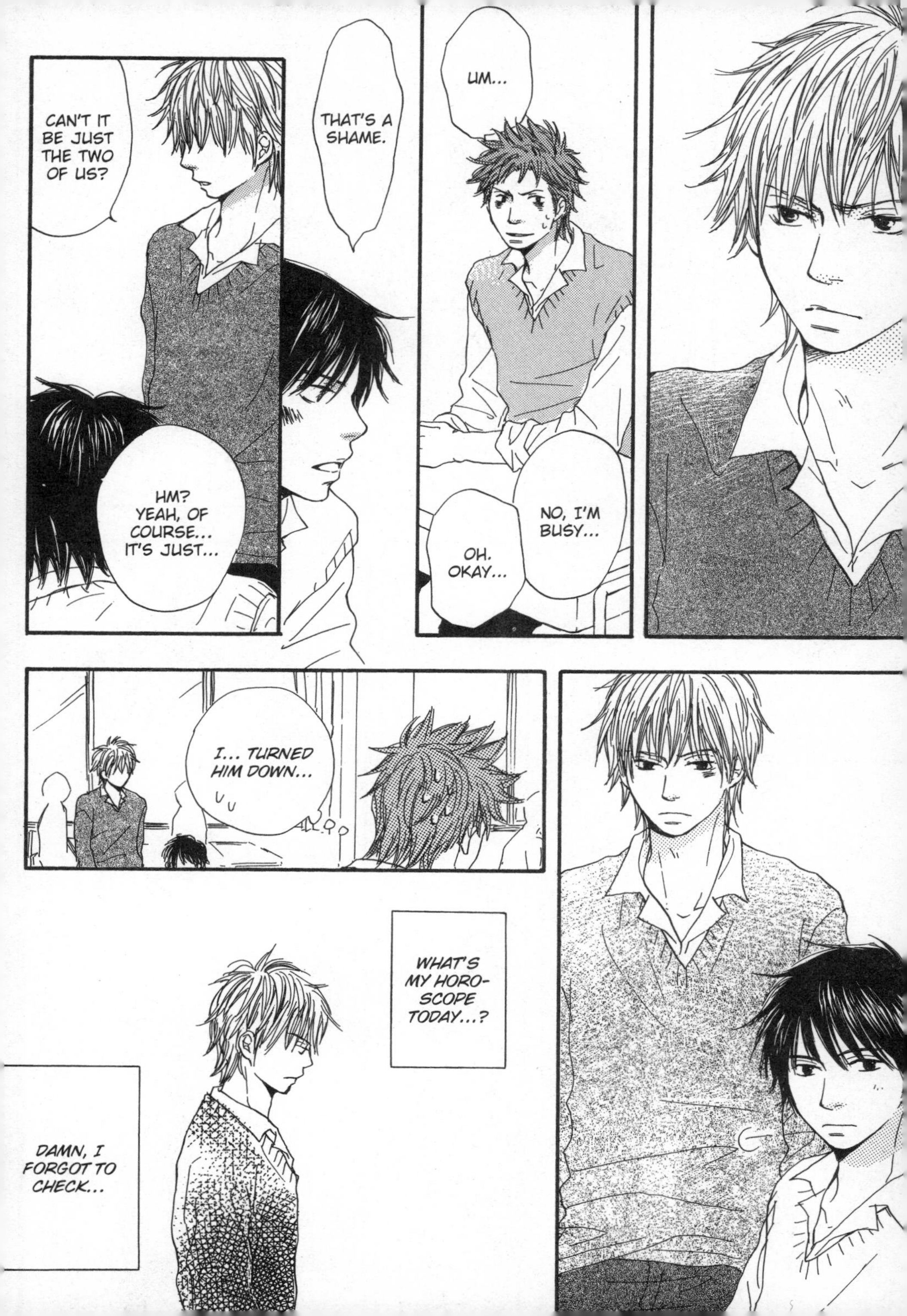
UM...
NO, I'M BUSY...
OH. OKAY...
THAT'S A SHAME.
CAN'T IT BE JUST THE TWO OF US?
HM? YEAH, OF COURSE... IT'S JUST...
I... TURNED HIM DOWN...
WHAT'S MY HORO-SCOPE TODAY...?
DAMN, I FORGOT TO CHECK...

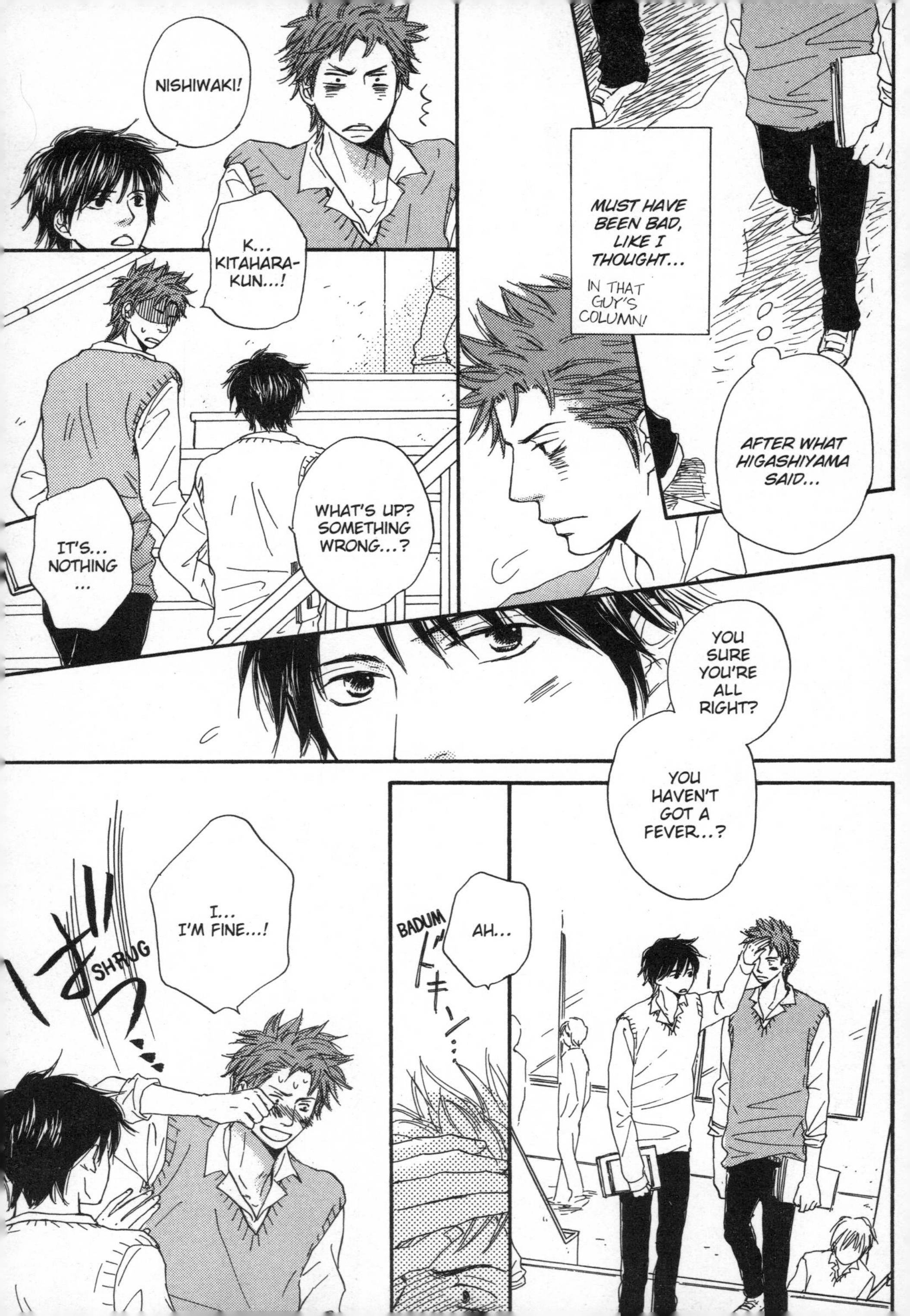
MUST HAVE BEEN BAD, LIKE I THOUGHT...
IN THAT GUY'S COLUMN!
AFTER WHAT HIGASHIYAMA SAID...
NISHIWAKI!
K... KITAHARA-KUN...!
WHAT'S UP? SOMETHING WRONG...?
IT'S... NOTHING ...
YOU SURE YOU'RE ALL RIGHT?
YOU HAVEN'T GOT A FEVER...?
AH...
BADUM
I... I'M FINE...!
SHRUG

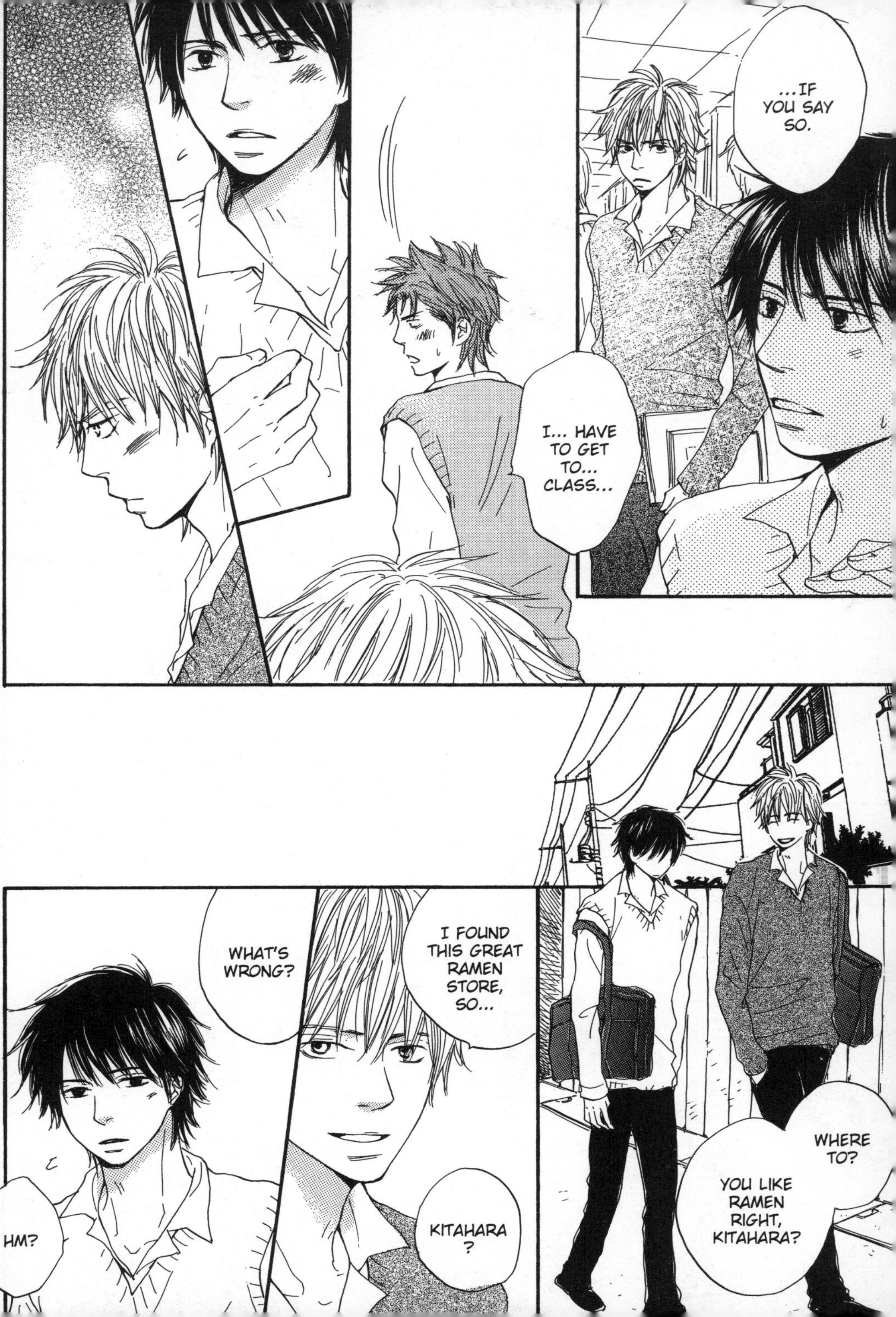
...IF YOU SAY SO.
I... HAVE TO GET TO... CLASS...
YOU LIKE RAMEN RIGHT, KITAHARA?
WHERE TO?
I FOUND THIS GREAT RAMEN STORE, SO...
KITAHARA?
WHAT'S WRONG?
HM?

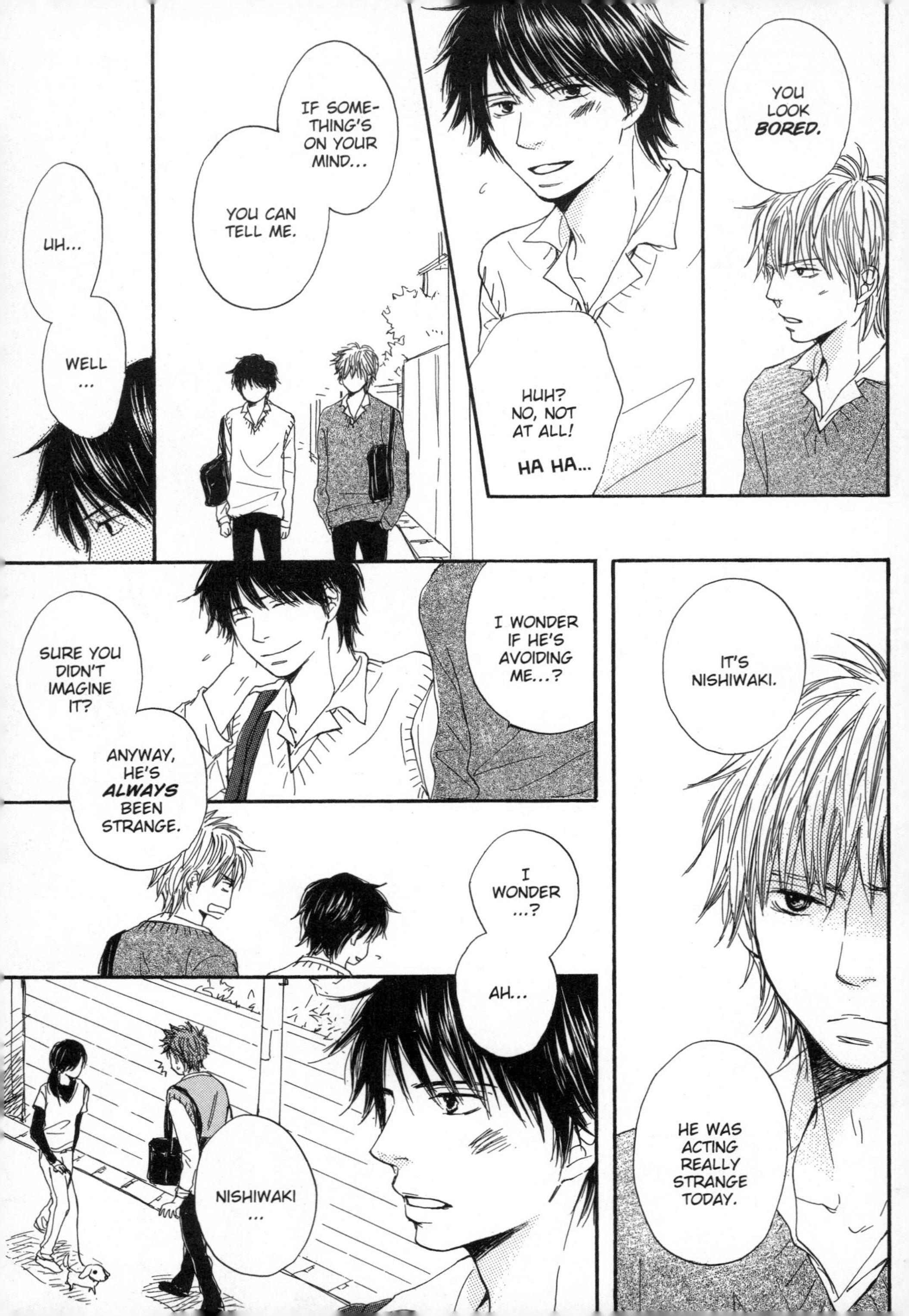
YOU LOOK BORED.
HUH? NO, NOT AT ALL!
HA HA...
IF SOME-THING'S ON YOUR MIND...
YOU CAN TELL ME.
UH...
WELL ...
IT'S NISHIWAKI.
HE WAS ACTING REALLY STRANGE TODAY.
I WONDER IF HE'S AVOIDING ME...?
SURE YOU DIDN'T IMAGINE IT?
ANYWAY, HE'S ALWAYS BEEN STRANGE.
I WONDER ...?
AH...
NISHIWAKI ...

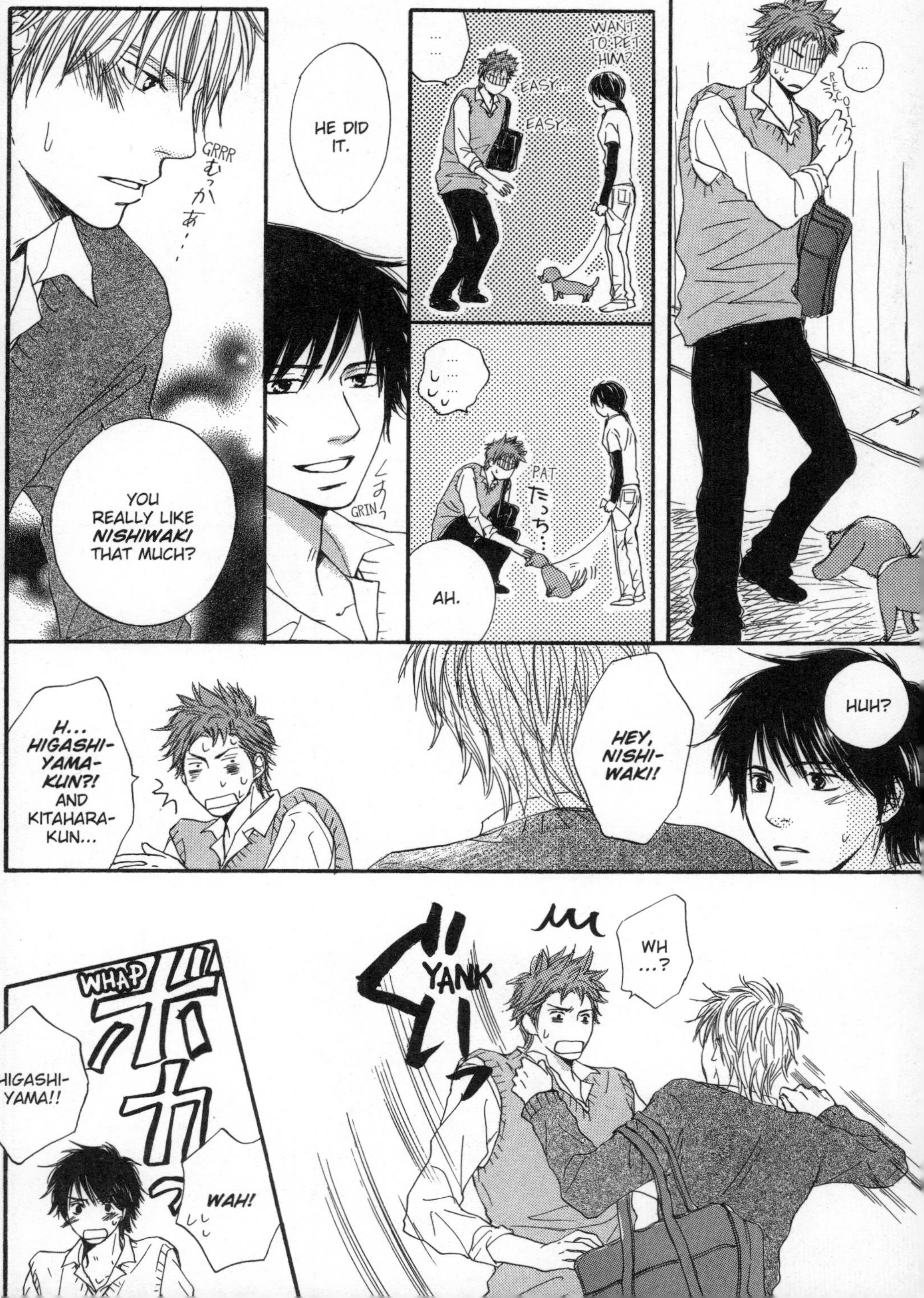
...
RECOIL
WANT TO PET HIM?
EASY
EASY
...
...
... ...
PAT
たっち...
AH.
HE DID IT.
GRIN
YOU REALLY LIKE NISHIWAKI THAT MUCH?
GRRR
むっかぁ・・・
HUH?
HEY, NISHI-WAKI!
H... HIGASHI-YAMA-KUN?! AND KITAHARA-KUN...
WH ...?
YANK
WHAP
HIGASHI-YAMA!!
WAH!

THEN WHY DON'T *YOU* DO THE SAME?!

IF YOU *DON'T* DO SOMETHING ABOUT IT...

I...

I *ENVY* YOU, HIGASHI-YAMA-KUN...

HOW YOU CAN SAY WHAT'S ON YOUR MIND...

SHRUG

YOU'LL BE THAT WAY FOR THE REST OF YOUR *LIFE.*

すた TIP
すた TAP
W...WAIT!
TIP
TAP すた
すた すた
TIP

GRAB

IT'S NOT FAIR, NISHIWAKI...

I WAS THERE FIRST.

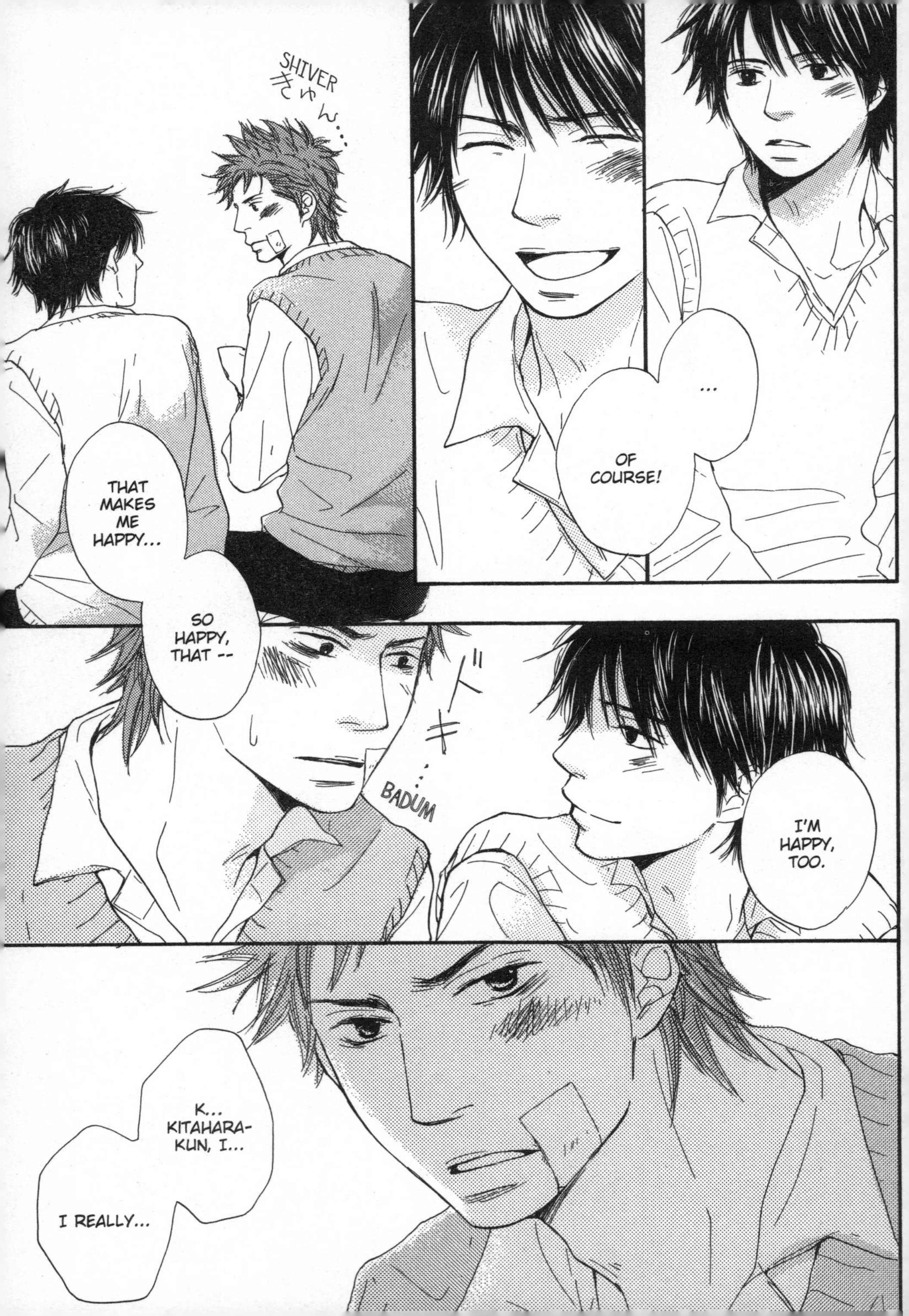
...
OF COURSE!
SHIVER
きゅん…
THAT MAKES ME HAPPY...
SO HAPPY, THAT --
I'M HAPPY, TOO.
ドキ…
BADUM
K... KITAHARA-KUN, I...
I REALLY...

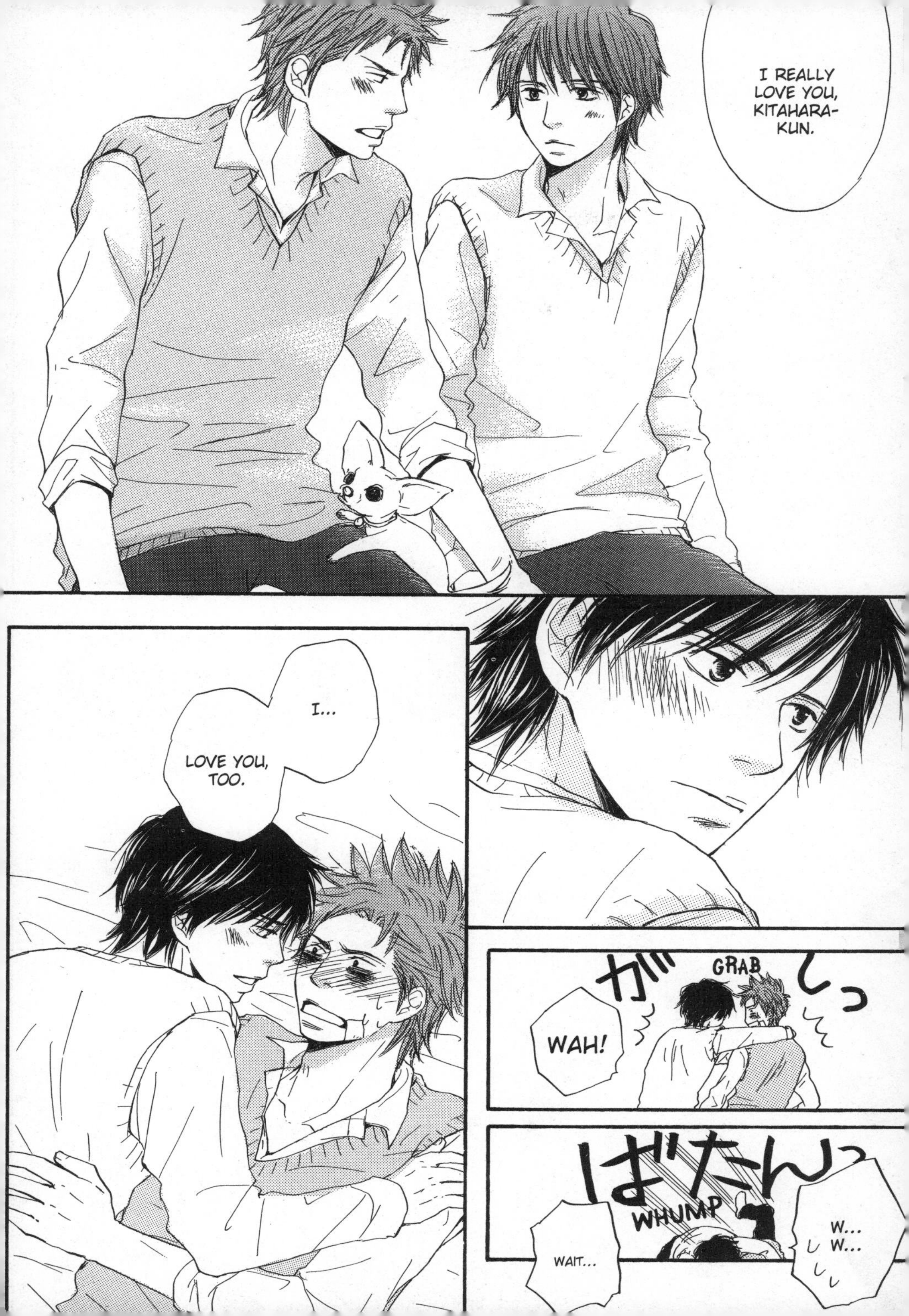
I REALLY LOVE YOU, KITAHARA-KUN.
しっ
GRAB
が
WAH!
ばたんっ
WHUMP
W... W...
WAIT...
I...
LOVE YOU, TOO.

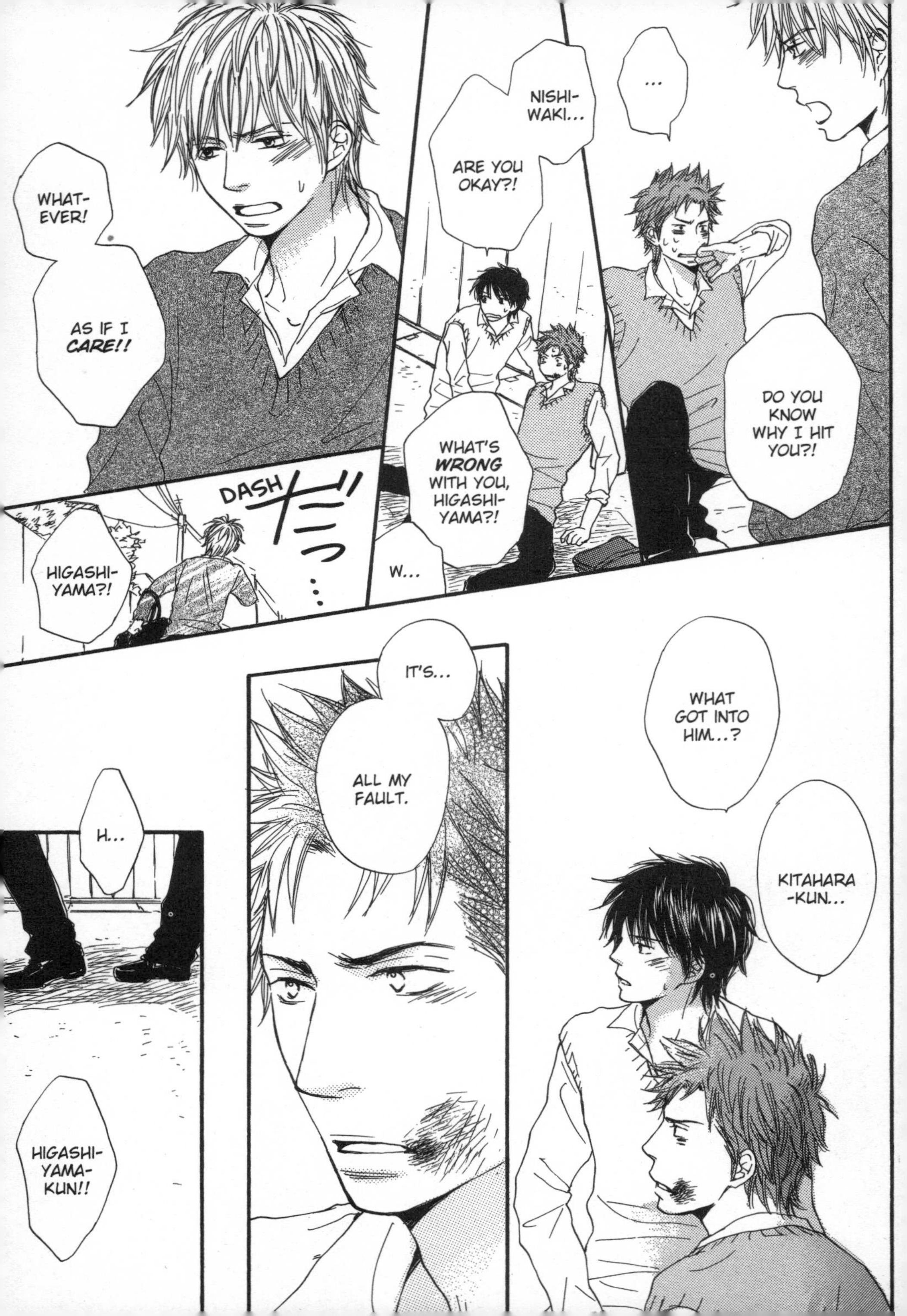
...
DO YOU KNOW WHY I HIT YOU?!
NISHI-WAKI...
ARE YOU OKAY?!
WHAT'S **WRONG** WITH YOU, HIGASHI-YAMA?!
W...
WHAT-EVER!
AS IF I **CARE!!**
DASH
HIGASHI-YAMA?!
WHAT GOT INTO HIM...?
KITAHARA-KUN...
IT'S...
ALL MY FAULT.
H...
HIGASHI-YAMA-KUN!!

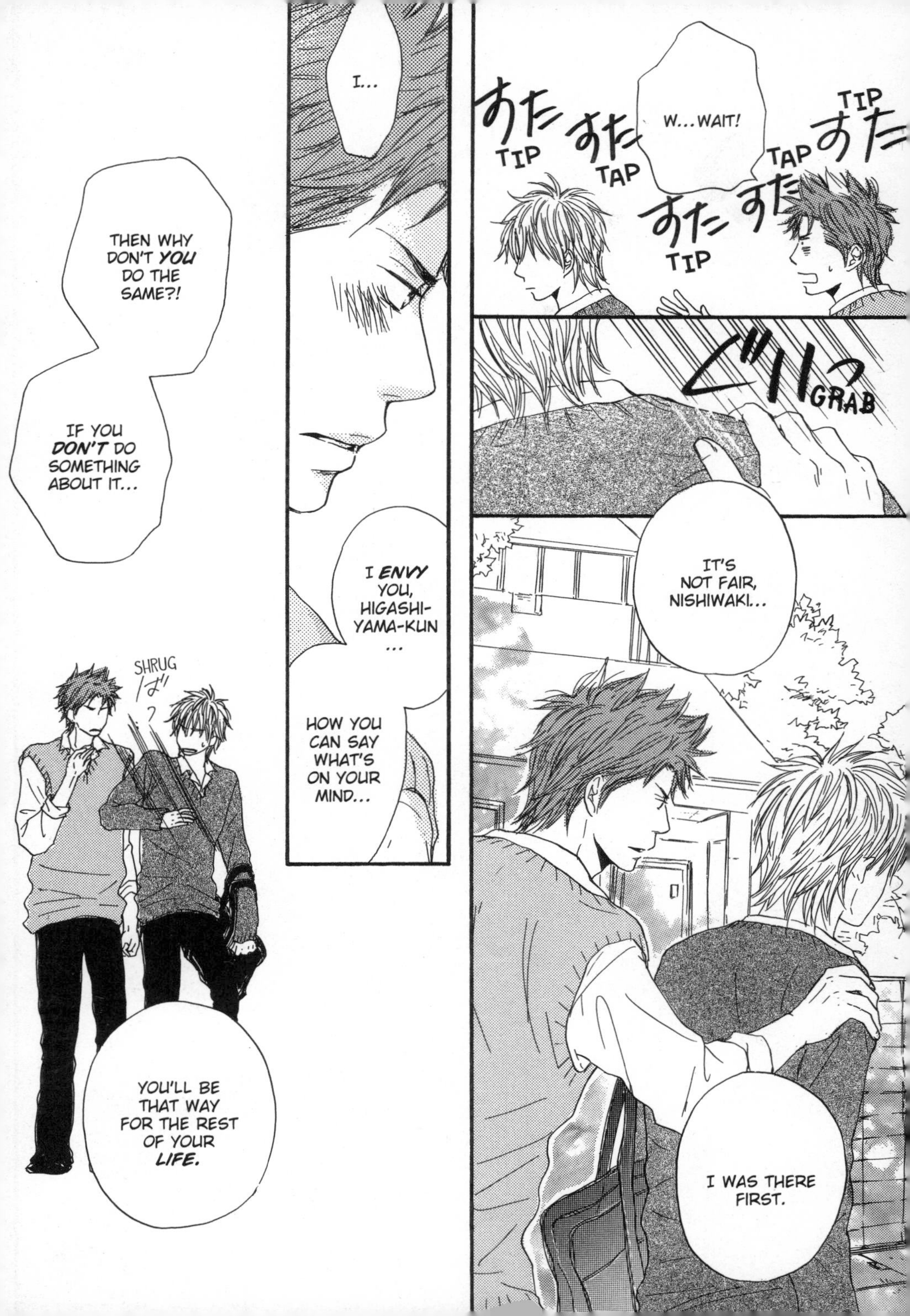
TIP すた
TAP すた
W...WAIT!
TAP すた
TIP すた
TIP すた
すた
ぐいっ GRAB
IT'S NOT FAIR, NISHIWAKI...
I WAS THERE FIRST.
I...
I ENVY YOU, HIGASHI-YAMA-KUN...
HOW YOU CAN SAY WHAT'S ON YOUR MIND...
THEN WHY DON'T YOU DO THE SAME?!
IF YOU DON'T DO SOMETHING ABOUT IT...
SHRUG ぱ
YOU'LL BE THAT WAY FOR THE REST OF YOUR LIFE.

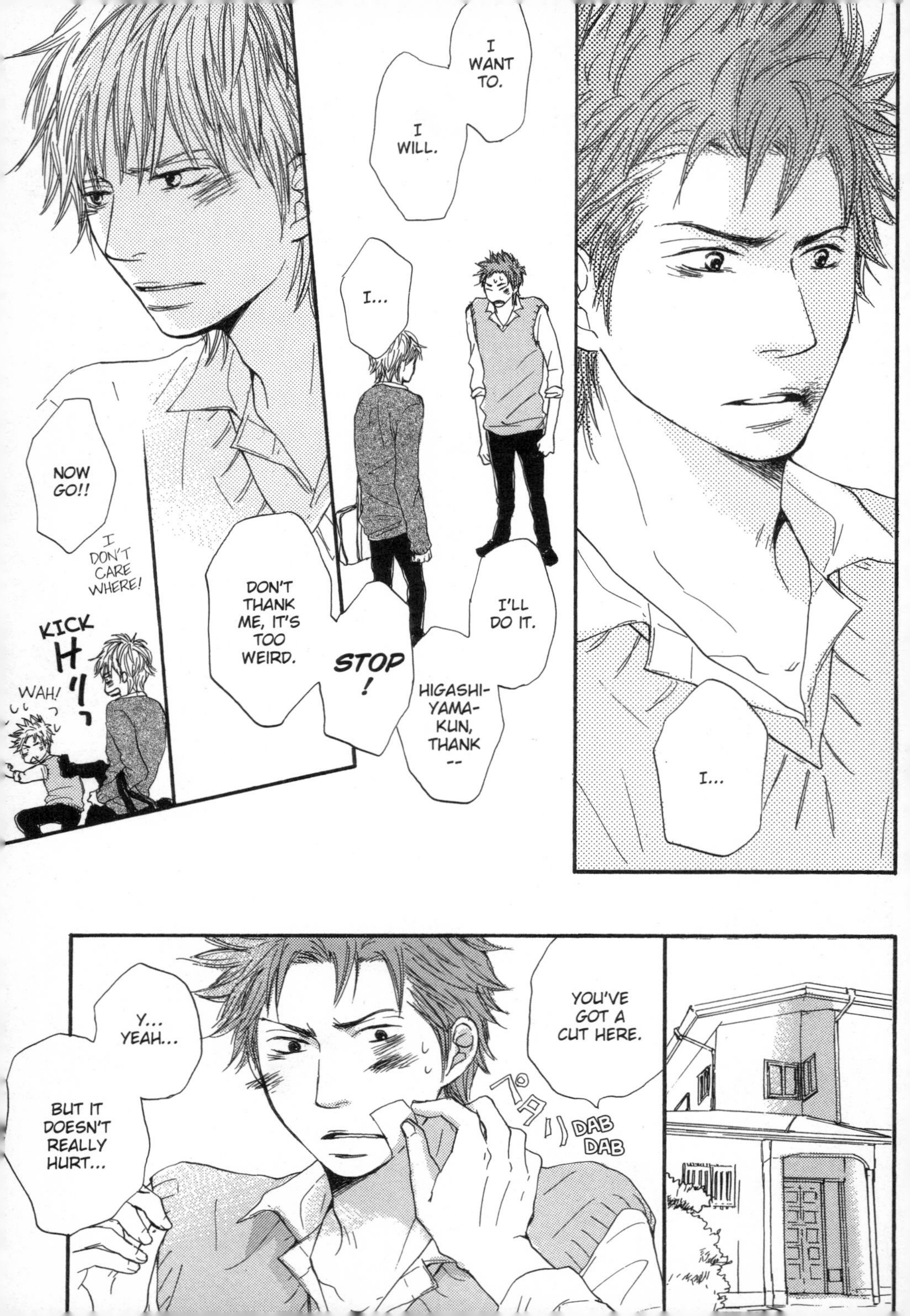
I...
I WANT TO.
I WILL.
I...
I'LL DO IT.
HIGASHIYAMA-KUN, THANK--
STOP!
DON'T THANK ME, IT'S TOO WEIRD.
NOW GO!!
I DON'T CARE WHERE!
KICK
WAH!
YOU'VE GOT A CUT HERE.
DAB DAB
Y... YEAH...
BUT IT DOESN'T REALLY HURT...

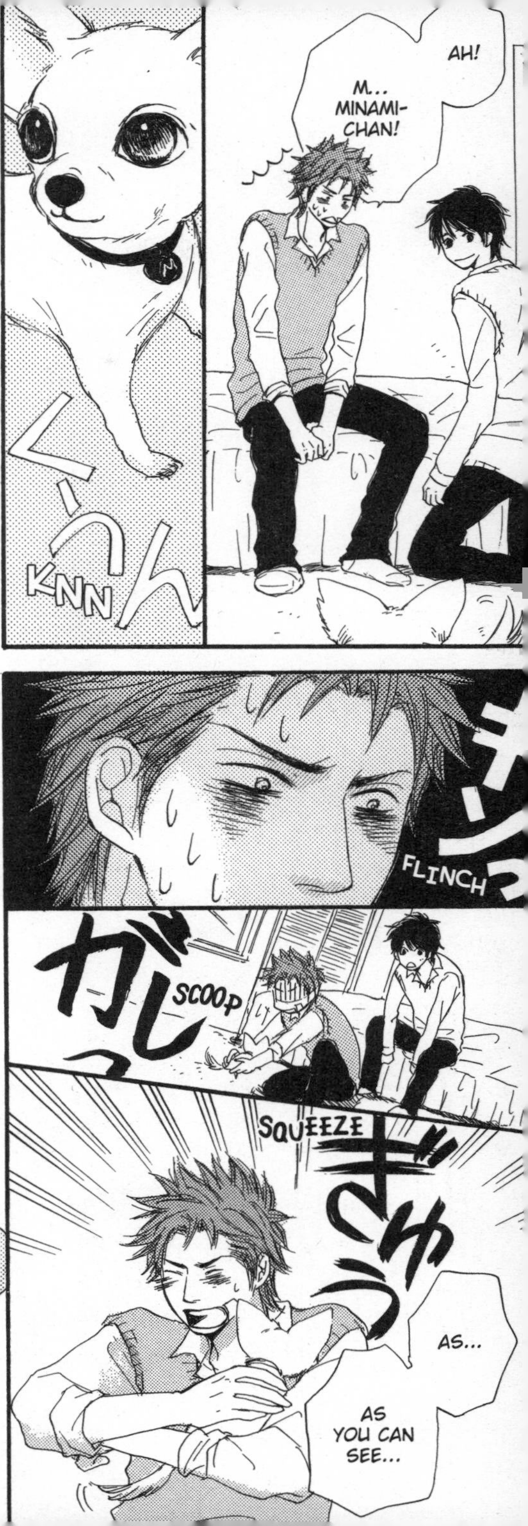
AH!
M... MINAMI-CHAN!
くぅん
KNN
FLINCH
がしっ
SCOOP
SQUEEZE
ぎゅう
AS...
AS YOU CAN SEE...

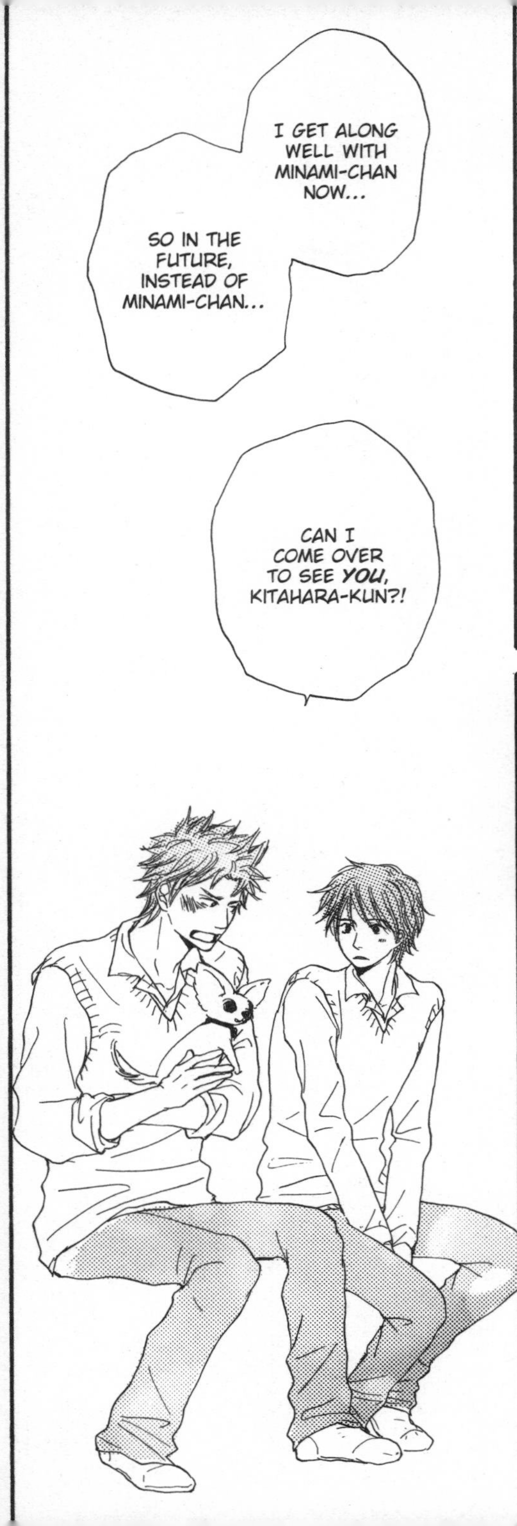
I GET ALONG WELL WITH MINAMI-CHAN NOW...
SO IN THE FUTURE, INSTEAD OF MINAMI-CHAN...
CAN I COME OVER TO SEE *YOU*, KITAHARA-KUN?!

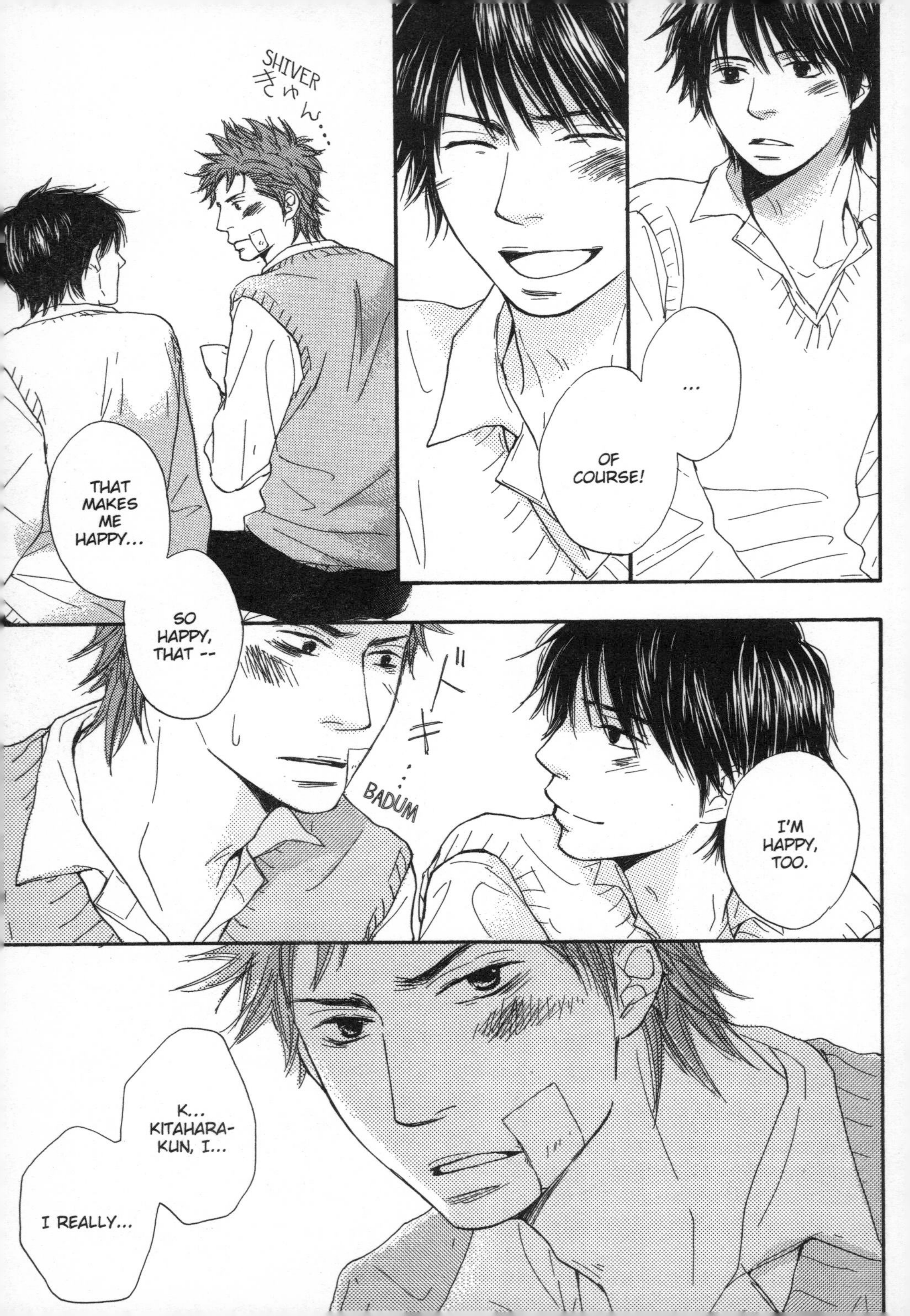
...
OF COURSE!
SHIVER
きゅん...
THAT MAKES ME HAPPY...
SO HAPPY, THAT --
ドキ...
BADUM
I'M HAPPY, TOO.
K... KITAHARA-KUN, I...
I REALLY...

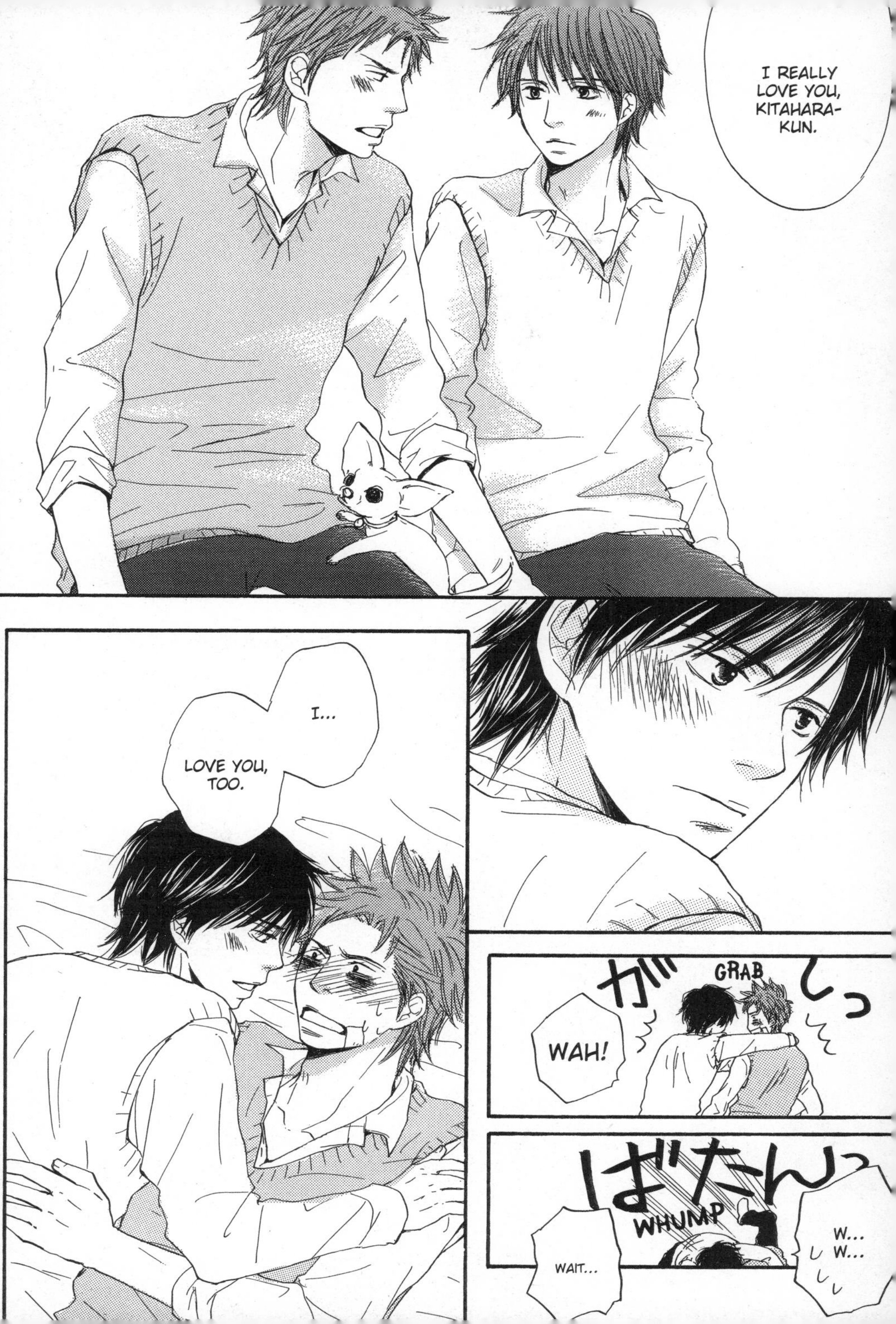
I REALLY LOVE YOU, KITAHARA-KUN.
WAH!
GRAB
がしっ
ばたんっ
WHUMP
W... W...
WAIT...
I...
LOVE YOU, TOO.

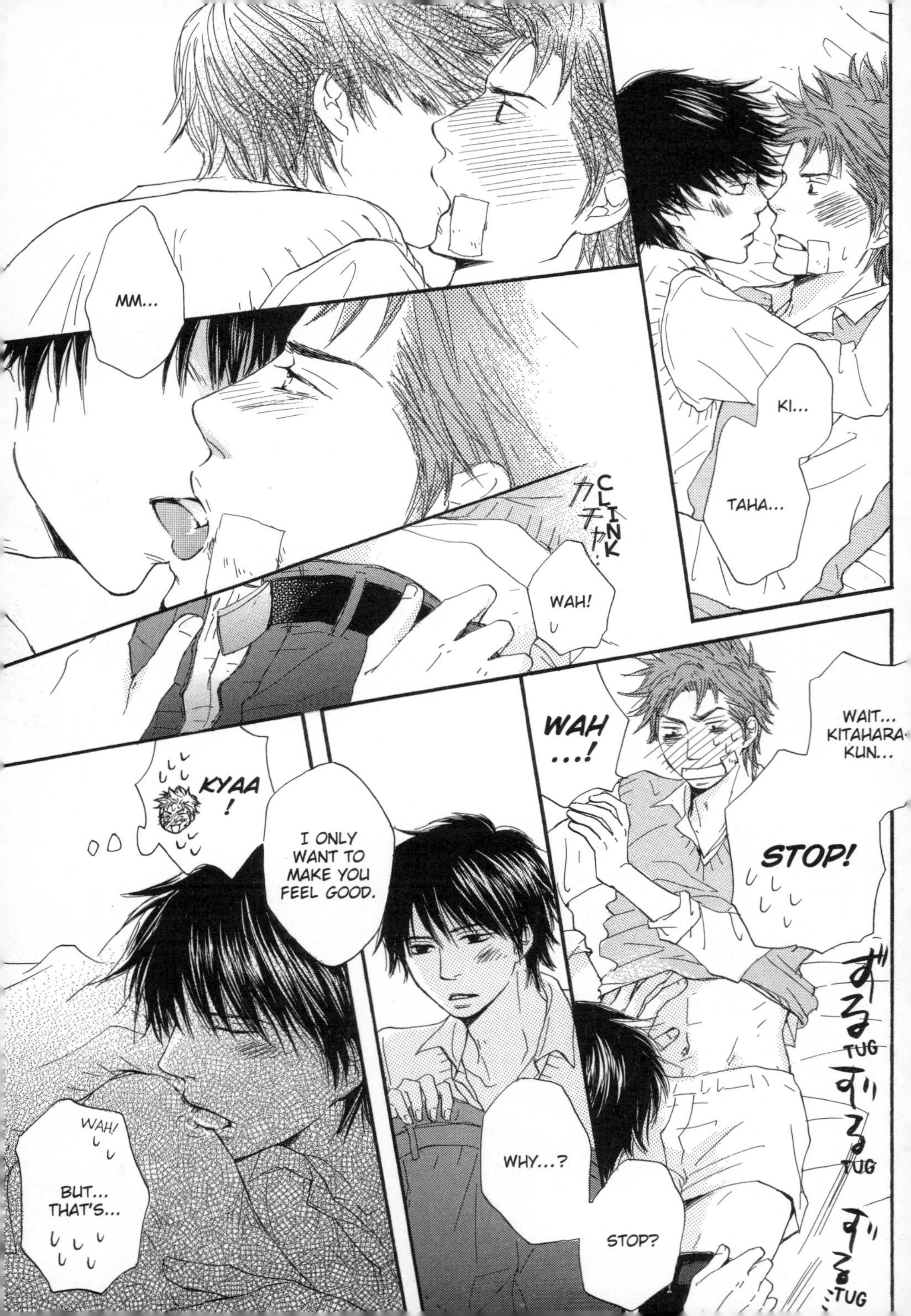
KI...
TAHA...
MM...
カチャ
CLINK
WAH!
WAIT... KITAHARA-KUN...
WAH...!
STOP!
ずる
TUG
ずる
TUG
ずる
TUG
WHY...?
STOP?
I ONLY WANT TO MAKE YOU FEEL GOOD.
KYAA!
WAH!
BUT... THAT'S...

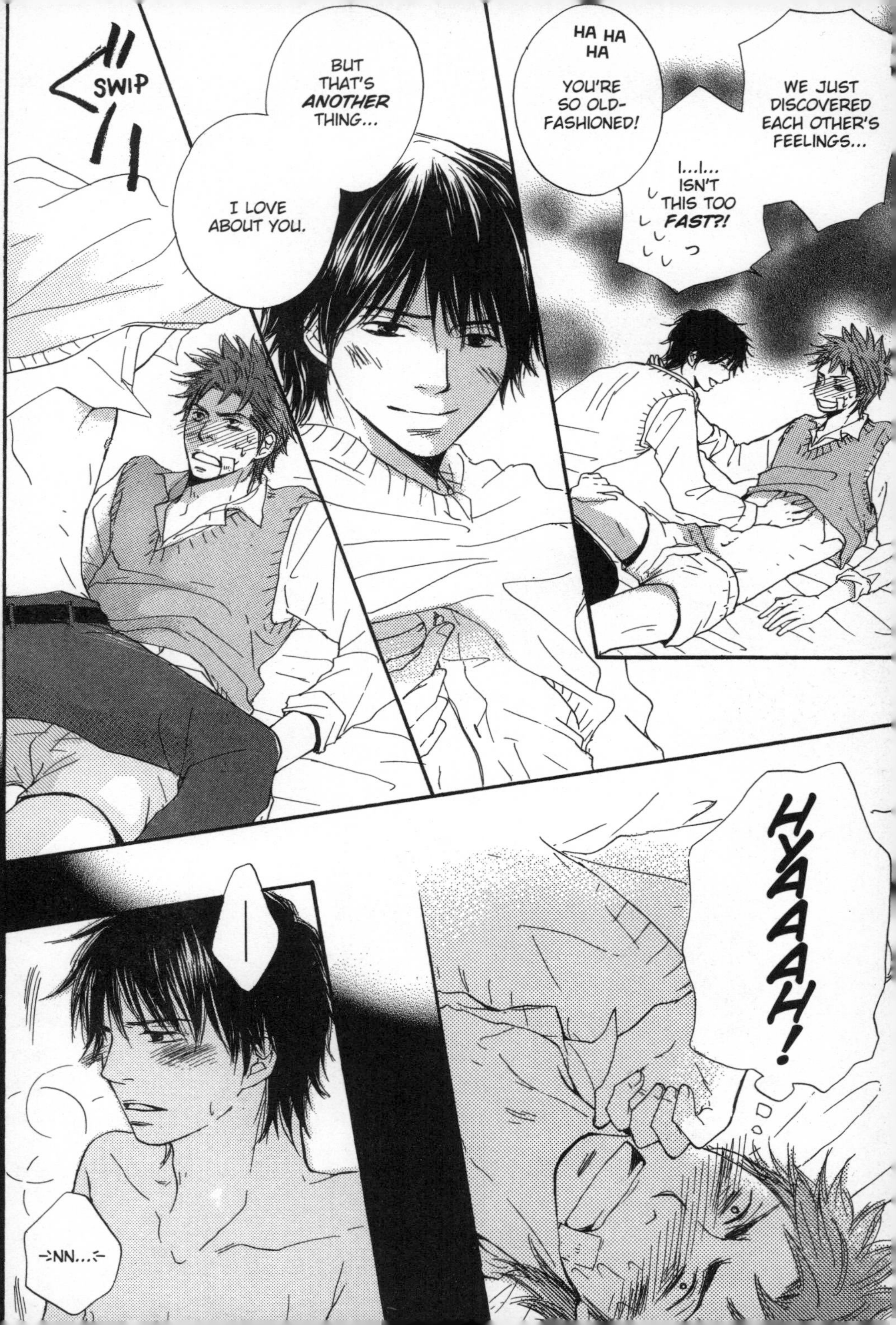
WE JUST DISCOVERED EACH OTHER'S FEELINGS...
I...I... ISN'T THIS TOO **FAST?!**
HA HA HA
YOU'RE SO OLD-FASHIONED!
BUT THAT'S **ANOTHER** THING...
I LOVE ABOUT YOU.
SWIP
HYAAAAH!
NN...

AH! I...

MADE ENOUGH FOR YOU TOO, HIGASHIYAMA-KUN!

HERE!

...

ISN'T THAT NICE, HIGASHIYAMA?

A HEART...

...

I M...MADE *CAKE* FOR DESSERT, TOO...

LIKE I PROMISED.

...

YAY!!

NISHIWAKI'S LUNCH BOXES ARE BEAUTIFUL!

I'M...

WH... WHAT?!

HI... HIGASHI-YAMA-KUN

...

BOX LUNCH?! GIVE ME A BREAK!

NEVER GOING TO ACCEPT THIS, YOU KNOW!!

I...

NAIVE LOVE TRIANGLE ● END

A TOWN IN THE EVENING

夕日の町

SAKAMOTO LIQUOR
坂元酒店

EVENIN'!!

YASU-SAN...

YOU'RE HERE *AGAIN*?

OH! NICE TO SEE YOU AS ALWAYS, YASUHIRO!

WHY DON'T YOU EAT WITH US?

I GOT SO MUCH YAKITORI*, I FIGURED I'D SHARE.

*GRILLED CHICKEN

FWIP

...

DAMN SUCK-UP...

HA HA

FLATTERY WILL GET YOU EVERYWHERE!

WOW! I *LOVE* YOUR COOKING AUNTIE -- THANKS!

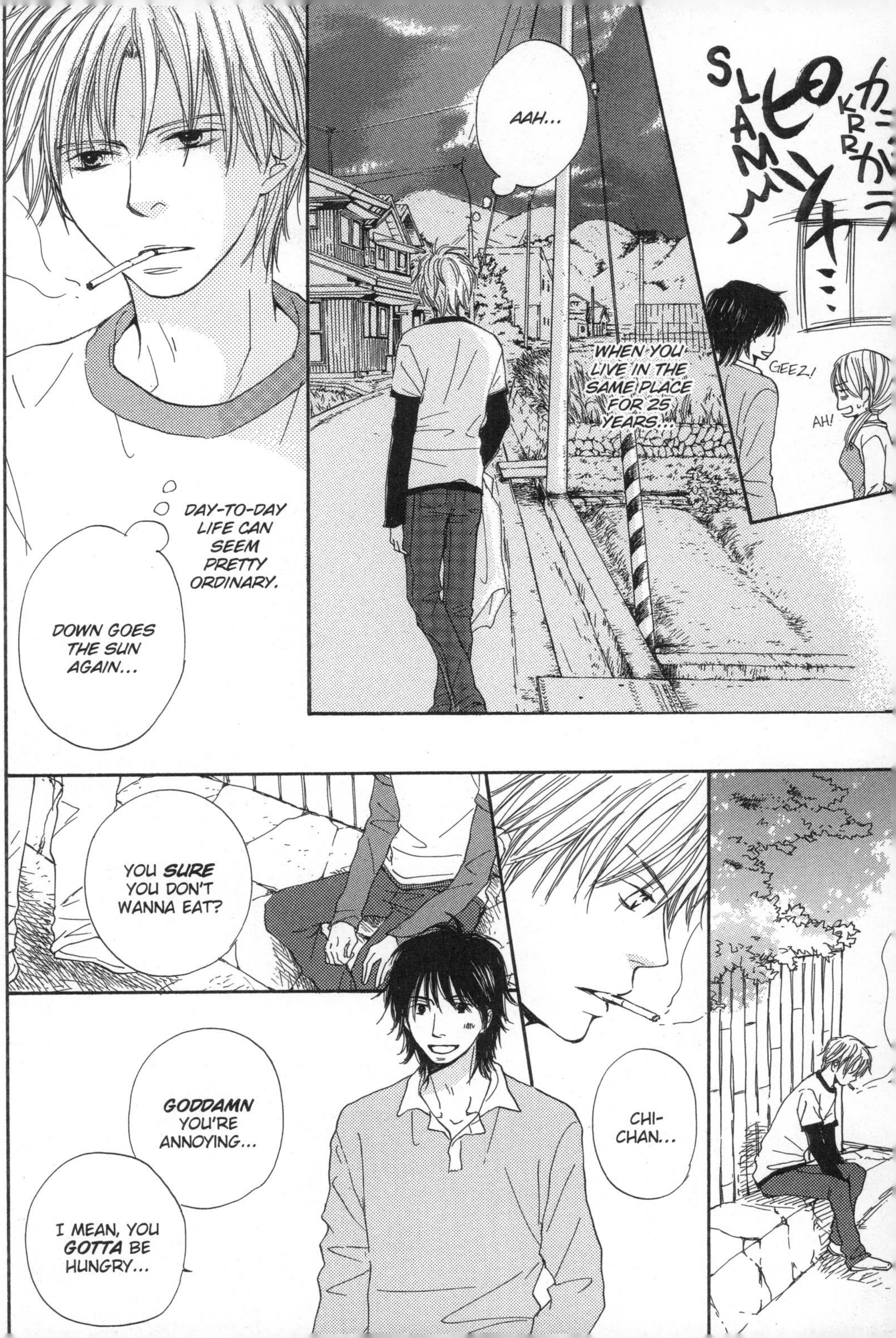
KRR
SLAM
GEEZ!
AH!
AAH...
WHEN YOU LIVE IN THE SAME PLACE FOR 25 YEARS...
DAY-TO-DAY LIFE CAN SEEM PRETTY ORDINARY.
DOWN GOES THE SUN AGAIN...
CHI-CHAN...
YOU **SURE** YOU DON'T WANNA EAT?
GODDAMN YOU'RE ANNOYING...
I MEAN, YOU **GOTTA** BE HUNGRY...

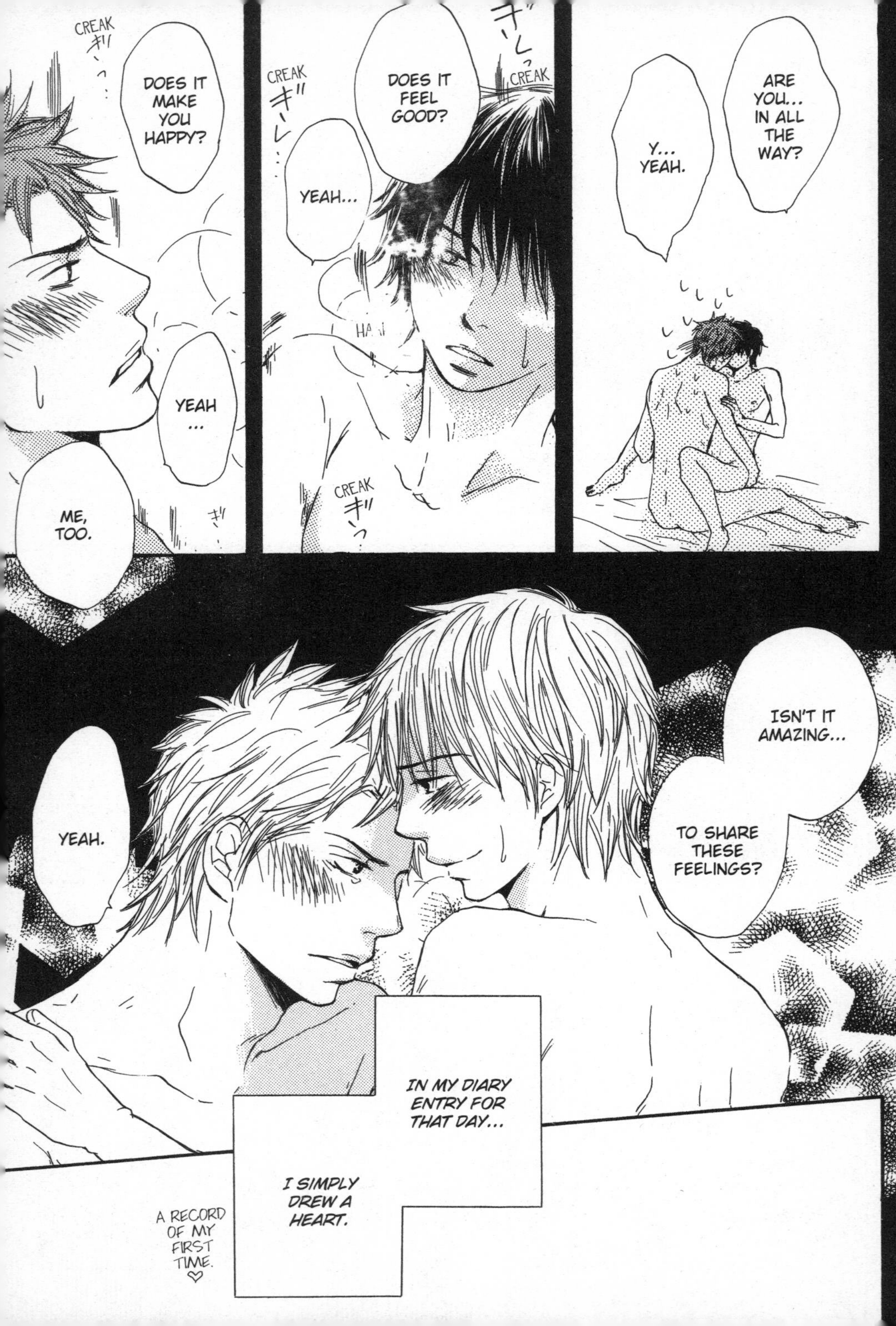
ARE YOU... IN ALL THE WAY?
Y... YEAH.
CREAK
CREAK
DOES IT FEEL GOOD?
YEAH...
CREAK
CREAK
DOES IT MAKE YOU HAPPY?
YEAH ...
ME, TOO.
ISN'T IT AMAZING...
TO SHARE THESE FEELINGS?
YEAH.
IN MY DIARY ENTRY FOR THAT DAY...
I SIMPLY DREW A HEART.
A RECORD OF MY FIRST TIME. ♡

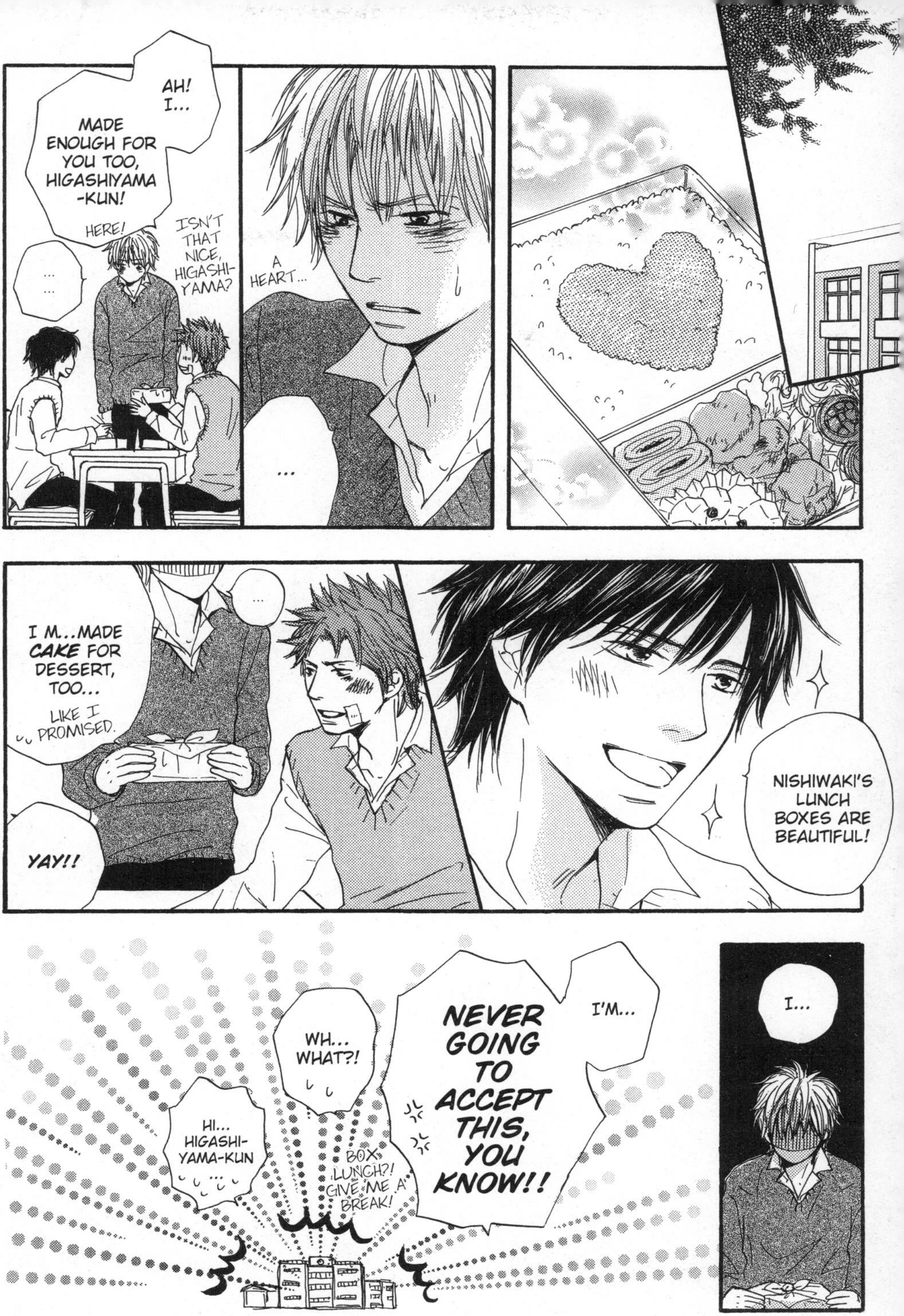
A HEART...
...
AH! I... MADE ENOUGH FOR YOU TOO, HIGASHIYAMA-KUN!
HERE!
ISN'T THAT NICE, HIGASHIYAMA?
... ...
NISHIWAKI'S LUNCH BOXES ARE BEAUTIFUL!
...
I M...MADE CAKE FOR DESSERT, TOO...
LIKE I PROMISED.
YAY!!
I...
I'M...
NEVER GOING TO ACCEPT THIS, YOU KNOW!!
WH... WHAT?!
BOX LUNCH?! GIVE ME A BREAK!
HI... HIGASHI-YAMA-KUN ...

NAIVE LOVE TRIANGLE ● END

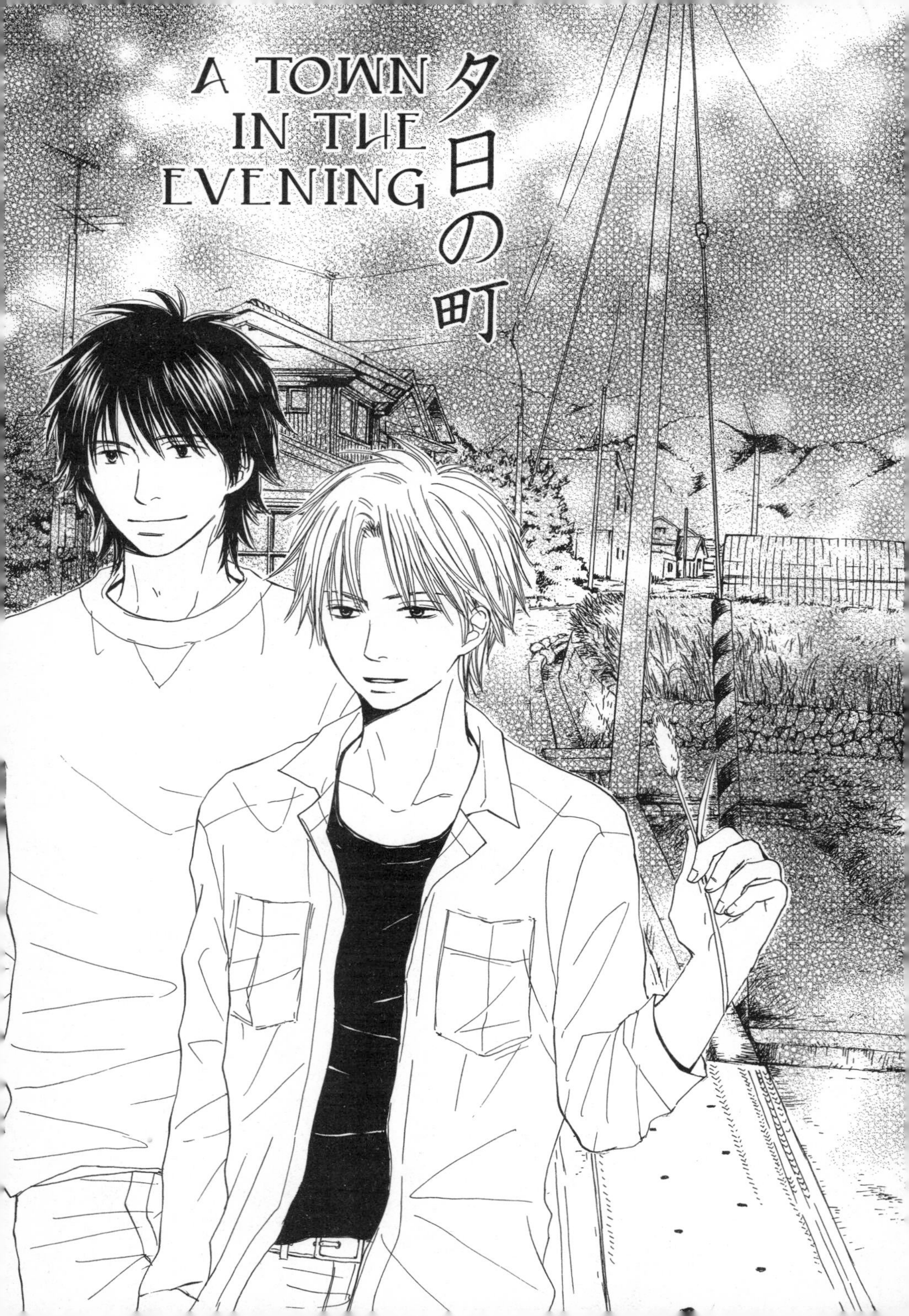
A TOWN IN THE EVENING
夕日の町

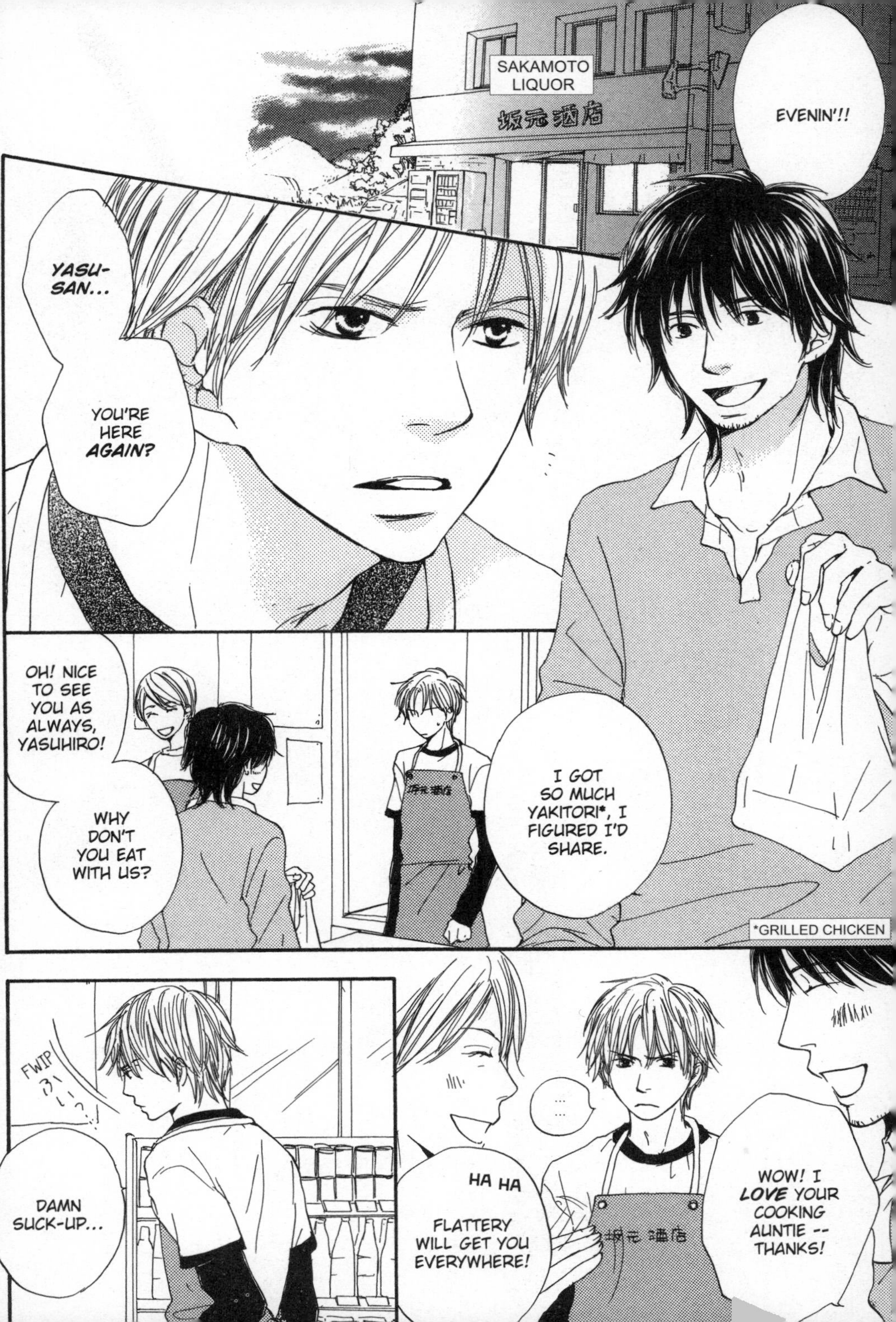
SAKAMOTO LIQUOR
坂元酒店
EVENIN'!!
YASU-SAN...
YOU'RE HERE AGAIN?
I GOT SO MUCH YAKITORI*, I FIGURED I'D SHARE.
*GRILLED CHICKEN
OH! NICE TO SEE YOU AS ALWAYS, YASUHIRO!
WHY DON'T YOU EAT WITH US?
WOW! I LOVE YOUR COOKING AUNTIE -- THANKS!
HA HA
FLATTERY WILL GET YOU EVERYWHERE!
......
FWIP
DAMN SUCK-UP...

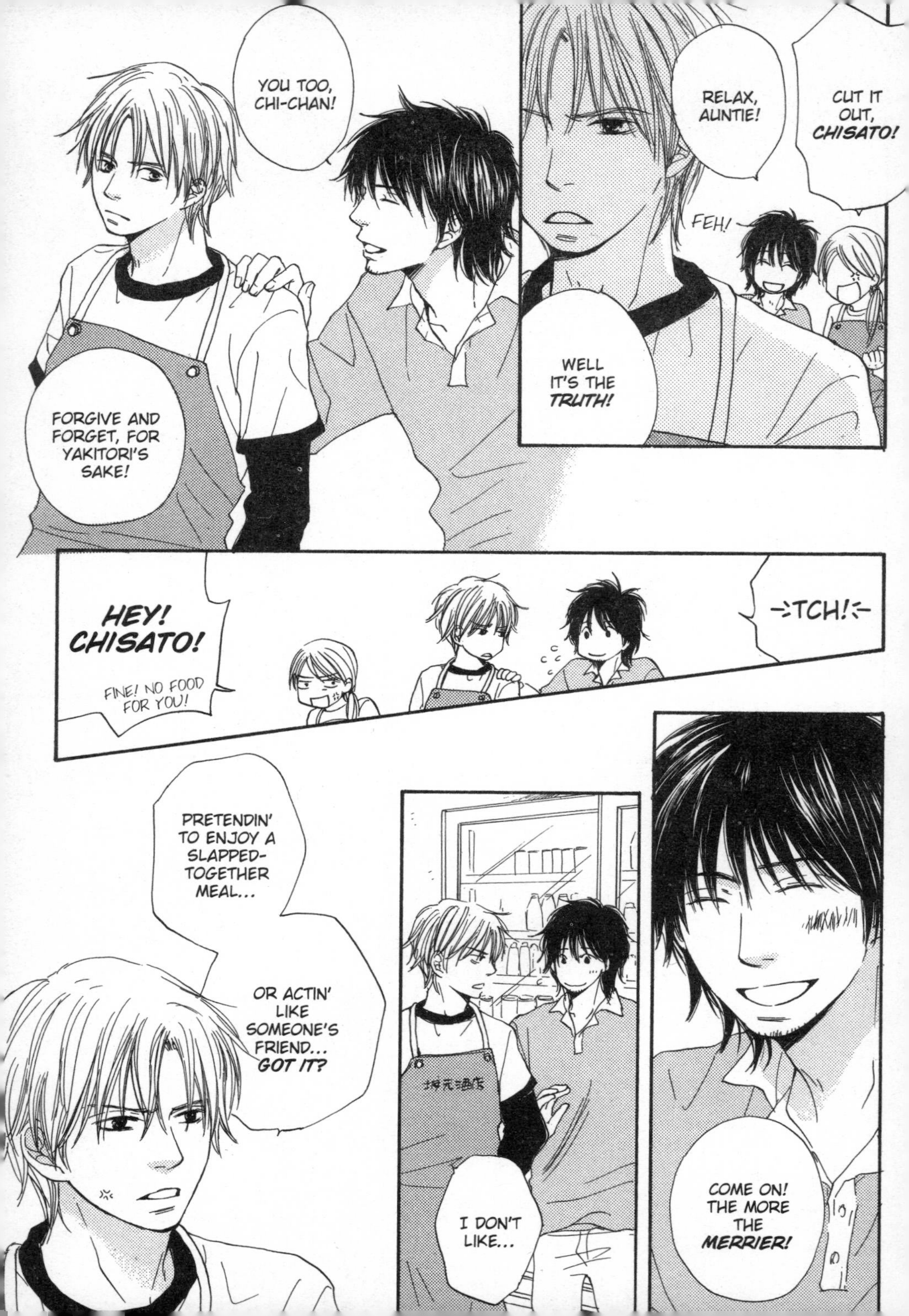
CUT IT OUT, CHISATO!
RELAX, AUNTIE!
FEH!
WELL IT'S THE TRUTH!
YOU TOO, CHI-CHAN!
FORGIVE AND FORGET, FOR YAKITORI'S SAKE!
TCH!
HEY! CHISATO!
FINE! NO FOOD FOR YOU!
COME ON! THE MORE THE MERRIER!
I DON'T LIKE...
PRETENDIN' TO ENJOY A SLAPPED-TOGETHER MEAL...
OR ACTIN' LIKE SOMEONE'S FRIEND... GOT IT?

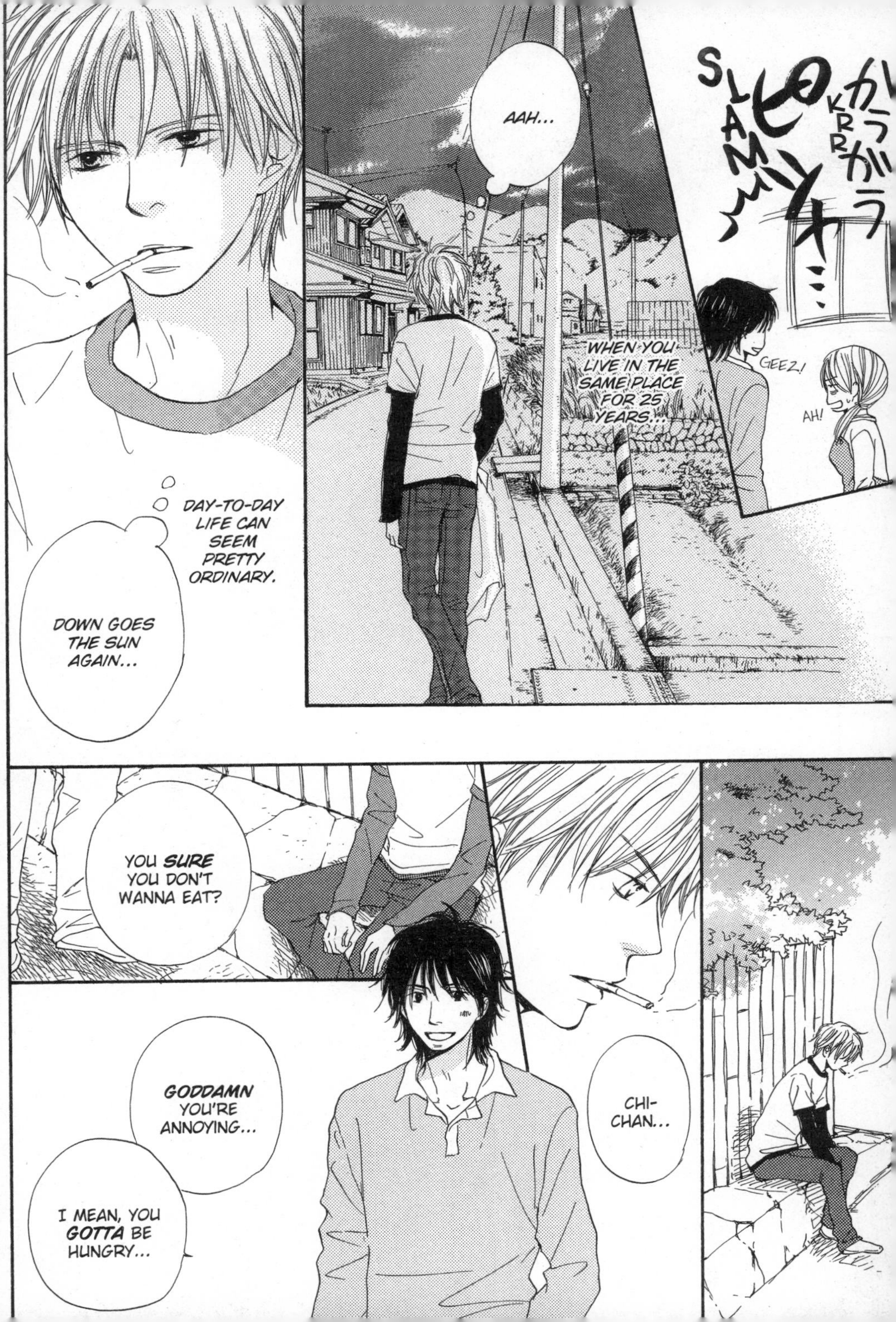
KRR
SLAM
GEEZ!
AH!
AAH...
WHEN YOU LIVE IN THE SAME PLACE FOR 25 YEARS...
DAY-TO-DAY LIFE CAN SEEM PRETTY ORDINARY.
DOWN GOES THE SUN AGAIN...
CHI-CHAN...
YOU **SURE** YOU DON'T WANNA EAT?
GODDAMN YOU'RE ANNOYING...
I MEAN, YOU **GOTTA** BE HUNGRY...

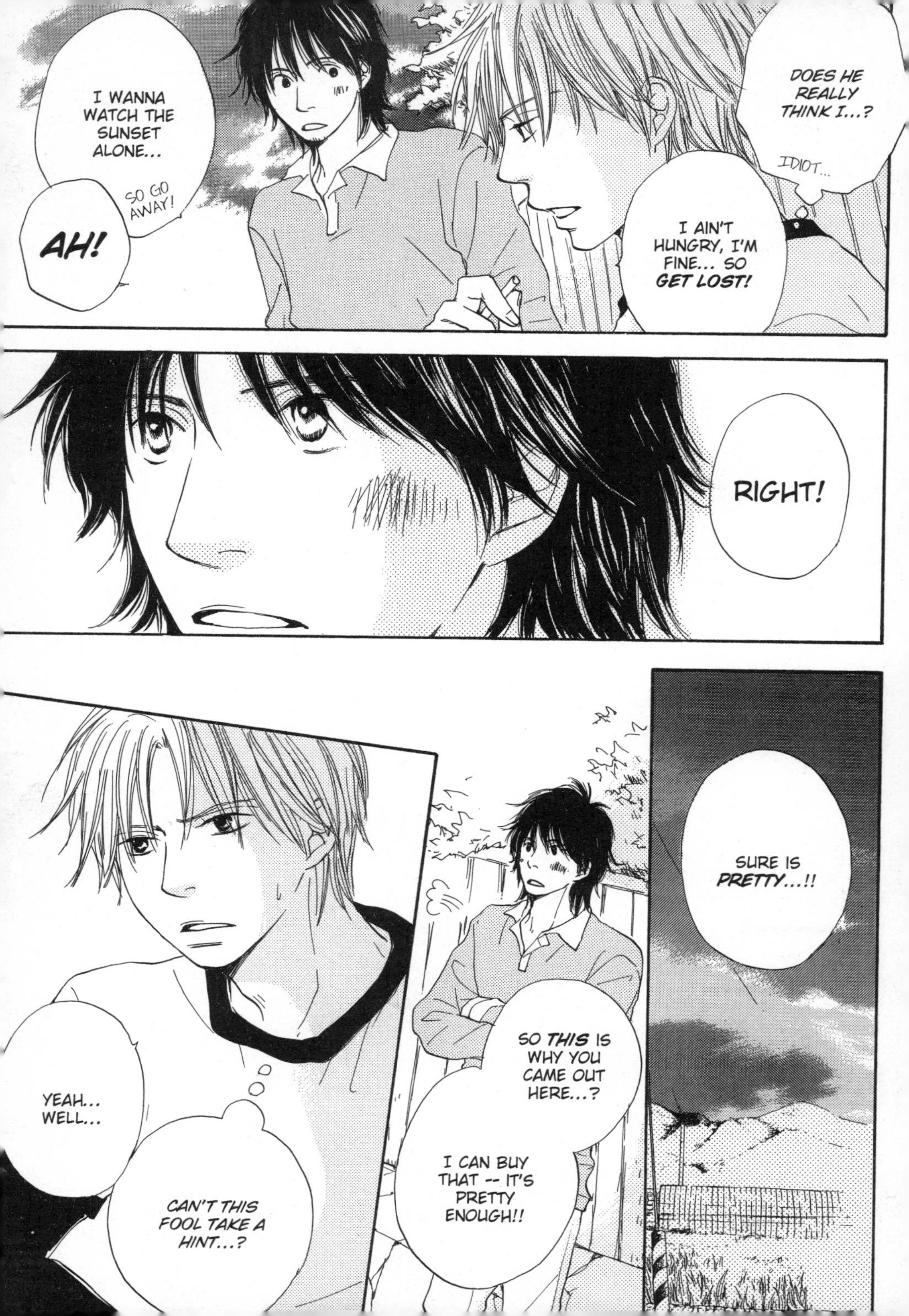
DOES HE REALLY THINK I...?
IDIOT...
I AIN'T HUNGRY, I'M FINE... SO GET LOST!
I WANNA WATCH THE SUNSET ALONE...
SO GO AWAY!
AH!
RIGHT!
SURE IS PRETTY...!!
SO THIS IS WHY YOU CAME OUT HERE...?
I CAN BUY THAT -- IT'S PRETTY ENOUGH!!
YEAH... WELL...
CAN'T THIS FOOL TAKE A HINT...?

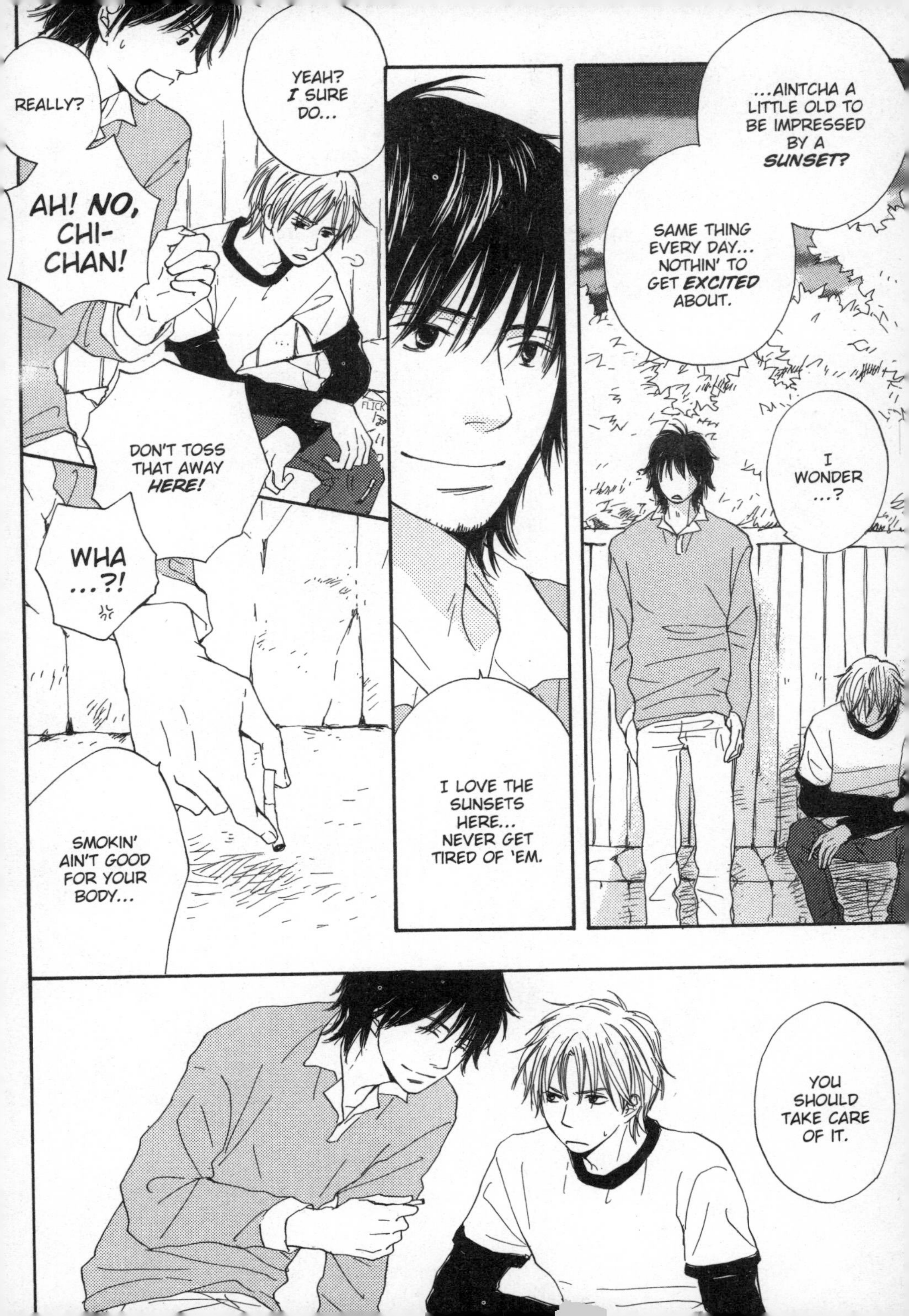
...AINTCHA A LITTLE OLD TO BE IMPRESSED BY A SUNSET?
SAME THING EVERY DAY... NOTHIN' TO GET EXCITED ABOUT.
I WONDER ...?
I LOVE THE SUNSETS HERE... NEVER GET TIRED OF 'EM.
YEAH? I SURE DO...
REALLY?
AH! NO, CHI-CHAN!
FLICK
DON'T TOSS THAT AWAY HERE!
WHA ...?!
SMOKIN' AIN'T GOOD FOR YOUR BODY...
YOU SHOULD TAKE CARE OF IT.

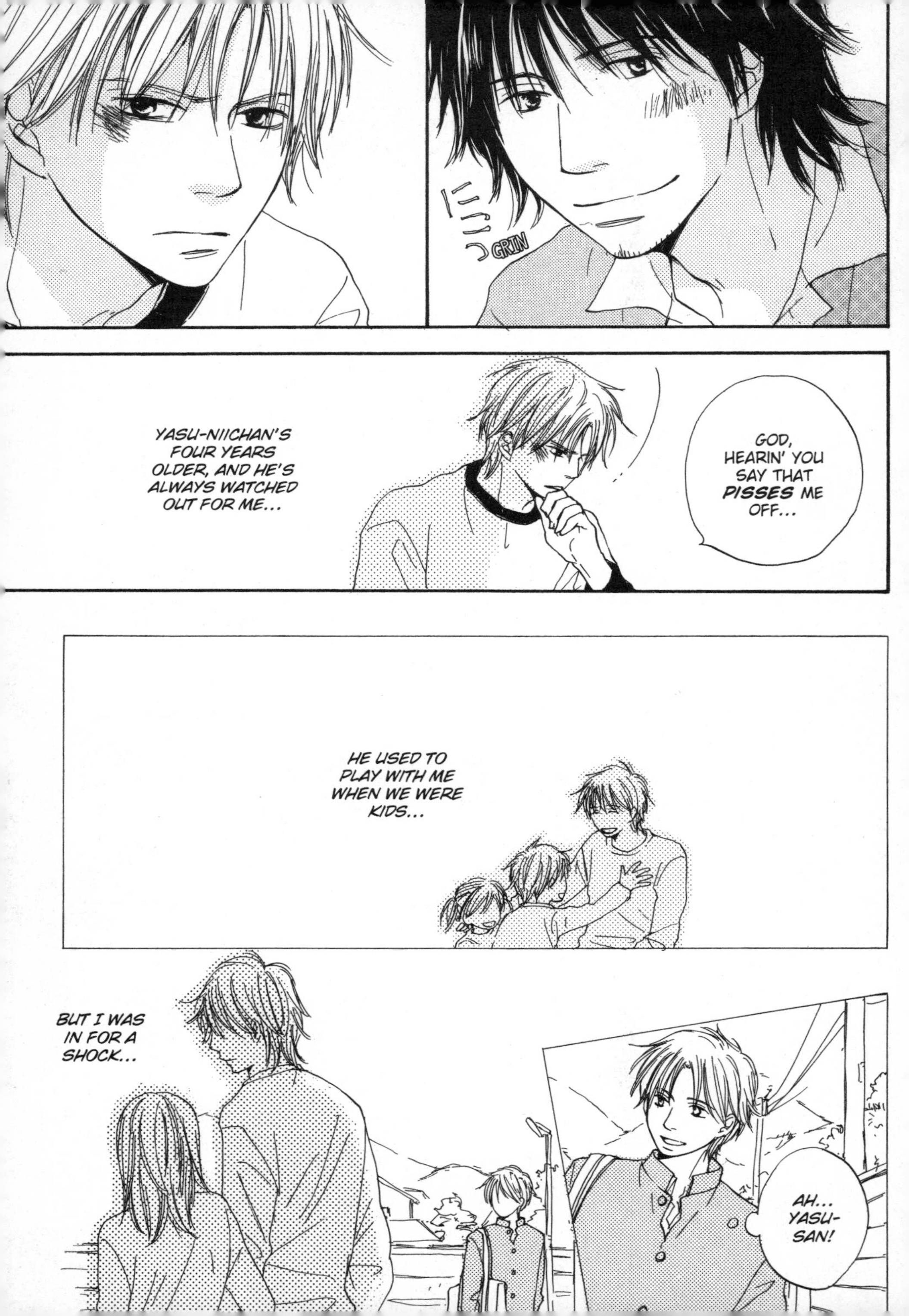
GRIN
GOD, HEARIN' YOU SAY THAT **PISSES** ME OFF...
YASU-NIICHAN'S FOUR YEARS OLDER, AND HE'S ALWAYS WATCHED OUT FOR ME...
HE USED TO PLAY WITH ME WHEN WE WERE KIDS...
AH... YASU-SAN!
BUT I WAS IN FOR A SHOCK...

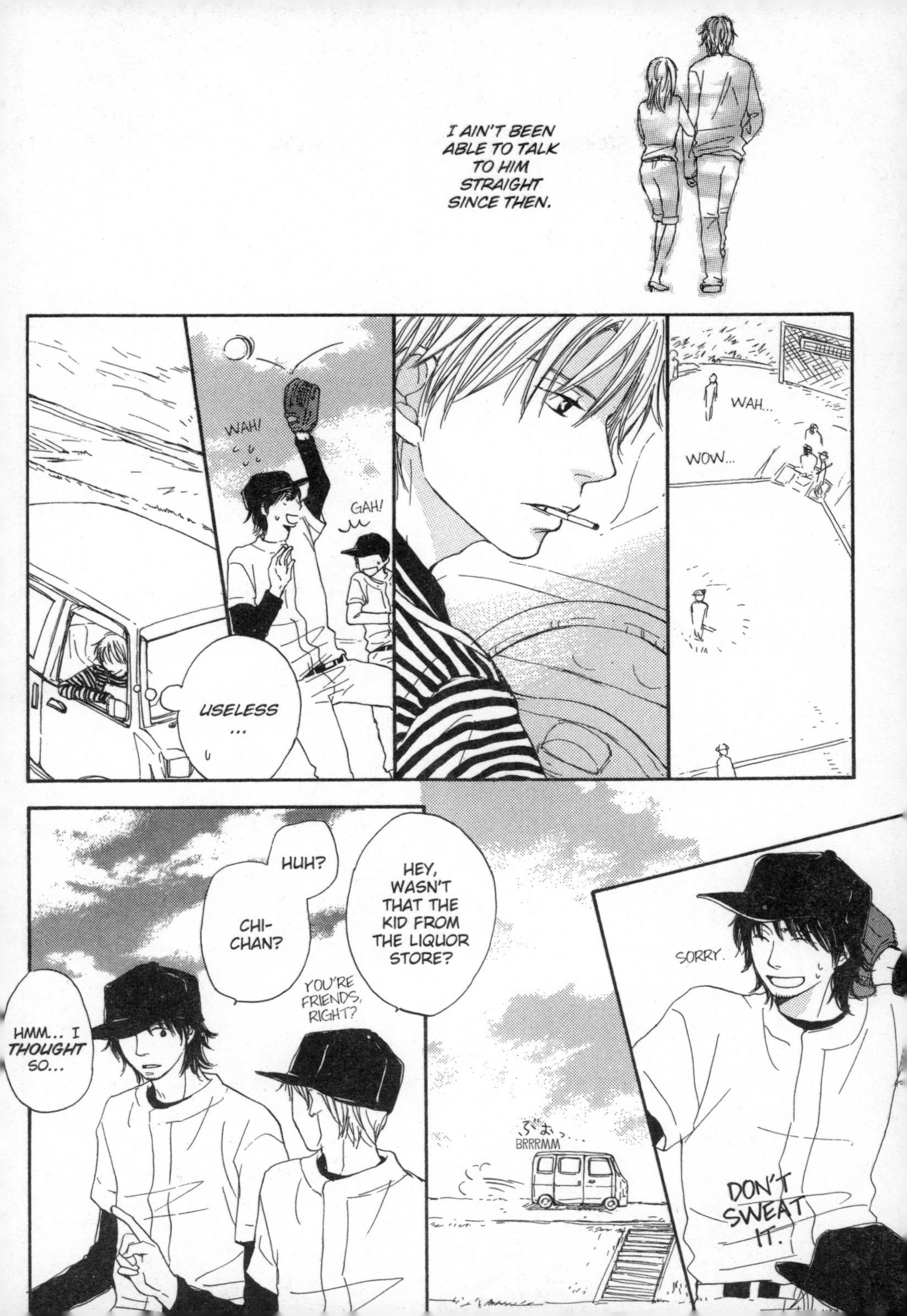
I AIN'T BEEN ABLE TO TALK TO HIM STRAIGHT SINCE THEN.
WAH...
WOW...
WAH!
GAH!
USELESS ...
SORRY.
DON'T SWEAT IT.
ぶおっ...
BRRRMM
HEY, WASN'T THAT THE KID FROM THE LIQUOR STORE?
HUH?
CHI-CHAN?
YOU'RE FRIENDS, RIGHT?
HMM... I THOUGHT SO...

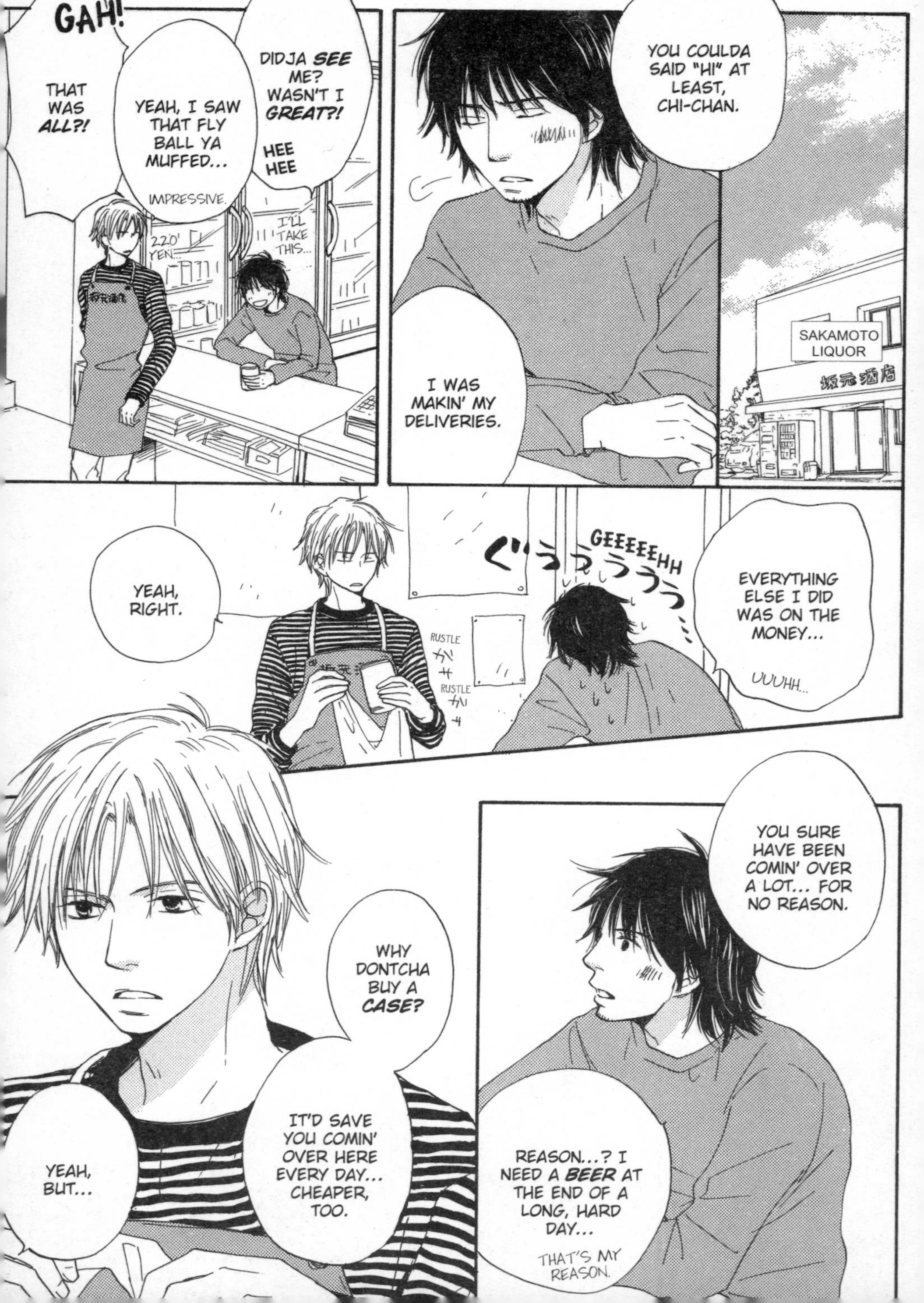
SAKAMOTO LIQUOR
坂元酒店
YOU COULDA SAID "HI" AT LEAST, CHI-CHAN.
I WAS MAKIN' MY DELIVERIES.
DIDJA SEE ME? WASN'T I GREAT?!
HEE HEE
YEAH, I SAW THAT FLY BALL YA MUFFED...
IMPRESSIVE.
I'LL TAKE THIS...
220 YEN...
GAH!
THAT WAS ALL?!
GEEEEEEHH
EVERYTHING ELSE I DID WAS ON THE MONEY...
UUUHH...
RUSTLE
RUSTLE
YEAH, RIGHT.
YOU SURE HAVE BEEN COMIN' OVER A LOT... FOR NO REASON.
REASON...? I NEED A BEER AT THE END OF A LONG, HARD DAY...
THAT'S MY REASON.
WHY DONTCHA BUY A CASE?
IT'D SAVE YOU COMIN' OVER HERE EVERY DAY... CHEAPER, TOO.
YEAH, BUT...

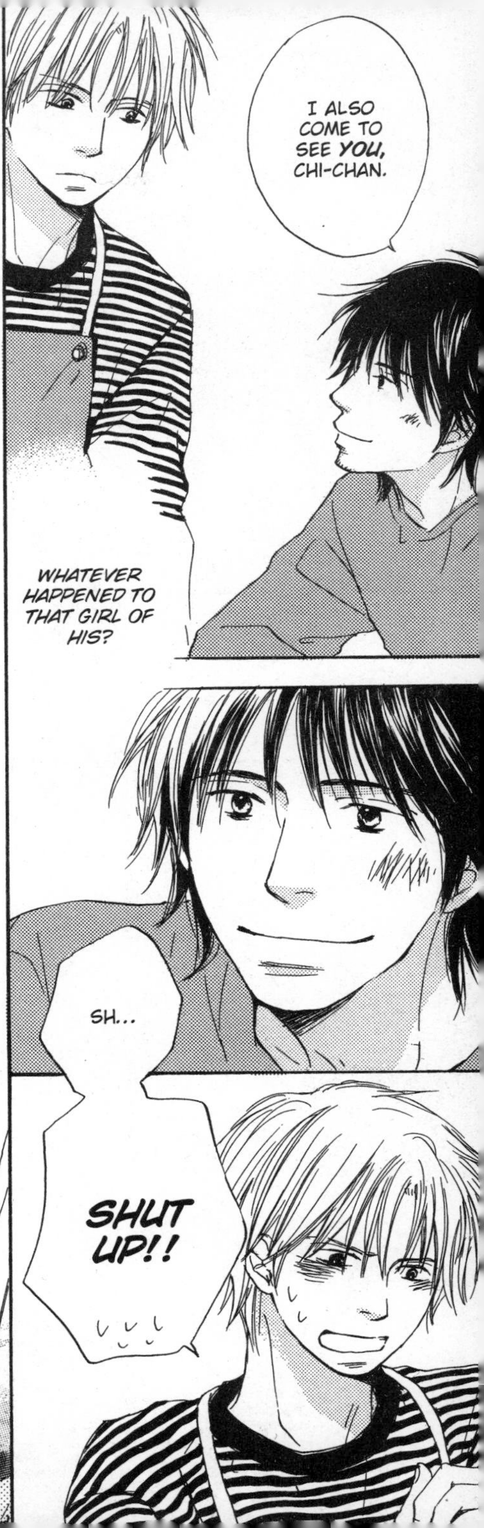
I ALSO COME TO SEE *YOU*, CHI-CHAN.
WHATEVER HAPPENED TO THAT GIRL OF HIS?
SH...
SHUT UP!!

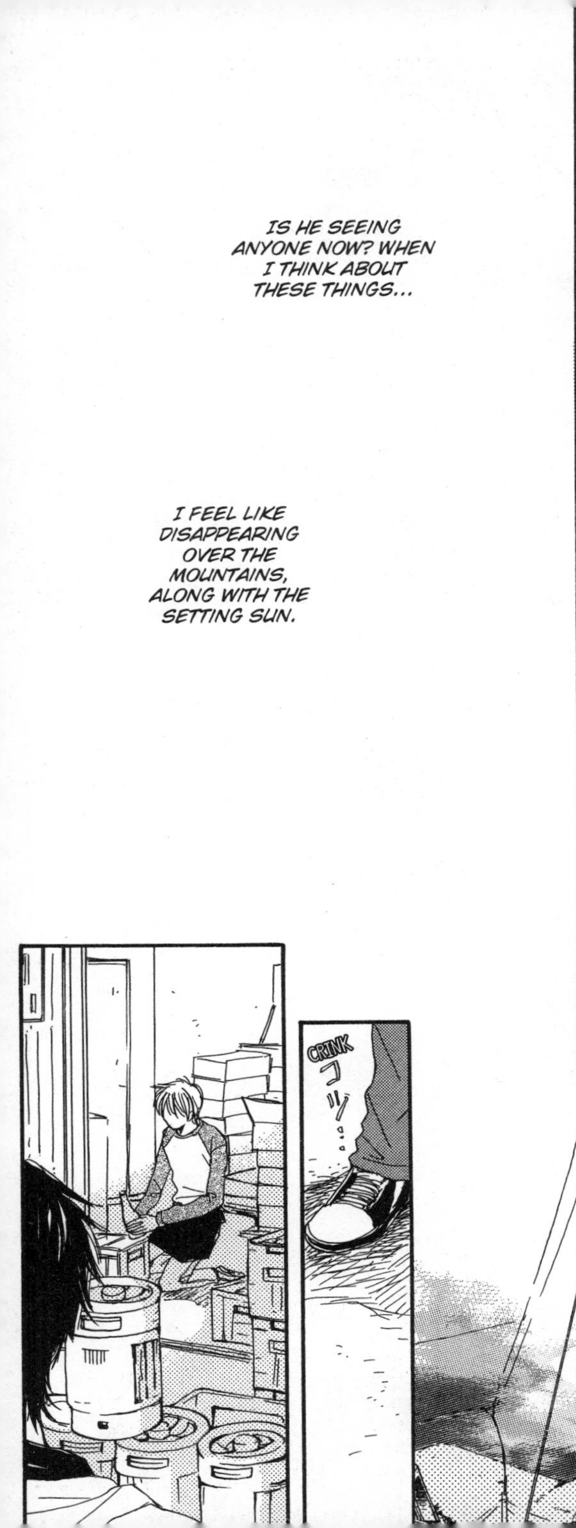
IS HE SEEING ANYONE NOW? WHEN I THINK ABOUT THESE THINGS...
I FEEL LIKE DISAPPEARING OVER THE MOUNTAINS, ALONG WITH THE SETTING SUN.
CRINK
コツ

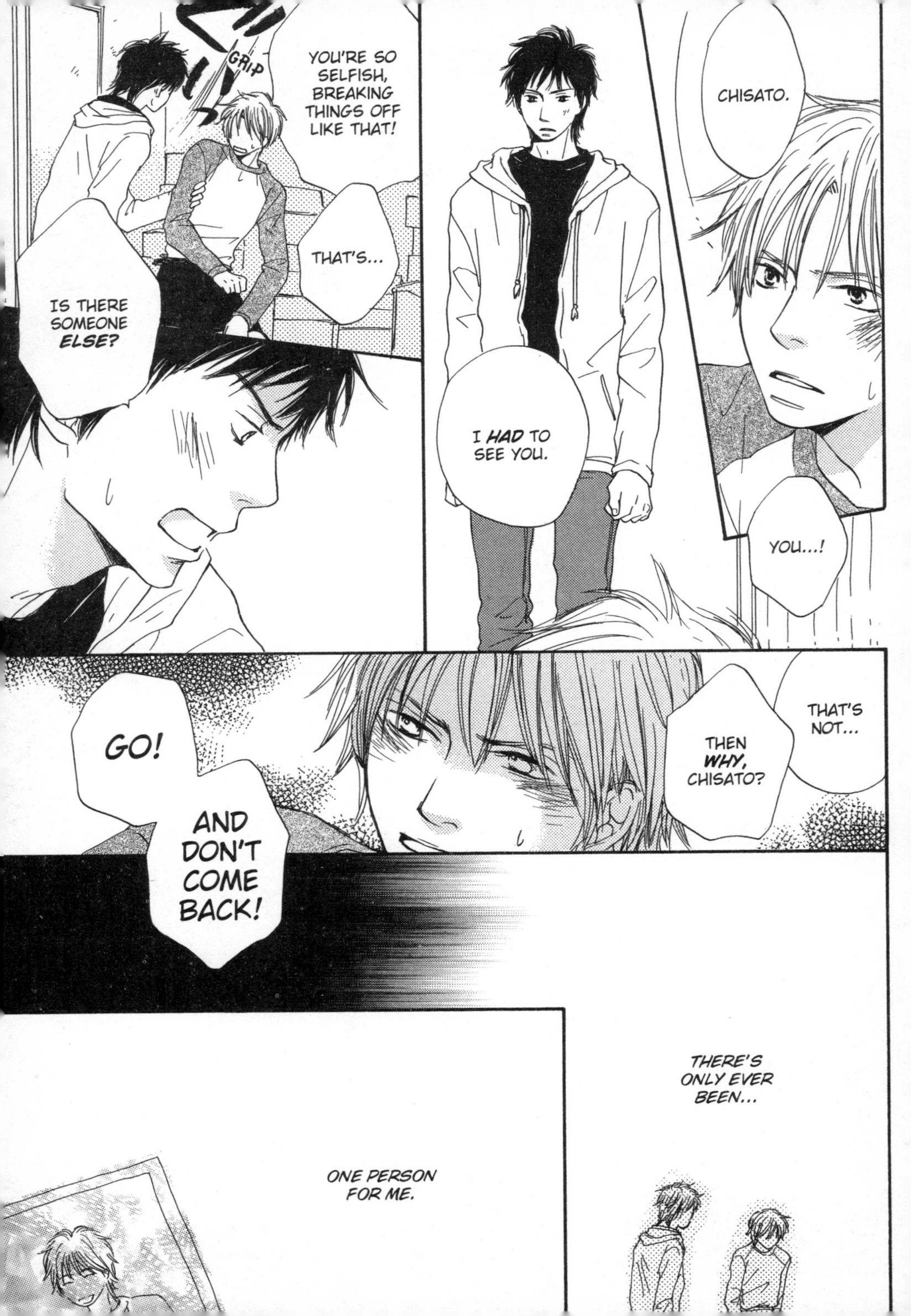
CHISATO.
YOU...!
I HAD TO SEE YOU.
YOU'RE SO SELFISH, BREAKING THINGS OFF LIKE THAT!
GRIP
THAT'S...
IS THERE SOMEONE ELSE?
THAT'S NOT...
THEN WHY, CHISATO?
GO!
AND DON'T COME BACK!
THERE'S ONLY EVER BEEN...
ONE PERSON FOR ME.

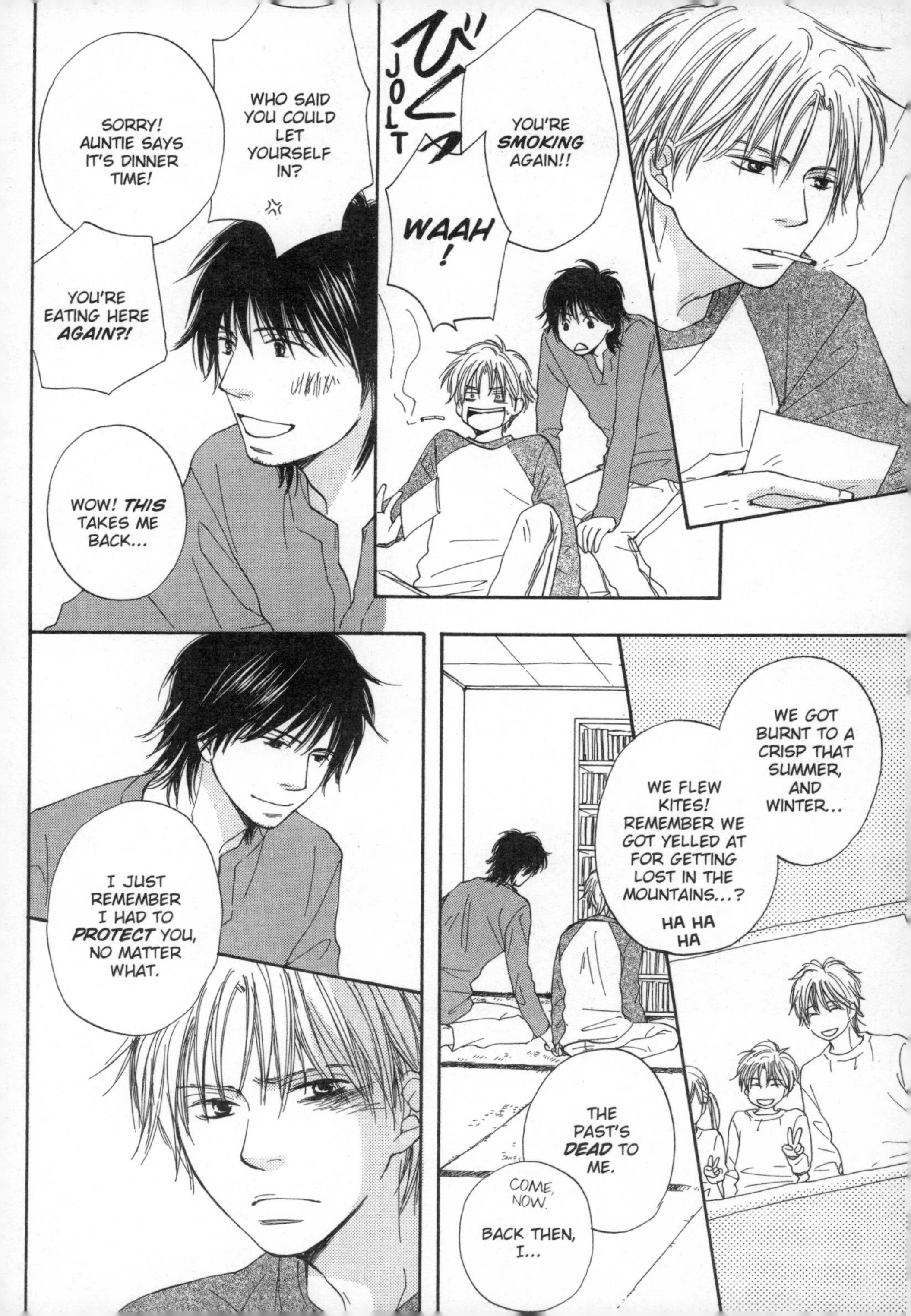
JOLT
YOU'RE SMOKING AGAIN!!
WAAH!
WHO SAID YOU COULD LET YOURSELF IN?
SORRY! AUNTIE SAYS IT'S DINNER TIME!
YOU'RE EATING HERE AGAIN?!
WOW! THIS TAKES ME BACK...
WE GOT BURNT TO A CRISP THAT SUMMER, AND WINTER...
WE FLEW KITES! REMEMBER WE GOT YELLED AT FOR GETTING LOST IN THE MOUNTAINS...?
HA HA HA
THE PAST'S DEAD TO ME.
COME, NOW.
BACK THEN, I...
I JUST REMEMBER I HAD TO PROTECT YOU, NO MATTER WHAT.

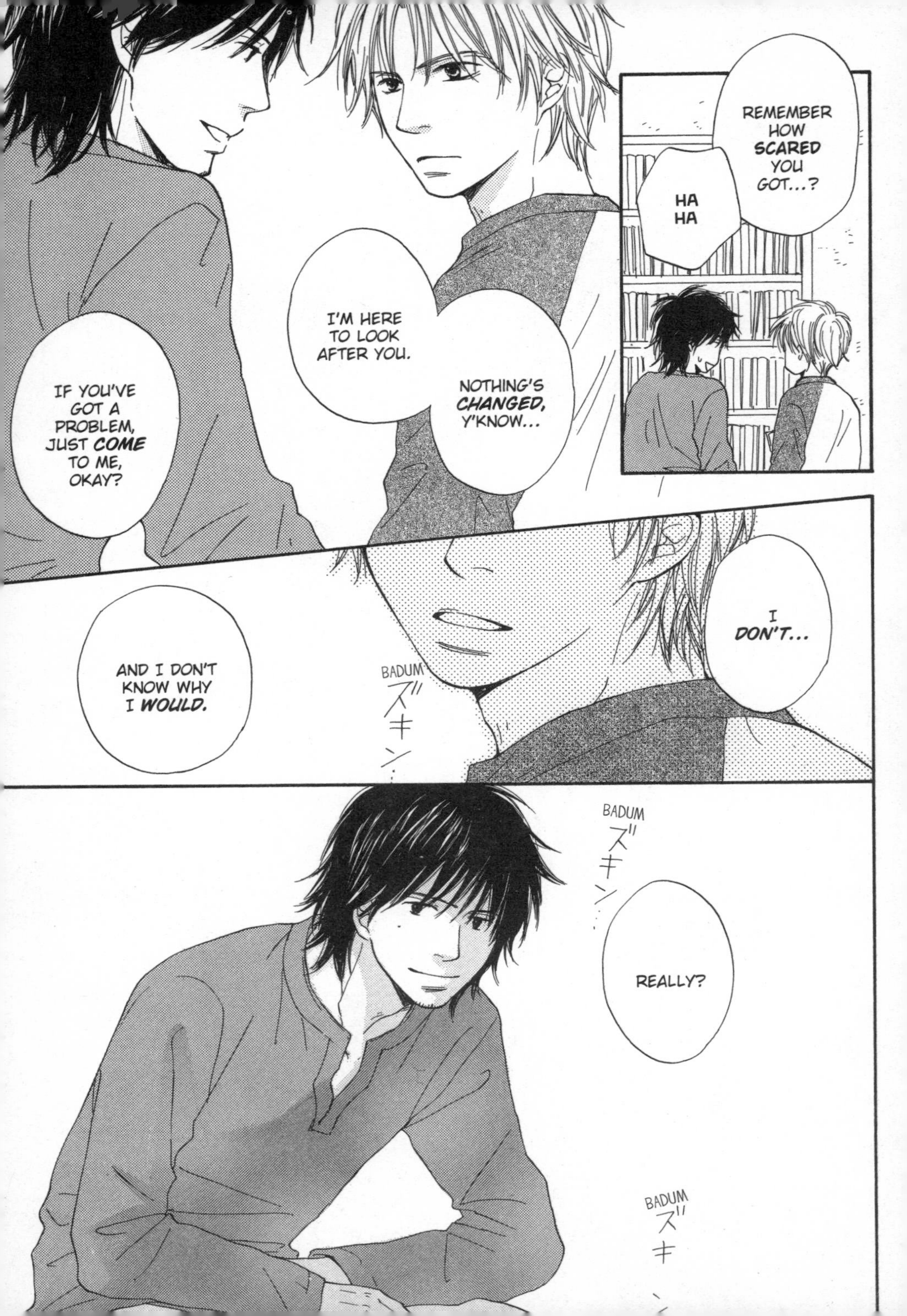
REMEMBER HOW **SCARED** YOU GOT...?
HA HA
I'M HERE TO LOOK AFTER YOU.
NOTHING'S ***CHANGED,*** Y'KNOW...
IF YOU'VE GOT A PROBLEM, JUST ***COME*** TO ME, OKAY?
I ***DON'T...***
BADUM
ズキン
AND I DON'T KNOW WHY I ***WOULD.***
BADUM
ズキン
REALLY?
BADUM
ズキ

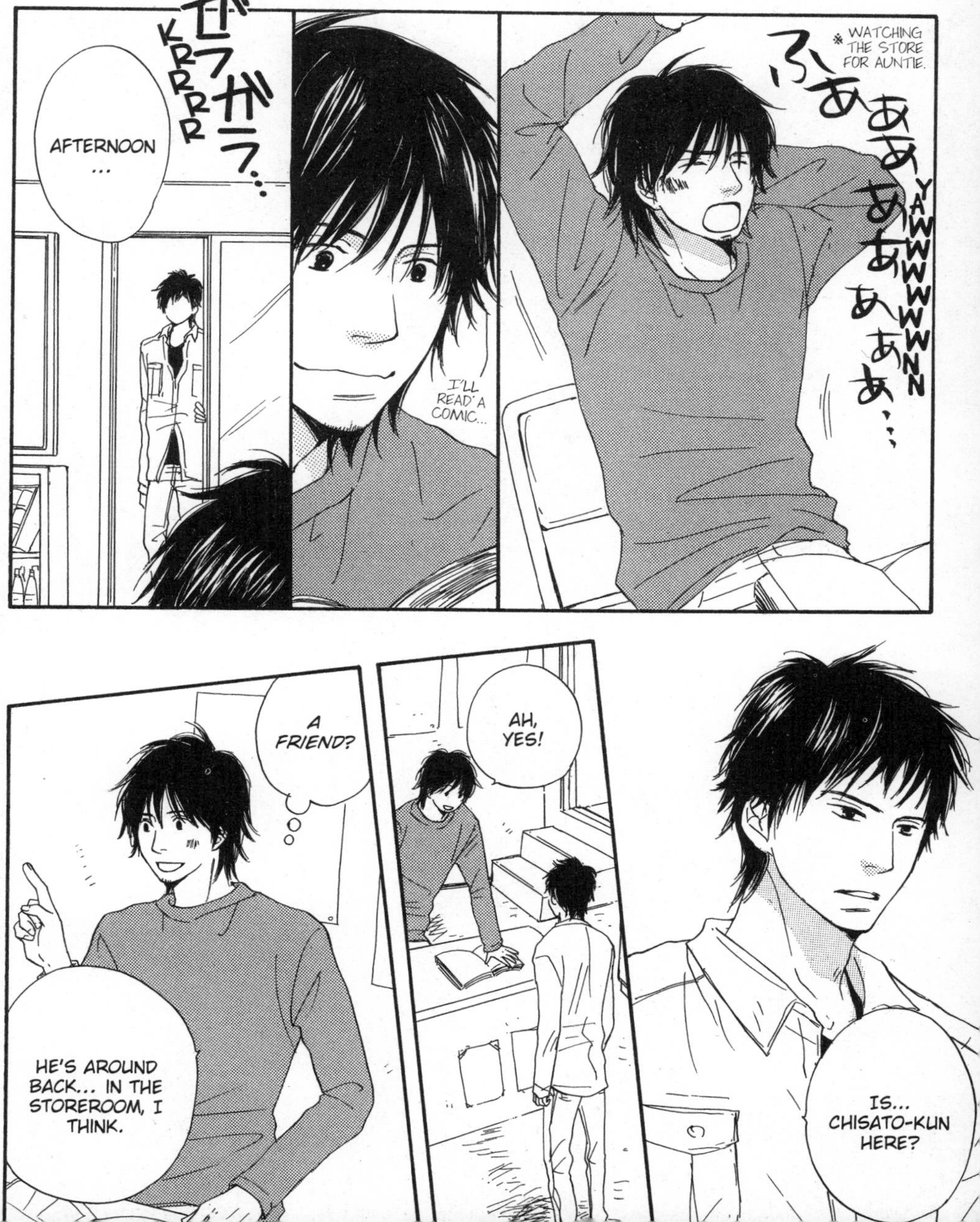
※WATCHING THE STORE FOR AUNTIE.
ふあああああああ…
YAWWWWWWWN
I'LL READ A COMIC...
ガラガラ…
KRRRR
AFTERNOON ...
IS... CHISATO-KUN HERE?
AH, YES!
A FRIEND?
HE'S AROUND BACK... IN THE STOREROOM, I THINK.

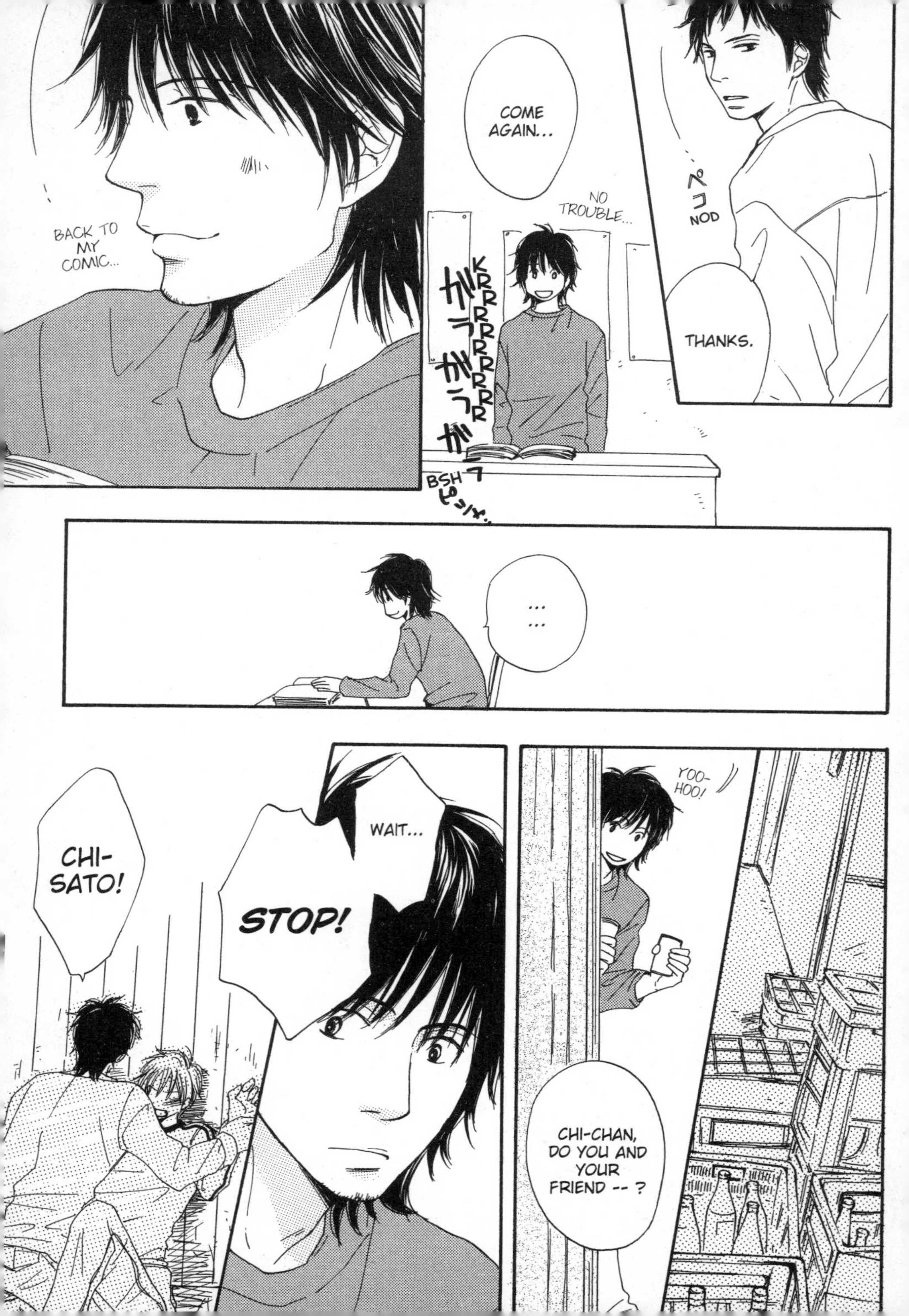
ペコ
NOD
THANKS.
COME AGAIN...
NO TROUBLE...
KRRRRRRRRR
BSH
BACK TO MY COMIC...
......
YOO-HOO!
CHI-CHAN, DO YOU AND YOUR FRIEND -- ?
WAIT...
STOP!
CHI-SATO!

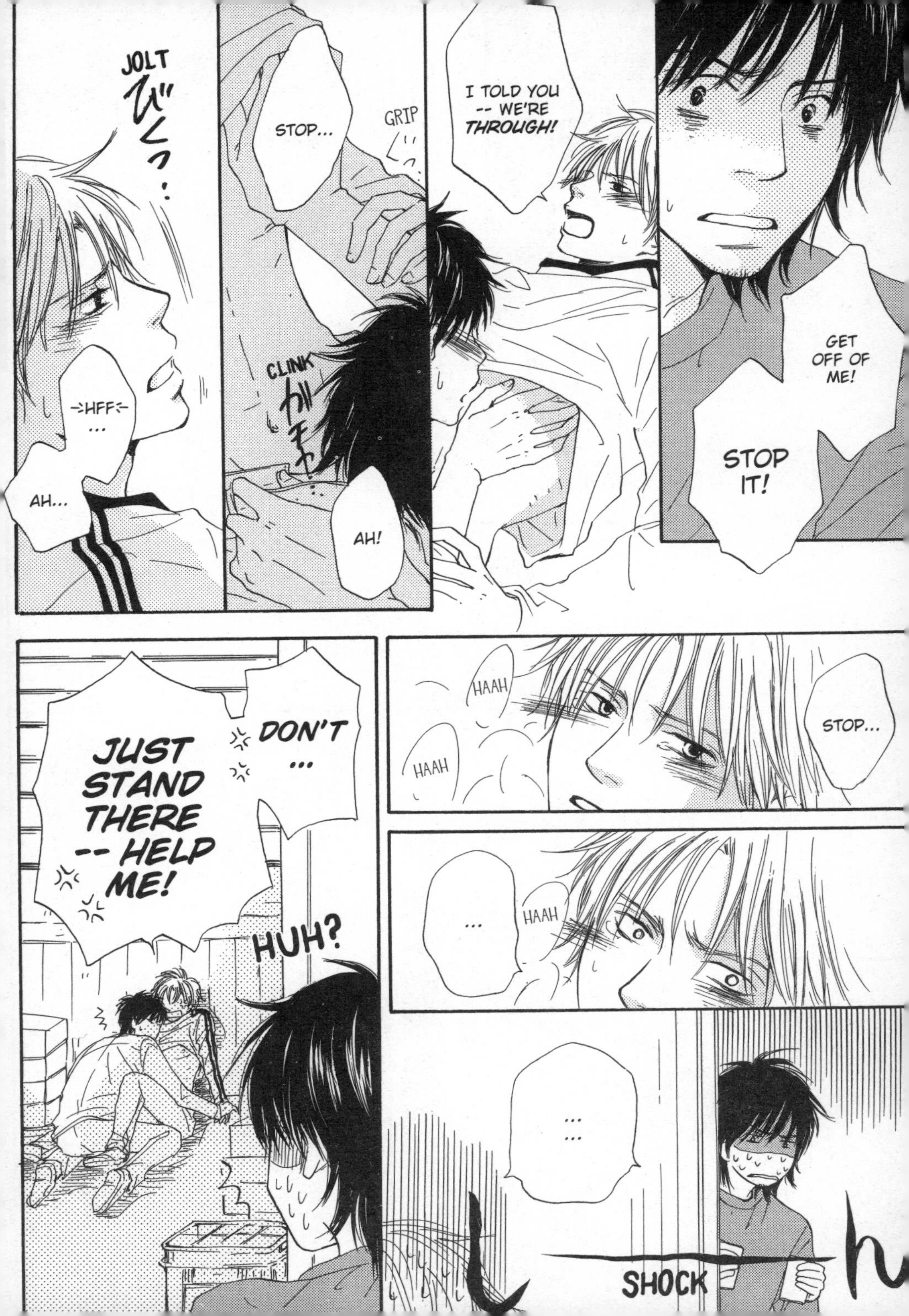
GET OFF OF ME!
STOP IT!
I TOLD YOU -- WE'RE THROUGH!
STOP...
GRIP
CLINK
AH!
JOLT
HFF ...
AH...
HAAH
HAAH
STOP...
...
HAAH
... ...
SHOCK
DON'T ...
JUST STAND THERE -- HELP ME!
HUH?

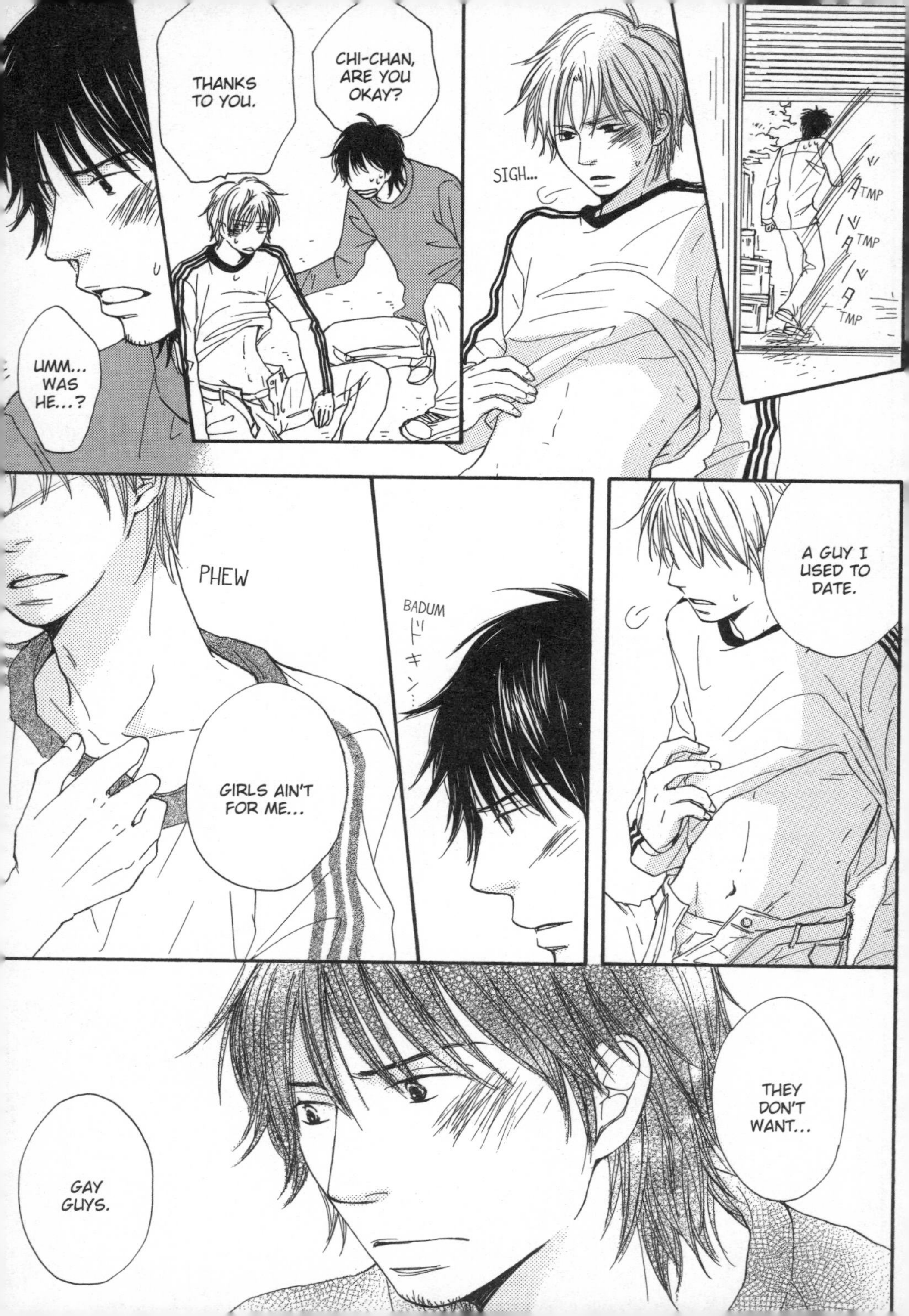
TMP
TMP
TMP
SIGH...
CHI-CHAN, ARE YOU OKAY?
THANKS TO YOU.
UMM... WAS HE...?
A GUY I USED TO DATE.
BADUM
ドキン…
PHEW
GIRLS AIN'T FOR ME...
THEY DON'T WANT...
GAY GUYS.

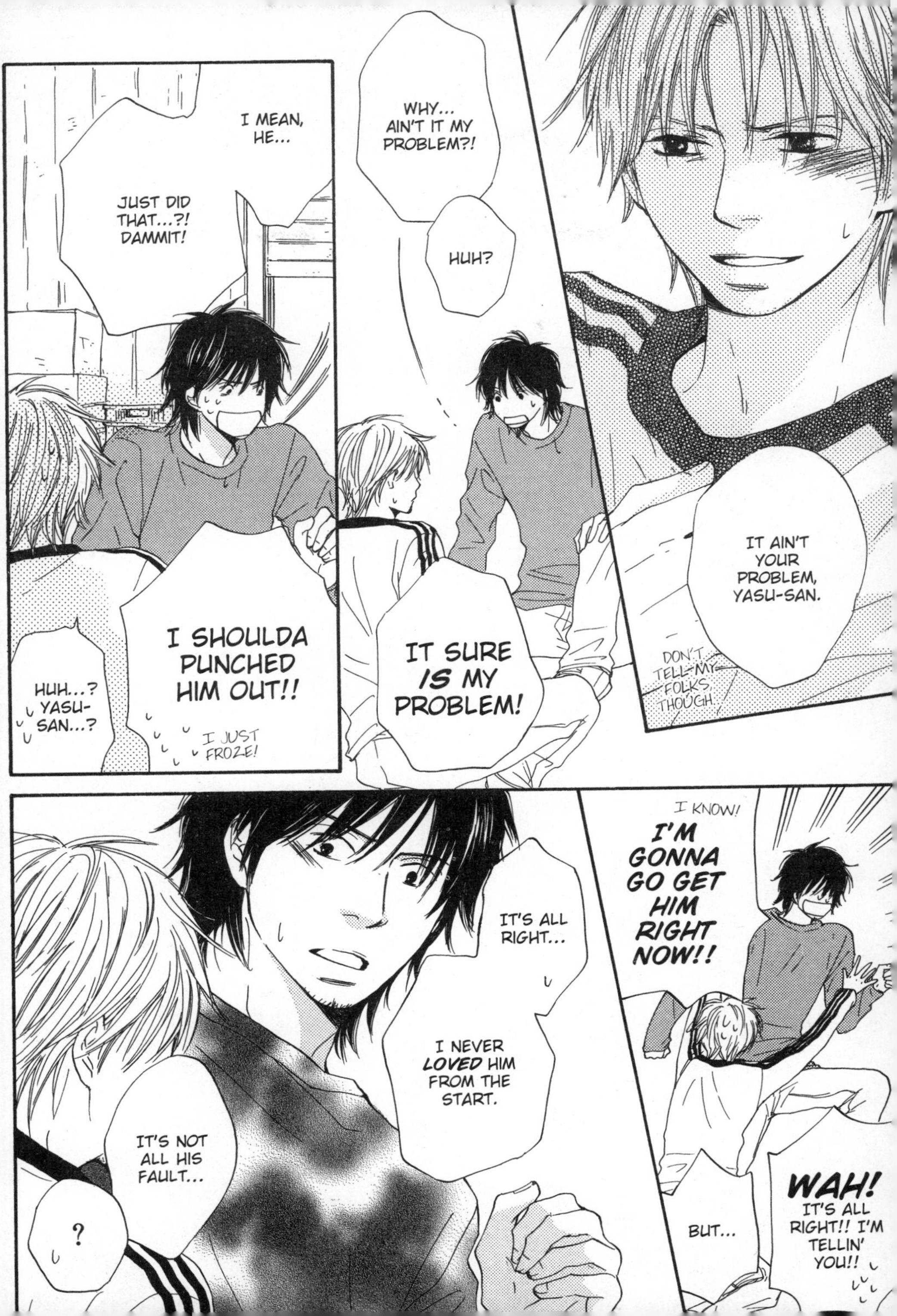
IT AIN'T YOUR PROBLEM, YASU-SAN.
DON'T TELL MY FOLKS, THOUGH.
WHY... AIN'T IT MY PROBLEM?!
HUH?
IT SURE *IS* MY PROBLEM!
I MEAN, HE...
JUST DID THAT...?! DAMMIT!
I SHOULDA PUNCHED HIM OUT!!
I JUST FROZE!
HUH...? YASU-SAN...?
I KNOW!
I'M GONNA GO GET HIM RIGHT NOW!!
WAH! IT'S ALL RIGHT!! I'M TELLIN' YOU!!
BUT...
IT'S ALL RIGHT...
I NEVER *LOVED* HIM FROM THE START.
IT'S NOT ALL HIS FAULT...
?

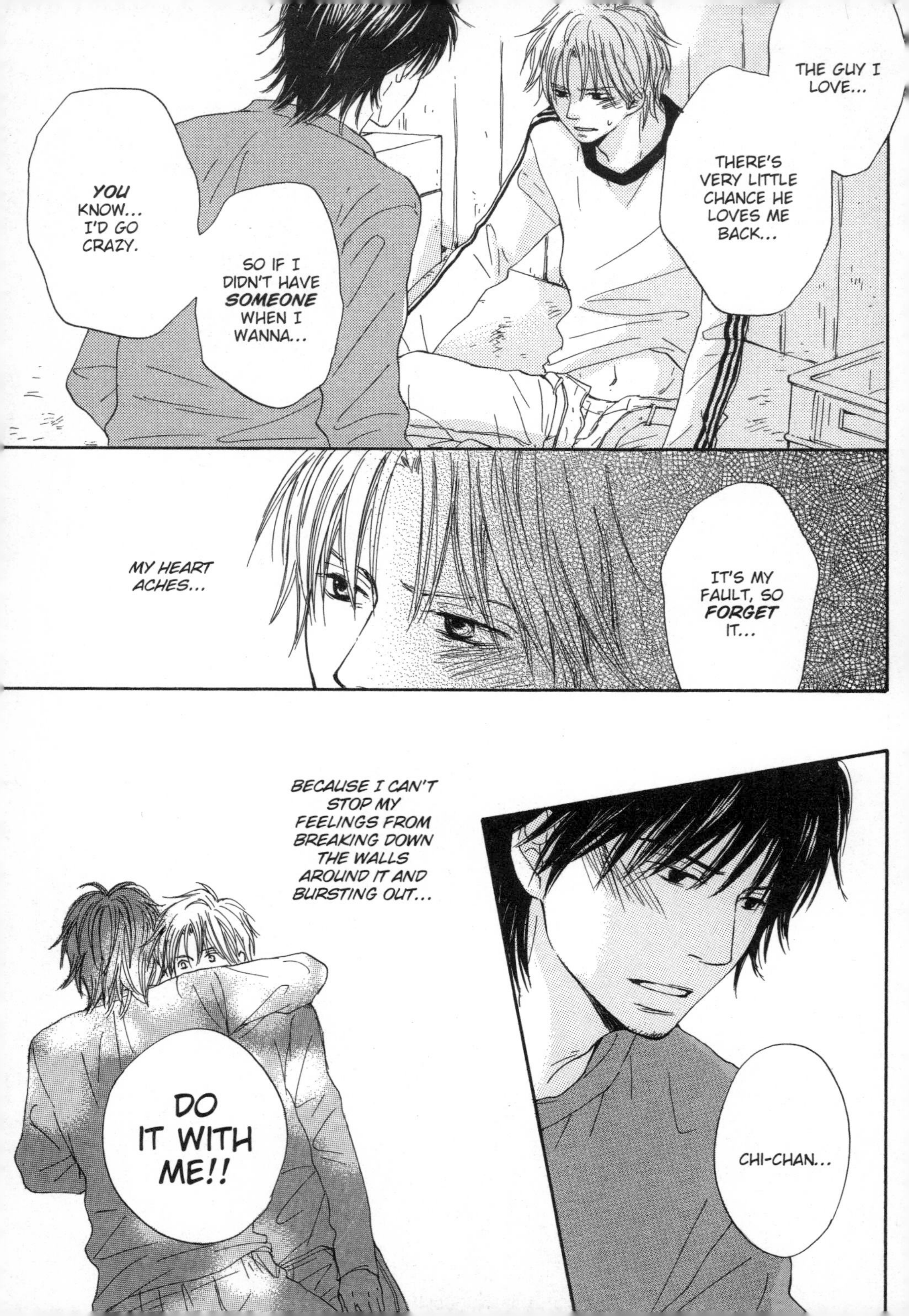
THE GUY I LOVE...
THERE'S VERY LITTLE CHANCE HE LOVES ME BACK...
SO IF I DIDN'T HAVE **SOMEONE** WHEN I WANNA...
YOU KNOW... I'D GO CRAZY.
IT'S MY FAULT, SO ***FORGET*** IT...
MY HEART ACHES...
CHI-CHAN...
BECAUSE I CAN'T STOP MY FEELINGS FROM BREAKING DOWN THE WALLS AROUND IT AND BURSTING OUT...
DO IT WITH ME!!

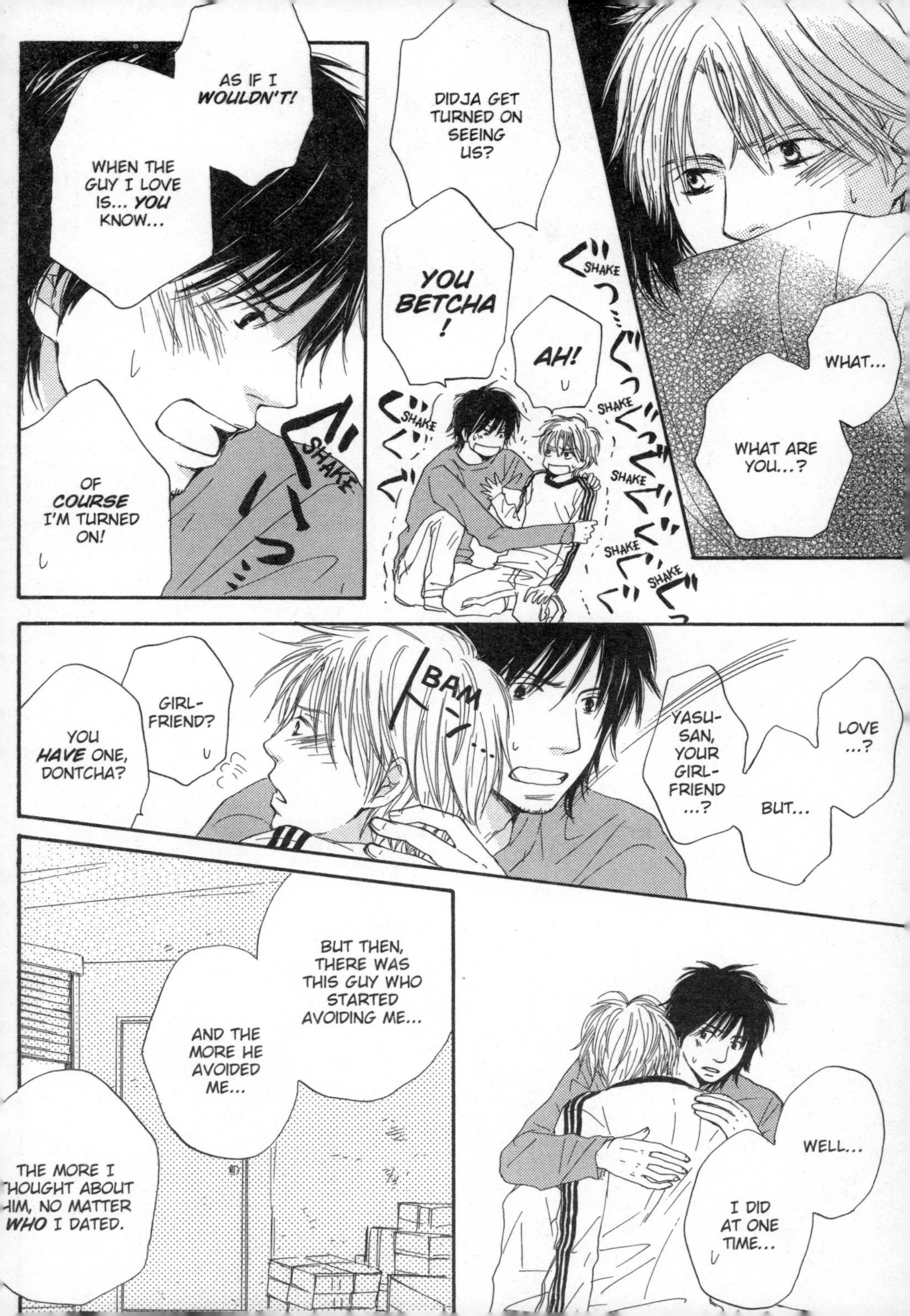
WHAT...
WHAT ARE YOU...?
DIDJA GET TURNED ON SEEING US?
YOU BETCHA!
AH!
SHAKE
SHAKE
SHAKE
SHAKE
SHAKE
SHAKE
AS IF I WOULDN'T!
WHEN THE GUY I LOVE IS... YOU KNOW...
SHAKE
OF COURSE I'M TURNED ON!
LOVE...?
BUT...
YASU-SAN, YOUR GIRL-FRIEND...?
BAM
GIRL-FRIEND?
YOU HAVE ONE, DONTCHA?
WELL...
I DID AT ONE TIME...
BUT THEN, THERE WAS THIS GUY WHO STARTED AVOIDING ME...
AND THE MORE HE AVOIDED ME...
THE MORE I THOUGHT ABOUT HIM, NO MATTER WHO I DATED.

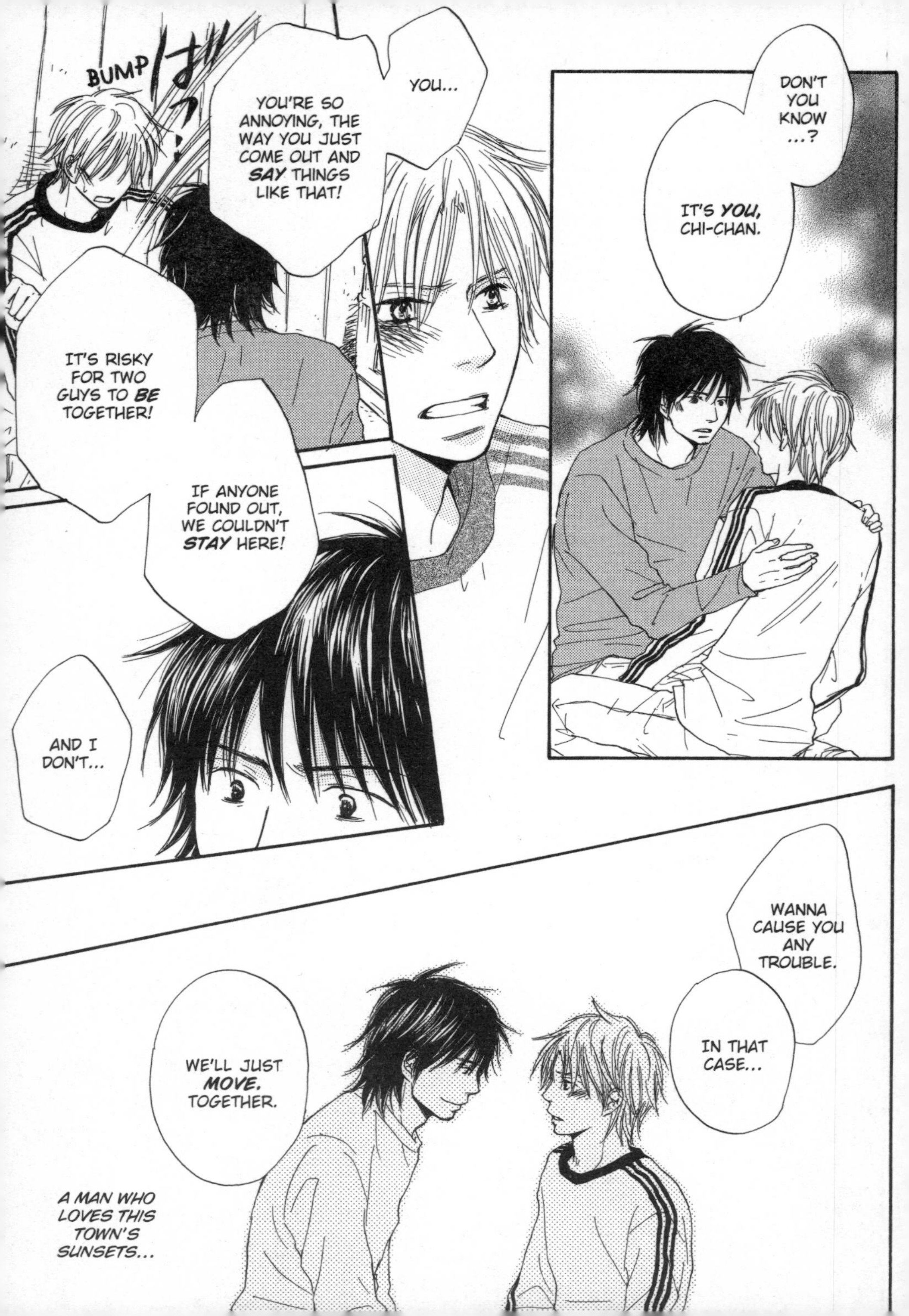
DON'T YOU KNOW ...?
IT'S YOU, CHI-CHAN.
BUMP
ばッ
YOU...
YOU'RE SO ANNOYING, THE WAY YOU JUST COME OUT AND SAY THINGS LIKE THAT!
IT'S RISKY FOR TWO GUYS TO BE TOGETHER!
IF ANYONE FOUND OUT, WE COULDN'T STAY HERE!
AND I DON'T...
WANNA CAUSE YOU ANY TROUBLE.
IN THAT CASE...
WE'LL JUST MOVE. TOGETHER.
A MAN WHO LOVES THIS TOWN'S SUNSETS...

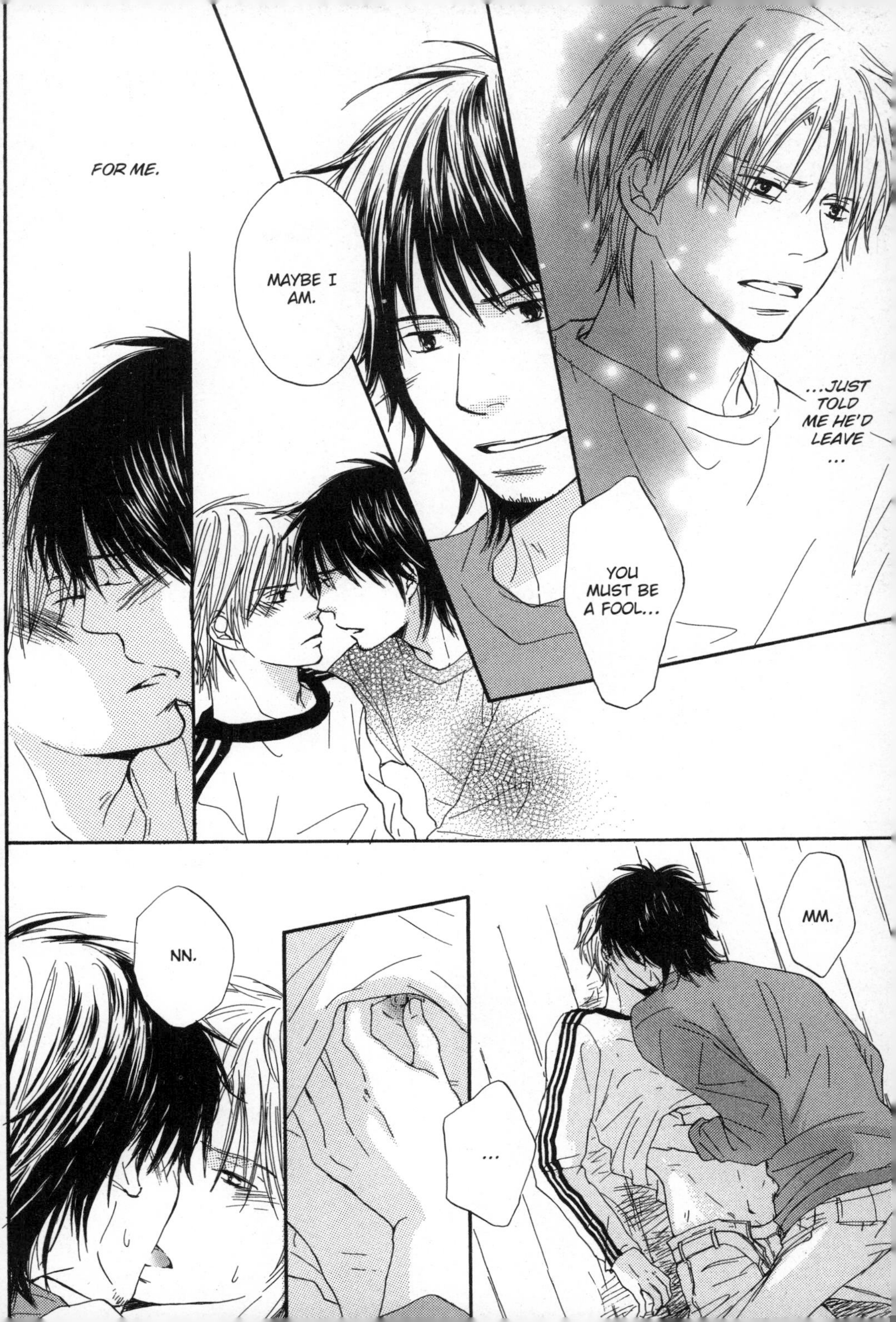

...JUST TOLD ME HE'D LEAVE ...
YOU MUST BE A FOOL...
MAYBE I AM.
FOR ME.
MM.
...
NN.

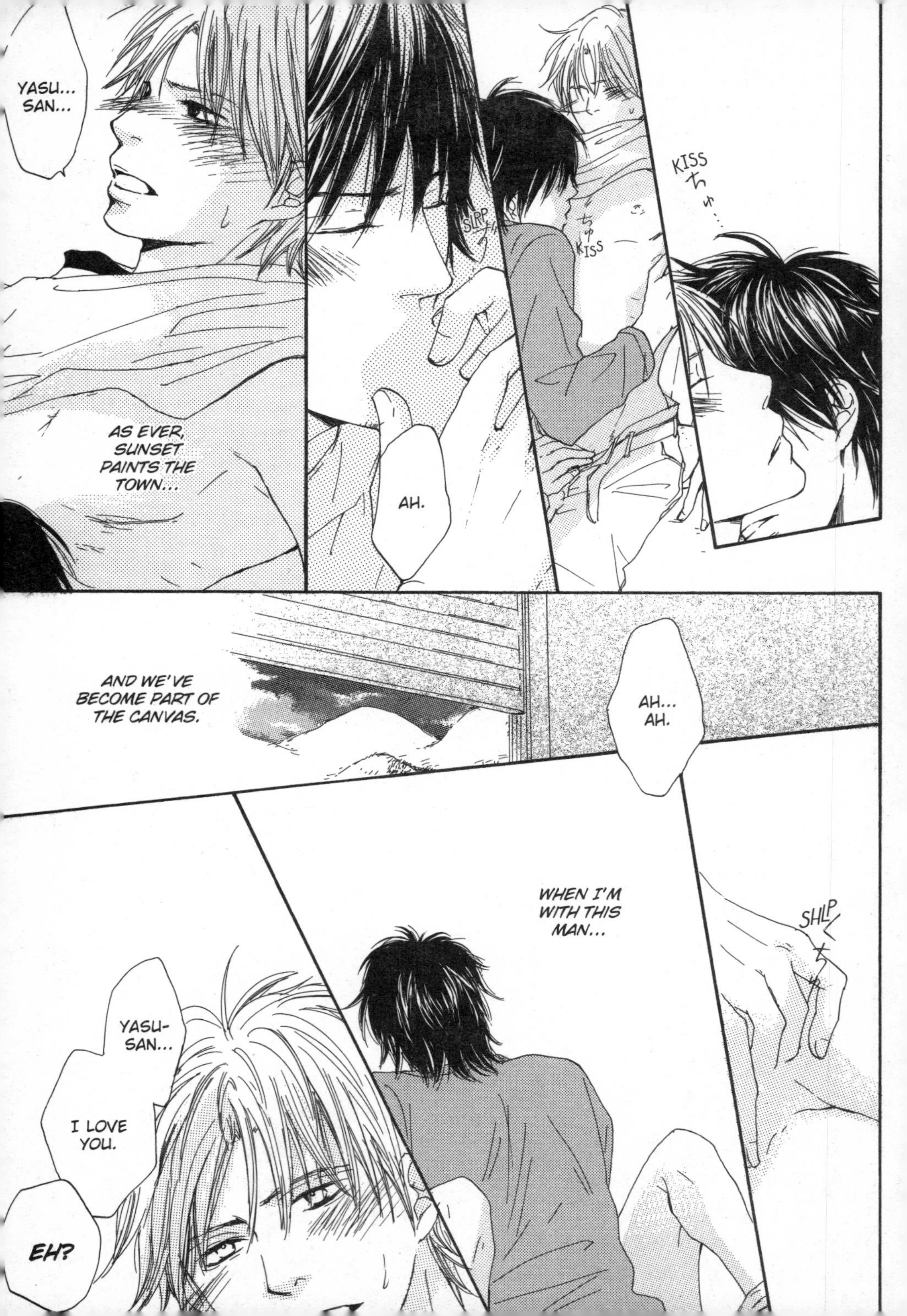
KISS
ちゅ…
SLRP
KISS
AH.
YASU... SAN...
AS EVER, SUNSET PAINTS THE TOWN...
AH... AH.
AND WE'VE BECOME PART OF THE CANVAS.
WHEN I'M WITH THIS MAN...
SHLP
YASU-SAN...
I LOVE YOU.
EH?

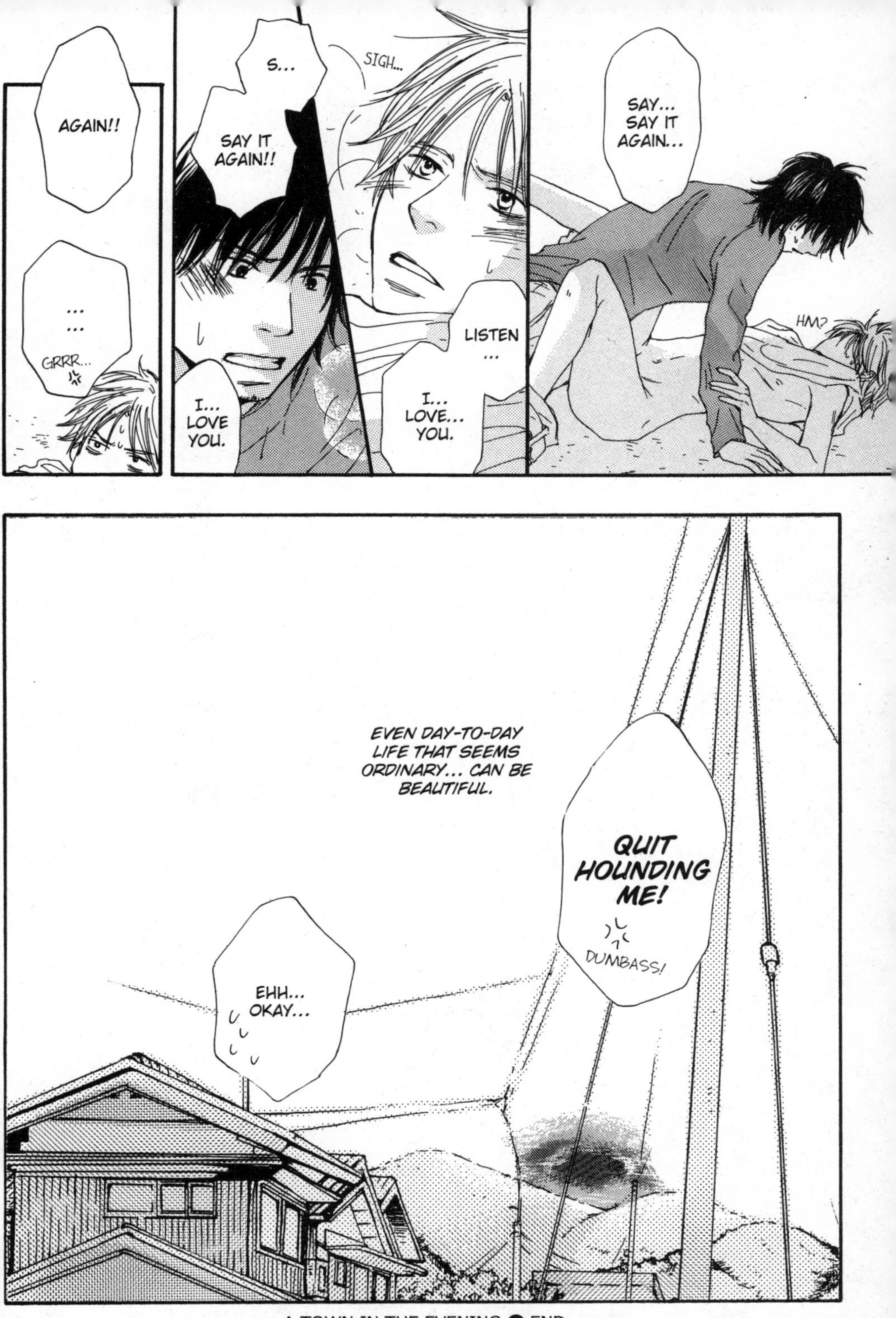
SAY... SAY IT AGAIN...
HM?
SIGH...
S...
SAY IT AGAIN!!
LISTEN...
I... LOVE... YOU.
I... LOVE YOU.
AGAIN!!
... ...
GRRR...
EVEN DAY-TO-DAY LIFE THAT SEEMS ORDINARY... CAN BE BEAUTIFUL.
QUIT HOUNDING ME!
DUMBASS!
EHH... OKAY...

A TOWN IN THE EVENING ● END

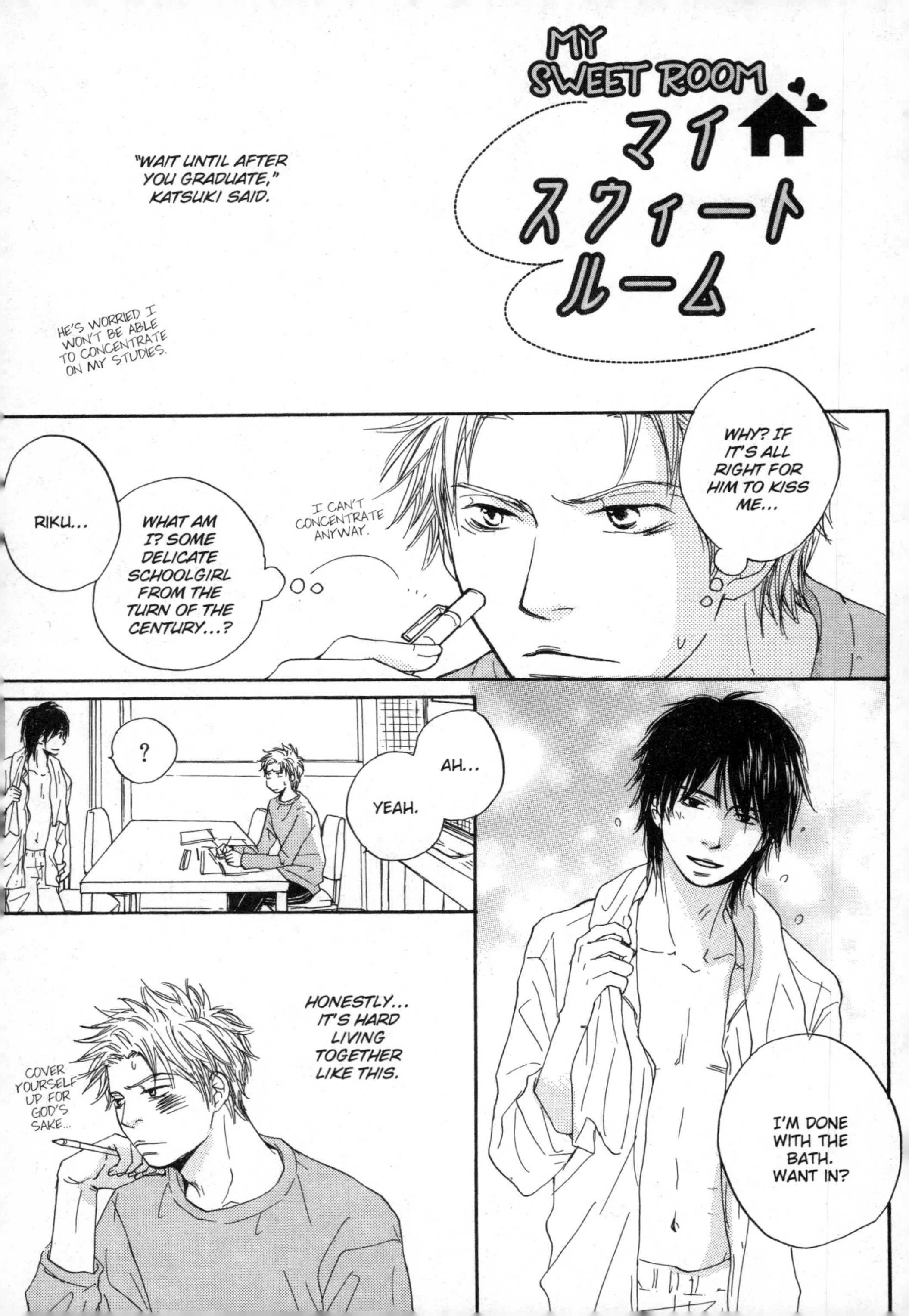
MY SWEET ROOM
マイスウィートルーム
"WAIT UNTIL AFTER YOU GRADUATE," KATSUKI SAID.
HE'S WORRIED I WON'T BE ABLE TO CONCENTRATE ON MY STUDIES.
WHY? IF IT'S ALL RIGHT FOR HIM TO KISS ME...
I CAN'T CONCENTRATE ANYWAY.
WHAT AM I? SOME DELICATE SCHOOLGIRL FROM THE TURN OF THE CENTURY...?
RIKU...
I'M DONE WITH THE BATH. WANT IN?
AH...
YEAH.
?
HONESTLY... IT'S HARD LIVING TOGETHER LIKE THIS.
COVER YOURSELF UP FOR GOD'S SAKE...

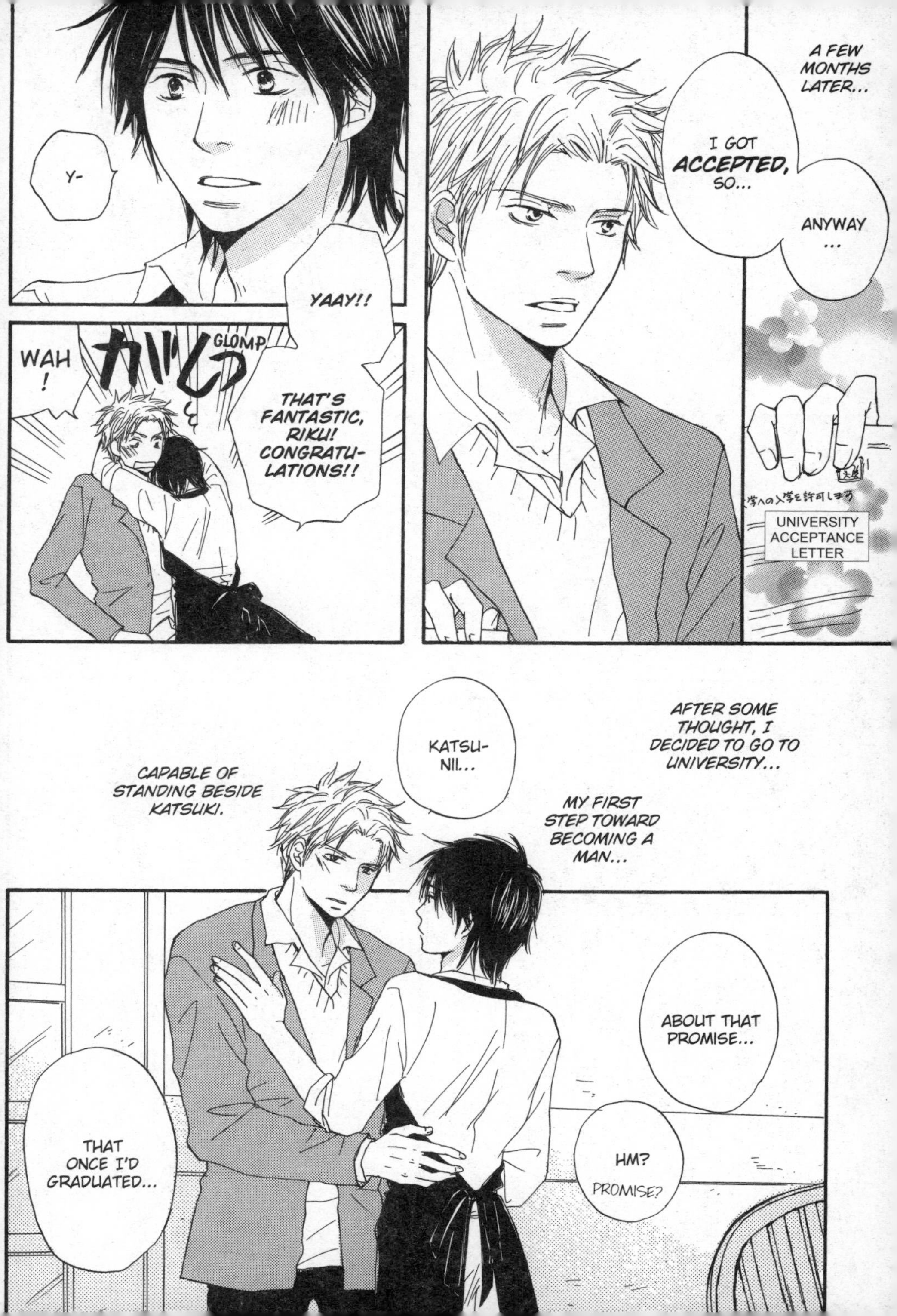
A FEW MONTHS LATER...
I GOT ACCEPTED, SO...
ANYWAY...
学への入学を許可します
UNIVERSITY ACCEPTANCE LETTER
Y-
YAAY!!
がしっ
GLOMP
WAH!
THAT'S FANTASTIC, RIKU! CONGRATULATIONS!!
AFTER SOME THOUGHT, I DECIDED TO GO TO UNIVERSITY...
KATSU-NII...
MY FIRST STEP TOWARD BECOMING A MAN...
CAPABLE OF STANDING BESIDE KATSUKI.
ABOUT THAT PROMISE...
HM?
PROMISE?
THAT ONCE I'D GRADUATED...

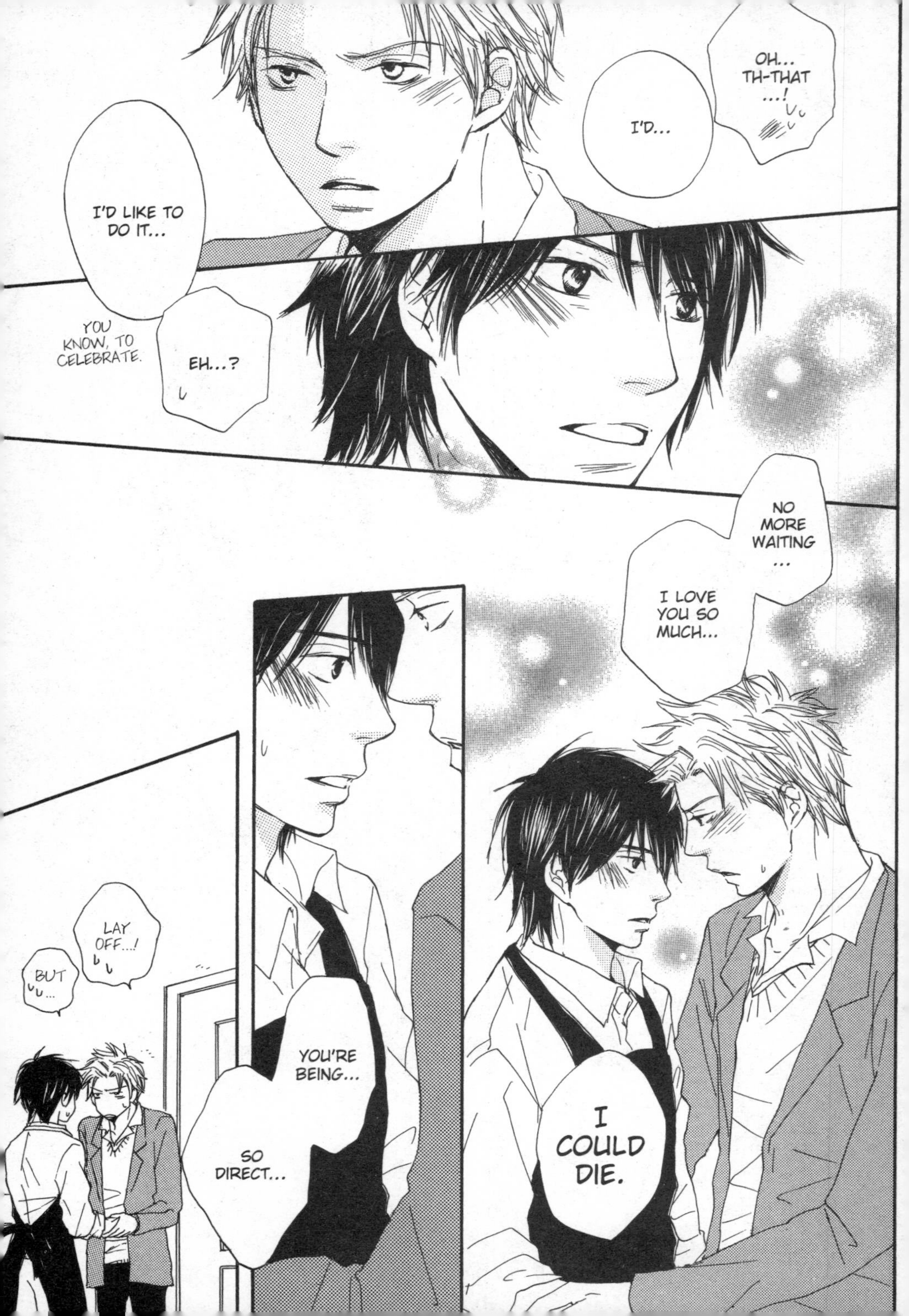
OH... TH-THAT ...!
I'D...
I'D LIKE TO DO IT...
YOU KNOW, TO CELEBRATE.
EH...?
NO MORE WAITING ...
I LOVE YOU SO MUCH...
I COULD DIE.
YOU'RE BEING...
SO DIRECT...
LAY OFF...!
BUT...

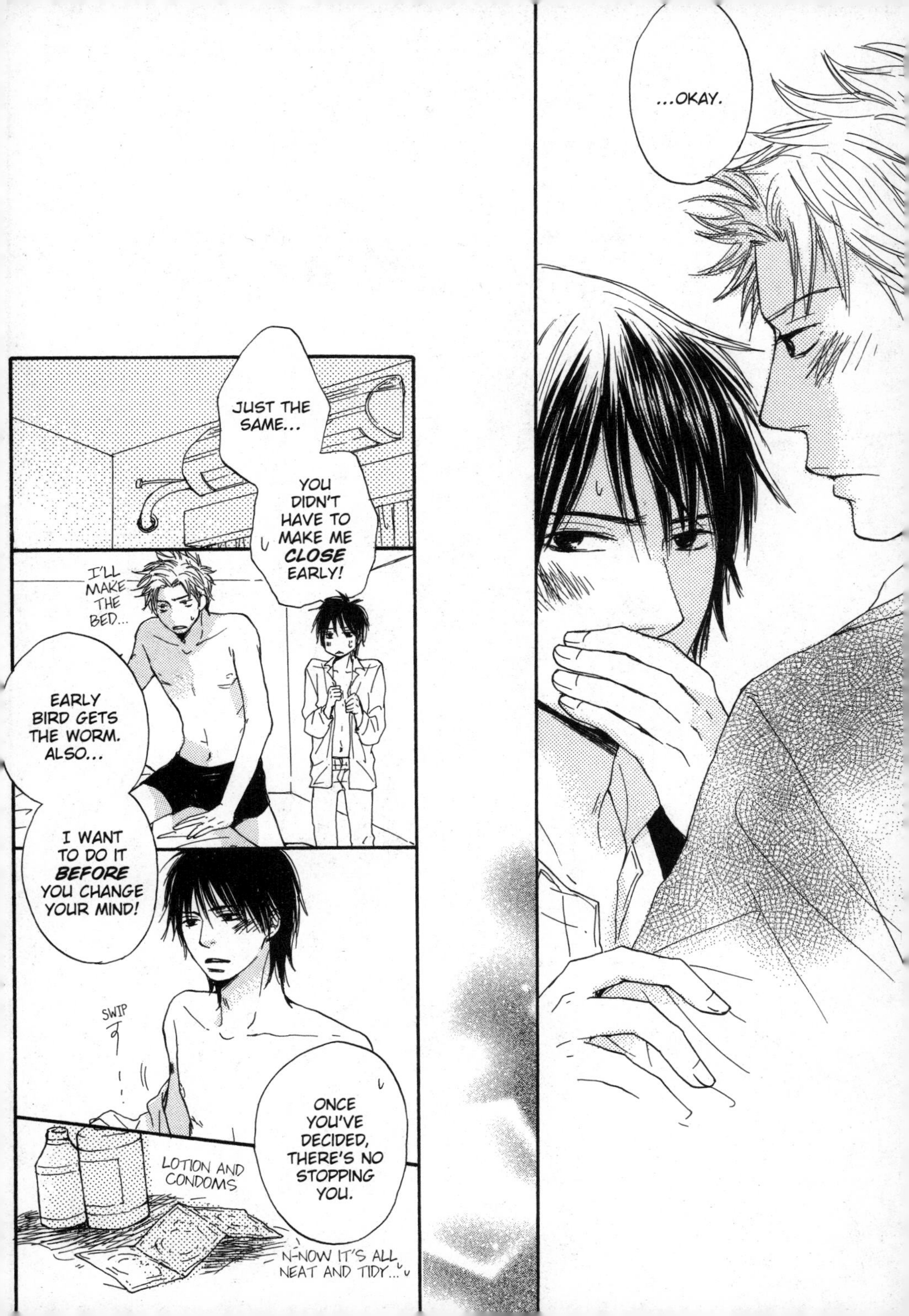
...OKAY.
JUST THE SAME...
YOU DIDN'T HAVE TO MAKE ME CLOSE EARLY!
I'LL MAKE THE BED...
EARLY BIRD GETS THE WORM. ALSO...
I WANT TO DO IT BEFORE YOU CHANGE YOUR MIND!
SWIP
ONCE YOU'VE DECIDED, THERE'S NO STOPPING YOU.
LOTION AND CONDOMS
N-NOW IT'S ALL NEAT AND TIDY...

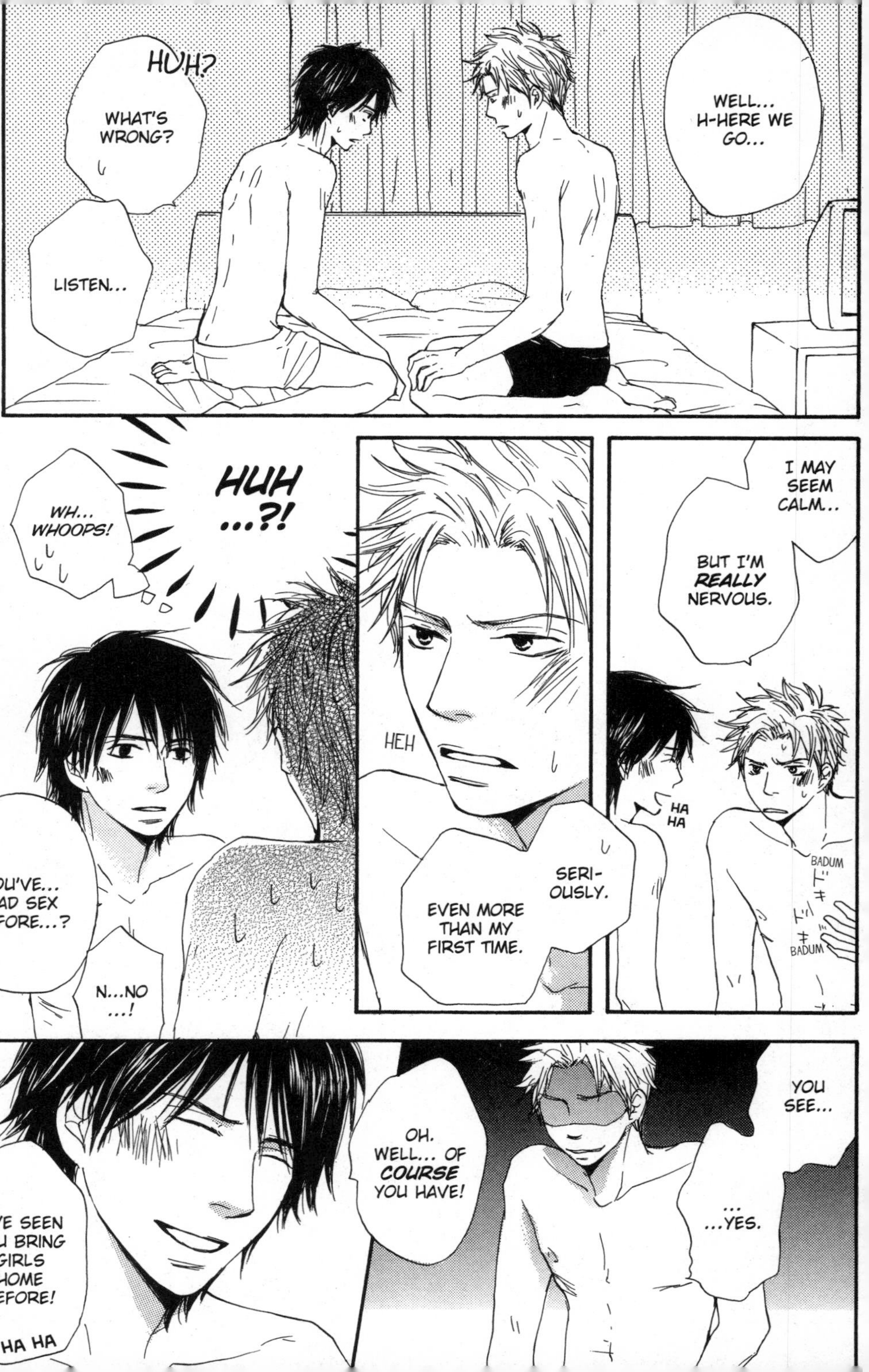
WELL... H-HERE WE GO...
HUH?
WHAT'S WRONG?
LISTEN...
I MAY SEEM CALM...
BUT I'M **REALLY** NERVOUS.
HA HA
BADUM
BADUM
HEH
SERI-OUSLY.
EVEN MORE THAN MY FIRST TIME.
HUH ...?!
WH... WHOOPS!
YOU'VE... HAD SEX BEFORE...?
N...NO ...!
YOU SEE...
... ...YES.
OH. WELL... OF **COURSE** YOU HAVE!
I'VE SEEN YOU BRING GIRLS HOME BEFORE!
HA HA

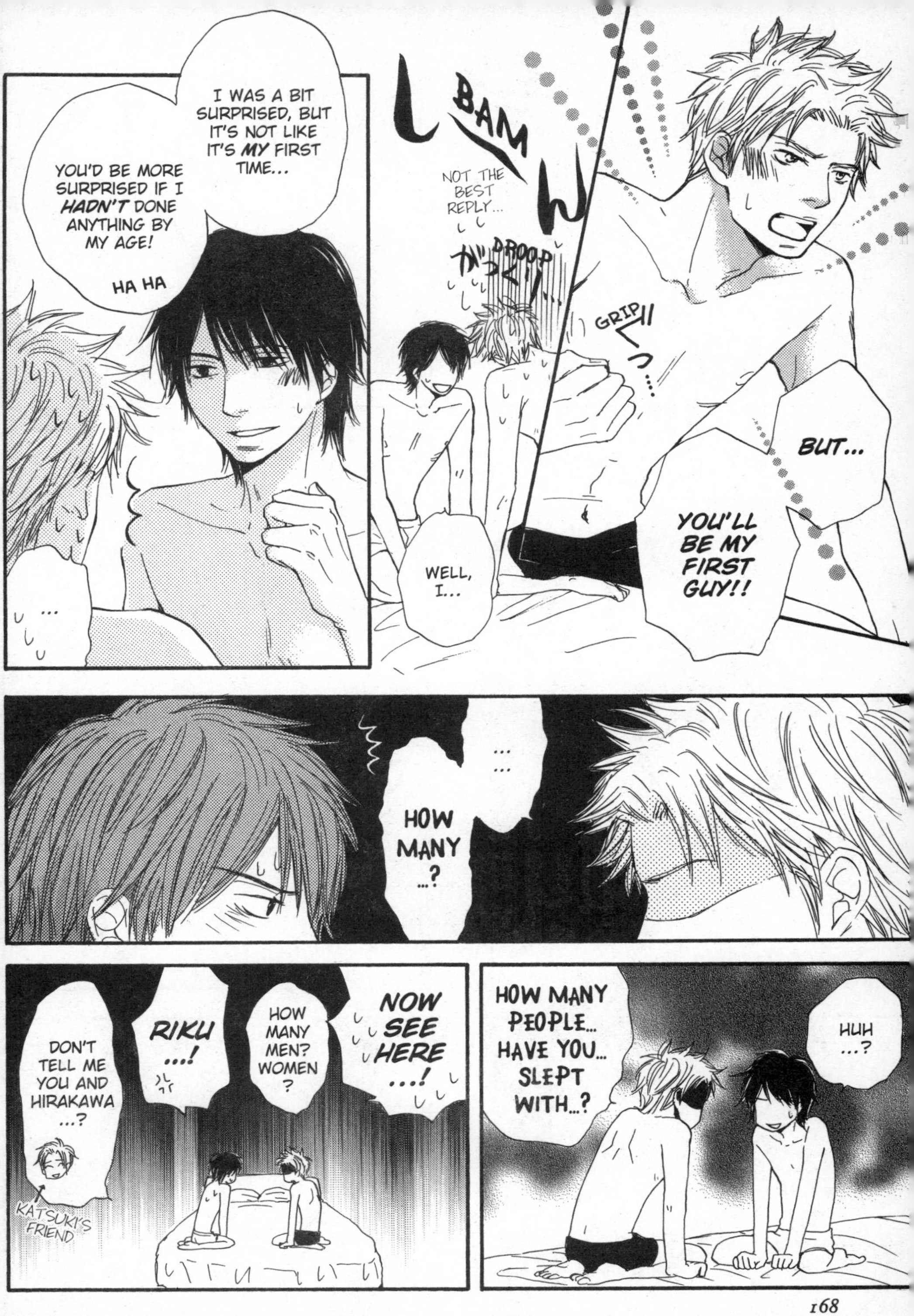
GRIP
BUT...
YOU'LL BE MY FIRST GUY!!
BAM
NOT THE BEST REPLY...
DROOP
WELL, I...
I WAS A BIT SURPRISED, BUT IT'S NOT LIKE IT'S *MY* FIRST TIME...
YOU'D BE MORE SURPRISED IF I *HADN'T* DONE ANYTHING BY MY AGE!
HA HA
...
...
...
HOW MANY ...?
HOW MANY PEOPLE... HAVE YOU... SLEPT WITH..?
HUH ...?
NOW SEE HERE ...!
HOW MANY MEN? WOMEN ?
RIKU ...!
DON'T TELL ME YOU AND HIRAKAWA ...?
KATSUKI'S FRIEND

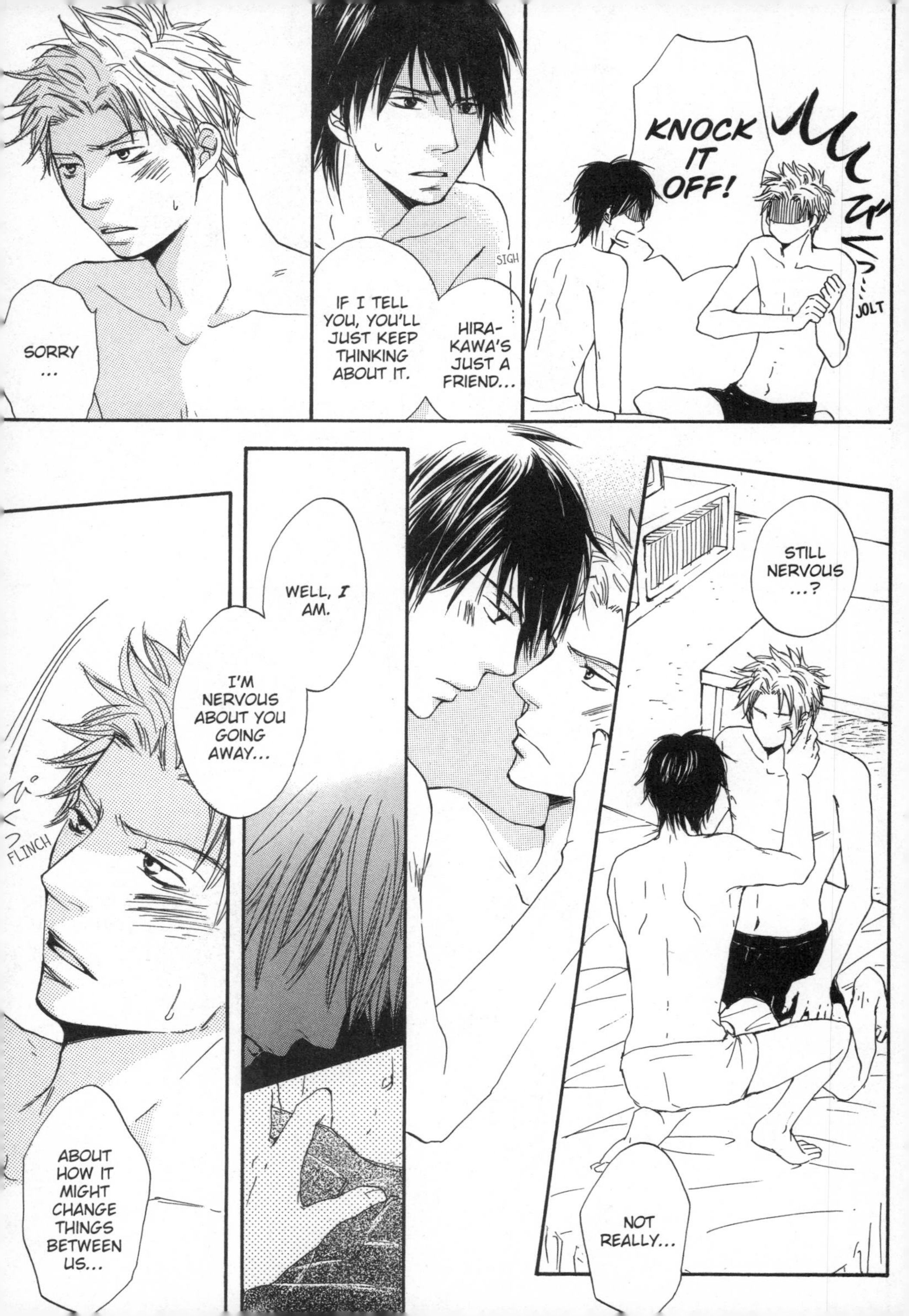
KNOCK IT OFF!
JOLT
SIGH
HIRA-KAWA'S JUST A FRIEND...
IF I TELL YOU, YOU'LL JUST KEEP THINKING ABOUT IT.
SORRY...
STILL NERVOUS...?
NOT REALLY...
WELL, I AM.
I'M NERVOUS ABOUT YOU GOING AWAY...
FLINCH
ABOUT HOW IT MIGHT CHANGE THINGS BETWEEN US...

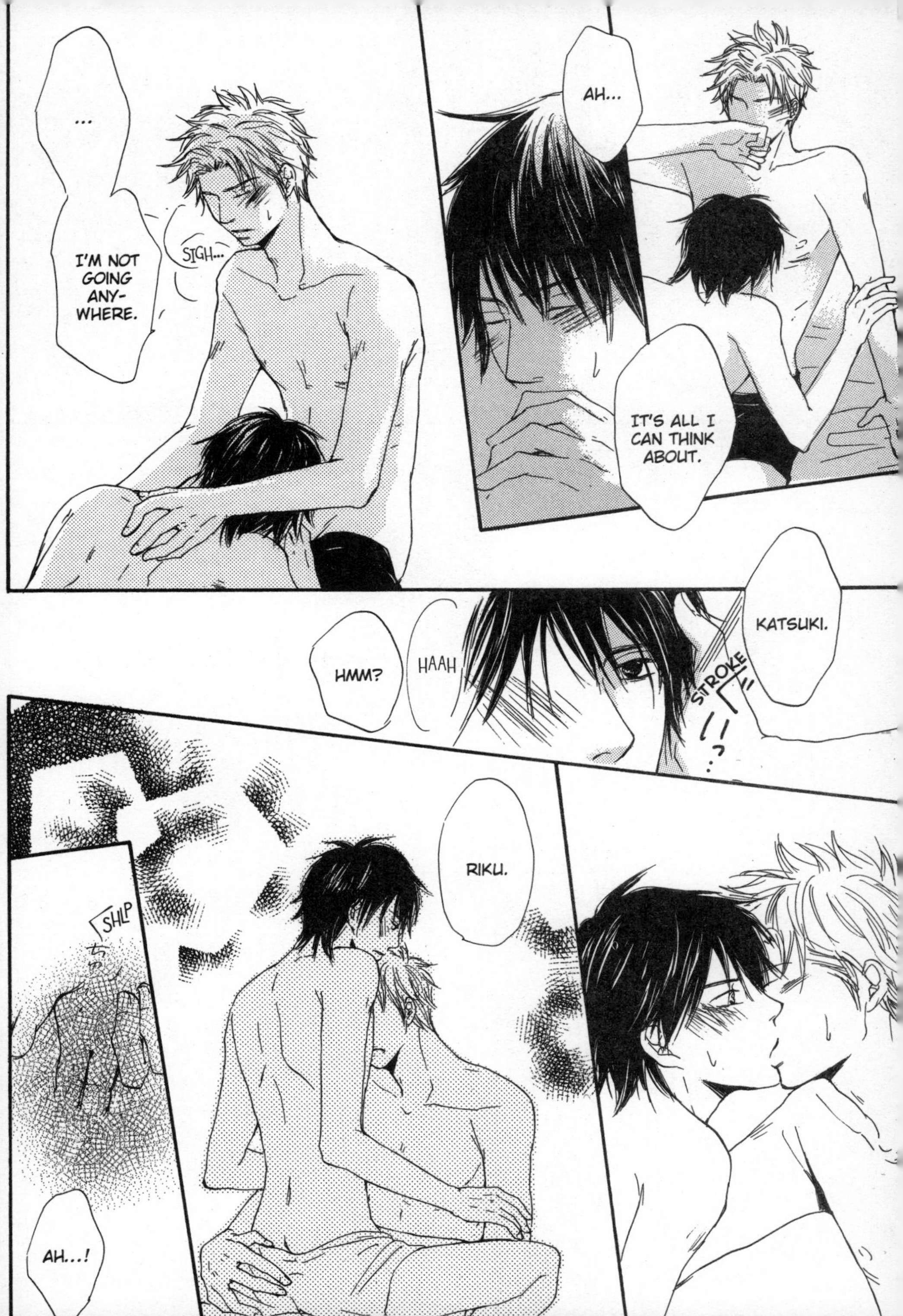
AH...
IT'S ALL I CAN THINK ABOUT.
...
SIGH...
I'M NOT GOING ANYWHERE.
KATSUKI.
STROKE
HAAH
HMM?
RIKU.
SHLP
AH...!

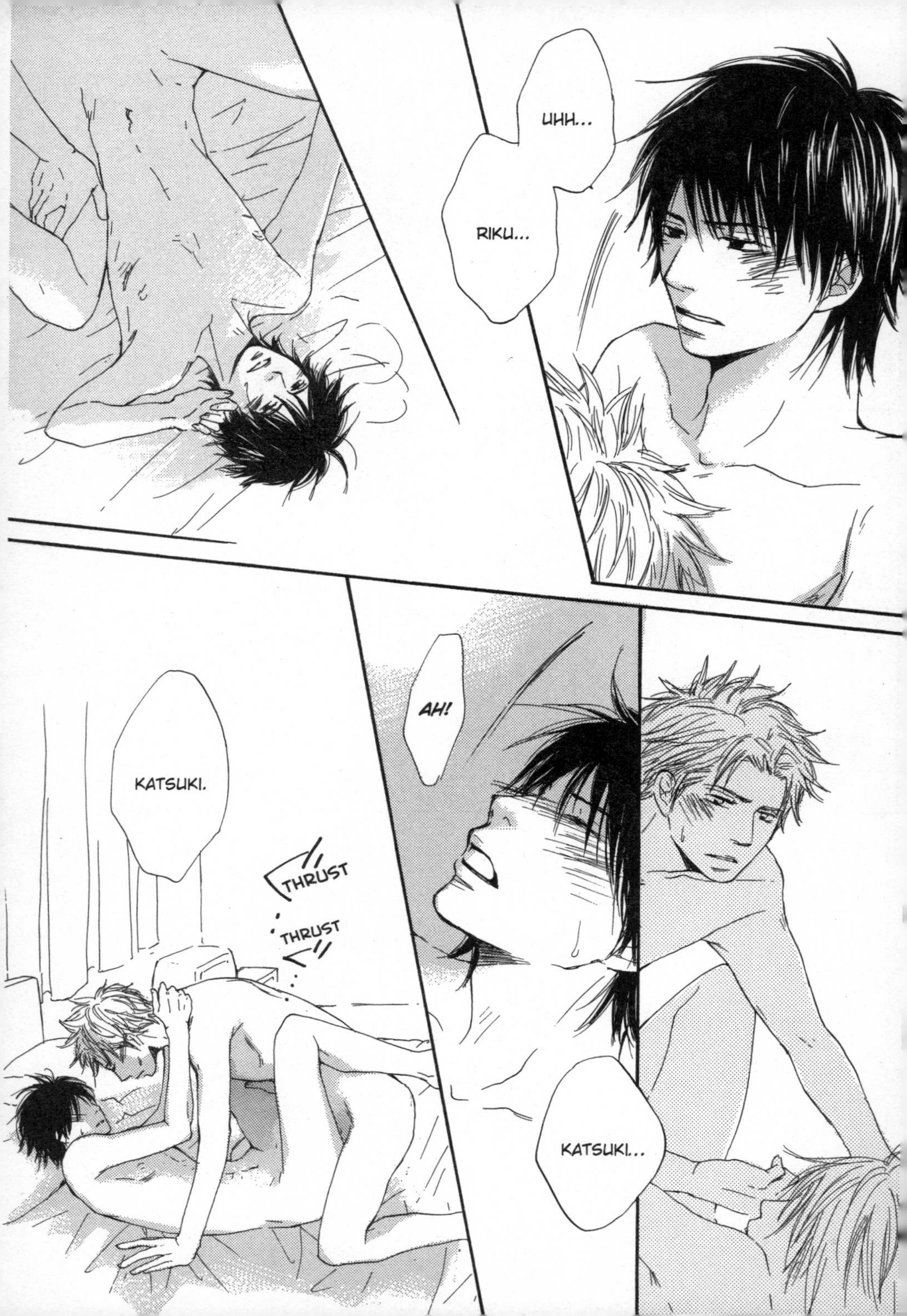
UHH...
RIKU...
AH!
KATSUKI...
KATSUKI.
THRUST
THRUST

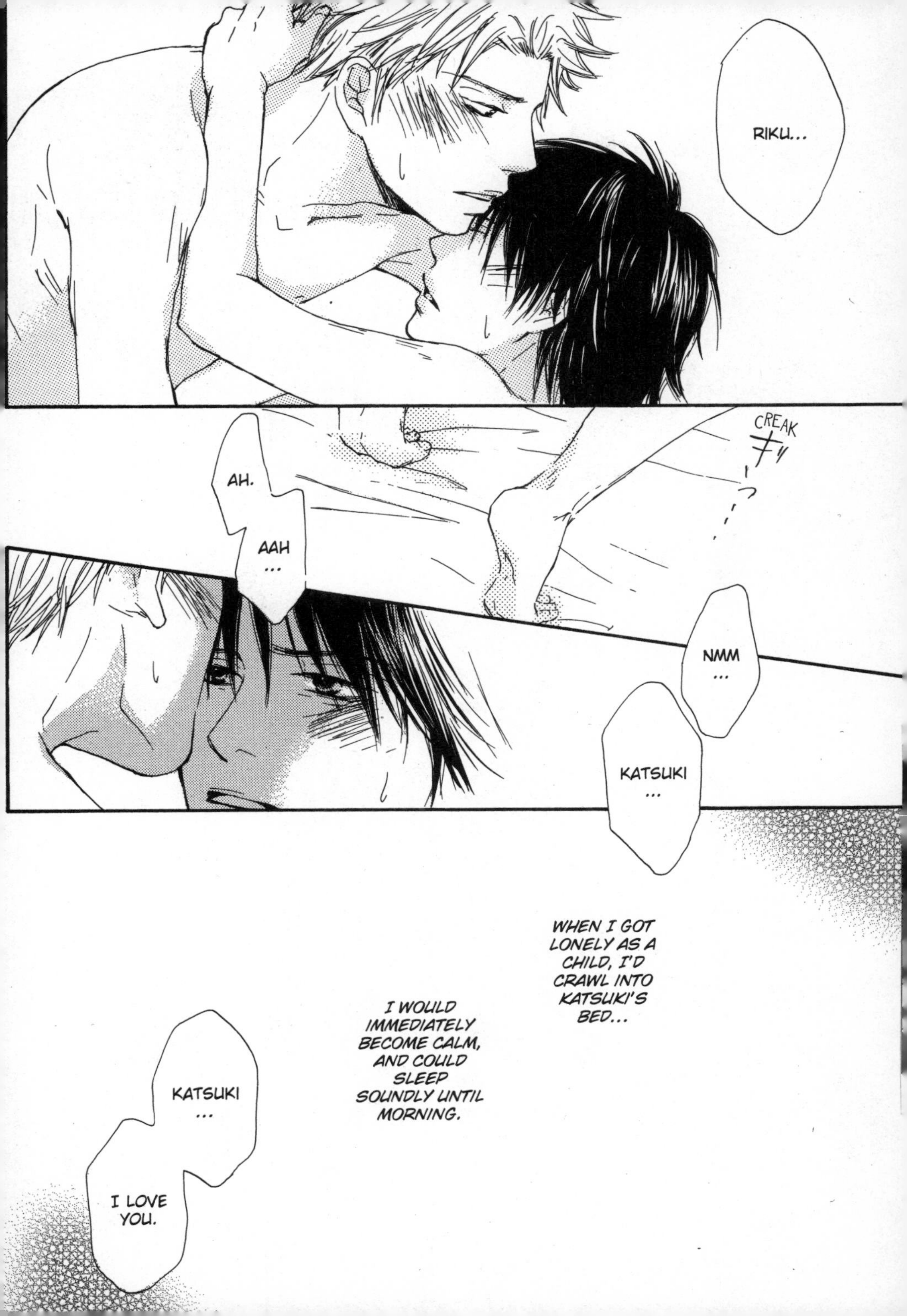
RIKU...
CREAK
AH.
AAH...
NMM...
KATSUKI...
WHEN I GOT LONELY AS A CHILD, I'D CRAWL INTO KATSUKI'S BED...
I WOULD IMMEDIATELY BECOME CALM, AND COULD SLEEP SOUNDLY UNTIL MORNING.
KATSUKI...
I LOVE YOU.

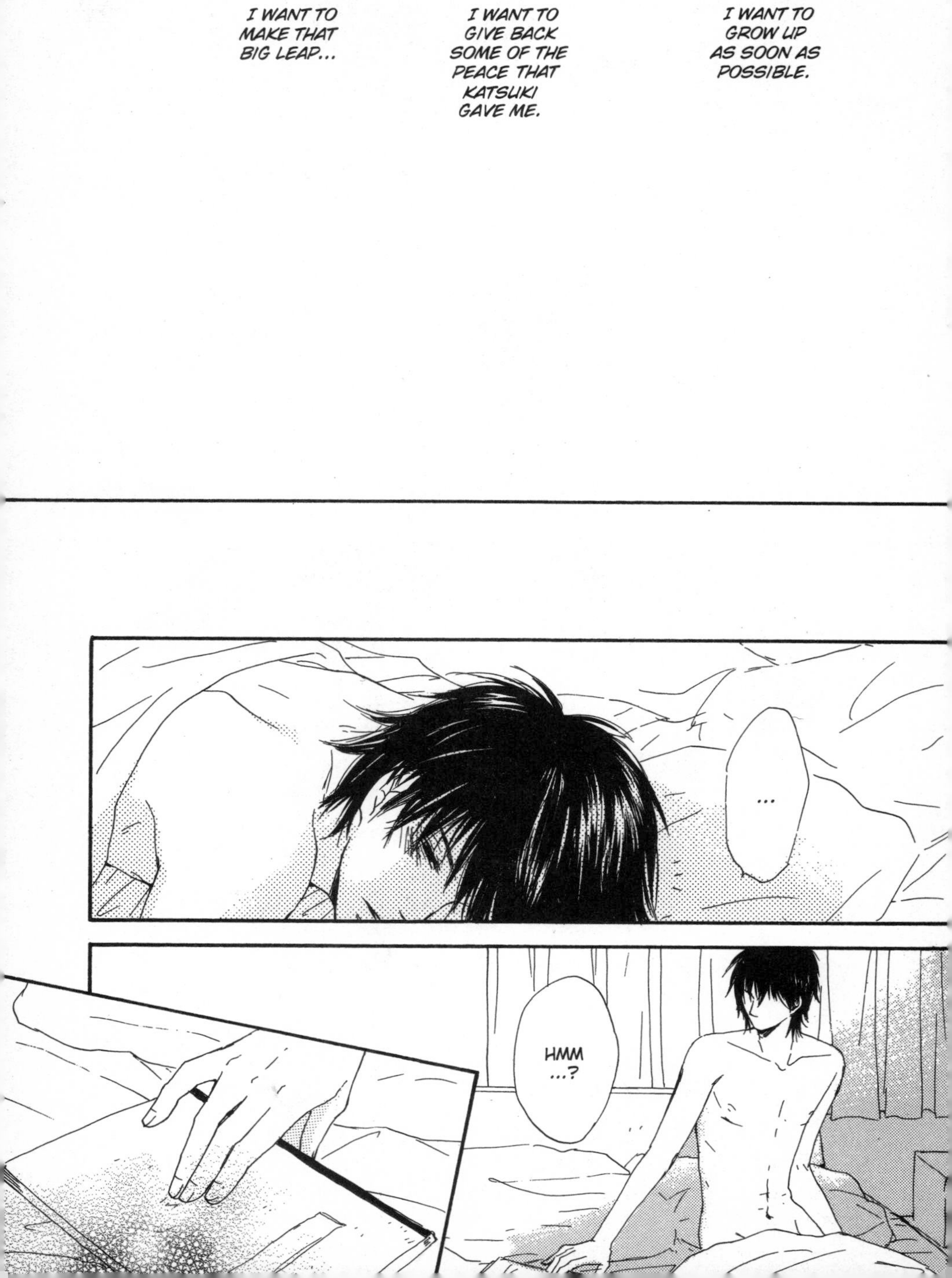
I WANT TO GROW UP AS SOON AS POSSIBLE.
I WANT TO GIVE BACK SOME OF THE PEACE THAT KATSUKI GAVE ME.
I WANT TO MAKE THAT BIG LEAP...
...
HMM ...?

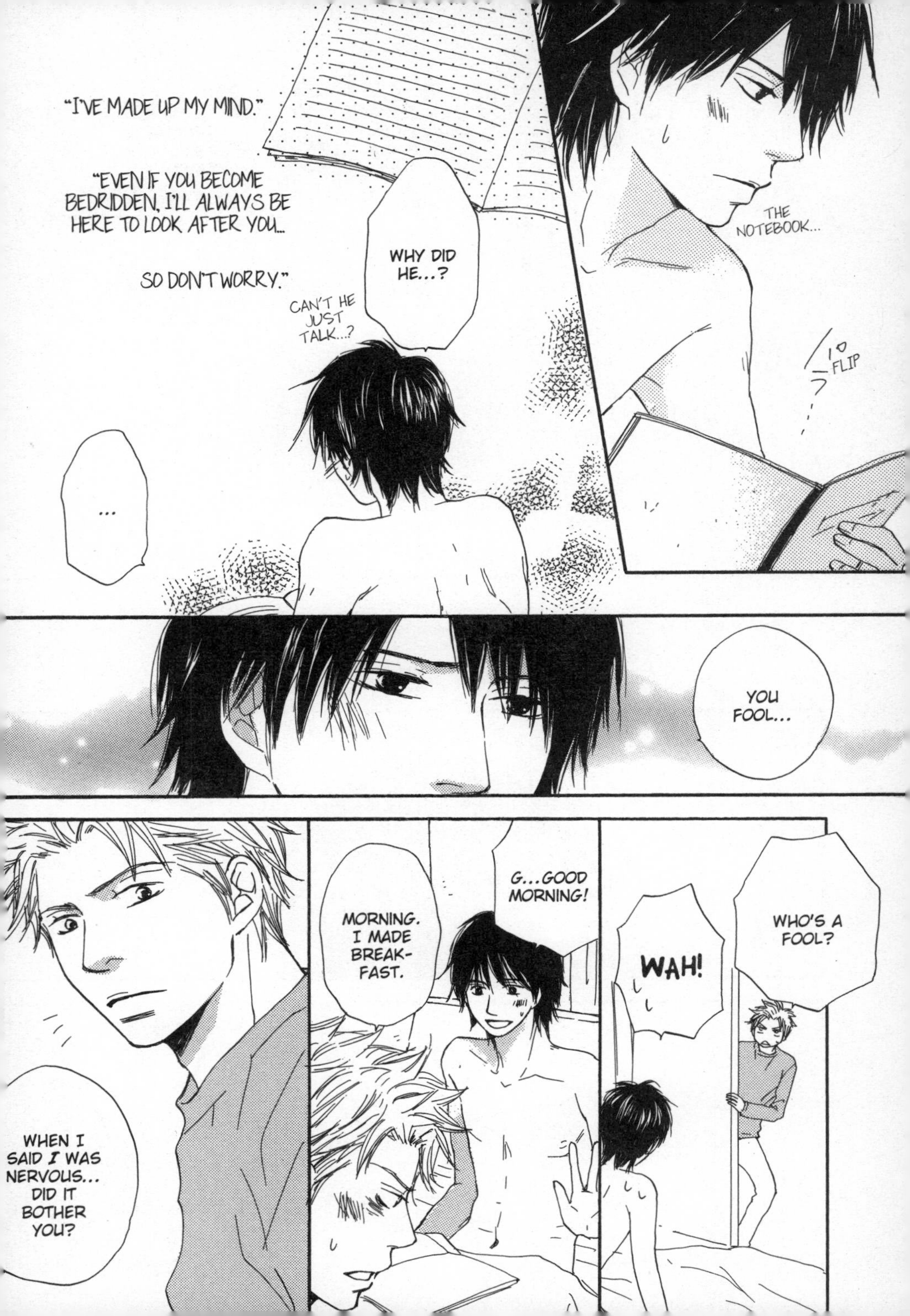
THE NOTEBOOK...
FLIP
"I'VE MADE UP MY MIND."
"EVEN IF YOU BECOME BEDRIDDEN, I'LL ALWAYS BE HERE TO LOOK AFTER YOU...
SO DON'T WORRY."
WHY DID HE...?
CAN'T HE JUST TALK...?
...
YOU FOOL...
WHO'S A FOOL?
WAH!
G...GOOD MORNING!
MORNING. I MADE BREAK-FAST.
WHEN I SAID *I* WAS NERVOUS... DID IT BOTHER YOU?

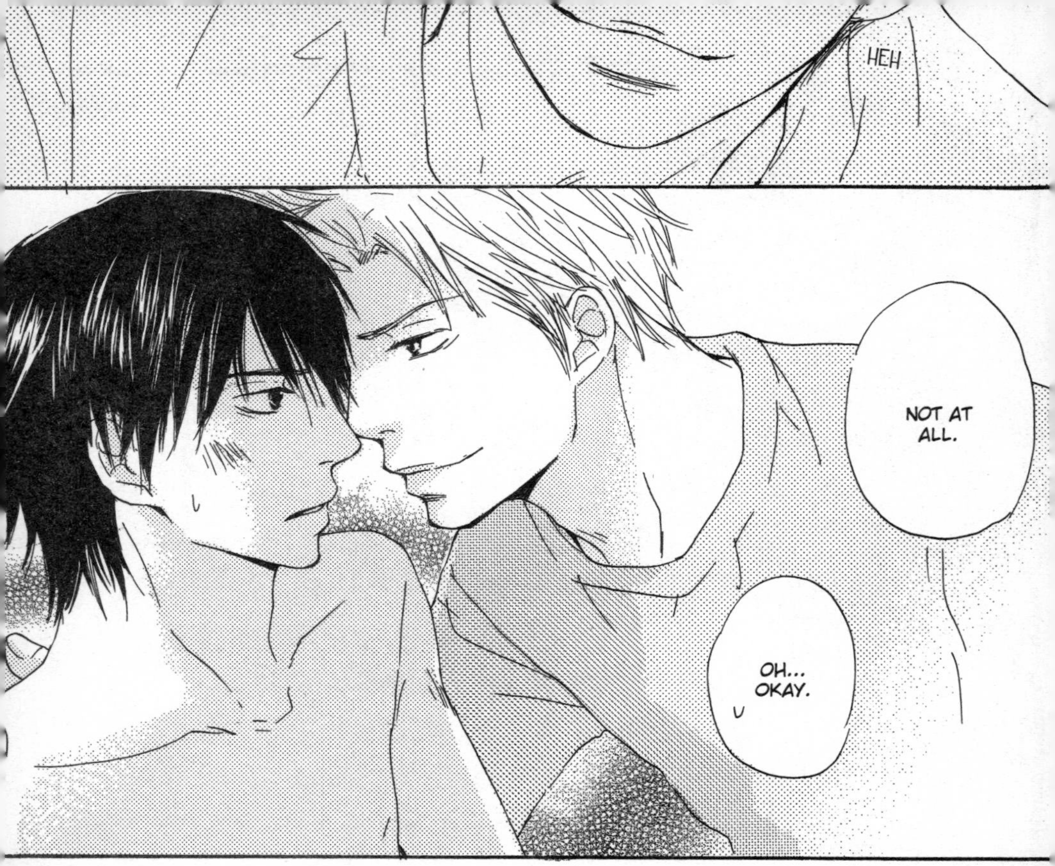
HEH
NOT AT ALL.
OH... OKAY.

I LONG FOR US TO BE TOGETHER...

TO CARE FOR EACH OTHER...

IN THIS SWEET ROOM.

MY SWEET ROOM ● END

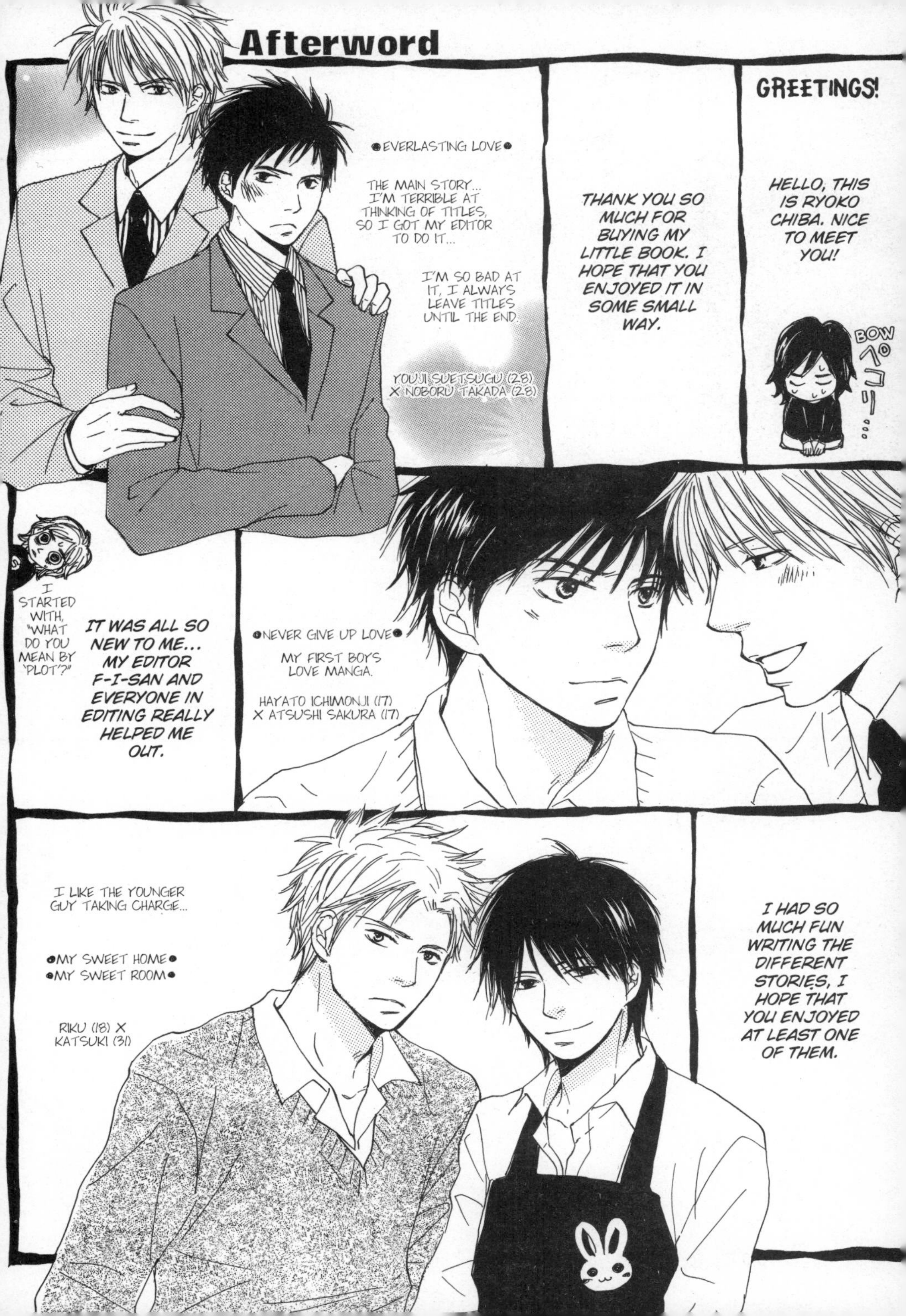
Afterword
GREETINGS!
HELLO, THIS IS RYOKO CHIBA. NICE TO MEET YOU!
BOW
ペコリ...
THANK YOU SO MUCH FOR BUYING MY LITTLE BOOK. I HOPE THAT YOU ENJOYED IT IN SOME SMALL WAY.
●EVERLASTING LOVE●
THE MAIN STORY... I'M TERRIBLE AT THINKING OF TITLES, SO I GOT MY EDITOR TO DO IT...
I'M SO BAD AT IT, I ALWAYS LEAVE TITLES UNTIL THE END.
YOUJI SUETSUGU (28) X NOBORU TAKADA (28)
●NEVER GIVE UP LOVE●
MY FIRST BOYS LOVE MANGA.
HAYATO ICHIMONJI (17) X ATSUSHI SAKURA (17)
IT WAS ALL SO NEW TO ME... MY EDITOR F-I-SAN AND EVERYONE IN EDITING REALLY HELPED ME OUT.
I STARTED WITH, "WHAT DO YOU MEAN BY 'PLOT'?"
I HAD SO MUCH FUN WRITING THE DIFFERENT STORIES, I HOPE THAT YOU ENJOYED AT LEAST ONE OF THEM.
I LIKE THE YOUNGER GUY TAKING CHARGE...
●MY SWEET HOME●
●MY SWEET ROOM●
RIKU (18) X KATSUKI (31)

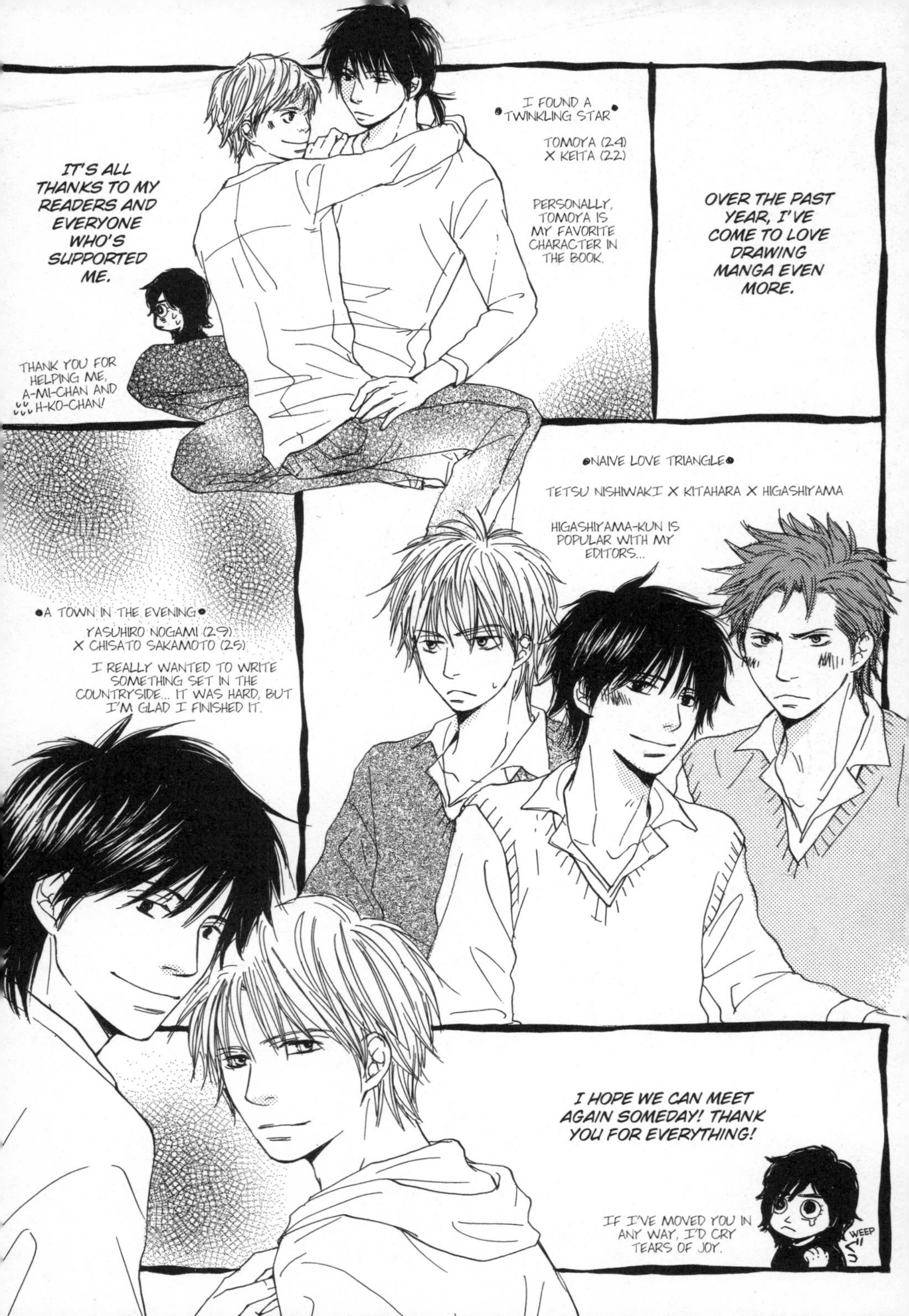

OVER THE PAST YEAR, I'VE COME TO LOVE DRAWING MANGA EVEN MORE.
•I FOUND A TWINKLING STAR•
TOMOYA (24) X KEITA (22)
PERSONALLY, TOMOYA IS MY FAVORITE CHARACTER IN THE BOOK.
IT'S ALL THANKS TO MY READERS AND EVERYONE WHO'S SUPPORTED ME.
THANK YOU FOR HELPING ME, A-MI-CHAN AND H-KO-CHAN!
•NAIVE LOVE TRIANGLE•
TETSU NISHIWAKI X KITAHARA X HIGASHIYAMA
HIGASHIYAMA-KUN IS POPULAR WITH MY EDITORS...
•A TOWN IN THE EVENING•
YASUHIRO NOGAMI (29) X CHISATO SAKAMOTO (25)
I REALLY WANTED TO WRITE SOMETHING SET IN THE COUNTRYSIDE... IT WAS HARD, BUT I'M GLAD I FINISHED IT.
I HOPE WE CAN MEET AGAIN SOMEDAY! THANK YOU FOR EVERYTHING!
IF I'VE MOVED YOU IN ANY WAY, I'D CRY TEARS OF JOY.
WEEP

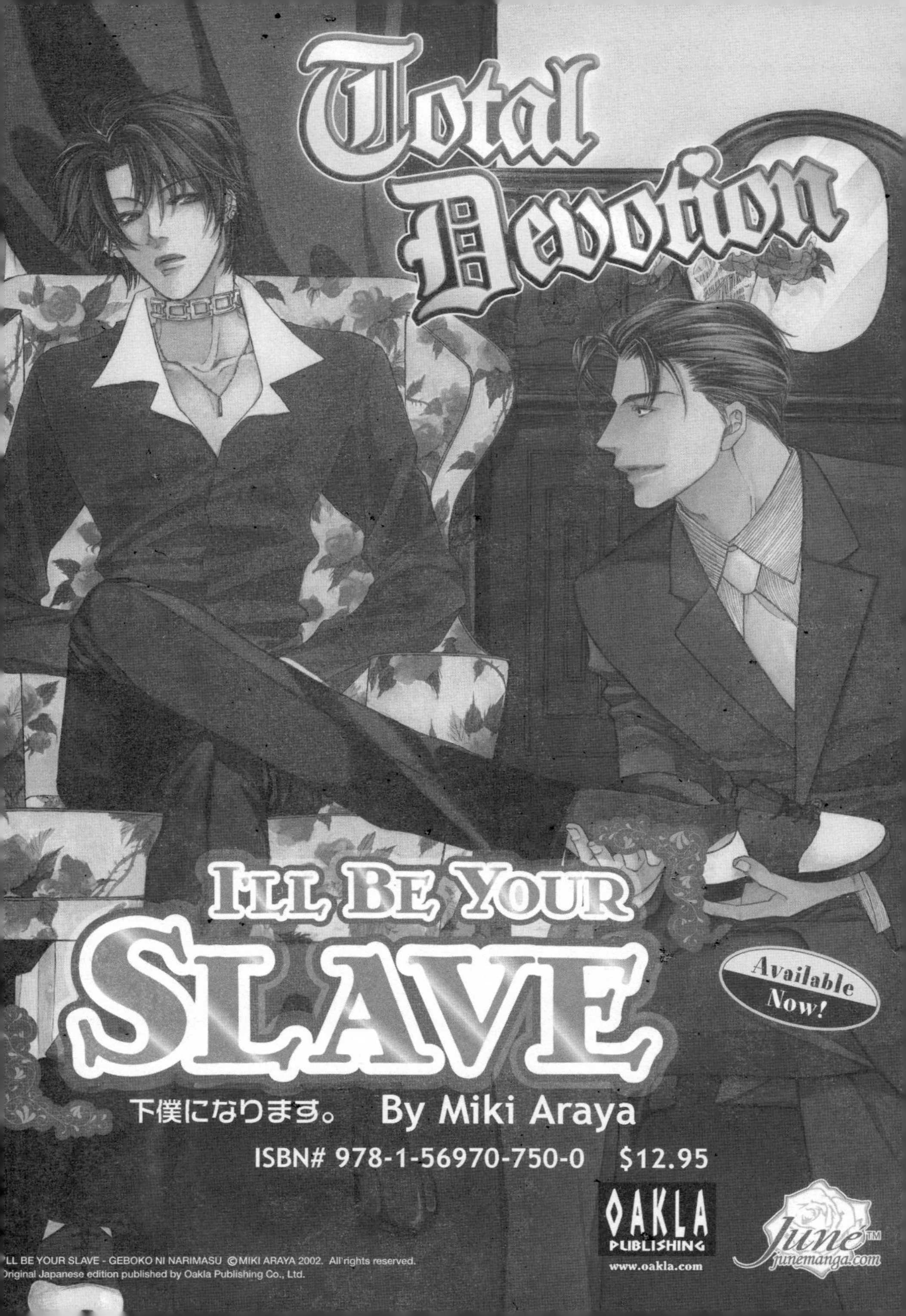
Total Devotion
I'LL BE YOUR
SLAVE
Available Now!
下僕になります。 By Miki Araya
ISBN# 978-1-56970-750-0 $12.95
OAKLA PUBLISHING
www.oakla.com
June™
junemanga.com
'LL BE YOUR SLAVE - GEBOKO NI NARIMASU © MIKI ARAYA 2002. All rights reserved.
riginal Japanese edition published by Oakla Publishing Co., Ltd.

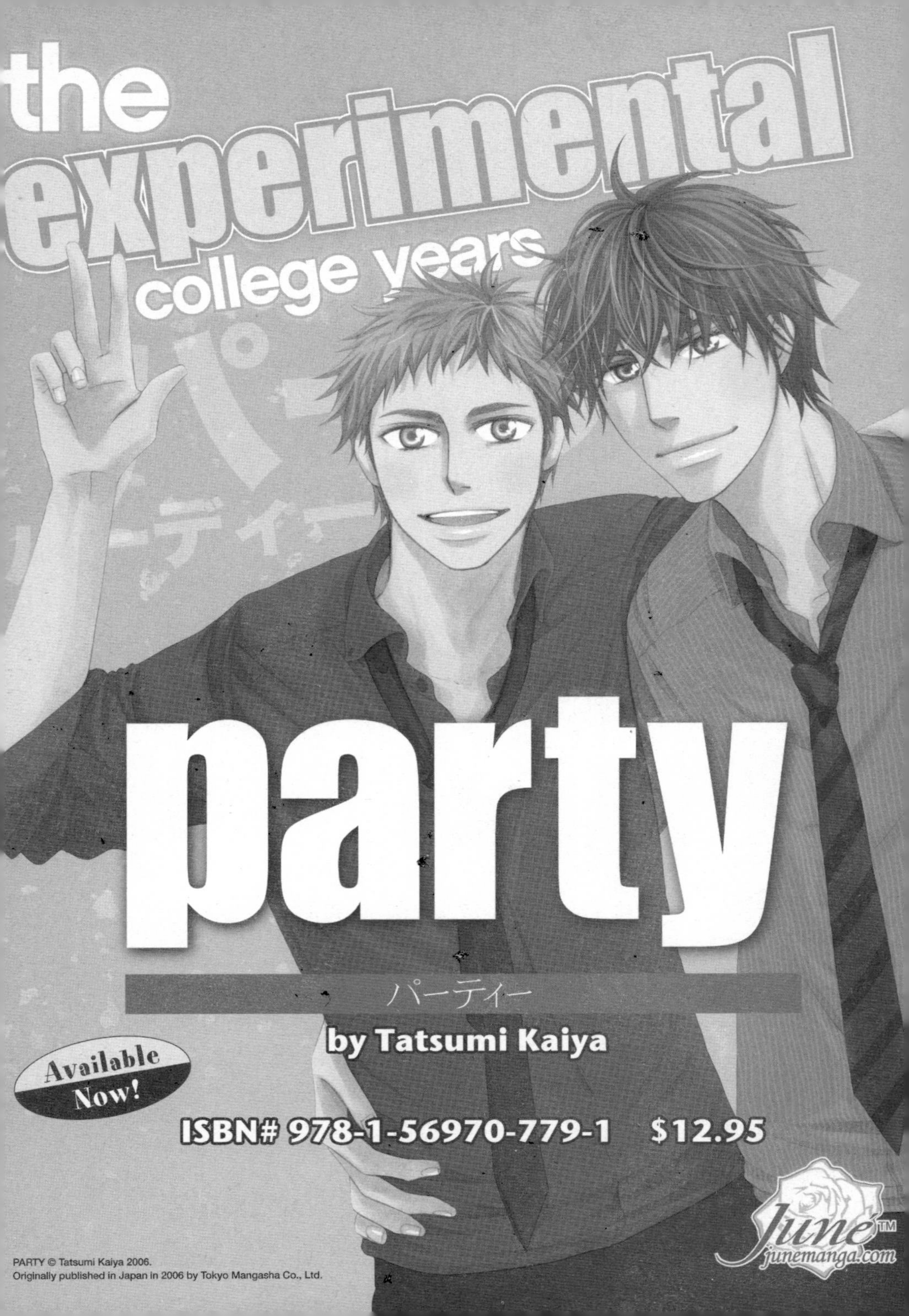
the experimental college years
パーティー
party
パーティー
by Tatsumi Kaiya
Available Now!
ISBN# 978-1-56970-779-1 $12.95
June™
junemanga.com
PARTY © Tatsumi Kaiya 2006.
Originally published in Japan in 2006 by Tokyo Mangasha Co., Ltd.

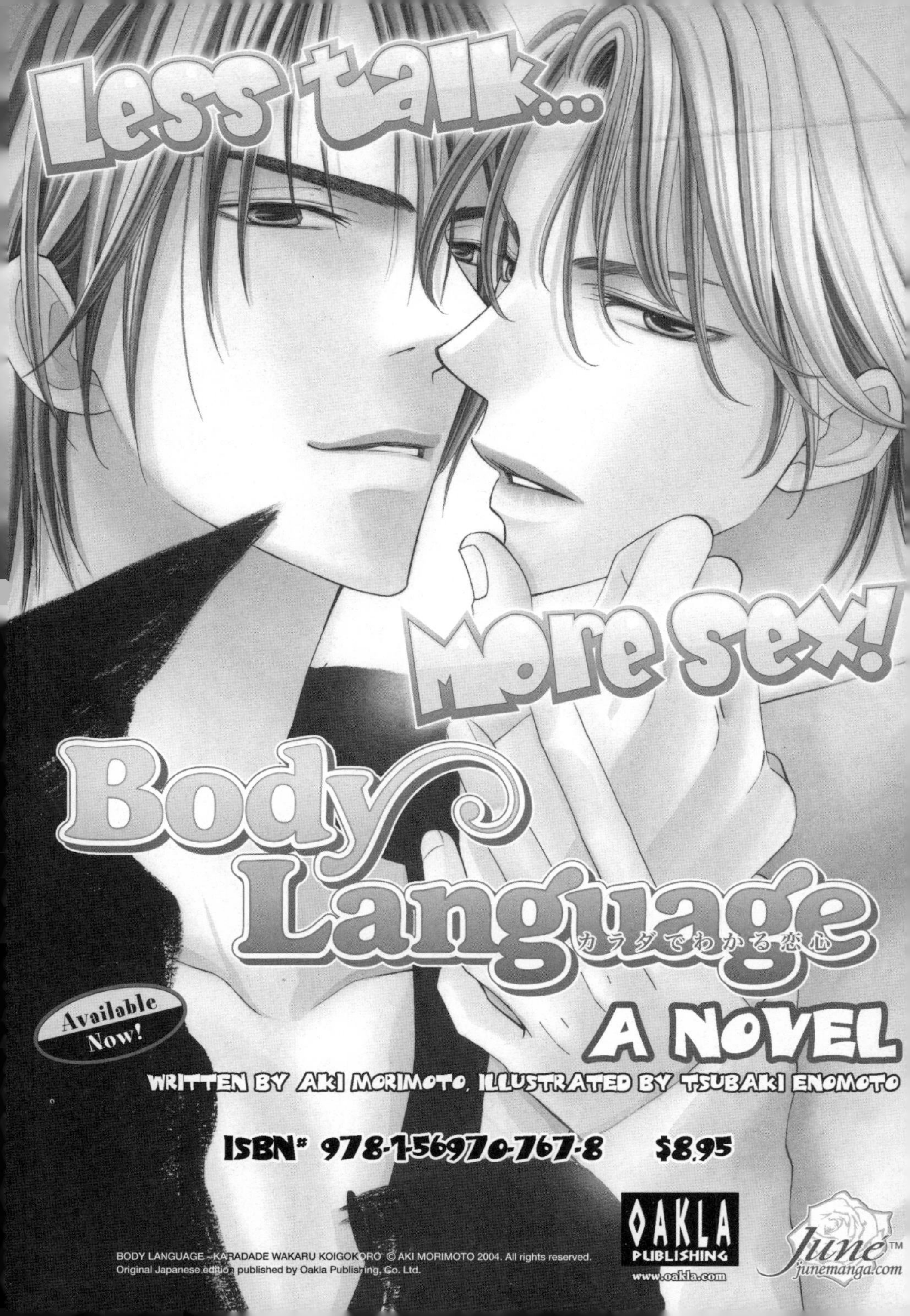
Less talk...
More sex!
Body Language
カラダでわかる恋心
Available Now!
A NOVEL
WRITTEN BY AKI MORIMOTO, ILLUSTRATED BY TSUBAKI ENOMOTO
ISBN# 978-1-56970-767-8
$8.95
OAKLA PUBLISHING
www.oakla.com
June™
junemanga.com
BODY LANGUAGE - KARADADE WAKARU KOIGOKORO © AKI MORIMOTO 2004. All rights reserved.
Original Japanese edition published by Oakla Publishing, Co. Ltd.

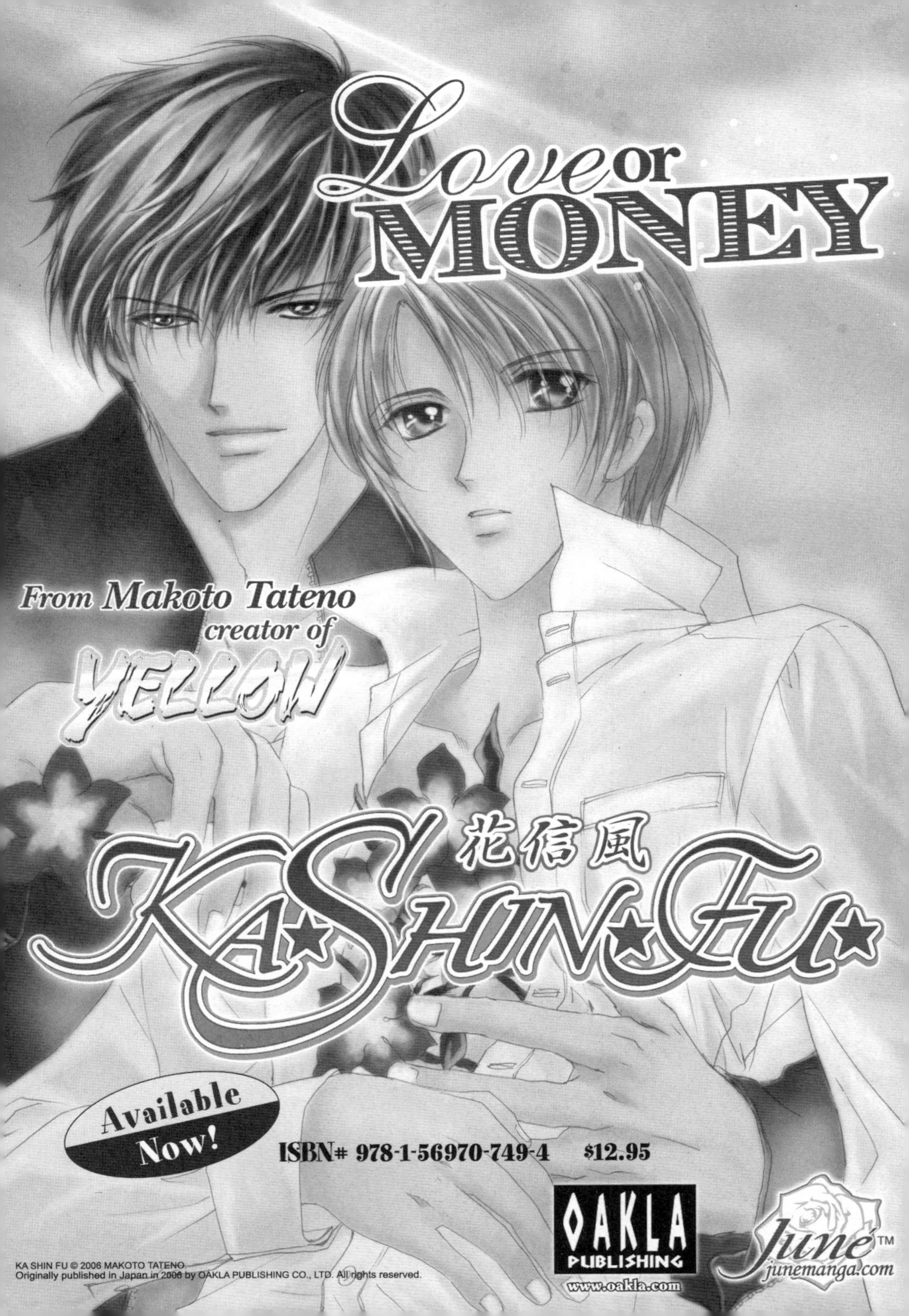
Love or MONEY
From Makoto Tateno
creator of
YELLOW
花信風
KA★SHIN★FU★
Available Now!
ISBN# 978-1-56970-749-4
$12.95
OAKLA PUBLISHING
www.oakla.com
June™
junemanga.com
KA SHIN FU © 2006 MAKOTO TATENO.
Originally published in Japan in 2006 by OAKLA PUBLISHING CO., LTD. All rights reserved.

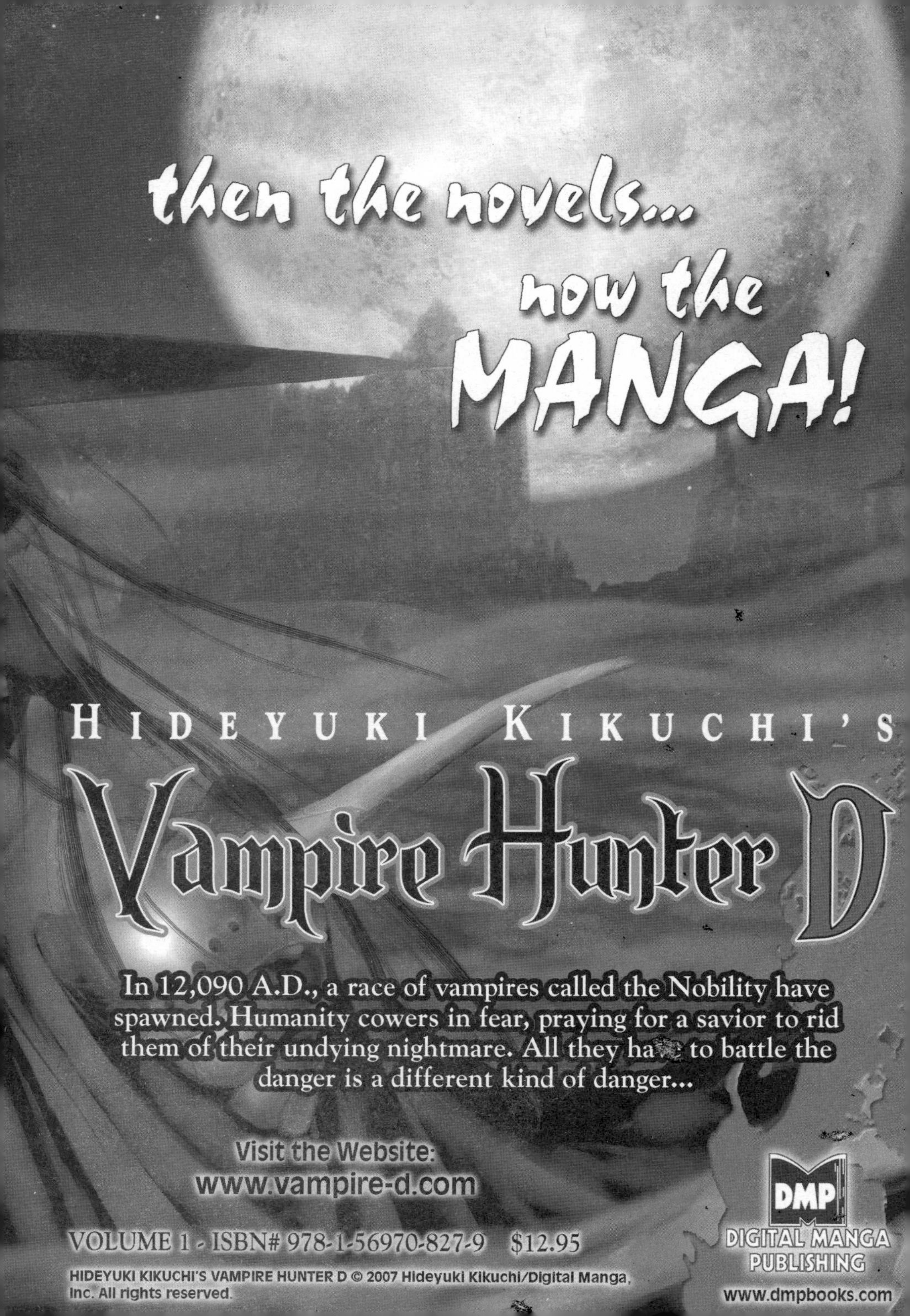
then the novels...
now the
MANGA!
HIDEYUKI KIKUCHI'S
Vampire Hunter D
In 12,090 A.D., a race of vampires called the Nobility have spawned. Humanity cowers in fear, praying for a savior to rid them of their undying nightmare. All they have to battle the danger is a different kind of danger...
Visit the Website:
www.vampire-d.com
VOLUME 1 - ISBN# 978-1-56970-827-9 $12.95
HIDEYUKI KIKUCHI'S VAMPIRE HUNTER D © 2007 Hideyuki Kikuchi/Digital Manga, Inc. All rights reserved.
DMP
DIGITAL MANGA PUBLISHING
www.dmpbooks.com

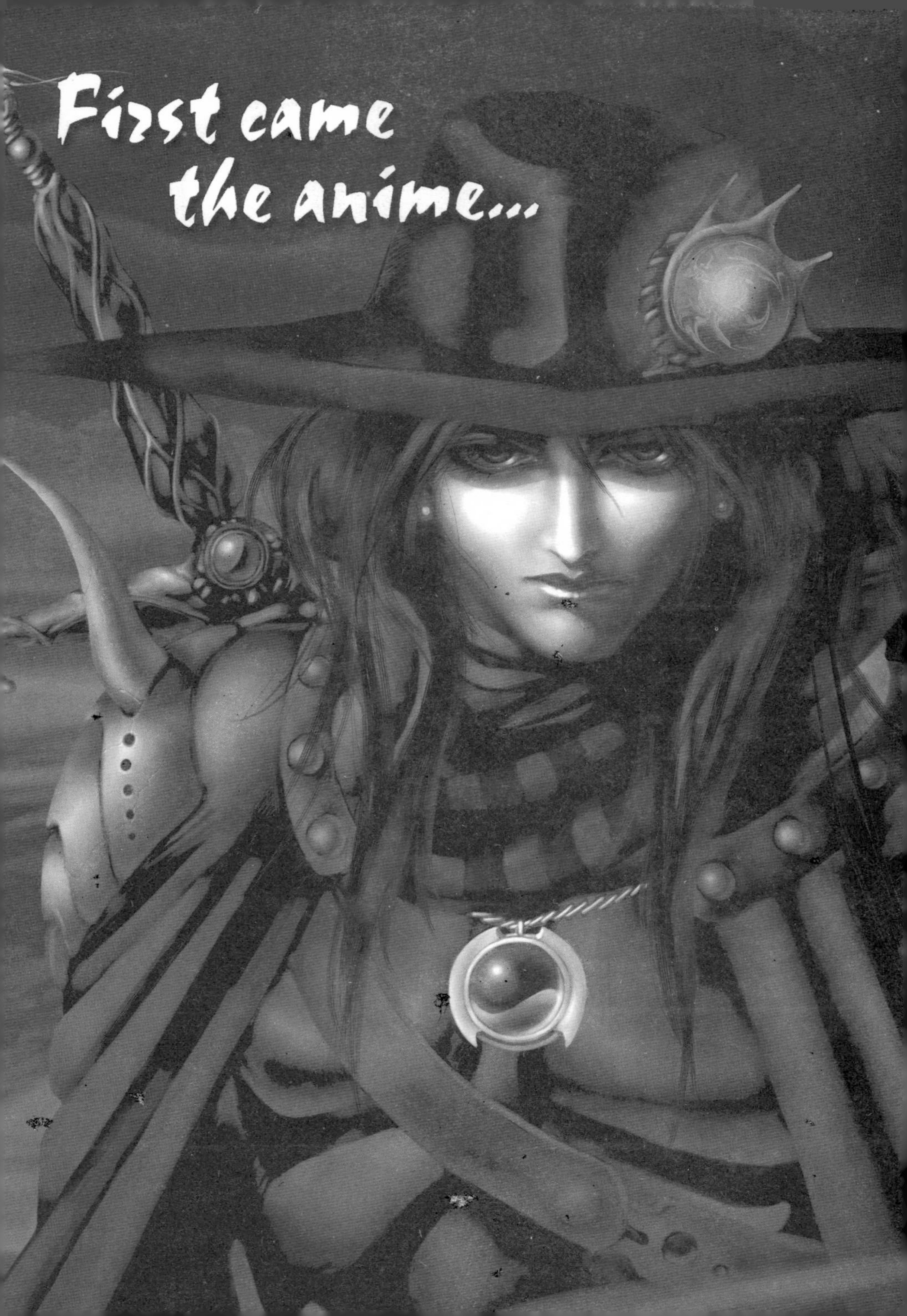
First came
the anime...

STOP

This is the back of the book!
Start from the other side.

NATIVE MANGA
readers read manga
from *right to left*.

If you run into our *Native Manga* logo on any of our books... you'll know that this manga is published in it's true original native Japanese right to left reading format, as it was intended. Turn to the other side of the book and start reading from right to left, top to bottom.

Follow the diagram to see how its done. *Surf's Up!*

NATIVE MANGA

READ RIGHT TO LEFT